Sacred Texts
and Buried Treasures

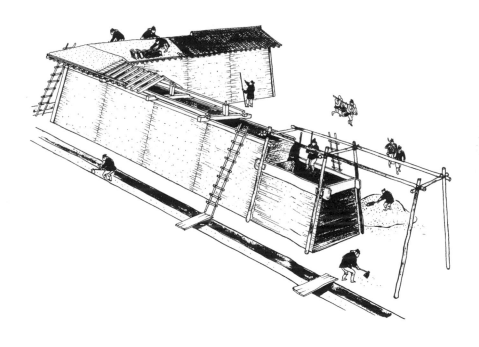

UNIVERSITY
OF HAWAI‘I
PRESS

HONOLULU

Sacred Texts and Buried Treasures

ISSUES IN THE HISTORICAL

ARCHAEOLOGY OF ANCIENT JAPAN

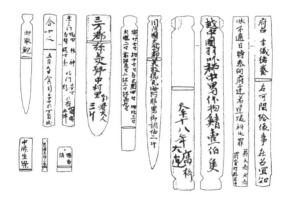

William Wayne Farris

Library of Congress Cataloging-in-Publication Data

Farris, William Wayne.
Sacred texts and buried treasures : issues in the
historical archaeology of ancient Japan / by
William Wayne Farris.
p.   cm.
Includes bibliographical references and index.
ISBN 0-8248-1966-7 (cloth : alk. paper). —
ISBN 0-8248-2030-4 (pbk. : alk. paper)
1. Japan—History—To 794. 2. Japan—
Relations—Korea. 3. Korea—Relations—Japan.
4. Japan—Capital and capitol—History. 5. Japan—
Antiquities. 6. Inscription, Japanese. 7. Wooden
tablets—Japan—History. I. Title.
DS855.F37   1998
952'.01—dc21   97–46014
                                          CIP

Permission to reprint passages from the following
sources is gratefully acknowledged.

The Manyoshu. Copyright © 1965 by Columbia
University Press. Reprinted with permission
of publisher.

*Nihongi: Chronicles of Japan from the Earliest
Times to A.D. 697* by W. G. Aston. Copyright © 1972
by Charles E. Tuttle Company, Inc. Reprinted with
permission of publisher.

Designed by Barbara Pope Book Design

To my two teachers, Al Craig and Kishi Toshio

CONTENTS

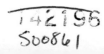

ACKNOWLEDGMENTS

I dedicate this book to two nurturing educators, Albert Craig of Harvard University and the late Kishi Toshio of Kyoto University. Craig introduced me to the world of American research on Japanese history; his command of the subject and ability to ask incisive and original questions have always inspired my own efforts. Kishi Toshio, the dean of Japanese historians on ancient Japan, taught me to search for the social and economic reality that lay behind the dry and often arcane laws and documents. In his later life this meant immersing himself in archaeology, an interest he sparked in me.

I would like to thank the Japan Foundation for a generous grant to allow me to learn more about Japanese archaeology during 1991–1992. I am also grateful to Professor Kamata Motokazu of Kyoto University for extending his hospitality and to Satō Yasuhiro for reading wooden tablets and other texts with me. Tateno Kazumi served as my liaison with the Nara National Cultural Properties Research Institute in Nara and Hashimoto Yoshinori in Asuka. I should also thank Sahara Makoto, Machida Akira, Nagashima Kimichika, Yoshida Takashi, Hayakawa Shōhachi, Yamanaka Akira, Shimizu Miki, Niiro Izumi, Walter Edwards, and numerous archaeologists who gave of their time. Special thanks go to Fujisawa Akiko and graduate students in the Department of Archaeology at Kyoto University. I should also like to thank Conrad Totman and Ted Kidder for reading a draft and making extensive comments; Gina Barnes for reading a shortened version of the chapter on Korea and pointing out many areas for improvement; two outside readers for the University of Hawai'i Press for filling pages with interesting and valuable points, not all of which I could incorporate into this work; Doris Gove and Jane Farris for suggesting numerous revisions in style and presentation; Wendi Lee Arms for assistance with the illustrations; and Patricia Crosby and Masako Ikeda for editorial assistance at the University of Hawai'i Press. The University of Tennessee generously provided funds to support publication. Any mistakes, of course, are the responsibility of the author.

Periods in East Asian Archaeology and History

China	Korea	Japan
		Jōmon Era 10,500 B.C.
	Bronze Age 1500 B.C.	
Zhou Dynasty 1122 B.C.		
Warring States 500 B.C.	Iron Age 400 B.C.	Yayoi Era 400–300 B.C.
Qin Dynasty 221 B.C.	Lo-lang established 100 B.C.	
End Later Han Dynasty A.D. 206		
Wei Dynasty A.D. 221		Yamatai and Himiko A.D. 240–250
		Tomb Era A.D. 250–300
Disunity A.D. 265	Three Kingdoms A.D. 300–668	A.D. 350 A.D. 450 Korean influence
		A.D. 538 Introduction of Buddhism
Sui Dynasty A.D. 589		A.D. 592 Beginning of Asuka century
Tang Dynasty A.D. 618		A.D. 645 Taika Coup
	Unified Silla A.D. 668	A.D. 663 Battle of Paekch'ŏn River
		A.D. 694 Fujiwara established
		A.D. 702 Taihō Codes
		A.D. 710 Nara established
		A.D. 745 Return to Nara
		A.D. 784 Nagaoka
		A.D. 794 Heian
		A.D. 805 End of Construction

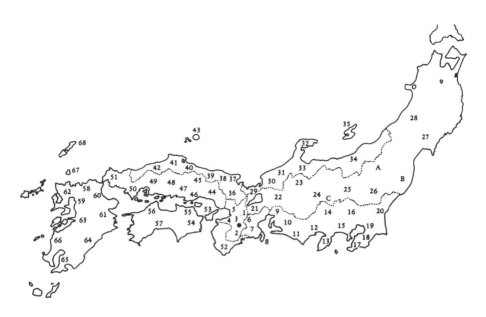

MAP 1 Provinces and Circuits of Ancient Japan. Reproduced by permission of the publisher from William Wayne Farris, *Population, Disease, and Land in Early Japan, 645–900*, Harvard-Yenching Institute Monograph Series, 24 (Cambridge: Harvard University, Council on East Asian Studies, 1985), pp. xviii–xix. © 1985 by the President and Fellows of Harvard College.

Key:

Kinai:
1. Yamashiro
2. Yamato
3. Kawachi
4. Izumi
5. Settsu

Tōkaidō:
6. Iga
7. Ise
8. Shima
9. Owari
10. Mikawa
11. Tōtōmi
12. Suruga
13. Izu
14. Kai

15. Sagami
16. Musashi
17. Awa
18. Kazusa
19. Shimōsa
20. Hitachi

Tosando:
21. Ōmi
22. Mino
23. Hida
24. Shinano
25. Kōzuke
26. Shimotsuke
27. Mutsu
28. Dewa

Hokurikudō:
29. Wakasa

30. Echizen
31. Kaga
32. Noto
33. Etchū
34. Echigo
35. Sado

San'indō:
36. Tanba
37. Tango
38. Tajima
39. Inaba
40. Hōki
41. Izumo
42. Iwami
43. Oki

San'yōdō:
44. Harima

45. Mimasaka
46. Bizen
47. Bitchū
48. Bingo
49. Aki
50. Suō
51. Nagato

Nankaidō:
52. Kii
53. Awaji
54. Awa
55. Sanuki
56. Iyo
57. Tosa

Saikaidō:
58. Chikuzen
59. Chikugo

60. Buzen
61. Bungo
62. Hizen
63. Higo
64. Hyūga
65. Ōsumi
66. Satsuma

Islands:
67. Iki
68. Tsushima

A. Iwashiro
B. Iwaki
C. Suwa

INTRODUCTION

The central contention of this book is that the rich archaeological discoveries of the past few decades have enabled historians to develop much more satisfactory interpretations of ancient Japan than was possible when scholars depended mostly on written sources. This truth is evidenced in four areas of inquiry: the hoary question of Yamatai; Japan-Korea relations; the creation of Chinese-type capital cities; and the appropriation of Chinese governing arrangements. These topics illustrate the broad process of historical evolution from a simple to a complex society, a process that in Japan's case is best viewed as occurring in two stages.

HISTORIOGRAPHIC OVERVIEW

Japan's philosophers and statesmen have long sought inspiration and legitimacy from the written record of their ancient past. The shaping of bygone eras to contemporary agendas began at least by the late seventh century, when members of the ruling elite compiled first *A Record of Ancient Matters* (*Kojiki*) and then *The Chronicles of Japan* (*Nihon shoki*). These books describe how a dynasty unbroken for ages had come to rule over divinely chosen islands. That interpretation survived over the next millennium despite the political decline and impoverishment of the imperial family.

Historical studies reached a new level of sophistication after 1700, when scholars of National Learning (*kokugaku*) performed philological and literary exegeses of ancient texts. Several writers envisioned a pure and innocent age of unique Japanese virtues before Chinese influence poisoned people's hearts

1

in the era after 700.[1] Modern oligarchs recreated the imperial institution after the Meiji Restoration of 1868, but *A Record* and *The Chronicles* served as the classical origins for many ideas expressed in the debate over the new ideology.[2] During the 1930s, a fundamentalist approach to these histories bolstered belief in the divine imperial throne and, by extension, Japan's war effort.

Not everyone agreed with the version of Japan's ancient period put forward in the court-sponsored histories. As early as the eighteenth century, Neo-Confucian rationalist Arai Hakuseki composed a radical critique of Japan's first chronicles.[3] After 1868, scholars avidly borrowed European historiographic techniques to interpret their distant past in light of findings elsewhere. These endeavors produced modern skeptics who claimed that the revered texts were contradictory and poorly substantiated, but until 1945 these critical scholars were a minority subject to harassment and even jail terms.

In the postwar period, historians analyzed and reinterpreted the ancient period as never before. With the imperial family no longer sacrosanct, scholars had more freedom to think and write about *A Record* and *The Chronicles* and to critique them using contemporary Chinese and Korean annals. They soon realized that the eighth century, when the formerly sacred texts had been compiled, really marked the beginning of Japanese written history, as it was the first century that could grant full scope to a historian's skills. That period produced an abundance of literary sources: law codes, poetry collections, detailed court chronicles, Buddhist stories, administrative documents. The age before 700, by contrast, was uncertain territory for textual experts. By the late 1970s, historians faced a crisis because they had virtually exhausted the plausible interpretations that could be gleaned from documents extant for the era until 800.

As Japanese historians depleted the written record, however, their colleagues in archaeology were hard at work. By the mid-1960s they had initiated an "archaeology boom" that continues today. A tide of hitherto unimagined original sources flooded the field, rejuvenating debates that had become arid and meaningless. Thanks to the efforts of innumerable archaeologists, scholars have never been so close to recreating the lives of long-vanished inhabitants of the archipelago, whether Yayoi peasants, Nara princes, or merchants outside Osaka Castle.

Like history, postwar archaeology had premodern roots but was influenced to a greater degree by European techniques.[4] The discovery of cultural artifacts dated back to the 600s, but men of learning did not make use of them until the eighteenth century. The American biologist E. S. Morse introduced modern archaeology to Japan in 1877 when he conducted the first scientific excavation at a prehistoric shell mound near Tokyo. Japanese academicians eagerly founded anthropological and archaeological associations and adopted the European periodization of antiquity: Old and New Stone Ages, Bronze Age, and Iron Age.

Between 1900 and 1945, archaeologists published research that laid the foundation for the postwar explosion of activity. Early in the century, Japanese scientists brought back basic new techniques from Europe, including typology and stratigraphy. By the 1920s, scholars had begun to employ local pottery styles to elaborate a chronology for ancient Japan unlike any proposed for the Mediterranean or Europe. About the same time, a leading thinker realized that it would be "difficult to utilize the periodization of *The Chronicles* as it is written."[5]

Two major discoveries stimulated archaeological interest after World War II. The first was the initial excavation of a Japanese Palaeolithic site at Iwajuku, several hours from Tokyo by train. The finds at Iwajuku suggested that human habitation of the archipelago was much older than previously believed. The second site was Toro, a third-century village that archaeologists unearthed complete with rice paddies and wooden tools.[6] Excavations proliferated thereafter, and by the late 1950s archaeologists had their hands full reporting on new sites and preserving old ones.

Beginning in 1962, the archaeology boom was in full swing. And with the information explosion, further specialization took place. Today Japan has an active archaeological community with more than four thousand members, about twenty times as many as in Great Britain, for example. In 1983 these scholars published over 1,600 site reports and received permits to dig at an estimated 14,500 excavations, seven times as many as in 1973.[7] In 1991, permits numbered a staggering 26,140, while expenditures amounted to 83.8 billion yen, almost $600 million.[8]

Archaeologists are largely responsible for a remarkable surge of interest in the ancient period, but they have had assistance from many quarters. In 1950, the Japanese Diet passed the Cultural Properties Preservation Law (no. 214 *bunka zai hogo hō*) requiring that an archaeological team be allowed to excavate prior to any major construction. The postwar building boom, which has laid bare so many acres for department stores and highways, has meant that the law has been frequently invoked. The press has played an important (although not always helpful) role, too, because it has fed the desire of Japanese citizens to know more about their ancient heritage.

Some say that the end of the prewar ideology should be cited as another reason for the archaeology explosion in postwar Japan. As noted earlier, the newfound freedom to treat historical sources critically has opened the way for many innovative interpretations that helped to destroy the myth of a single dynasty ruling a unified country from time immemorial. Yet ideology still places limits on archaeological research. The Imperial Household Agency bars excavation of more than one hundred tombs believed to predate the eighth century because they may contain the remains of once-sacred emperors (*tennō*) or their kin, a ban enforced since the late 1800s.

Today scholars of ancient Japan are obliged to know both written and material records. Sometimes archaeological and historical sources contradict each other; on other occasions they reinforce one another. The overlapping of two differing disciplines has been a healthy development, invigorating study of a long-lost era through the publication of many volumes of good scholarship.

FOUR TOPICS OF CONSEQUENCE

This book examines four major topics located at important points in the ancient Japanese past, defined in this case as the period until 800. The first issue is one of the oldest: the question of Yamatai. According to a third-century Chinese historian, somewhere in Japan was Yamatai, "the queen's country," an alliance of twenty-odd "countries" that paid tribute to the Central Kingdom. The location of this Yamatai has stumped Japanese scholars for centuries and continues to bedevil historians and archaeologists today. Two points of contention, the degree of political unity and the level of social and economic development of the archipelago, are implicit in the Yamatai debate.

The second problem is not as old as the controversy over Yamatai, but it is at least as laden with political meaning: what was the relationship between Japan and Korea from 350 to 700? Japanese written sources state that Japan conquered southern Korea and the Japanese court benefited from tributary items that flowed from the peninsula, but many Japanese and all North and South Korean scholars no longer accept this view. What does archaeology on both sides of the Korean Straits have to say about this interpretation? Does it support or refute the written sources?

The third subject too deals with Japan's ties to the mainland. Commencing in the seventh century, the Japanese ruling class imported Chinese-style institutions to bolster its power; one of the best-known imports was the Chinese-style, symmetrical capital city. What continental metropolis served as the prototype for Japanese capitals? Were the Japanese recreations real cities, and if so, how were they erected? What can the attempt to apply this Chinese idea to

Japan tell scholars about the last two centuries of Japan's political and economic development?

The fourth topic continues the examination of the archipelago's apprenticeship to Chinese civilization between 645 and 800, but it relies on a different archaeological source. Scientists have excavated some 170,000 wooden tablets throughout Japan. These artifacts were used for official business, and they bear dates and other information that shed new light on old historical questions. How quickly and thoroughly did the court attempt to copy Chinese-style government? How did it adapt Chinese bureaucratic procedures and revenue arrangements to Japan? What were the economic foundations and composition of the Nara aristocracy, and how did they change with the implementation of Chinese-style law?

Although these four areas of inquiry may appear to have little in common, they were not chosen randomly. Two criteria guided these selections. First, each topic encompasses both written records and material evidence, thereby illuminating how historical archaeology has developed in Japan over the past thirty years. This means that I have left to other researchers the undocumented prehistoric age before A.D. 100, despite its significance and appeal. Second, each topic contains clues as to how Japan developed from a simple into a complex society, or perhaps from barbarism to civilization.

The creation and spread of complex societies are subjects that have engaged scholars throughout the nineteenth and twentieth centuries.[9] Although there are many controversies, social scientists have agreed on a seminal definition that can be applied relatively well around the globe to groups as diverse as the Aztecs, the ancient Romans, the Guptas, and the West Africans. Complex society (also known by the more judgmental and therefore less satisfactory term "civilization") has occurred wherever one occupation—usually agriculture—has become so productive that a surplus accumulates, allowing some people to turn to other jobs such as soldiering, ruling, crafting goods, or praying to the gods.[10]

The degree and mix of specialization in each society depends on many factors. They may be similar or radically different in various areas, but usually the initial stages of complexity involve inventions, such as metallurgy and writing, and the erection of large monuments and urban centers.[11] Complex societies have social classes and are based on inequality. They have spread around the globe because they result in greater wealth and better control of the environment than the known alternatives.

Not every group has desired (or been productive enough) to settle down and become complex. Simple societies, where livelihoods such as hunting, herding, and gathering prevail, have faced intense competition from their specialized neighbors. In some cases, simple societies have been overwhelmed by invasion; in others, some members became aware of the challenges from a more powerful and complex neighbor and copied that culture as far as their own economy, social structure, and other factors would permit. The eventual result over millennia has been the diffusion of complex cultural patterns to most areas of the world.

OUTLINE OF JAPANESE BEGINNINGS

The story of ancient Japan may be divided for the purposes of this book into three parts: prehistoric, protohistoric, and fully historic.[12] Prehistoric Japan, for which no written sources are extant, includes the traditional archaeological periods of the Palaeolithic (180,000?–10,500 B.C.) and Jōmon (conventionally 10,500–300 B.C.).[13] During these epochs, almost all inhabitants lived by hunting, fishing, and gathering. Jōmon people used polished stone tools, lived in pit dwellings, and built elaborate "rope-pattern" pots by hand. Jōmon natives had a lively religious life, buried their dead in garbage heaps of shells and bones, and practiced tooth pulling as a rite of passage. The population probably never exceeded 300,000. Jōmon culture thrived in eastern Honshu and Hokkaido; there are few Jōmon sites in the area west of modern Nagoya.

The Jōmon era may seem typical of Neolithic times in other parts of the world, but in fact it was not. To be sure, the Jōmon people used polished stone tools and a few practiced horticulture late in the period. But agriculture, which was the foundation of Neolithic societies in China, the Middle East, and Europe, remained undeveloped. Two reasons help to explain Japan's relatively late adoption of farming: not only were hunting, fishing, and gathering such rich livelihoods that agriculture was an afterthought, but the nutrient-poor soil and limited plains area discouraged more settled occupations. Nonagricultural pursuits continued to flourish even into modern times, especially in mountainous regions.

Beginning in the fourth century B.C., the technologies of wet-rice agriculture and metallurgy entered northern Kyushu from southern Korea, initiating an epoch identified archaeologically as the Yayoi (conventionally 300 B.C.–A.D. 300). The effect of the new livelihood on western Japan was immediate, as population surged and settlements multiplied. Eastern Honshu resisted agriculture, and residents of Hokkaido relied mainly on hunting and fishing until the nineteenth century. The metals brought into the archipelago were first iron and then bronze, reversing the order known in other parts of the world. Iron was used primarily for tools; bronze was cast into swords, halberds, and ritual bells. The immigrants who bore the new technologies were taller than the natives, and one may infer that both warfare and intermarriage took place between the two groups.[14]

The protohistoric age began after A.D. 100, when texts and artifacts begin to play equally important roles. An important theme of protohistoric Japan is state formation, a gradual and painful process. Until 300, Japan remained under the control of numerous regional chieftains, each ruling an area of 100 to 150 square kilometers.[15] These chiefs formed alliances, especially with hegemons of the Kinai (the Kyoto–Osaka–Nara area).[16] By the late third century, Kinai chiefs had started building large keyhole tombs and filling them with valuable goods. Archaeologists call the years between 300 and 645 the Tomb period (*kofun jidai*) after these impressive monuments.

The fourth century is typically characterized as a time of increasing political unity in the archipelago. Archaeologically, the Kinai-style keyhole tombs spread outward to southern Kyushu and to northern Honshu by the end of the 300s. Historically, this era comprises a "century of mystery," for there is no contemporary written evidence. Myths recount stories of conquest and founding heroes, but scholars remain uncertain about the boundaries of the new state (or states) or the degree of centralized control.

Chinese histories record contact with Kinai hegemons from 421 to 502, the era of the Five Kings. According to Chinese annals, these Five Kings claimed suzerainty over numerous "countries" in eastern and western Japan and southern Korea. Historians believe that the leaders who dispatched missions to China ruled the Kinai and should be associated with truly mammoth tombs containing horse trappings, gold ornaments and crowns, massive amounts of iron tools and weapons, and pottery. Slowly an organized state structure with an aristocratic court was taking shape, but until the 500s succession wars were frequent. As a rule, the victor in these wars moved the palace away from the site of his predecessor, a custom that reduced the court's stability.

The years from 500 until 645 mark the heyday of the Yamato state, named after the province in the Kinai where rulers presided over an increasingly sophisticated court. In this epoch, the government underwent rapid development due at least partly to influence from the continent. Sometime in the first half of the sixth century, Buddhism was introduced. The court granted to aristocrats and local notables titles (*kabane*) and surnames (*uji*) that indicated their status and function, and the court organized units (*tomo; be*) to supply goods and services to members of the ruling elite.[17] The monarch provided legitimacy for the group, and the ruling ideology was first written down. Rulers also designated about 120 notables from other parts of Japan to be *kuni no miyatsuko* ("provincial servants"). The degree of centralized control is again an issue, but evidence suggests that a Yamato king could oust a rebellious notable and convert the area into a royal demesne (*miyake*).

State machinery underwent increasing elaboration from 645 to 800. A palace coup in 645, a disastrous military defeat in Korea in 663, and a civil war in 672 paved the way for an aggressive line of sovereigns who aspired to direct control over Japan's land and people based on Chinese models. In 701, the court completed the first set of Chinese-style penal and civil statutes. The ruling class modeled its tax, military, inheritance, census, land tenure, bureaucratic, religious, police, and market systems after Chinese examples. The first major urban centers were designed and constructed with reference to Chinese cities. The court assimilated many aspects of Chinese culture, including music and the arts, writing, medicine, and costume. The plenitude of written sources makes the eighth century fully historic; from this point on, there is less dependence on archaeology to supply basic data. Intensive analysis of the four subjects noted here should lead to greater insight into how Japanese civilization developed.

CHAPTER 1

THE LOST REALM

OF YAMATAI

The location of Yamatai is one of the oldest and most heated controversies in Japanese scholarship. Compiled in A.D. 280 from Chinese emissaries' reports, the description of Yamatai figured in the Japanese court's political agenda in the early eighth century as authors tried to fit its ruler into an unbroken line of divine sovereigns.[1] When interest in the ancient past revived in the eighteenth century, Yamatai became a major scholarly concern, with writers placing the "country" in Kyushu or the Kinai according to their beliefs about the antiquity and strength of the imperial dynasty. From 1868 to 1945, the volume of books and articles examining this problem may have surpassed output on any other historical question.

After World War II, historians expanded their inquiries into the ancient text and archaeologists utilized sites and artifacts in more convincing and exciting ways. By the late 1960s, a "Yamatai boom" was under way. The news media pounced on each discovery, trying to explain what it meant for the debate. Novelists wrote stories imagining life under a queen-shaman in third-century Japan. Taxicab drivers and housewives found it necessary to expound whenever anyone broached the topic of the long-lost realm.

As Yamatai became a national obsession, scholars changed their attitude toward the controversy. Today many are appalled by the amateurish attention and avoid the subject altogether. A prominent Japanese archaeologist has captured the new feeling in this revealing passage:

> Speaking of Yamatai, I have received this direct and simple question from newspaper reporters:
> "Prof! Prof! Was Yamatai in Kyushu or the Kinai?"

At this time, I always recall filling out an entry application when I went on an international trip some time ago. In the documents of that era, there was a line for religious affiliation. No matter how I considered it, I wasn't really much of a believer in any religion. But if I wrote "None" in the line for religion, I remembered the admonition of a senior colleague who said that "Europeans and Americans will think that you are strange if you don't fill it in," and so in that spirit I wrote "Shinto" or "Buddhism" in the space.

Isn't it useless to ask an unbeliever to confess his religion? When I get this kind of question about Yamatai, I feel the same way. . . . Excuse me, but I want to say it doesn't matter.[2]

While the question of Yamatai's location may no longer hold the fascination it once did, other issues—the nature of its society, economy, and polity—do matter profoundly. How unified was Japan in the third century? How far along the path to a complex society had the archipelago come? Because a scholarly retreat from Yamatai means neglecting crucial evidence bearing on these questions, an examination of the Chinese text from both historical and archaeological perspectives is in order.

THE HISTORY OF THE WEI DYNASTY

The first step in analyzing the record of Yamatai is a description of the author's career, the structure and contents of the composition, and the vicissitudes of the Yamatai controversy.[3] Historian Chen Shou was born in A.D. 233 in the southern Chinese country of Shu. At the time, civil war had torn the Middle Kingdom into three rival states, of which Shu had the most diverse and least sinicized populace. It therefore seems likely that Chen had contact with foreigners early in his life and may have begun to develop an interest in alien customs and things, a proclivity that is apparent in his later writing.

Although intelligent and well educated, Chen did not serve in an official capacity in the land where he was born. When he was thirty-one, the Jin dynasty destroyed Shu, but Chen found a patron, Zhang Hua, to promote his interests. On the recommendation of Zhang, a high officeholder at the Jin court, Chen assumed a position as an official historian for the dynasty. Zhang was probably a big influence on Chen's life. Two points in Zhang's career are particularly noteworthy: first, he had written a long book about geography, zoology, and botany, a fact that must have reinforced Chen's interests; second and more important, Zhang later oversaw Jin's defenses in the area around modern Beijing, where he studied routes to the distant lands of northeastern Asia, especially Korea.

In 280, the Jin unified China and Chen completed *The History of the Three Kingdoms,* which described the sixty years of Chinese history since the collapse of the Later Han dynasty (A.D. 25–220). These sixty years had witnessed internecine warfare among the states of Shu, Wei, and Wu, and the author wrote separate histories for each kingdom. Chen was especially careful to legitimize the Wei by giving the most space to that dynasty (thirty fascicles [*juan*] as opposed to fifteen for Shu and twenty for Wu), because the Jin ruling house claimed descent from the Wei. Zhang liked the work so much that he asked Chen to edit the annals of the Jin dynasty as well. Chen succeeded to other posts after 280, but he died at the age of sixty-five in 297.

After Chen's death, *The History of the Three Kingdoms* became renowned for its excellent prose style and for the moral lessons the author found in the past. Soon others made copies (one has been unearthed in the deserts of western China) and annotated the text. Eventually Chinese scholars recognized *The History of the Three Kingdoms* as the fourth official Chinese dynastic chronicle after the history of the known world (*Si ji*) written by Si-ma Qian and the records of the Former and Later Han dynasties. Chen's composition differed from these earlier accounts only in that *The History of the Three Kingdoms* contained neither annals (*biao*) nor treatises (*zhi*) on various topics. As John Young has pointed out, Confucian scholars composed their histories from original documents after the dynasty under study had fallen. *The History of the Three Kingdoms* adheres to the same relatively high standards of reliability and objectivity achieved by other official compilations.[4]

Chen devoted the thirtieth fascicle of *The History of the Wei Dynasty,* the relevant section of the *History of the Three Kingdoms,* to two major groups of non-Chinese: the Xian-bi (and related Mongols) and nine eastern peoples. Five of the nine "Eastern Barbarians" were from Manchuria, including the Puyŏ and the Kingdom of Koguryŏ; the other four comprised three southern Korean bands (the Ma-han, the Chen-han, and the Bian-chen) and the Wa, or Japanese (in Chinese, Wo).[5] Of these nine peoples, the author consigned by far the most space to the Wa (sixty-one lines) compared to fifty lines for all three southern Korean groups combined and forty-four for Koguryŏ. Chen Shou also covered details of Wa life not touched upon in other accounts. It seems clear that the Wa had special meaning to Chen and the Wei dynasty.

The "Account of the Wa" (in Japanese, *Wajin den*), as well as the reports on the other Eastern Barbarians, may be subdivided into three parts.[6] In the first

section, Chen wrote of the geographic location of the group under consideration, as well as its internal administrative divisions. For the Wa this part
includes the all-too-famous description of the route from the Chinese com-
mandery of Dai-fang near modern-day Seoul to the queen's country of Yamatai somewhere in Japan. The explanation of the route to Yamatai lists both
directions and distances, expressed sometimes in "leagues" (*li*) and sometimes
in travel time. The author also mentioned titles for local officials and the number of households in each of the Wa's "countries." As John Young has suggested, strict adherence to the distances and directions leaves one on the high
seas south of Kyushu. Alteration in the distances could steer the traveler to
Kyushu while adjustment of the directions could place one in the Kinai, the
historic home of Japan's imperial family.

Of the *Wajin den*'s eight stops along the way from the southern tip of Korea
to Yamatai, Japanese scholarly consensus has identified the first five: Tsushima,
Iki, Matsuro (Matsuura district in Hizen province), Ito (Ito district in Chikuzen province), and Na (somewhere in the Fukuoka plain).[7] Writers have
advanced many interpretations for the location of the final three sites. Usually
they presume that the last country (Yamatai; in Chinese Ye-ma-tai) refers to
Yamato, because the two words seem to resemble each other so closely. Yamato is best known as the province in the Kinai where the imperial dynasty built
its palaces in the seventh and eighth centuries, but it is a common place-name
found also in Kyushu.

Until 1945, this seemingly trivial disagreement over the location of Yamatai
had important political overtones. Because the Kinai was the traditional home
of the imperial dynasty, placing Yamatai in the Kinai seemed to affirm the
ancient origins of the imperial house, as the prewar ideology posited. Conversely, an argument for northern Kyushu signified rejection of claims for the
antiquity of the imperial family as ruler of the realm. In the years since 1945,
however, Japanese historians have proved the old way of thinking to be in
error. In the liberated atmosphere of contemporary Japan, only the most
confirmed rightists and traditionalists believe the imperial family existed as
such in the third century.

Even so, this innocent-looking dispute contains significant implications for
the level of political centralization in third-century Japan. Since the "Account
of the Wa" states that all eight places (plus twenty-one mentioned later) are
subservient to the queen of Yamatai and that only the Kingdom of Kunu to the
south of Yamatai resisted her rule, situating Yamatai in the Kinai could mean
that some powerbroker had already unified most of Japan from Nara down
the Inland Sea to the northern region of Kyushu by A.D. 250. If one follows this

line of reasoning, then Japan was unified early. If Yamatai turns out to have been in Kyushu, however, then Japan might still have been politically fragmented into many competing centers of power.

There seems to be little textual evidence to resolve this debate. Some have asserted that it is more likely that Chinese emissaries to Yamatai would have erred in tabulating distance rather than direction, but either is possible. One historian has reasoned that Chen exaggerated the distance of the northeastern peoples from the Chinese capital in *The History of the Wei Dynasty* in order to praise the accomplishments of his friend and patron Zhang Hua; such an interpretation favors the Kyushu theory.[8] One thing is certain: the difficulty of the problem has been matched only by the energy devoted to its resolution.

The second section of the "Account of the Wa" describes social customs and the economic base and government of the region. Conventions discussed in detail include tattooing, especially of fishermen as a ploy to avoid sea monsters; burial of the dead in a coffin with a small mound; funerals with a mourning period of up to ten days; unusual forms of dress like the poncho and the headband; a practice of journeying with a "fortune-keeper" who would try to bring travelers good luck by his virtuous behavior; habits such as squatting to convey respect to superiors; and divination. Mention is also made of the use of cosmetics, liquor, and wooden eating utensils; the clapping of hands during worship; separate sleeping arrangements for "father and mother, elder and younger"; and polygamy.

The second part also deals briefly with economic matters. The Wa cultivated grains including rice, as well as hemp plants and mulberry trees, and they wove fine silk. The climate was warm and mild and there were no oxen, horses, tigers, leopards, or sheep. Chen Shou listed many kinds of plant life, minerals such as cinnabar, and precious gems like jade and pearls. One important passage states that the Wa had both granaries and markets, where exchange occurred under the watchful eyes of officials.

The author devoted more attention to the government of the Wa. Fighters used spears, shields, and wooden bows with bamboo arrows tipped with iron or bone. Crime was rare, but punished harshly; taxes were collected. A man once ruled the Wa, but there were so many uprisings for seventy or eighty years that eventually leaders turned to Himiko, an unmarried female shaman, to govern them. She had a thousand women attendants, as well as a younger brother who "served her food and drink and acted as her medium of communication." Few saw Himiko, as she lived in a guarded palace surrounded by towers and stockades. The "Account of the Wa" also describes an official stationed in Ito in northern Kyushu who kept the residents "in a state of awe and fear" and acted as an inspector for emissaries coming from the continent to see the queen.

Chen concluded the second section by describing an island of dwarfs and lands of naked men and black-toothed people, all of which adds an air of unreality to the narrative. Twice during the second part of the account the author refers to the Wa as resembling or residing near peoples of southern China. As one observant scholar has noted, the comparisons to southern China generally fit well with the depiction of the customs of the Wa, suggesting that the Wa were related to or heavily influenced by the peoples of southern China and Southeast Asia.[9] There is relatively little in Chen's account to argue for the importance of Northeast Asian, especially Korean, elements in Wa society. All these facts might also be taken to indicate that Yamatai was in southern Kyushu.

The third part of the "Account of the Wa" deals with Yamatai's diplomatic relations with the Wei.[10] In A.D. 238, Himiko dispatched a representative to Dai-fang, an outpost recently brought under Chinese control. The governor sent the representative to the Wei capital at Luo-yang, and in the twelfth month of that year the Chinese emperor issued a proclamation to Himiko calling her the "Queen of Wa Friendly to the Wei." In return for presents from Himiko, the emperor awarded her a gold seal with a purple ribbon, various lengths of colored fabrics, one hundred bronze mirrors, two swords, gold, jade, and beads. In 240, the governor of Dai-fang had a representative take the proclamation and presents to the queen, who proceeded to send another emissary to thank the emperor. In 243, Himiko ordered yet another embassy to go to Luo-yang and pay tribute; two years later the Chinese court rewarded the emissary.

In 247, when a new governor of Dai-fang arrived in Korea, Himiko reported that she was at war with the recalcitrant king of Kunu. The Chinese tried to buttress Himiko's position as an ally, but at the same time they advised reconciliation. Then Himiko died, and "a great mound was raised, more than a hundred paces in diameter." A king tried to assume Himiko's place, but disorder prevailed until a girl of thirteen related to Himiko became queen and peace once again reigned. The governor of Dai-fang proclaimed her the new leader of Yamatai, and she then sent a delegation of twenty persons to Luo-yang with presents. The "Account of the Wa" in *The History of the Wei Dynasty* stops at this point. Except for the mention of one mission in A.D. 265 in a different Chinese history, Chinese written sources are silent on the Wa until the beginning of the fifth century.

THE CONTROVERSY OVER YAMATAI:
A HISTORICAL PERSPECTIVE

The "Account of the Wa" had a direct effect on Japan's first historians.[11] In the early eighth century the imperial house ordered a committee of courtiers to create a history of Japan emphasizing the dynasty's divine origins and unbroken lineage. In 720, compilers completed *The Chronicles of Japan,* and they referred to Chen Shou's history three times in the annals of Empress (*kōgō*) and Regent (*sesshō*) Jingū (r. 201–269, according to *The Chronicles*).[12] The references described the missions sent back and forth from the Wa to the Wei in the third century. According to John Young, the authors of *The Chronicles* wanted to equate Himiko with Jingū and Yamatai with Yamato in the Kinai to reinforce the imperial family's claim to rule from antiquity. The appropriation of Chen's work for political purposes had begun. Later scholars would also note that the detailed narratives about Jingū marked a dividing line in the Japanese compilation as it moved from mythology to a more factual record.

For the next millennium, Japanese historians barely mentioned Yamatai or Himiko. The scholarly debate over the "Account of the Wa" really dates back about three centuries, a span of time that one expert, writing in 1982, has divided into five periods:[13] the premodern era to 1868; the years after the Meiji Restoration from 1868 to 1910; 1910 to 1930, the high point of research before World War II; 1930 to 1945, when censorship and war stymied research; and 1945 to 1971. In turn, the decades since World War II have seen such a flood of new interpretations that the same expert has analyzed the writings for that era and divided it into four more subperiods. To comprehend the Yamatai controversy in its historical context, it is necessary to review here the copious work of Japanese scholars.

Study of the Yamatai problem began auspiciously in the early eighteenth century with Arai Hakuseki, the famous philosopher-statesman. Arai flatly stated that the story of Yamatai in *The History of the Wei Dynasty* was reliable; this assertion immediately prompted criticism from a scholar of the Mito school, who accepted the veracity of *The Chronicles* and dismissed Chinese compilations. Arai traced the route of the Chinese emissaries as far as northern Kyushu. Early in his life he argued that Yamatai was in the Kinai, while later he seems to have favored northern Kyushu. Thus the origin of the debate over the location of Yamatai resides in the work of one scholar.[14] Arai also equated Himiko with Jingū and criticized the dating of both Japanese and Chinese sources. Most current Japanese historians see Arai Hakuseki as the pioneer of objective research into the controversy.

Motoori Norinaga, another renowned philosopher who was a member of the chauvinistic National Learning school, addressed the problem of Yamatai in the 1770s and 1780s. Unlike Arai, Motoori argued that the Chinese record was filled with inaccuracies; the true account of Japan in the third century A.D. was available only in *The Chronicles*. Motoori rejected the entries from *The History of the Wei Dynasty* in the annals of Jingū in *The Chronicles* as later accretions. Specifically, the National Learning scholar believed that a king of the warlike peoples (*kumaso*) of southern Kyushu, which Jingū had yet to pacify, had dispatched to the Wei emissaries who masqueraded as officials of Jingū's court in the Kinai. Therefore Himiko was indeed a reference to Jingū, but the inhabitants of southern Kyushu had fooled the Wei emperor, whose ambassadors had traveled only as far as Kyushu. Yamatai had to be in Kyushu, as Motoori's analysis of the route and customs also supposedly proved. Motoori's usurpation hypothesis (*gisen setsu*) carried great weight for the next century.

A crucial discovery on Shiga Island in northern Kyushu in the spring of 1784 soon added weight to Motoori's view. A farmer repairing a ditch to his rice paddy happened upon an unusual treasure: "As small stones gradually appeared, there was a large rock that could be carried only by two men. When we removed the rock with a crowbar, there was a shining object among more stones."[15] The prize was a golden seal with an inscription of five characters, which contemporary scholars were uncertain how to read. All agreed that the inscription stated that the Former Han dynasty (206 B.C.–A.D. 8) had sent the seal to a king in Japan; some thought the chief ruled Ito, while others regarded the seal as belonging to the monarch of southern Kyushu. Motoori argued that both positions were possible, but he clearly believed that the discovery supported his previously stated view that Yamatai was in Kyushu.[16] The seal was soon widely accepted as a key element in the more popular Kyushu theory.

With the coming of the Meiji Restoration in 1868, European historical scholarship flooded Japan for the first time. In particular, the German school of historiography led by Leopold von Ranke encouraged Japanese historians to be critical of their sources and avoid contemporary political and religious biases. In his own words, Ranke emphasized a "strict presentation of the facts, contingent and unattractive though they may be, [as] the highest law."[17] Perhaps the Neo-Confucian tradition of the Edo period (1600–1868) predisposed many scholars to follow Ranke, whose methods remain influential today.

At the same time, a second trend had an opposite and more deleterious effect on historians. Because the Meiji ideology formulated in the late nineteenth century made the emperor sacrosanct, the government could view criticism of *The Chronicles* or other early Japanese texts as an attack on the imperial system. While some writers deferred to the times and became more nationalistic, several lost university posts because of their actions and writings during the 1890s.[18]

Despite these limitations, one brilliant contribution forever changed the way Japanese looked at their history. Beginning in 1878, Naka Michiyo wrote a series of articles maintaining that the chronology of *The Chronicles* was totally inaccurate. He argued that compilers had artificially backdated the reign of the first Emperor Jimmu (r. 660–585 B.C.) by six hundred years to make his enthronement appear to have been an epoch-making act.[19] Naka's theory affected the dating for later rulers as well; in his chronology Jingū became a fourth-century queen whose reign could not possibly have coincided with Himiko's. Motoori's usurpation hypothesis, along with Arai's Himiko–Jingū equation, had to be wrong.

Just as these theories lost their credibility, another insight heartened those looking for Yamatai in Kyushu. In 1892, a Japanese scholar correctly read the inscription on the golden seal found on Shiga Island as "The King of the Country of Na of the Wa from the Han Dynasty." Na was one of the place-names identified as being on the way from Dai-fang to Himiko's residence in Yamatai. It appeared that communication between northern Kyushu and China had originated even before the Wei. Bolstered once again by the seal, scholars reasoned that Himiko must have been a local chieftain unrelated to the imperial line and tried to pinpoint Yamatai in southern or northern Kyushu. One well-known historian even wrote that the argument about the location of Yamatai was over.[20]

The year 1910 began a new era in the controversy over Yamatai when advocates of both the Kyushu and Kinai interpretations solidified their arguments. The main supporter of the Kyushu theory, Shiratori Kurakichi of Tokyo University, asserted three points: first, the directions in the "Account of the Wa" were generally correct but the distances had been exaggerated; second, Yamatai had lost its war with Kunu (also in Kyushu) as a result of the collapse of its ally Wei in Korea and eventually had fallen to forces from the Kinai in the fourth century; and third, Himiko's power was religious and this fact had tempted the compilers of *The Chronicles* to equate her with Jingū.

The leading adherent of the Kinai theory was Kyoto University's Naitō Torajirō, who believed that the distances were accurate but all directions should be changed from south to east. He also argued that titles for Wa officials were synonymous with those used later at the imperial court, that Himiko was the high priestess of the imperial shrine at Ise, and that Wa leaders had even brought southern Korea under their control. Other historians soon took sides, deriving place-names and reading the text to suit their own purposes.

By the 1910s archaeology was a serious discipline in Japan, and these scholars hesitantly began to consider the Yamatai problem. They debated the nature of the site where the golden seal was found. Was it the tomb of the king of Na? Was it a hiding place? If the seal belonged to the king of Na, then why was it buried on Shiga Island and not in Na? These questions were difficult to answer, but one archaeologist offered a widely accepted interpretation: the Shiga seal was identical to one that the author of *The History of the Later Han Dynasty* had referred to as being sent to the king of Na in A.D. 57.[21] According to the same record, thereafter other Wa communities dispatched missions, but the Later Han could not make presents due to its own internal strife. The collapse of the Wa ally also initiated an epoch of warfare in Japan in the middle and late second century A.D., as described in *The History of the Later Han Dynasty*.

Archaeologists from Kyoto University led by Umehara Sueji seized upon hitherto ignored artifacts as proof that Yamatai was located in the Kinai. According to this view, all bronze mirrors dug up in Kyushu dated from the Early Han or Wang Mang interregnum (up to the first years A.D.). Yet mirrors picturing Chinese gods and animals in relief (*hanniku bori shinjū kyō*), found almost exclusively in the Kinai, contained a few Chinese characters that seemed to provide evidence for limiting the date of manufacture to the Wei or Liu Sung (A.D. 420–478) dynasties.[22] One specific type of these mirrors (later termed a "triangle-rimmed deity and beast mirror," *sankakuen shinjū kyō*) was especially interesting. A fragment excavated in the Kanto had a partial date that seemed to be A.D. 265, a year during which the Wei dynasty existed. Because most triangle-rimmed deity and beast mirrors were recovered in the Kinai, surely that region was Yamatai.[23]

Yet many found flaws in the archaeological argument.[24] First, there was disagreement over the dating of the mirrors; most bore no writing by which scholars could easily fix the year of manufacture.[25] How could one be sure that the deity and beast mirrors were indeed the ones sent to Himiko? Archaeologists often based their decisions on typology, very much a matter of interpretation. The problem became even more complicated when one realized that archaeologists had found the so-called Wei mirrors in giant keyhole-shaped tombs, which scholars of the prewar era dated to the late third or early fourth centuries, several decades after Himiko's death. Second, there was the problem of sample. Most triangle-rimmed deity and beast mirrors, it was true, came from the Kinai, but because there was an official ban against digging the imperial tombs, no one really knew how representative the sample was. Moreover, many mirrors unearthed before the Meiji Restoration had made their way via antiquities dealers into private collections and museums after leaving the tombs, with their provenances thus unknown.[26] Finally, critics pointed out that third-century owners could have moved the mirrors far beyond the point of entry into Japan. In some cases, users of the mirrors had rubbed them smooth, which suggested long service and even inheritance. Broken ones had been mended with rope. Umehara tried to prove that triangle-rimmed deity and beast mirrors had been interred soon after their importation, but advocates of the Kyushu theory seized upon these methodological weaknesses to reject the testimony of Kyoto archaeologists.

In fact, archaeologists soon came to the conclusion that there were two distinctive cultural centers in the first two centuries A.D. One was the Kinai, where bronze bells (*dōtaku*) were important ritual objects; the other was northern Kyushu and western Honshu, where bronze swords, spearheads, and halberds were common. The existence of this cultural variation raised many questions: Was one region superior to the other? Had rulers of the Kinai dominated northern Kyushu from the outset? Or had Kyushu been stronger and later conquered the Kinai, as Tsuda Sōkichi, the iconoclastic historian, insisted? Despite so many doubts, the contribution of archaeologists in the prewar period provided a foundation for further refinement in the postwar era when ideological restrictions lessened and the number of excavations increased dramatically.

By 1930, the debate over Yamatai was being swept up in a new wave of intellectual endeavor.[27] Marxism and its materialistic interpretation of history had entered Japan in the late nineteenth century, but their effect on historiography became evident only in the 1920s. By 1929, writers who studied slavery in Yamatai began to use terms like "the form of property ownership" and "modes of production," indicating the influence of Marxist thought. Marxism can be a rigid dogma, but the materialistic interpretation did raise many problems never before considered, such as the economic basis of Himiko's rule and the nature of the social structure.

Marxist thinkers of the 1930s considered the "Account of the Wa" an important historical record and were not afraid to synthesize many different approaches. Most liked archaeology and argued that Yamatai was in the Kinai because of the preponderance of mirrors there. A few wrote that the debate over the location of Yamatai did not matter, but most believed that a resolution of the conflict could provide a significant step in defining third-century Japanese society and government. All Marxist authors concluded that the Wa had a class society with private property and a primitive state. One historian pointed to the phrase "the people agreed upon a woman for their ruler" after the era of civil war and reasoned that Yamatai was a tribal confederacy.[28]

Non-Marxist historians also contributed to the deepening interest in the nature of Wa society. One scholar asserted that Himiko was really Yamato-toto-momo-so-hime-no-mikoto, aunt of the legendary Emperor Sūjin on his father's side, because her supposed tomb at Hashihaka in Nara measured about a hundred paces in diameter, the measurement given for Himiko's grave. This theory gained adherents in the postwar period. Another saw in Himiko an expression of women's political authority in early Japan.[29]

As the 1930s wore on, however, Japanese political leaders became more and more intolerant of original thinking on Japanese history in general and Yamatai in particular. After 1935 censorship ruined most attempts to analyze Yamatai or Wa society; books from 1935 to 1945 contain long passages with nothing but x's where text should have been.[30] Along with the constant bombing and harsh realities of war, government censors dealt a death blow to objective scholarship until 1945.

The end of World War II liberated Japanese scholars from these conditions, and research on Yamatai and all Japanese history soon showed the benefits. Writing in 1972, an authority on the "Account of the Wa" divided the decades of postwar study into four periods: the beginning of new research from 1945 through 1949; an era of reaction and searching for new paradigms from 1950 through 1954; the decade 1955–1964 when major advances were stimulated by archaeological finds; and 1965 to 1972, the epoch of the "Yamatai boom."[31]

The first five postwar years were really a period of rediscovery. Textbooks began to include the record of Himiko for the first time since the 1920s, and historians again became conscious of the importance of the "Account of the Wa" and began to propose new interpretations. One author, noting that Himiko controlled a fairly large area and carried on foreign relations with China, concluded that Japan was not as primitive as some had believed. An advocate of the Kyushu location argued that Wa officials of northern Kyushu actually used written documents to communicate with Himiko. Yet a third scholar asserted that Yamatai was a loose confederation of communities that frequently fought among themselves; Queen Himiko could not even pass along her power safely to an heir. This same author believed that Yamatai was in Kyushu and that the bronze mirrors had been imported into the Kinai after Himiko's death and the resulting civil war.[32]

Two trends appeared in studies done between 1950 and 1954. The first was a reaction that reemphasized prewar myth-history. Just as in Motoori's day, scholars wrote that Chen Shou had based his descriptions of the Wa on hearsay evidence. Watsuji Tetsurō, who had first proposed the existence of two cultural centers in Kyushu and the Kinai, tried to reconcile the "Account of the Wa" with the myth-history in The Chronicles.[33] These five years also saw the rise of "people's history," the use of Marxist categories, and the reemployment of linguistic methods. Historians tried to define Himiko's era as a slave society or time of communal property and looked for a heroic age similar to the Homeric legends of Mediterranean history. Sakamoto Tarō suggested that Yamatai was originally in Kyushu and that the conqueror symbolized by the first Emperor Jimmu had taken the place-name with him when he subjugated the Kinai.[34]

The ten years from 1955 through 1964 comprised an epoch of great advances, as archaeologists made new and stunning contributions. The most striking work centered on a tomb excavated near Kyoto which contained numerous bronze mirrors that may date from the third century. This research still constitutes the most solid foundation for resolving the debate over the location of Yamatai, and it is discussed later in detail.

In addition to the archaeological contribution, historians tried to define the character of Yamatai and Wa society more seriously than ever before. Ueda Masaaki and Inoue Mitsusada carried on an extended debate on the nature of the Yamatai polity.[35] Ueda, a professor from Kyoto University and an advocate of the Kinai theory, argued that Himiko's was a despotic state with a generalized slave system (*sōtaiteki dorei sei*), a term borrowed from Marx's *Pre-Capitalist Formations*. Inoue, a Tokyo University supporter of the Kyushu position, replied that Yamatai was a "balance of small states," or loose alliance of communities, and even allowed for popular political expression. Ishimoda Shō fueled the debate by constructing four criteria for state formation and suggesting that Yamatai was not yet a state by his definition. From this point on, it became common for Kyoto University historians and archaeologists to argue for the Kinai theory while scholars from Kyushu and Tokyo generally favored the Kyushu hypothesis.

Still other discussions focused on social structure and the international scene. The "Account of the Wa" used three terms to describe members of Wa society, and scholars tried to define the words more precisely. In the end, historians decided that the Wa had three classes below Himiko: tribal chiefs (*daijin*), village headmen and commoners (*geko*), and slaves (*seikō*). Writers on the international aspect of Himiko's power concluded that Yamatai was a fragile creation dependent upon the political fortunes of China and its possessions on the Korean peninsula: when China was strong and controlled Korea, Wa chieftains could look for its support in their internal battles; when China was weak, the Wa descended into civil war. The inscribed seal conferred by the Han emperor on the king of Na showed that Chinese symbols of authority wielded great influence among the Wa.[36]

The final period, from 1965 through 1972, ushered in the "Yamatai boom."

These years coincided with the beginning of the archaeology explosion in Japan, but other scholars still insisted on having their say. In 1969, one historian proposed a particularly inventive theory based on careful scrutiny of Chen's spelling.[37] Noting that the text actually read "Yamai" or "Yamaichi" rather than "Yamatai," this critic shocked the academic world by arguing that the entire three-century debate was a product of willful misreading of *The History of the Wei Dynasty*. He bolstered his interpretation by suggesting that the Chinese character "*tai*" was a taboo word that compilers would never have employed to describe a non-Chinese kingdom. Not surprisingly, advocates of this theory located "Yamaichi" in Kyushu.

Criticism of the Yamaichi reading was quick and devastating.[38] The oldest extant text of Chen's work was a Sung edition dated 1003, and the printers had indeed used "*ichi*" instead of "*tai*." But an earlier compilation, *A View of the Great Peace* (*Tai ping yu lan;* 984) included portions of the "Account of the Wa" from *The History of the Wei Dynasty* and utilized Yamatai, not Yamaichi. When one considered that *The History of the Later Han Dynasty, The History of the Liang Dynasty,* and *The History of the Sui Dynasty* all wrote of Yamatai, it seemed that Yamaichi was probably a misprint and that the bold attempt to resolve the controversy had failed. The collapse of the "Yamaichi" theory showed the bankruptcy of linguistic methods, although one benefit was enhanced textual criticism.

In the years since 1972, three characteristics have marked the Yamatai controversy. First, the number of articles and books focusing on the "Account of the Wa" has grown immensely. Some works were of high quality and examined such topics as how the ancient Chinese conducted foreign relations. Archaeologists took up the debate and tried to illustrate Chen's text with the artifacts and remains that they were uncovering. Scholars from disciplines outside history and archaeology utilized comparative data to analyze Wa society and kinship.

Second, the debate became more diffuse and amateurs joined what was becoming a cacophony. The "Account of the Wa" became a national obsession popularized in print and the media. Mystery writers looked for the secret of Himiko's hold over the populace. Every time a sensational new archaeological find occurred, newspapers asked if the site could have been Yamatai. Owners of coffee shops discussed the Wa with their customers, and housewives enlightened their neighbors on possible locations for "the queen's country."

Third, professional scholars began to retreat from the debate. As one might expect, under these circumstances myth-history and ideology made a bid for a comeback. Nationalists claimed the existence of the Miyashita ("under the shrine") documents, which "proved" among other things that the mythical first Emperor Jimmu was a real person. A sample of this attitude is manifest in the following excerpt in which a nationalist put Chen on trial:

> The "Account of the Wa" in *The History of the Wei Dynasty* that you wrote runs the gamut from Japanese and Korean geography to Queen Himiko and her customs. As noted in the complaint, the mistakes, confusion, omissions, and imperfections in the account are extreme; for this reason people have come to doubt the true outline of Japanese history and have even gone to the point of changing the organization of the ancient Japanese past. The controversy has wasted the valuable time and money of numerous Japanese historians and others. This waste hurts not just the Japanese people but the entire human race. Thus your crime is not merely a minor offense.[39]

In this atmosphere, research into the "Account of the Wa" could only suffer. Nevertheless, the description of Wa society written by Chen Shou is an invaluable source. Can one use archaeology and related disciplines to illuminate the Chinese historian's work?

CHEN SHOU'S "ACCOUNT OF THE WA" AS A PICTURE OF YAYOI JAPAN: AN OVERVIEW

Two questions have been implicit in the Yamatai controversy over the last three hundred years. First, how unified was the archipelago in the third century? Did Himiko rule a confederation based in the Kinai and embracing much of western Japan, or was she merely the shaman of one isolated community in northern Kyushu? Second, how advanced was Japan around A.D. 250? Had the archipelago made large strides toward becoming a complex society with a productive economy, or was it relatively backward?

These two issues have assumed their own form among Japan's archaeologists. For most, the "Account of the Wa" describes the Yayoi period (usually dated 300 B.C.–A.D. 300), when clothed cultivators and anglers lived in many populous communities with nascent social distinctions and political affiliations, fought and traded among themselves, and communicated with the continent. But for some, Chen's writing portrays a more complex society making the transition from the Yayoi to the Tomb period (conventionally dated A.D. 300–645), with Himiko commanding chieftains along the Inland Sea and building a huge tumulus for her burial. Which of these two competing views is more accurate? Only an evaluation of the account from an archaeological perspective can suggest an answer. As a first step, let us check the general accuracy of Chen's text by comparing it to the archaeological record of late Yayoi Japan with respect to the natural environment and population, the society and its customs, and the economy. (The polity will be examined in the next section.)

But before undertaking this analysis, let us define some terms. The words Jōmon ("rope pattern") and Yayoi (a section of downtown Tokyo) originally referred to two different types of hand-built earthenware. As noted in the Introduction, scholars have customarily dated the Jōmon to 10,500–300 B.C. and the Yayoi to 300 B.C.–A.D. 300, but because archaeologists use pottery styles to construct relative sequences, few absolute dates are reliable. Increasingly scholars are pushing the date for the beginning of the Yayoi era back to 400 B.C. or earlier, and many scientists, especially those envisioning Himiko as a transitional figure of the late Yayoi and early Tomb eras, now place the end of the Yayoi period no later than A.D. 250.[40] By extension, Jōmon and Yayoi have come to mean the distinctive cultural systems of those eras—that is, Jōmon alludes to the hunter-gatherer society of polished stone users and Yayoi refers to the settled agricultural peoples who cast bronze and forged iron tools. The boundary between these eras and systems is no longer as clear as it once was, however, and there was always great regional variation. By Yayoi I mean the cultural system of rice growing and metallurgy that entered Japan gradually from Korea as early as 400 B.C. and predominated in the western half of the archipelago until the late third century A.D.[41]

The Natural Environment and Population

Chen's account lists nine varieties of trees and three types of bamboo as native to Wa. Although scholars do not agree on exactly how the Chinese words translate into modern scientific terminology, there is consensus that the description of vegetation fits western Japan in the late Yayoi period (third century) fairly accurately.[42] One expert has argued that Chen's inventory of trees and bamboo is closer to the glossy-leaved plants found in the warm climes of Kyushu, but it is probably going too far to use the catalog of vegetation in the "Account of the Wa" to decide the location of Yamatai. Analyses of pollen and pieces of wood found at Yayoi sites throughout western Japan show that third-century Kyushu had only one more species than the Kinai in Chen's tally of trees and bamboo.[43]

Chen's account also mentions four types of jewels as Wa possessions: pearls, "green jade," "white gems," and "carved jade." Once again the precise nature of these terms is open to question, but one scholar has suggested that the four referred to pearls, jasper, carved shells, and jadeite curved beads (*magatama*), respectively.[44] If one accepts these characterizations, then archaeologists have uncovered evidence of all four in late Yayoi sites in western Japan, especially in northern Kyushu.[45]

Just when it seems that Chen Shou's narrative is a perfectly accurate portrayal of Yayoi Japan, however, other points raise doubts. His account asserts, for instance, that Wa had a "warm and mild climate." This characterization fits fairly well with pollen analyses done at some third-century sites near modern Osaka and in northern Kyushu. Gina Barnes has presented evidence that argues for a rise in the water level in the Kawachi inlet (modern Osaka) about A.D. 100.[46] But Japan's leading expert on climate history disagrees, arguing that Himiko's time was a global Little Ice Age.[47] This scholar utilizes evidence such as the depth of the Nile River and the testimony of European historians to bolster statistics from Korean records. A pollen analysis conducted for the Kodera site in Ehime prefecture supports the claim for a Little Ice Age to a certain extent by suggesting cool summers during the late Yayoi era.[48] The climate historian goes on to argue that the sudden burst of cold weather led to famine conditions responsible for civil wars before and after Himiko's reign. One therefore wonders: was Chen, a historian writing hundreds of miles away from Japan in northern China, misled because he believed that the Wa lived in a tropical zone far to the south, near Taiwan and South China?

The view of population that one sees in the "Account of the Wa" also presents a mixed result. Chen characterizes Wa communities as densely settled: Yamatai was supposed to have had 70,000 households, a figure that some take to be exaggerated. This picture of dense population corresponds well to what archaeologists know as the Yayoi demographic explosion, which saw the number of inhabitants increase from about 260,000 in the mid-Jōmon (3500–2400 B.C.) to between 1 and 4 million by the end of the third century A.D., a leap of between fourfold and sixteenfold.[49] In western Honshu and Kyushu, where the hunting, fishing, and gathering occupations of the Jōmon had done poorly but Yayoi agriculture flourished, population growth was an astounding thirty-two times.[50]

Other aspects of the archaeological record give rise to doubt as well. For instance, Chen's account states that "the people live long, some to one hundred and others to eighty or ninety years." While there has been little work on longevity during the Yayoi period, studies of Jōmon skeletons and eighth-century census registers suggest an average life expectancy at birth of fifteen years during the Jōmon and about twice that (twenty-seven to thirty-two years) in the 700s.[51] Of course, a few people always outlive the average, but it is difficult to see how Chen could have deemed third-century Japanese to "live long."

Even the name given to the Japanese by Chen—"Wa," or "small person"— stirs debate. Archaeologists have uncovered skeletons from Yayoi sites in northern Kyushu and western Honshu: men averaged as much as 163 centimeters (5 feet 3½ inches) and women about 152 centimeters (just under 5 feet). Although these persons may seem short by modern American standards, they were taller than average for western Japanese of the Jōmon epoch, taller than Japanese of the Tomb era, and about the same height as southern Koreans. Thus the skeletal evidence does not seem to provide a rationale for the Chinese epithet. In discussing the term "Wa," however, it is important to remember Chen's perspective. The Japanese may have received such an epithet simply because they were more diminutive than northern Chinese, who were in some cases more than 170 centimeters tall. One should remember that Chen was born in southern China but wrote his account in a northern Chinese city (Luo-yang).[52]

Society and Social Customs

A major controversy concerns the family arrangements of Wa commoners, which the "Account of the Wa" describes as follows: "Father and mother, elder and younger, sleep separately." This assertion is difficult to interpret: do all four relations (fathers, mothers, elder and younger children) each sleep in different quarters, or do parents and their offspring sleep in their own rooms? An ethnologist has constructed a speculative but thought-provoking argument based on this passage.[53] Following the second interpretation—that parents and children sleep in separate rooms—he writes that "elder" and "younger" probably referred to grown progeny with their own families. He then compares these arrangements to those of certain southern Chinese and Southeast Asian peoples (whom Chen would have known about) and argues that Chen's description was intended to show that both the Wa and his native southern Chinese shared a similar form of kinship.

Usually when one thinks of kinship patterns, the first to come to mind are patrilineal or matrilineal norms in which a family traces its descent through the father's or mother's line, respectively. Yet there is another common form of kinship called bilateral relations in which kin can claim descent through either parent. In contrast with patrilineal and matrilineal kinship, bilateral forms are highly flexible and "pragmatic." Bilateral kinship grants power to women, often allowing them to live separately from their husbands and hold their own property. This ethnologist has interpreted Chen's statement to mean that the Wa utilized bilateral kinship forms, like residents of southern China and Southeast Asia.

The archaeological record provides limited support for this claim. The best-known example comes from a burial ground on the western tip of Honshu at Doigahama.[54] Archaeologists uncovered about 4,200 square meters of a graveyard with 207 human skeletons at Doigahama and concluded that the site was from the early Yayoi era. The archaeologist who wrote the report on Doigahama divided the area into two parts: the eastern and northern sections. In the eastern section there were 122 skeletons (69 males, 28 females, and 25 infants), while in the north villagers had interred 11 males, 12 females, and 1 infant. Although almost all the dead in the eastern section possessed jewelry and accessories, few in the north did. Moreover, the overwhelming majority of skeletons in the eastern plots had participated in ritual tooth pulling (60 of 70); only about half of those interred in the north were missing teeth.

The two sections of the burial ground seemed to distinguish two different groups of people, and ethnologists have argued that the distinction was founded on the birthplace of those interred. The eastern section, where infants were buried, represented persons who had always lived in the village; the northern graveyard, which contained one-half males and one-half females and almost no children, represented outsiders who had come to Doigahama to live. In the northern section, about half had had their teeth pulled, a condition implying that they attained adulthood at their native settlement before they reached Doigahama.[55] One of the strongest reasons for adults to come to Doigahama from another village was marriage, and since the "outsider" burial ground contained almost equal numbers of males and females, the kinship system could not have been unilateral. It must have been bilateral.

Later historical evidence strongly supports this reading of Doigahama's graveyard and the Chinese historian's text.[56] When the Japanese court adopted Chinese law in the eighth century, for inheritance and mourning purposes it borrowed Chinese patrilineal terminology to describe Japanese families: the Chinese distinguished between the father's relatives and the mother's by different words for each. But in one interpretation of the Taihō Code written around 730, an ancient legal expert known for his realism wrote that there was no difference in Japanese terms for one's father's and mother's relatives. In Chinese, for example, two separate words distinguished between one's father's sister and one's mother's sister, but in Japanese the terms were the same (oba).[57] Taken together with other evidence on marriage, adoption, and inheritance, this testimony supports a bilateral kinship system for the eighth-century Japanese. Heian literature confirms this picture as well.[58]

Could bilateral kinship date back as far as the Yayoi period? The inference is tempting, given the strength of Nara and Heian written evidence and the comparative data from southern China and Southeast Asia, both of which are possible sources of Yayoi culture. It should be noted, however, that this ethnologist's interpretation of Chen's text is open to dispute. One needs more archaeological finds before drawing conclusions about this interesting thesis.

Chen also wrote of the Wa that "in their meetings and in their deportment, there is no distinction between father and son or between men and women." As in the passage on sleeping arrangements, it is difficult to determine what his words mean. Assuming that he was comparing the Wa to northern Chinese, one may conclude that Chen was describing a lack of age and gender differentiation in Wa society. How well does the archaeological record correspond to the author's statement?

Some archaeologists would argue that certain regions of late Yayoi Japan had abundant signs of differentiation by age and gender. One example comes from the Tenjinmae site in Chiba prefecture, admittedly distant from Yamatai but still a valuable reference. At Tenjinmae and several other excavations in central Honshu, scientists have found evidence of skeletons that villagers buried once, dug up, and then reinterred. Archaeologists uncovered only about 60 square meters at Tenjinmae but discovered seven pits each with from one to seven pots inside. The pots were small (about 40 to 60 centimeters in height) but contained fragments of human bones from different adults. Most important, the chief archaeologist concluded that the pots could not have held a corpse; the relatives must have interred the dead once, waited for the body to decompose, unearthed the bones, and reburied them inside a pot.[59]

One explanation for such a custom is based on the existence of age distinctions in some Yayoi villages. As people of a given age and the same sex passed through rituals together, they formed bonds; as members grew old and began to die, the dead individuals were buried once as corpses. When the dead turned to bones, relatives unearthed the skeleton and preserved the bones in a pot. As members of the age cohort passed away, the number of pots increased until the entire age group died off and all pots were then buried together at one time in the same pit.

Two pieces of evidence support the idea that Tenjinmae's residents practiced the ceremonial reburial of age cohorts. First, many pots showed signs of long term preservation, such as repeated mending, before burial. Second, all those interred were male and thus could have been of the same cohort. It should also be noted that Jōmon society was highly age-conscious. Assuming some degree of continuity in this area, one may posit that Yayoi society is not a good match for the Wa if Chen meant that the Wa did not observe gender and age distinctions.[60]

Chen's description of the cloth and clothing worn by the Wa, however, corresponds fairly well to the archaeological record of the late Yayoi era. Chen's account lists ramie (*karamushi*) and mulberry trees among the vegetation of Japan, and the remains of both plants have appeared at Yayoi excavations. Archaeologists have also found examples of what they believe to be hemp (*taima*) cloth pressed into pottery for designs. At Tateiwa, a site in northern Kyushu, excavators have discovered a rare piece of silk attached to a sword.[61] Artisans cast several bronze bells with pictures showing persons holding reels for dyed thread, probably for silk cloth.[62] Taken together with many Yayoi sites that have revealed spindles and parts for looms, these artifacts suggest that ramie and hemp clothing was widely available by the third century. It is probably best, however, to think of the production of silk cloth as limited to a few locations in Kyushu and the Kinai until A.D. 400.[63] The archaeological record even confirms the style of dress described by Chen. Material remains from the Yayoi era supply evidence for the hairstyles, headbands, and ponchos mentioned in his account.[64] Footprints uncovered from rice paddies and other areas confirm that some third-century people went about barefooted, just as the Chinese historian noted.

Chen also wrote that the Wa produced vermilion and cinnabar in order "to smear their bodies with pink and scarlet." Cinnabar and vermilion have the chemical composition of mercury sulfide and ferric oxide (hematite), respectively; residents of the archipelago used these minerals widely during the Yayoi era to paint combs, shields, bronze mirrors, and pottery. Moreover, archaeologists have uncovered a large amount of red powder in a burial urn for a chieftain at Yoshinogari, a northern Kyushu site sometimes equated with Yamatai (to be discussed later).[65] The idea of applying these cosmetics probably entered Japan from China and proceeded up the Inland Sea to the Kinai.[66]

The "Account of the Wa" lists weapons such as "spears, shields,... wooden bows made with a short lower part and long upper part," and "bamboo arrows... sometimes tipped with iron or bone." The description is once again a generally accurate picture of Yayoi archaeology, especially if one assumes that Chen was implying that arrowheads were usually of stone. Yet the Chinese historian omitted some Yayoi weapons, such as the halberd and slingshot, remains of which turn up occasionally in excavations.[67] One point, however, catches the eye because it is an observation that all experts in Japanese weaponry recognize. The configuration of the Wa bow with its short bottom and long top corresponds perfectly to the few artifacts available from the Yayoi period. This arresting detail suggests that Chen based his writing on the testimony of eyewitnesses who had seen the Wa, whether at Luo-yang or in their native land.

The account of Wa customs says that the people served their food "on wooden and bamboo trays, helping themselves with their fingers." A careful investigation of the terms used by Chen suggests that these trays were pedestals (*takatsuki*). Many such wooden dishes have appeared at Yayoi sites like Toro, products of what is widely considered to have been a technological improvement in woodworking.[68] The problem is that by Himiko's reign the Japanese had a 10,000-year-old tradition of making their own clay pottery, and clay pedestals are among the most common finds in archaeological sites for the third century. Why did the Chinese historian not mention Japanese pottery?

One scholar believes that the Chinese were probably trying to emphasize the utter barbarity of the Wa, a people without the ability to make rudimentary pots. In this connection it is interesting to note that the same phrase about eating habits appears in descriptions of other non-Chinese peoples of northeastern Asia. But Chen's reference to using the hands at meals seems to have been correct: the earliest chopsticks found to date are from late seventh- or eighth-century palaces.[69]

Finally, Yayoi archaeologists have shown that Chen's account accurately portrayed other practices of the Wa. Yayoi pottery has pictures of people with streaks running from their foreheads to their cheeks, probably representing either pigments or tattoos. One expert on the Yayoi era believes that different communities applied tattoos in varying patterns as marks of geographic origin. Archaeological sites also reveal abundant evidence of divination using both turtle carapaces and deer bones from at least the middle of the Yayoi period.[70]

*Economy*_____

Chen reports that the Wa had "no oxen, horses, . . . or sheep," a passage that has engendered one of the most heated controversies among Yayoi archaeologists. On the face of it, artifacts would seem to contradict Chen's claim, since scientists have excavated horse and cattle bones in Yayoi sites.[71] But as Sahara Makoto has asserted, there is a strong probability that these bones originated from a time long after the Yayoi era and just happened to have been interred at those sites. Sahara gives two reasons for his belief: first, scientists recovered most horse and cattle bones in the nineteenth and early twentieth centuries when dating techniques were much less sophisticated; second, these horse and cattle bones contained considerably less fluorine than other animal bones found in the same excavations. (Bones accumulate fluorine over time.) If one accepts these arguments, then all evidence of horses, cattle, or sheep for Yayoi Japan is tainted and Chen's attribution may indeed have been accurate.[72]

Not all archaeologists agree with Sahara's argument, however. One writer on the Tomb era has noted that several late Yayoi sites have bronze bells similar to those that Koreans and Chinese attached to horses.[73] Another archaeologist has upheld the original dating assigned to bones excavated from late Yayoi and even Jōmon sites.[74] But the same author has admitted that horses were probably rare in Japan before the end of the third century A.D., even if there is some evidence of domesticated pigs and cows.

Testimony from later Japanese history tends to favor the conclusion that the Japanese of the Yayoi age possessed no livestock. Livestock and the plow have never played a prominent part in Japanese agriculture; humans have provided most of the labor. Castration of livestock or humans was unknown among the Japanese until the nineteenth century, and the Japanese have never managed large herds of any animal, not even flocks of chickens.[75] Until an archaeologist can provide unequivocal evidence of a horse or cattle bone that can be dated from before A.D. 300, it is probably safe to assume that Chen's statement was an accurate portrayal of Yayoi Japan.[76]

If they had no livestock and did not even keep chickens in flocks, what did the average inhabitant of the archipelago consume in the Yayoi era? This question is at the heart of a major debate raging among archaeologists: the place of rice agriculture in the life of Yayoi peasants. The controversy over how people of the Yayoi period made their living is intimately bound up with the way Japanese archaeologists date sites and artifacts.

Despite the invention of radiocarbon dating, Japanese archaeologists have preferred to rely on relative sequences of pottery styles to periodize the Yayoi era.[77] This rather subjective method has resulted in relative dates for the pottery of different areas of Japan but also has caused great confusion, since there is disagreement on how the style of one region and period corresponds to the pots of another area. The problem of relative dating was especially confusing for the end of Jōmon and beginning of Yayoi because the pottery of the two periods is almost indistinguishable. Recently, leading archaeologists have ceased using pottery to date the transition from Jōmon to Yayoi. Today the preferred yardstick is livelihoods: Jōmon is viewed as a time of hunting, gathering, and fishing whereas Yayoi saw rice agriculture introduced from the continent through Korea.

Rice is the only crop that Chen mentions by name in his "Account of the

Wa," and most archaeologists, along with many historians and the over-whelming majority of the Japanese people today, think of their countrymen as having always subsisted primarily on rice. There can be little doubt that rice cultivation played a prominent role among the livelihoods of western Japan in the Yayoi era. The massive demographic increase in that region is testimony to the observation that rice can support a denser population than any other grain in the world. Evidence for rice cultivation during the Yayoi era is so common as to be routine, as archaeologists can attest by the numerous hoes and shov-els, stone reaping knives and sickles, rice paddies, and grains of rice unearthed from Kyushu to the northern tip of Honshu.

The most famous example of rice farming from the late Yayoi epoch comes from the Toro site in Shizuoka prefecture, where excavators uncovered seven hectares (17.4 acres) of large rice paddies for the first time in 1947.[78] For some years thereafter, archaeologists rarely discovered rice fields, but since the 1980s paddies have come to light with increasing frequency from northern Kyushu to northern Honshu.[79] By 1988, the Japanese had dug up 214 examples of rice acreage from the past, over twenty of which dated from the Yayoi era.[80] Most of these paddies were located in western Japan.

One's view of contemporary farming methods naturally affects any judg-ment about the prominence of rice agriculture among livelihoods of the Yayoi period. If one thinks that rice cultivation was advanced, then Yayoi paddies would have been highly productive and rice would have played a large role in the diet, as Chen implies. Conversely, more primitive methods would have been less productive, other livelihoods would have been more attractive, and there would have been less rice to go around.

As I argued in *Population, Disease, and Land in Early Japan, 645–900,* Yayoi rice agriculture was more primitive than cropping of the late premodern epoch (especially after the Kamakura age, 1185–1333).[81] Yayoi rice acreage was usually located in low-lying, swampy areas, where access to water was easy but the quality of the soil was poor. Irrigation ponds, fertilizer, double-cropping, and multiple strains of rice were all unknown. Cultivators normally made their hoes, shovels, sickles, and harvesting knives of wood, stone, and even shell until the last century of the Yayoi period.[82]

Yet over the past decade, many archaeologists have been upgrading their opinions of Yayoi rice farming. It was once thought that Yayoi peasants broad-cast seed over paddies for the spring planting (called *jikamaki*). Sahara Makoto now argues that peasants drilled holes for their seeds to prevent birds from consuming the grains. What is more, the same scholar believes that trans-planting seedlings from prepared beds into flooded paddies—a process known as *taue* and assumed to have been a relatively recent development—may actually have preceded drilling because it required less labor for weeding.[83] J. Edward Kidder connects the adoption of transplanting with the appearance of wooden mashers to crush plant matter for use as fertilizer.[84]

In excavations of ancient paddies, archaeologists have come to recognize a greater sophistication among Yayoi cultivators in their use of land. There seems to have been a difference between larger fields cut out of swamps, like those at Toro, and smaller ones often located on floodplains or even slopes. To one scholar the two types of fields suggest different farming technologies borrowed from the continent at the beginning of the Yayoi and adapted to varying soil and topographic requirements.[85] Yayoi farmers adjusted their planting techniques to different paddies, as well, using the drilling technique on low-lying fields while reserving transplanting for the higher paddies.

The same archaeologist who has analyzed Yayoi land use also believes that iron-sheathed farming tools were available even in the early Yayoi era and were nearly universal by the first century A.D.[86] Other analyses support this belief in the widespread dispersal of iron-covered agricultural implements by revealing that although there are few remnants of iron-sheathed tools before the third century, the variety of wooden implements decreases drastically by the later Yayoi, implying that iron pieces for tools may simply have rusted or been carried away.[87]

It is unwise, however, to carry this optimistic line of reasoning too far. Very few iron shoes for farm tools have appeared in Yayoi excavations, and almost all come from northern Kyushu just across the Korean Straits. The typical mode of harvest was to employ a stone (or shell or metal or even wooden) knife and painstakingly cut each ear of rice from the stalk in a process that must have consumed intensive labor and weeks of time. Gina Barnes has pointed out that ancient Japanese rice paddies commonly mixed rice seedlings with reeds, a condition that must have inhibited growth and complicated the harvest.[88]

Information on yields could help to settle the dispute over the sophistication of Yayoi rice agriculture and the place it occupied among livelihoods and in the diet. Direct evidence is difficult to come by, however. One scholar estimated yields at less than one-fifth the amount normally anticipated from a twentieth-century rice paddy of the same size (about 500 kiloliters), but his conclusion was based exclusively on comparative data from Southeast Asia. Another appraisal, derived from statistics from the Nara (710–794) and Heian (794–1185) periods, states that a poor Yayoi paddy would have yielded only 63.5 kiloliters per unit, while a good field would have produced a mere 100 kiloliters. One should be careful about relying too heavily on any of these estimates.[89]

Chen also states that the Wa planted other grains, implying dry cropping. Archaeologists have found evidence of many different types of grains, implying that Yayoi peasants harvested wheat, barley, two types of millet, buckwheat, peas, and soybeans along with rice. Yet evidence of dry fields is almost nonexistent.[90] One also wonders how many farmers practiced swidden cropping, a form of agriculture dating back to the Jōmon era, but the "Account of the Wa" makes no mention of this livelihood.

The debate over the place of rice farming in the late Yayoi economy is liable to continue for many years. Archaeologists need to uncover more artifacts to determine how widely and how well rice cropping was practiced in Himiko's age. At the same time that archaeological testimony confirms Chen's observation that the Wa planted rice and other grains, it also allows scholars some latitude in assessing the precise level of Japan's agricultural development, an important factor in judging third-century Japan's progress toward a complex society.

How else might Yayoi people have sustained themselves? The Chinese historian devotes a large portion of his narrative to fishing. This occupation was already thousands of years old by the time Chen wrote, but artifacts suggest that the Yayoi era saw important improvements in fishing technology that provided the foundation for anglers for a millennium to come. From the earthen weights for nets, iron hooks, bone harpoons, and wooden traps uncovered at Yayoi sites, archaeologists have been able to show that the design of weight manufacture improved, that fishhooks became more complicated and added the barb, that makers forged many implements from iron by the end of the third century, that anglers invented the octopus trap, and that specialized communities traded in salt manufactured from seawater. The calm Inland Sea between Honshu, Shikoku, and Kyushu was the site of many fishing activities. Residents of the archipelago were still a long way from the advanced forms and technology used in the Muromachi (1333–1573) and Edo eras, but as was the case for clothing, woodworking, and agriculture, ancient anglers owed much to their Yayoi forebears.[91]

Fishing and farming populations needed each other, and the "Account of the Wa" and artifacts from China and Korea recovered in Japan suggest that people traded, perhaps as Chen wrote, "under the supervision of Wa officials." Archaeologists have unearthed evidence for trade in a few materials from the early Yayoi period. For example, Tateiwa village in northern Kyushu produced stone reaping knives, sickle blades, swords, halberds, and arrowheads. Partially finished tools at Tateiwa and the distribution of similar implements throughout northern Kyushu suggest that workers at Tateiwa manufactured their stone implements for adjacent settlements as well. Imayama village, also located in northern Kyushu, was a major source for stone axes. Further up the Inland Sea, archaeologists have traced the origin of stone tools found from Hiroshima to the Kinai to two mountains, Mount Kana in Shikoku and Mount Nijō on the border between Osaka and Nara.[92]

The exchange of lithic tools should come as no surprise to those familiar with Jōmon Japan or Stone Age societies the world over, but archaeologists have uncovered more exciting examples of trade in the Yayoi era. Perhaps as early as 150 B.C., certainly by A.D. 100, inhabitants of the archipelago were casting their own bronze ceremonial bells (dōtaku), swords, and halberds.[93] Analyses of the lead-isotope content of these Japanese artifacts have shown that all the copper and tin came from either China or Korea, suggesting international trade in these metals.[94]

A few casting molds excavated in western Japan imply the existence of artisans producing bronze bells and swords, but as in the case of rice farming, archaeologists debate how sophisticated craft organization really was. Sahara Makoto, who argued for advanced rice cropping techniques and high yields, not surprisingly also sees bronze manufacture during the Yayoi era as highly developed. He believes that settlements where archaeologists have unearthed many bronze artifacts and molds were homes to independent, full-time craftsmen. Sites containing only a few bronze articles probably received their items through trade or casting by an itinerant worker.[95] Yet many scholars disagree with Sahara and think that third-century Japan had only a few part-time, wandering bronze makers.[96]

No matter how many specialists cast bronze items, it seems safe to assert that trade was one method by which these items arrived at smaller and more isolated settlements. One scholar has reconstructed a trade network for the Kinai region based on Yayoi sites and artifacts and argues that his map of trade routes fits Chen's description of "markets in each province, where necessaries are exchanged under the supervision of Wa officials." It should come as no surprise that this same archaeologist sees the Kinai as the home of Yamatai and regards late Yayoi society and economy as specialized and advanced.[97]

Summary

The preceding discussion of diverse aspects of the "Account of the Wa" suggests that the Chinese historian's narrative serves as a generally accurate portrayal of late Yayoi society.[98] To be sure, some of the most important features of Wa life, such as the existence of livestock and the nature of kinship, are matters of controversy among archaeologists. Yet excavations have not only confirmed that Chen was correct in his overall picture of third-century Japan but also support the Chinese author on important details such as the species of vegetation, the style of clothing, the use of cosmetics, the shape of the bow, and eating with the hands.

Of the many areas discussed so far, only five have revealed a disparity between Chen's description and archaeological finds. In the case of age and gender distinctions, the difficulty may have been that all sites for secondary burials come from eastern Japan, which was not home to the Wa. The other four aspects—climate, the longevity and height of the population, and the use of wooden dishes—all suggest that Chen may have been an advocate of Chinese ethnocentrism. He may have believed that the Wa were "barbarians" who lived far to the south of his home in northern China.

This illustration of Chen's work using sites and artifacts has begun to reveal two sides of a scholarly debate about third-century Japan. One side sees rice farming as the dominant livelihood, iron tools as ubiquitous, craft organization as sophisticated, and trade as commonplace. The other side delineates a society in which rice cropping was only one among many occupations, iron implements were rare, a few itinerant artisans could fill demand, and trade was unusual.

The difficulty of filtering out the writer's bias complicates this debate considerably. Chen may have underestimated the Wa because he considered them "barbarians." Conversely, his terminology derived from Chinese culture and may have been too imprecise and sophisticated to apply to simpler Japanese society. Such problems are manifest, too, when one examines politics.

A SOCIETY CONSTANTLY AT WAR

In 1947, archaeologists unearthed Toro, a third-century rice-farming village in central Honshu. For scholars and tourists alike, Toro is one of three "must-see" excavations for the Yayoi period (the other two are Yoshinogari and Tatetsuki) and one of the most important sites in all Japanese archaeology. Among the pottery shards, wooden agricultural implements, stone tools, glass beads, pieces of cloth, and boards for homes and fields that came to light, however, one type of artifact was notable for its rarity: weapons.[99] Coming as it did after Japan's most disastrous war, the discovery of Toro seemed to convey to a war-weary public a much-needed impression of their ancient ancestors as peace-loving families of rice cultivators.

The "Account of the Wa" called such an image into question, at least for the Yayoi epoch. Chen described how "for some seventy or eighty years after [the demise of a male ruler] there were disturbances and warfare." When Himiko assumed leadership of Yamatai, she went to war with the neighboring kingdom of Kunu. Then, following Himiko's death, "assassination and murder" were the rule and "more than one thousand" were slain. Other Chinese historians agreed with Chen. *The History of the Later Han Dynasty* reported that "during the reigns of Huan-di [A.D. 147–168] and Ling-di [A.D. 168–189], the country of the Wa was in a state of great confusion, war and conflict raging on all sides." Were these accurate statements or just the imaginings of ethnocentric Chinese historians?

Consider the following archaeological facts uncovered since 1947. Of the more than five thousand skeletons excavated from Jōmon sites, only about ten give evidence of violent death. Scientists have about a thousand skeletons for the Yayoi era, but remains reveal that over one hundred persons probably died from wounds inflicted by weapons. Iron and stone arrowheads are among the most common finds at Yayoi sites—and those dating from the middle and late Yayoi age are much heavier and more deadly than hunting arrowheads found in the Jōmon period. While many bronze swords, spears, and halberds found in northern Kyushu were too large for actual combat, their size means that residents had a ceremonial use for armaments. Relatives often buried smaller bronze weapons with their departed owners. In the words of Sahara Makoto, "the people of northern Kyushu worshiped weapons."[100]

To someone grounded in anthropological theory, these conclusions probably come as no surprise because one hypothesis holds that early farming societies are often war-ridden. According to Jacob Bronowski, who first put forth such a theory for Neolithic Jericho, agricultural technology produces groups of haves and have-nots. The development of social classes may not necessarily beget conflict as Marx ordained, but tensions are inherent when a primitive society becomes sophisticated enough to have persons with different jobs. Why do some people rule and others pay taxes? Why do some contribute to society's well-being in one way and others in another? What are the relative values of different occupations? Above all, farming produces the economic underpinning for the state, and one of the most important functions of government is to make war in defense of its tax producers.[101]

Excavations of Yayoi villages indicate that defense was very much on the minds of residents. Even before World War II, archaeologists noticed that small hamlets of three to five households were often situated 200 to 400 meters above sea level. These homes undoubtedly functioned as bases for the clearance of dry fields or even wet-rice paddies, but not long after the war it became apparent that cultivation was not the major activity of such householders. As Japan entered the postwar archaeology boom, the number of upland sites increased and scientists gave them the special name of "highland settlements" (*kōchisei shūraku*). Soon it became clear that although highland settlements had existed all over Japan, the overwhelming majority were concentrated in western Japan, especially along the Inland Sea. Many hamlets dated from as early as 200 B.C., but they seemed to be particularly common in the middle to late (A.D. 50–200) and very end of the Yayoi era.

The leading expert on highland settlements was a geographer who suggested that these villages could have served four functions: locations for hunting and slash-and-burn farming; land clearance sites; ceremonial centers; and military posts.[102] Then archaeologists made two more exciting discoveries: scorched earth and ashes (perhaps beacons) and weapons.[103] Although some scholars still deny that every upland habitation had a military purpose, by the 1980s it was the consensus that most had served as lookouts for scouts keeping watch for an attack.[104] Most important, the dating and geographical situation of these hamlets seemed to fit exactly with Chen's contention that the Wa descended into civil war in the second and third centuries A.D.[105]

Archaeologists who believe most fervently that highland settlements are evidence of Wa internecine warfare point to several other facts. First, it was usually possible to send smoke signals from one base to another; the Osaka Prefectural Museum of Yayoi Culture actually performed experiments to prove this point. Second, these mountain hamlets were frequently within a short run of a major Yayoi settlement of many hundreds of households.[106] Finally, the appearance of highland settlements seemed to coincide with the production of heavier and more deadly arrowheads and widespread evidence of burnt homesteads.[107]

Yet not all scholars are quite so certain. Some archaeologists have asserted that these military upland villages actually reached their peak in the first century B.C., well before the Wa civil war described by Chinese historians.[108] The problem with matching artifacts to the written record is that pottery styles used to periodize Yayoi sites yield only relative and not absolute dates. It is therefore a question of interpretation of local ceramic styles as to whether one believes that the construction of highland settlements actually corresponded to the two centuries of intermittent civil war noted by Chinese historians of the Later Han and Wei dynasties. Although many scholars agree that the appearance of upland households implies that Yayoi Japan was violent, most would also say that one cannot therefore apply the description in Chen's account literally to a specific site.

Mountain lookouts were not the only defensive arrangements in the Yayoi period. Many large and well-known settlements located on plains (as well as some upland habitations) were protected by ditches (*kangō shūraku*). From the end of World War II until 1990, excavators uncovered seventy-nine such villages located from Kyushu to northeastern Honshu and dating from 300 B.C. to the third century A.D.—at which point they suddenly disappear, not to be seen again until after 1200.[109] A typical example might be Ōtsuka in Kanagawa prefecture, where an oval trench measuring 20 by 130 meters in diameter was 4 meters wide and 2 meters deep. At Ōgidani in Kyoto prefecture there were two encircling ditches about a kilometer in length. Diggers undoubtedly piled much of the contents in front of the trench for defense. One archaeologist has estimated that the dirt moved to make the ditches at this site could have filled a thousand 10-ton dump trucks.[110]

In some cases residents of these settlements took extraordinary precautions to ensure their own safety. At the huge Asahi site in Aichi prefecture, there were three trenches, the outer one 5 to 7 meters wide and 1.5 meters deep enclosing 10 hectares. The second and third ditches were only 1.5 to 2 meters wide, but inside the trenches villagers had implanted stakes, planks, and twisted branches that made access to their homes exceedingly difficult. Further outside the last ditch was another line of thigh-high stakes and planks. The only way in and out of Asahi would have been by bridge.[111]

The origin of this type of large fortified settlement was probably continental. Most Neolithic (early agricultural) societies, whether in China or Europe, experimented with fortifications. And while Chinese examples come from 5000–3000 B.C. and scholars cannot directly connect them with Japan's habitations, recently archaeologists have excavated a village with encircling ditches in southern Korea that dates from about 400 B.C. Like metallurgy and rice farming, large settlements surrounded with trenches are another example of the Yayoi's continental legacy.[112]

Currently the most famous fortification from the Yayoi age is the northern Kyushu site of Yoshinogari, where in the late 1980s archaeologists found a double-ditched 25-hectare settlement of possibly 1,000 to 1,500 residents located on the highest point of a low hill.[113] The outer trench was 7 meters wide and 3 meters deep with a V-shaped cross section while the inner one was about 2 meters wide with an earthen embankment on the outside surrounding an area of 15,000 square meters. Settled throughout the Yayoi period, Yoshinogari had grown considerably by 50 B.C. and probably held at least a hundred pit dwellings at its apogee during the first three centuries A.D. In addition, the village contained storage pits and fifty granaries; a 40 by 30-meter burial mound where residents interred about twenty persons of distinction as evidenced by the daggers, headdress, and vermilion found there; an equally impressive cemetery with almost 2,500 jars, cists, coffins, and holes for commoners, some of whom had met violent ends; silk and hemp cloth; stone, bone, and iron tools; molds for bronze casting; human hair; and beads.

Yoshinogari is particularly important because it supplies new data on the nature of politics and social ranking. In his writing Chen utilized terms he was familiar with to describe the Wa as having many "countries" (*guo*) with their own "kings" (*wang*). Yoshinogari seems to have been the center of one of these units, a point that some archaeologists have argued from casts for bronze weapons found there; products seem to have circulated to nearby hamlets. Moreover, ritual vessels unearthed within Yoshinogari suggest that people of neighboring villages came there to pay their respects.[114] If Yoshinogari was indeed the capital of a "country," then some have surmised that its borders may have stretched nearly to the boundaries of the eighth-century district of Kamisaki in Hizen province, over 110 square miles.[115] Two archaeologists estimate the average size of a Yayoi "country" at 60 to 90 square miles.[116] Yet once again, as with so many other attempts to equate the age of Himiko with the late Yayoi period, there are cautionary voices about how to read Chen's account. Gina Barnes, an American archaeologist of ancient Japan, has argued that these Chinese descriptions "exhibit the tendency of any sophisticated society to interpret simpler social systems in terms of their own sophisticated organizations."[117] Stated another way, the Chinese could only describe the unknown in terms of what they knew, like Columbus in his voyages to the New World.

Several sites excavated in northern Kyushu contain Chinese mirrors, glass beads, and other signs of political recognition from the mighty emperors of the Middle Kingdom, but the problem is one of interpretation. How can scholars be sure that some brave and skilled seaman from one of these Wa communities did not cross the Korean Straits, journey to a Han outpost, and receive or trade for a mirror or even a seal? What qualifications did a person need to obtain Chinese recognition? It is tempting to assume that grave goods such as mirrors, beads, and weapons almost always signify elite status, but one archaeologist has written that both the Chinese terms "king" and "country" exaggerate the political development of Japan in the third century: "kings" ran the gamut from adventurers to figures with extraordinary but temporary communal leadership positions; "countries" were no more than villages, certainly not states.[118] Given the evidence of elite burials at Yoshinogari, it is perhaps best to think of these "countries" as chiefdoms.

The same interpretive debate runs throughout discussions of social ranking in the Yayoi period. Chen Shou notes in his descriptions of forms of worship, marriage, and personal address and meeting that the Wa were conscious of a social hierarchy. And the separate burial mound, shell bracelets preventing physical labor, and possible example of an elite residence at Yoshinogari all support the Chinese historian to a degree.[119] Most sites in western Japan give some evidence of separate interment in mounds or moated precincts for a few families.[120]

But it is easy to push this line of thinking too far. According to a scholar of the Yayoi epoch, even when the village interred members of an elite in separate burial mounds, grave goods usually amounted to no more than a single bronze mirror or an iron implement. Accessories that indicate a highly developed system of social classes are missing in Yayoi excavations to date.[121] Even at Yoshinogari there were only six elite burial chambers out of nearly 2,500 interments. Compared to other chiefly societies, status differentiation in Yayoi Japan appears to have been slight.[122]

These two points about late Yayoi Japan's political development and status differentiation suggest one possible answer to the debate over Yamatai. Maybe third-century Japan was too fragmented to have had one dominant polity. Put another way: "The superordinate role of Yamatai . . . is not apparent from the [Yayoi] archaeological record."[123] Chen's Yamatai, which he said achieved paramountcy over nearly thirty small communities, may have been a figment of the author's imagination. Such reasoning comes closer to placing Yamatai in northern Kyushu than the Kinai, because a Kinai confederacy would have been too large.

Was Yoshinogari Yamatai? The news media in Japan have bandied this question about since excavation began in the late 1980s. The best evidence in favor of such a conclusion resides in the foundations of what are believed to be watchtowers. Within Yoshinogari's inner trench, archaeologists unearthed three semicircular projections dating from the third century A.D., two of which contained six large postholes in a 2 by 3 arrangement.[124] If these foundations indeed supported watchtowers as most archaeologists believe, then Yoshinogari comes reasonably close to Chen's description of Himiko's palace, "surrounded by towers and stockades, with armed guards in a state of constant vigilance." One other point also favors Yoshinogari, or at least northern Kyushu: the peaks of ditch building in northern Kyushu seem to correspond to the periods of warfare mentioned in the "Account of the Wa," whereas the Kinai was on a different cycle.[125] Taken together with the fact that five of eight places on the way to Yamatai were located in northern Kyushu, these arguments suggest that Yamatai, too, most likely was in that area.

The arguments against Yoshinogari, however, are at least as strong. Yoshinogari had too small a population, even if Chen did exaggerate the count at

Yamatai. The burial mound at Yoshinogari is too small and too early to have been Himiko's. Another archaeologist objects that Himiko lived after villages with trenches had begun to lose their popularity or had even disappeared altogether.[126] Finally, in the spring of 1992, archaeologists discovered a picture of a watchtower scratched on a Yayoi pottery shard from Karako-Kagi, a large settlement in the Kinai, indicating that watchtowers existed outside northern Kyushu.

Archaeologists have uncovered only about half of Yoshinogari thus far, of course, so there is always a chance that another exciting discovery will bolster the arguments of those equating it with Yamatai. But to many, the near-absence of one particular artifact is the most powerful argument against Yoshinogari's being Yamatai. Apart from three small fragments, archaeologists have found no Chinese mirrors there.

Looking for Yamatai: Mirrors, Graves, and Iron

To this point we have seen that Chen's description of the Wa fits sites and artifacts from the late Yayoi period fairly well. Of course, the Chinese historian could not compose a perfectly accurate record from such a great distance, and some of his locutions betray Chinese ethnocentrism. But so long as one assumes that the Yayoi period extends to A.D. 300, the match of Chen's description with Yayoi archaeology seems secure.

As with so many scholarly questions, however, the solution depends on how the problem is framed. To many archaeologists, the Yayoi period ended not in A.D. 300 but in A.D. 250; because sequences of pottery styles cannot reveal absolute dates, no one can be sure. If the Yayoi period terminated in A.D. 250, Himiko was a transitional figure, the last Yayoi shaman and possibly the first occupant of one of Japan's giant keyhole tumuli. Which of these visions of third-century Japan is more accurate from an archaeological point of view? Each alternative places Yamatai in a different place and uses different types of evidence: mirrors, graves, and iron.

"Mirror, mirror, . . . "

In March 1953, as employees of Japan National Railways graded a slope next to a nineteenth-century line running from Kyoto to Nara, workers noticed odd-looking, shiny fragments in the discarded earth. Impressed by their finds, some removed and hid them. It was only later that the railway company asked the police and prefectural government to perform an archaeological survey on the burial chamber at the circular end of the keyhole-shaped tomb at Tsubai Ōtsukayama. Among the swords, armor, and iron fishing and farming tools, scientists also eventually recovered thirty-six bronze mirrors.

Bronze mirrors were prized possessions in early Japan. One of the most famous myths about the Sun Goddess, the chieftain of the ancient Japanese pantheon, records how her fellow gods and goddesses used a mirror, among other devices, to reflect her brilliance and lure her out of a cave to illuminate a dark world. For this reason ethnologists often associate mirrors with the sun and the Japanese imperial family, who long ago designated the mirror as one of three sacred treasures. Mirrors also call to mind the one in charge of the spiritual life of the ancient community: the shaman. At Doigahama, the Yayoi site described earlier, the skeleton of an elderly female interred in the eastern cemetery holds in its hand a wooden carving of a bird. One archaeologist has written that peoples of the Yayoi age believed the bird to have magical powers because it could fly up to heaven and the sun. The old woman was probably a shaman, just like her more famous sister-in-magic Himiko.[127]

According to the "Account of the Wa," the Wei emperor sent Himiko one hundred bronze mirrors. Although Chen Shou did not specify the type of mirror the Chinese sent to Japan, prewar scholars had thought that the triangle-rimmed deity and beast mirror seemed a likely candidate to be the mirrors of Yamatai. Thirty-two of the mirrors found at Tsubai Ōtsukayama were triangle-rimmed deity and beast mirrors, thereby adding enormously to the cache of artifacts considered relevant to the Yamatai debate and enflaming passions once again.

The central figure in the controversy was Kobayashi Yukio of Kyoto University's Archaeology Department. After analyzing the mirrors recovered from Tsubai Ōtsukayama and thirteen more uncovered at Kurumazuka Tomb in Okayama prefecture, Kobayashi concluded that the triangle-rimmed deity and beast mirrors were Chinese products: the makers named on the mirrors had Chinese names; the place-names engraved on the mirrors were located in Chinese regions famous for the manufacture of mirrors; and phrases listed on the mirrors drew heavily from Chinese philosophy. Kobayashi followed his prewar teachers at Kyoto University in believing that craftsmen had cast these mirrors during the Jin and especially the Wei dynasties.[128]

Kobayashi's most original achievement came in recognizing that numerous sets of mirrors, each set comprising items cast from the same mold, had turned up in many different tombs. Among the triangle-rimmed deity and beast mirrors found at Tsubai Ōtsukayama, for example, Kobayashi noted that twenty-two had same-mold duplicates recovered from nineteen other tombs located from the Kanto to northern Kyushu.[129] The archaeologist drew up a complex diagram to show the network of relationships among the tombs. To Kobayashi, the distribution of mirrors was no accident, as some historians had asserted in the prewar period, but rather the result of elaborate gift giving among Japanese political leaders in the third and fourth centuries A.D. Presumably the most powerful chieftain gave his ally in another region some mirrors (up to five) to symbolize the ally's submission and acceptance into the chieftain's confederacy. When the ally died, he or she had the mirrors buried with the body. Accepting this reasoning, Kobayashi then assigned a date of between A.D. 280 and 350 to Tsubai Ōtsukayama.[130]

While Kobayashi was cautious in addressing the Yamatai question, the implications of his theory were clear. Himiko received the one hundred triangle-rimmed deity and beast mirrors from the Wei emperor, and after she died in the mid-third century A.D., Himiko's followers started giving them to her allies. Then her thirteen-year-old follower and sister-shaman Daiyo received even more mirrors and steadily distributed them to her allies throughout Japan. As Daiyo and her henchmen expired, they had the mirrors placed in their tombs.[131] The center of Himiko's confederacy (that is, Yamatai) had to be in the Kinai because most of the mirrors originated in that region; in fact Tsubai Ōtsukayama was a strong candidate for such a center because it was situated near a major waterway.[132] Some even said that Tsubai Ōtsukayama was Daiyo's tomb.

Kobayashi's thesis has found support from many different quarters. By 1988, archaeologists had uncovered 233 triangle-rimmed deity and beast mirrors of seventy-six varieties, all supposedly brought from China. Excavators recovered over 50 percent in the Kinai, while only 12 percent had come from northern Kyushu. Mirrors of similar design manufactured in Japan show a like distribution.[133] Moreover, artisans cast Chinese-style dates on a few mirrors: one indicated A.D. 239 and three indicated A.D. 240.[134] The importance of this discovery could not be overemphasized: not only was the dating system associated with the Wei dynasty, but Himiko's ambassadors were in the Wei capital in A.D. 239–240. Surely triangle-rimmed deity and beast mirrors were the mirrors of Yamatai.

But as with every scholarly hypothesis, there were doubters. The first group of critics argued that the evidence that triangle-rimmed deity and beast mirrors were ever manufactured in China was weak. To date, archaeologists have found none in China.[135] How could the Japanese have cast Chinese reign periods, personal and place-names, and phrases from Chinese philosophy on the mirrors? They did not have to, because the makers of the mirrors were Chinese and Korean refugees from wars on the continent. Another group of skeptics found timing to be a problem.[136] Triangle-rimmed deity and beast mirrors have never come to light from Yayoi sites; all have come from keyhole tumuli associated with the subsequent Tomb era. If Himiko died around A.D. 250 and the Tomb age did not begin until A.D. 300, as most archaeologists believed in Kobayashi's era (1960), what happened to the mirrors during the fifty-year gap? How accurately could the distribution of mirrors in fourth-century tombs reflect political relationships of Himiko's age? These same doubters also noted that if one limited the search to mirrors other than triangle-rimmed deity and beast mirrors uncovered from Yayoi graves, then nearly 80 percent came from northern Kyushu.

A Chinese archaeologist has voiced the most imaginative interpretation so far.[137] Wang Zhong-shu, an expert on Chinese mirrors, has argued that the triangle-rimmed deity and beast mirrors were not products of the Wei dynasty, but resembled those cast in southern China, specifically the Kingdom of Wu (A.D. 222–280). While the resemblance was clear enough, there were also differences between the Japanese mirrors and the designs supposedly used for Wu mirrors. (Remember that no duplicates have appeared from Chinese sites.) Wang therefore concluded that Wu craftsmen had traveled to the archipelago and manufactured Japan's triangle-rimmed deity and beast mirrors based loosely on Chinese models. In fact, on some mirrors there is writing which Wang interpreted to mean that casters "had used copper and arrived east of the sea," an apparent reference to Japan.

As so often happens, a new discovery came along that seemed to bolster the Wang theory. In late 1986, archaeologists unearthed from a tomb near Kyoto another triangle-rimmed deity and beast mirror with a date. The time listed was the fourth year in the "Brightness for the First Time" (in Chinese *Jingchu;* in Japanese *Keisho*) reign of the Wei emperor Ming-di, which would have worked out to A.D. 240. The problem was that Ming-di had died in the first month of the third year of the Brightness for the First Time era, or early in 239, and it was the Chinese custom to change the slogan for a reign every time an emperor died. Those who supported Wang, as well as others who believed that craftsmen in Japan made all the triangle-rimmed deity and beast mirrors, pointed to the suspect date and argued that news of the emperor's death had not yet reached Japan and so casters continued to use old dates just as if nothing had happened.[138]

But the Wang hypothesis also has its critics. If Wu artisans made the mirrors, they asked, then why did they use the Wei dating system? Moreover, the phrase "had used copper and arrived east of the sea" was probably not a reference to Japan but a phrase from Chinese philosophy that describes a paradise for immortals east of the sea.[139] Finally, it is also possible to explain the existence of a mirror made in China with an erroneous date. Artisans cast most mirrors while Ming-di was still alive. Assuming that he would still be on the throne in the next year when Himiko's ambassadors returned to Japan, they merely used the next year in Ming-di's reign period, the fourth year of the Brightness for the First Time era. Scholars have noted other examples of this practice in Chinese history.[140]

Certainly the existence of a mirror with a suspicious date and the lack of any triangle-rimmed deity and beast mirrors in what was supposed to be its native land are telling criticisms of the Kobayashi theory that places Yamatai in the Kinai. But apart from questions about evidence, Kobayashi's reasoning has at least two serious flaws. First, the dating is based on circular logic. Kobayashi believed that Japanese owners may have passed their triangle-rimmed deity and beast mirrors along to at most one generation, unlike other earlier mirrors imported from China.[141] Since this was true, it was possible to date the tombs sharing same-mold mirrors with Tsubai Ōtsukayama to the late third and fourth centuries A.D. At the same time, however, Kobayashi also assumed that because the tombs could all be dated to sometime in the late third to fourth centuries, the owners of the mirrors must not have handed them down for many generations. This reasoning is like a house of cards waiting to collapse.

More important is Kobayashi's assumption that the distribution of grave goods may be equated with a hierarchy of political relationships.[142] Nowhere does it say that members of the ruling elite from the late third through the fourth centuries gave mirrors out as signs of political preference. The distribution of mirrors could just as easily have been the result of trade between independent communities or pillage after a war.

Because of these weaknesses, Kobayashi does not have an airtight case proving that Yamatai was in the Kinai. While almost all archaeologists who received their training at Kyoto University follow Kobayashi's theory, many are still supporters of northern Kyushu. Yet the concentration in the Kinai of the triangle-rimmed deity and beast mirrors, which probably are the mirrors of Himiko, is undoubtedly the single most convincing argument in the debate over Yamatai because it integrates archaeological and historical evidence. Most scholars, whatever they believe, cite it when the controversy comes up.

Burial Practices _____

One implication arising from Kobayashi's hypothesis is that both Himiko and Daiyo lived, not in the Yayoi era, but in a transitional epoch just as Japan was moving from the Yayoi to the Tomb period. After all, as the "Account of the Wa" stated, "when Himiko passed away, a great mound was raised, more than a hundred paces in diameter." The existence of so many tombs in the Kinai had seemed to bolster advocates of that theory ever since the 1920s. The circular section of Hashihaka Tomb even measured about one hundred paces in diameter according to some estimates. Were Himiko and Daiyo Yayoi shamans, or figures of the Tomb era, when grave goods were much richer and elite burials considerably larger? What do burial practices of the third and fourth centuries A.D. have to contribute to the debate over Himiko's polity? The answers to these two questions depend on how one reads the archaeological and historical records.

Japanese archaeologists have identified as many as twelve different types of graves in the Yayoi period, and the form of individual burial (simple earthen pits, jars, stone or wooden coffins) varied widely by region and date.[143] Jars were the characteristic form of interment in northern Kyushu, especially in the middle Yayoi era (about 100 B.C.–A.D. 100), though no one else in East Asia adopted a similar technique; the Kinai followed the mainland custom of using wooden coffins. Among all these variables, the one constant is that Yayoi cemeteries almost always contain large groups such as extended families or whole villages.

In contrast, builders constructed the subsequent giant tombs for only one or two persons. Therefore, while the size of the largest graves greatly increased from the first through the fourth centuries, the number of persons who could afford to be so interred was severely limited. In other words, most archaeologists assume that over these centuries Japan moved from a relatively egalitarian society to one with clearly defined social and political elites, as evidenced by the "energy expenditure" on leaders' burial.[144]

The problem seems to be the rather simple-looking task of locating Himiko and Daiyo along the sequence from one burial type to the other. But this job is a good deal more difficult than it appears on first consideration because the difference between Yayoi burial modes and the later Cheops-sized tombs is so great. To be sure, archaeologists have closed this breach to a degree with the discovery of Tatetsuki and other mounded interment sites (*funkyū bo*) constructed during the middle and late Yayoi epoch. At Tatetsuki in Okayama, the mound is situated on a hill commanding the valley below and measures 43

meters wide and 4.5 meters high with a wooden coffin for the deceased chieftain near the center. Two earthen projections, presumably places where residents conducted burial rites and transferred power to the next generation of
chiefs, extended from either end of the mound. Archaeologists have uncovered large clay cylinders, forerunners of the figures of the Tomb period, which
locals probably used in ceremonies. A few tall megaliths also dot the mound.
Cinnabar, beads, and large stones decorated in a swirling pattern have come
to light within the burial precincts.[145]

Another piece of evidence in the search for the grave of Himiko comes
from a burial type called "extended four-cornered graves" (*yosumi tosshutsu
bo*) found near Izumo on the Japan Sea.[146] This burial type, dating to the end
of the Yayoi, was a square or rectangular mound with four projections from
the corners. Stones surrounded the grave, which usually contained at least two
or three persons; the largest grave was 65 meters to a side (including the exten-
sions) and about 5 meters high. Like other mounded interments, this kind too
was probably the scene of elaborate rites for the dead and possibly a ceremony
signifying transfer of power to the chief's heir.

A similar trend toward the segregated burial of a small group of the community is also apparent in other parts of Japan. In the Kinai, archaeologists
have recently discovered a small keyhole-shaped tomb that fits the description
of a transitional form between the Yayoi and Tomb epochs, while in northern
Kyushu there is the grave at Yoshinogari, the largest interment mound found
to date for the Yayoi era.[147] Thus most of Japan seems to have been on the
track to a hierarchical society, led by a small political elite, as early as the first
century B.C. in northern Kyushu and considerably later in western Honshu.

But it is unwise to see too many similarities between late Yayoi and Tomb-
period graves. Sahara Makoto, a reticent supporter of the Kinai theory, has
pointed out that all the Yayoi mounded interments—Tatetsuki, Yoshinogari,
and the others—are poor in grave goods. At the most, these elite burials contain a mirror or one iron artifact, a far cry from the rich grave goods in later
keyhole tombs. Moreover, the late Yayoi mounded interments are tiny beside
the keyhole tombs: Sahara uses a diagram that fits four of the most famous
Yayoi elite cemeteries in less than half the area of Hashihaka Tomb. So the distance from the Yayoi epoch to the age of tombs remains a large gulf.[148]

Given the archaeological record, two possibilities seem likely. First, one can
accept Chen's description as accurate and envision Himiko as a transitional
figure—a late Yayoi shaman interred in the first huge tumulus. In this view,
the Yayoi period is deemed to have ended around A.D. 250, not 300. Furthermore, Yamatai would have been in the Kinai, where most of the keyhole tombs

exist today. Japan would have been unified from the Kinai to northern Kyu-shu, and Japanese society would have been more complex than Yayoi archae-ologists originally conceived because of the greater richness of grave goods and giant size of elite burials in the Tomb period.

A senior scholar who was the first to argue for A.D. 250 as the beginning of the Tomb era has pointed out supporting evidence for this view of Chen's text.[149] He has asserted that northern Kyushu was much later than either Okayama or the Kinai to adopt and build large tombs for an elite. In fact, late-Yayoi northern Kyushu is relatively poor in artifacts and shows strong influences from the Kinai in pottery and other elements of culture.[150] More-over, this interpretation of the "Account of the Wa" and the archaeological record fits nicely with Kobayashi's argument about the triangular-rimmed deity and beast mirrors. But one would like the answers to further questions before accepting this perspective. What percentage of all large tombs have sur-vived until the present? How many tumuli have been flattened by generations of farmers and builders? What chance is there that Himiko's tomb has survived to the twentieth century? Scholars are a long way from being able to answer these queries.

The second alternative is that Chen Shou was exaggerating. There are three reasons for believing that Chen may have erred in describing Himiko's grave. First, Chen made mistakes on other aspects of Wa burial practices, such as his claim that the Wa did not use outer coffins.[151] Second, it makes sense that Chen would want to exaggerate the size of Himiko's burial mound, since it served as a symbol of the power of a badly needed ally. Third, by the time Himiko died around A.D. 250, Wei missions to Yamatai had ceased and there was only one Wa embassy to their patron in China. Therefore, despite the gen-eral validity of the "Account of the Wa," perhaps the Chinese historian was gravely mistaken on this important point!

Iron and Yamatai

Chen Shou's description of the Wa and their customs is not restricted to the treatise entitled "Account of the Wa." Just before Chen began his controver-sial report, he wrote of the Han people of southern Korea. In a short but revealing segment on the Bian-chen (in Korean, Pyŏnjin) tribes of southeast-ern Korea, ancestors of the kingdoms of Kaya and Silla, Chen said that "the country produces iron; the Han [southern Koreans] . . . and the Wa all pursue and take it." Chen concluded by adding that "all markets use iron like the Chi-nese use cash."

This quotation raises the problem of iron and metallurgy in the Yayoi era, a complex issue subject to heated debate. Almost all archaeologists now believe that iron implements entered Japan at the beginning of the Yayoi era, before bronze, but they disagree on the rate of dispersion thereafter. Many assert that for the first two-thirds of the Yayoi era (until A.D. 50–100), both wood and stone were more popular materials.[152] Metalworkers made almost all weapons, mirrors, ceremonial bells, and many other objects from bronze; only tools for woodworking and farming contained iron, and most of these did not appear until after the middle of the Yayoi period.[153] In this view, Japan did not follow the Mediterranean or Middle Eastern model of succeeding Stone, Bronze, and Iron ages, but had in the Yayoi epoch a Stone–Bronze–Iron Age all in one.

Other Japanese scholars are more optimistic. Sahara Makoto, for example, has argued that iron implements existed in relatively large numbers from the advent of the Yayoi age, with stone items playing merely a secondary role.[154] This archaeologist explains the abundance of wooden implements and the absence of iron in late Yayoi sites like Toro by referring to the great value of iron in Japan, which meant that farmers were likely to recycle iron pieces, not leave them behind for an archaeologist to find centuries later. Another scholar noted for his study of iron farm tools uses a similar argument, asserting that hoes and spades with iron coverings over wooden blades, as well as sickles with iron cutting edges, had almost totally replaced wooden implements all over Japan by about A.D. 100.[155]

The source and dispersion of iron technology in early Japan is thus an important topic. To understand this issue, it is necessary to examine the role of iron technology in world history.[156] Bronze is an expensive metal because the elements from which it is made, copper and tin, are relatively rare and must be combined in just the right proportions (Cu:Sn = 9:1) by the sophisticated process of casting at high temperatures. Because only a few people have access to this metal, Bronze Age societies, like ancient Sumer or Shang China, tend to be aristocratic. Iron is much more common than copper and tin and does not need to be cast: artisans can smelt iron from ore or river sand in small ovens called bloomeries, and the product (called a bloom) can then be forged at a lower temperature on an anvil. For most of the world's population, metal tools first became available with the dawn of the Iron Age.

One problem that hindered the immediate replacement of bronze products with iron had to do with the properties of iron: it is too brittle to use when cast or forged by itself. Around 1400 B.C. in eastern Turkey, the Hittites learned to mix smelted iron ore with charcoal. The product was flexible, and as tough as bronze, but cheaper and easier to make. The only shortcoming of the new metal was that it rusted, which made it unsuitable for decorative purposes. The Hittites tried to keep their technological advantage a secret, but soon it spread to other parts of the world.

By 400 B.C. iron products had begun to spread into Korea and Japan. The first iron tools of the Yayoi period were cast iron axes probably made in China and shipped via Korea.[157] It seemed as though Yayoi peoples were about to receive the benefits of iron technology, even without a proper Bronze Age. But there was one major impediment to Japan's entering the Iron Age in a major way: the country was iron-poor. Most iron in Japan came from the bottom of rivers as iron sand, a fact that the residents of the archipelago probably did not discover until long after the Yayoi period had ended. Japanese archaeologists have been unable to find any evidence for iron smelting in Japan until the late fifth century.[158]

This apparent fact may have had a fundamental significance for early Japan. Not only did it require that Japan stay in constant contact with southern Korea, the best source of iron according to Chen Shou and archaeologists on both sides of the Korean Straits, but the shortage of iron made the metal more expensive and limited its use to an elite. In the rest of the world, the Iron Revolution democratized metal technology and civil wars drove Bronze Age aristocracies from power; in Japan, the ruling class remained a tiny elite because for several centuries one had to cross a hundred miles of ocean to get iron.

Because access to iron ore meant political power, the problem of this technology is also relevant to the debate over Yamatai. In 1980, a scholar tabulated all the iron artifacts that had appeared in Yayoi sites and found that excavations in northern Kyushu possessed 663 pieces while the Kinai had only 79.[159] Moreover, the count for late Yayoi was 524 versus 72, and weapons showed northern Kyushu ahead 97 to 17. In a word, northern Kyushu was much closer to Korea and the iron from which to forge tools for more productive agriculture and industry and weapons for a stronger army. So long as one confines the argument to iron artifacts and their great potential, northern Kyushu seems the more logical place for the location of Yamatai.

RECAPITULATION

Chen Shou, the Chinese historian who authored the "Account of the Wa" in *The History of the Three Kingdoms*, was from southern China and served as an official historian of the Jin dynasty. His patron's interest in the geography and cultures of Northeast Asia probably influenced Chen. *The History of the Three Kingdoms,* which emphasized the accomplishments of the Wei dynasty, became a classic of Chinese historiography. Within *The History of the Wei Dynasty* one fascicle dealt with the northeastern "barbarians" and focused on the Wa, a term that referred to inhabitants of the western Japanese archipelago. The "Account of the Wa" may be subdivided into three parts: a description of the route to the dominant "country" of Yamatai; a passage relating the natural environment, population, social structure and customs, economy, and government; and a narrative of the diplomacy between Himiko, the queen of Yamatai, and the Wei dynasty between A.D. 238 and 247.

It did not take Japan's first historians long to use Chen's story for their own purposes, as they created the Empress and Regent Jingū whose rule in *The Chronicles* coincided with Himiko's age. In the Edo period, philosophers Arai Hakuseki and Motoori Norinaga ignited a controversy over how credible Chen's account really was and just where Yamatai was situated: northern Kyushu or the Kinai. A seal discovered on Shiga Island seemed to tilt the argument in Kyushu's favor. With the Meiji Restoration, European historical techniques encouraged the Japanese to perform textual exegeses at the same time Naka Michiyo asserted that *The Chronicles* was historically inaccurate until A.D. 400 or so. Between 1910 and 1930 the debate over Yamatai settled down to an argument between two camps, one advocating northern Kyushu and the other the Kinai. By the 1930s the contributions of archaeologists and Marxist thinkers had broadened the debate, but war and censorship intervened to stop all fruitful publication. After World War II, intellectuals rediscovered the "Account of the Wa" and began a search for new paradigms amid a brief period of reaction. By 1955, historians had raised many interesting new questions, notably regarding the nature of Himiko's rule and Wa social structure, even as archaeologists started to supplement Chen's text with evidence and ideas of their own. By 1965, the Yamatai boom was on and specialists reevaluated Chen's text and dealt more carefully with new topics like ancient Chinese diplomacy.

In the 1970s, serious Japanese scholars started to retreat from the controversy. For historians and linguists, the end to fruitful work on Chen's text probably came because they had exhausted their approaches. Archaeologists introduced many new angles to consider, but they too began to avoid larger questions raised by the Yamatai debate. In the vacuum, mystery writers and other amateurs followed their own interests. Nationalists regained a foothold, attacking Chen for daring to describe ancient Japan in terms other than those contained in the eighth-century classics.

In response to these troubling trends, this chapter has evaluated the

"Account of the Wa" from both historical and archaeological perspectives. Initially the analysis revealed that the story of the Wa is a generally reliable description of the late Yayoi environment, society and customs, and economy. A comparison of politics with Yayoi archaeology also suggests that Himiko's time was, as Chen and other Chinese historians wrote, an epoch of widespread warfare. To be sure, some points are controversial or belong to the realm of interpretation, but no historian would ever insist that Chen's account was "the whole truth" anyway.

There seem to be at least three ways in which Chen's biases are apparent. First, he seemed at times to be emphasizing the barbarity of the Wa. One can criticize Chen for this shortcoming, but the Chinese lived in a more technologically and culturally advanced society than the Wa. Second and conversely, Chen also tried to build up the Wei ally as a powerful state ruled by a queen with a thousand servants and a huge tomb. This bias arose from the nature of Chinese historiography, committed as it was to the ruling dynasty. Finally, Chen had no choice but to write of the Wa in terms that he knew—words like "country" and "king" that no anthropologist would ever have used. If one filters out these biases, the "Account of the Wa" can still be informative reading.

Among archaeologists the debate over the location of Yamatai turns on a disagreement about dating that has significant implications. For many, Chen's text is a record of the late Yayoi period, which terminated in A.D. 300. According to this vision, society tended to be less complex and the economy less productive, and the chances of Himiko's ruling a confederation uniting western Japan were slim. For others, the Yayoi era ended in A.D. 250 and Himiko and Daiyo were transitional figures who ruled a western Japanese confederation centered in the Kinai. The first large tombs and rich grave goods suggest a more complex society and productive economy. While Kobayashi's theory of the mirrors and evidence from burial practices favor the Kinai, the distribution of iron tools and arrowheads encourages one to lean toward northern Kyushu.

Which of these two pictures of Yamatai and third-century Japan is more accurate? The answer depends on how one evaluates Chen's biases and how one reads the archaeological record. Both portraits are plausible. Thus the only honest response to queries about the location of Yamatai is the disappointing one: no one knows for sure. But no matter which vision of Yamatai and third-century Japan one chooses, scholars must use *all* the evidence to debate the relevant issues.

One's inability to decide between these alternatives should not, however, obscure the significance of the Yayoi period in ancient Japanese history. These centuries witnessed great changes in population; livelihoods such as rice farming, fishing, woodworking, metalworking, and trade; and the social division of labor, even taking into account Chen's propensity to exaggerate the accomplishments of Wei's ally. The new materials and technologies introduced from the continent beginning in 400 B.C. formed the social and economic underpinning for the next millennium and more.

Sahara Makoto has compared the Yayoi centuries to the Meiji period, another time of rapid change. Japan's culture in both epochs had items and technologies that entered from the outside, indigenous traditions that resisted change and remained resilient, and new elements developed by the residents of the archipelago. Foreign items and technologies included mirrors, glass beads, iron tools and weapons, rice farming, metallurgy, granaries, silk weaving, divination, and certain religious beliefs. Most of these things were the latest in Han Chinese culture, but some, such as bronze weapons, were so old that the Chinese had forgotten all about them. Traditional elements that carried over from the Jōmon period were pit dwellings, pottery techniques, hunting and gathering, ritual tooth pulling, and lacquer technology. Elements peculiar to Yayoi culture invented by the inhabitants of the islands were the worship and burial of weapons and ceremonial bells, stone short swords, iron halberds, bronze and shell bracelets, the jar burials of northern Kyushu, and perhaps the reinterment of remains found in eastern Japan. Western Japan was entrepôt for the new, while residents of eastern Japan were more traditional.[160]

No matter how high one's evaluation of the Yayoi period, Japan still had one more age of great social and economic growth to go through before it entered reliably documented history around 700. The next stage would be spread out over the four centuries following the Yayoi, and the agent of change would once again be the continent.

CHAPTER 2

ANCIENT JAPAN'S
KOREAN CONNECTION

After Himiko died around A.D. 250, Japan entered a "century of mystery" without written records. This gap is unfortunate, because archaeological finds suggest that the archipelago was undergoing important changes. The close of the third century marks the inception of the Tomb age, which scholars usually divide into early (the 300s), middle (the 400s), and late (500–645) eras. During these 350 years, the size and number of elite burials grew enormously, and grave goods indicate that many items became available on a hitherto unimaginable scale. New or expanded technologies included the ferrous industries, horsemanship, hydraulic engineering, the potter's wheel and kiln, stonemasonry, gold and silver metallurgy, writing, and methods of statecraft.

Most scholars agree that the stimulus for the development of these skills, if not the products themselves, came from the continent. Many also concur that the spread of these technologies coincided with a trend toward larger political units, resulting in unification wars in Korea and China and court-led efforts at centralization in Japan. These points of agreement, however, mask serious disputes about how these techniques were dispersed and which country's leadership was dominant. In particular, the relationship between the inhabitants of the Korean peninsula and the Japanese archipelago has been an area of contention.

This chapter examines the role of peninsular peoples in the formation of Tomb-age society, economy, and government. Did natives of the Japanese islands indeed conquer and rule southern Korea, as *A Record of Ancient Matters* and *The Chronicles of Japan* would have readers believe? Or, as some scholars assert, did equestrian ancestors of modern Koreans invade Japan and found the imperial house? Analysis of these problems once again calls for a thorough examination of both historical and archaeological materials.

HISTORY OF THE CONTROVERSY

Few relationships are as difficult and sensitive as that between modern Japan and the two Koreas. From 1910 to 1945, Japan ruled and exploited the peninsula about as harshly as any imperial power has ever dominated a possession. Not content to wrest away Korea's natural resources, the Japanese government tried to eradicate Korean culture and language by reeducating the inhabitants in Japanese civilization, based on the belief that all things Korean were inferior. Japanese treatment of the occupied populace has left a legacy of bitterness and hatred among Koreans, while many Japanese still harbor prejudice toward their closest neighbors.

These feelings color every discussion of ties among the three states, but such emotions reach the boiling point when it comes to relations among the ancient polities of Korea and Japan. There are at least five good reasons for such passion. First, origins are always a delicate subject for nation-states; the same would be true for the United States or any European nation as well. Second, there are few written records for the period from 300 to 700, and most that have survived for these four centuries date from well after the events they claim to describe. Third, all pertinent historical materials are products of a distinctive ideology with a definite perspective. Fourth, archaeology is still in its infancy in North and South Korea (although it is expanding rapidly in the south), while the same field in Japan is usually restricted to salvage projects. Fifth, the great tombs presumably hiding the treasures of persons that the sacred texts describe as Japan's first emperors are off-limits to archaeological investigation, even though scholars advocated opening them after World War II. In combination, these elements would seem to make a thorough and dispassionate analysis of the connections among the ancient peoples and cultures of the peninsula and archipelago virtually impossible. Despite these odds, many educators in Japan, North and South Korea, China, Western Europe, and the United States have tried to shed light on this topic, and miraculously a great deal of progress has resulted. The following pages survey the historiography of this topic, concentrating on crucial works in Japan where most research has taken place.

But before we delve into historiography, we should pause for a caveat.

Nationalism is a modern emotion that often leads citizens and governments to claim the distant past to legitimize or explain current conditions. Japanese and North and South Koreans are fond of seeing "Japanese" or "Korean" characteristics in ancient societies, yet neither the Korean peninsula nor the Japanese archipelago was unified for most of the period under consideration. Because connections between modern nation-states and ancient polities and cultures are tenuous, it is wise to use the words Korea and Japan sparingly, and even then only as geographical terms.

Unfortunately, the words employed during the ancient period all have drawbacks as well. There were four states on the Korean peninsula: Koguryŏ, Paekche, Silla, and Kaya. (See Map 2.1.) Boundaries were ill defined and mutable, and the ethnic and linguistic differences among societies are difficult to discern. The term "Wa," usually assumed to mean Japan, probably referred to a disunified ethnic group comprising several regional chiefdoms and occupying the western archipelago and perhaps the southern coast of Korea as well.[1] "Yamato" is a Japanese word usually designating an area in the southern Kinai. By extension it refers to the chiefly state that came into being there about 300. The development of this state is shrouded in uncertainty and the subject of great controversy, but most agree that by the early sixth century the Yamato king led an aristocratic court and was bringing a growing unity to the islands. By 720, this same line of sovereigns sponsored the compilation of *A Record* and *The Chronicles*, which glorified its presumed Yamato ancestors by naming them the emperors of Japan from time immemorial.

Research History

One justification for modern Japan's colonization of Korea and the underpinning for Japan's (and by default the world's) scholarly consensus until the 1920s lay in the first court history, *The Chronicles of Japan*. According to these annals, Empress and Regent Jingū subdued the three southern Korean states of Kaya, Silla, and Paekche in the forty-sixth through fifty-second years of her reign (A.D. 246–252 in *The Chronicles* chronology as converted to Gregorian years). In their narrative the authors favored Paekche, describing how its desire to send tribute to Japan was the beginning of Jingū's inroads into Korea. In contrast they pictured the Kingdom of Silla as deceitful and untrustworthy. Jingū conquered Kaya, located between Paekche and Silla, because she wished to have a base from which to protect Paekche and attack Silla.

For the next fifteen reigns and three hundred years, *The Chronicles* portrayed Japan's sovereigns as directly controlling Kaya, which annalists called

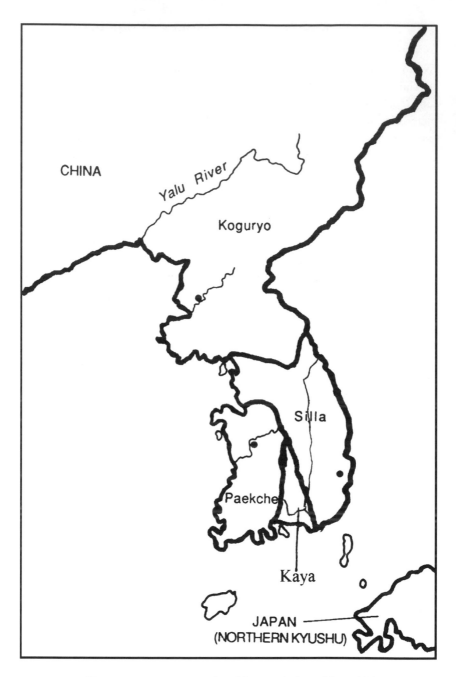

MAP 2.1 Korea, ca. A.D. 500. Reproduced by permission of the publisher from William Wayne Farris, *Heavenly Warriors: The Evolution of Japan's Military, 500–1300,* Harvard East Asian Monographs, 157 (Cambridge: Harvard University, Council on East Asian Studies, 1992), p. 24. © 1992, 1995 by the President and Fellows of Harvard College.

Mimana, and as receiving tributary items from both Paekche and Silla. In 562, Mimana fell to Silla, and the Yamato court planned but never dispatched several expeditions to punish Silla and regain its foothold, even as Paekche became more dependent on Yamato and Silla continued to send tribute. Paekche resisted Silla and Koguryŏ, its bellicose neighbor to the north, for another century. Finally in 663 a combined Silla and Chinese fleet humiliated the forces of Japan and Paekche in battle and Paekche was destroyed. Silla unified most of Korea, and writers characterized relations between the Japanese ruling class and Silla's aristocracy as hostile for the duration of the seventh and eighth centuries.

The Chronicles was explicit about Japan's superiority over the Korea states. Here is a typical speech from a Paekche king:

> The immense benevolence of the honorable country [i.e., Japan] is more weighty than Heaven and Earth. What day, what hour shall we presume to forget it? The sage sovereign dwells above, illustrious as the sun and moon; thy servants now dwell below, solid as a mountain or hill. We will always be the western barbarian land, never to the last showing double hearts.[2]

Emperor Yūryaku, portrayed by The Chronicles as a tyrant, was not merely harsh in his dealings with inhabitants of the archipelago. In the following passage, he raped and murdered a Korean woman with impunity:

> Iketsu hime of Paekche, in spite of the Emperor's intention to favor her [i.e., have intercourse with her], had [another] amour. . . . The Emperor was greatly enraged, and giving his commands . . . stretched the four limbs of the woman on a tree. The tree was placed over a cupboard, which was set fire to, and she was burnt to death.[3]

And Japan's armies annihiliated Korean (especially Silla's) armies:

> [The Japanese general] and the rest accordingly entered Silla, striking as they went [through] the districts along their way. . . . The King of Silla heard by night on all sides the drums of the [Japanese] government army, and becoming aware that they had completely conquered the land of Tok, fled in confusion with several hundred horsemen. Thereby ensued a great defeat.[4]

It is little wonder that the prewar Japanese government used the first court history, *The Chronicles*, to justify its twentieth-century domination of Korea.

Until 1920, most Japanese historians accepted descriptions in *The Chronicles* as close to, if not the literal, truth.[5] They revered the classics, especially the story of Jingū's invasion and conquest of southern Korea, even as they watched modern Japan win victories over the Chinese in 1895 and Russians in 1905 that gave them control of Korea and southern Manchuria. At the same time, the Meiji state was busy elaborating an ideology based on the divinity of the imperial house. Since the earliest histories of Japan reinforced such an interpretation, it was lèse-majesté to criticize *The Chronicles* too aggressively.

A few historians dared to perceive things differently. Naka Michiyo (who discovered that the ascension of the first Emperor Jimmu in 660 B.C. was a fabrication and argued that the chronology of later reigns was inaccurate by at least 120 years) expressed doubts about the early stories of the court's conquest of Korea. In 1888, Naka wrote that *The History of the Three Kingdoms* (*Samguk sagi*) and *Record of the Three Kingdoms* (*Samguk yusa*), Korean chronicles written in the late twelfth and fourteenth centuries respectively, were more credible than the Japanese annals.[6] In 1892, another scholar cast doubt on the reliability of *The Chronicles*' dating of Jingū's subjugation of southern Korea.[7] These voices encountered protest from most historians, who asserted, for example, that the compilation of Korean sources took place too long after the events they portrayed to be accurate. Even as Naka and others were voicing their suspicions, however, the trend toward uncritical belief in the sacrosanct texts gained momentum with the discovery of two important artifacts claiming origins from the third through the early fifth centuries.

The first was an inscribed seven-branched sword (*shichishi no katana*) located in Isonokami Shrine in Nara in 1873. While scholars did not agree on the reading of the gold-inlaid, rusty inscription, the sword seemed to be a gift from a Paekche monarch to the king of the Wa. Most experts surmised that the seven-branched sword was identical to one mentioned in the fifty-second year of Jingū's era in *The Chronicles*, whereby Paekche presumably cemented its tributary status with Yamato. The inscription also contained a difficult-to-read date, thought to be a Chinese reign period in the middle to late third century, about the time annalists wrote that Jingū had lived. Finding a Paekche sword in a Japanese shrine known in legend for its ties to the founder of the imperial house (Jimmu) and to a family of military aristocrats (the Mononobe) seemed to provide further vindication for proponents of the conventional view.

The second discovery took place in southern Manchuria. In 1884, an officer in the General Staff Headquarters of the Japanese Imperial Army returned from a spy mission against the Chinese with a rubbing from a stone monument situated on the northern bank of the Yalu River. The stele, which Ching-dynasty officials had discovered and begun caring for in 1880, stood more than 6 meters high and had over 1,800 characters carved into its surface. Copies of the ink rubbing, which had been done by Chinese artisans soon after the discovery, came into the possession of Ching scholars of epigraphy. At first, Japanese educators obtained their copies through the imperial army, but eventually many tourists and scholars journeyed to the Yalu and made their own versions. All texts were difficult to read, with many unusual characters and occasional gaps, seemingly due to weathering of the stele. In essence, the inscription stated that the Wa and Koguryŏ had competed for suzerainty over Paekche, Kaya, and Silla in the late fourth century. The two powers fought in the southern part of the peninsula and the Wa suffered a smashing defeat. Because most scholars believed that the Wa meant the Yamato court, the stone monument seemed to support the Japanese scholarly consensus and the Meiji ideology, although some were uncomfortable with any evidence of a Japanese military reversal. By 1908, scholar Shiratori Kurakichi, an advocate of the Kyushu theory in the Yamatai controversy, was leading a movement to relocate the stele to Japan. The imperial army aided in the planning (it was never carried out).[8]

With the conquest of Korea and southern Manchuria, the Japanese government assumed control of the South Manchurian Railroad. In 1908, the Manchurian Railway Research Institute (Mantetsu chōsa bu), specializing in the history and geography of Northeast Asia, was established at Tokyo Imperial University.[9] The iconoclastic Tsuda Sōkichi, a Shiratori student from Tokyo, became a member of the institute. Tsuda began twenty years of research into the two classics, A Record and The Chronicles, at about the same time. After analyzing the sections of these works that dealt with Korea, he came to a startling conclusion: a large portion of the Jingū annals was an invention of mid-sixth-century historians. Tsuda argued that as the Yamato court was about to lose its foothold in Kaya (Mimana) to Silla around 550, chroniclers fabricated Jingū's invasion story to assert the priority of their court's claims of supremacy over Kaya and Silla. Editors also borrowed descriptions from Paekche records that dated from the years when Yamato and their country first opened friendly relations around A.D. 372 and then inserted them in Jingū's reign 120 years earlier to give them greater antiquity (and thereby authority). Even the Paekche documents had undergone many alterations by reciters anxious to please their audience. Tsuda believed that another section of the

Japanese tale of conquest contained a kernel of truth, but he thought it could never have taken place in the mythical Jingū's era. Instead he argued that Yamato had first invaded and subjugated Silla and Kaya during the reign of Emperor Ōjin, the reputed son of Jingū. Adding 120 years to the dates of The Chronicles as Naka argued, Tsuda proposed that Ōjin had lived in the late fourth century. Although Tsuda doubted the reliability of the sacrosanct texts, he trusted the stele in southern Manchuria. He asserted that in the late fourth century Yamato had pressured Silla militarily, made an alliance with a dependent Paekche, and dominated Kaya, an occupation that continued for about two centuries until 562. Even Tsuda's critical attitude toward The Chronicles resulted in an interpretation that gave the Yamato court control of southern Korea for two centuries. A few scholars such as Ikeuchi Hiroshi followed Tsuda's lead.[10]

At the same time that Tsuda was formulating his views, archaeologists began cautiously addressing the problem of Japan's Tomb-age relations with the rest of East Asia. In particular, Hamada Kōsaku and Gotō Shuichi acknowledged that the archipelago had absorbed elements of higher culture from the continent. The precise origin of the outside influences was left undefined, however, perhaps because detailed studies were simply not yet available. Moreover, archaeologists usually argued that Japan had assimilated these foreign influences into an indigenously derived social matrix that was inherently superior.[11] As in the case of the Yamatai, prewar archaeology laid a foundation for later research. It could have supplied ammunition to scholars desiring to undermine the conventional interpretation, but such potential remained untapped until after World War II.

By the late 1920s, the tides of history were flowing against those holding unorthodox opinions. The Great Depression overtook Japan, and the army expanded into Manchuria and provoked war with Nationalist China. Scholars expressing doubts about the authenticity of The Chronicles or A Record suffered jail terms and other deprivations. The military-led government banned Tsuda's writings in 1939 and found him guilty of lèse-majesté and incarcerated him in 1942. In this atmosphere, chauvinistic interpretations of the relations among the ancient states of Korea and Japan became the norm and good research came to a halt amid censorship and the rubble of war.

In the ruins of postwar Japan, rejection of the prewar ideology and criticism of previous scholarship were universal, and these trends affected how historians saw ties to the ancient Korean states. Iconoclastic interpretations like Tsuda's came into vogue in the late 1940s, but nothing could have prepared scholars for the shocking views first voiced by Egami Namio in 1948.[12]

As an ethnologist and archaeologist, Egami created his own unorthodox periodization of the great tombs of Japan by dividing them into early and late eras. He then argued that the archipelago had witnessed a sudden invasion by militaristic nomads of North Asia at the end of the first period in the early fourth century. These aristocratic equestrians had ridden down the peninsula and crossed the Korean Straits in boats, founding kingdoms in Korea and Japan as they went. Egami also used the Japanese classics to support his contentions, even naming the tenth Emperor Sujin ("Mimaki") as the foreign conqueror of Japan.

The horserider theory was a brilliant synthesis of archaeology, history, and ethnology and it had at least three attractions. First, it attempted to explain a period for which there was no written evidence to contradict the thesis. Second, it seemed as though there was some truth to the archaeological trends that Egami proposed, such as the influx into Japan of horse-riding equipment and massive amounts of weapons during Egami's late Tomb period. Third and most important, the theory linked Japan to Korea and the peoples of Northeast Asia. Japanese scholars had previously proposed such a connection, calling the hypothesis *Nissen dōso ron* ("Japanese and Koreans have the same ancestor"). The horserider hypothesis addressed the problem of why the Japanese court of the sixth, seventh, and eighth centuries fought so hard to retain its base in southern Korea by claiming that the leaders of Japan, Paekche, Silla, and Kaya were all relatives.

The response of Japanese scholars raised on the prewar ideology and authenticity of *The Chronicles* was predictable: disdain and disapproval. Egami met resistance from Japanese archaeologists on his reading of the record; most said that while tombs contained many grave goods, there were no horse trappings for a century after Egami's postulated invasion. Others argued that the change from pacific, agricultural peoples of the early Tomb era to the later horseriders was neither sudden nor revolutionary, as would befit an invasion.[13] Many contradicted his interpretation of the classics, and most noted that while the third and fourth centuries were indeed a time of nomadic incursions and political upheaval in China, Egami had not presented direct evidence to prove that this unrest had reached Japan. Thanks to Egami's untiring defense, the horserider theory continues to be influential. Although the overwhelming majority of Japanese scholars have rejected it, the thesis gained popularity among the growing community of scholars of Korean history in Korea, Europe, and the United States.[14] These scholars came to view the horserider theory as a necessary antidote to insular, chauvinistic interpretations put forward in Japan.

By the early 1960s, Japanese historians had reached a consensus about ties between ancient Japan and the Korean states.[15] According to this view, even as early as the middle of the third century Yamato had come into possession of Mimana-Kaya and considered southern Korea as its political and economic base of continental operations. In 313, Koguryŏ destroyed the Chinese-controlled districts of Dai-fang and Le-lang in Korea, and by 369 Yamato, which had unified western Japan, sent an enormous expedition to aid Paekche, force the capitulation of Kaya, and harass Silla. As a result of these battles, the Yamato court came into direct control of Kaya and subjugated Paekche and Silla as the outer wall of defense against Koguryŏ.

Historians then invoked the stele on the northern bank of the Yalu River to describe Koguryŏ's advance into the southern peninsula, which Yamato used as an excuse to strengthen its hold over Paekche. Rulers of Silla tried to adhere to Koguryŏ to escape Yamato's grasp. In this interpretation, Yamato's control over southern Korea was at its height during the age from 400 to 475; in the latter year Koguryŏ defeated Paekche in battle and drove the ruling class south, a move that also represented the weakening of Yamato's power in Korea. In the sixth century, both Paekche and Silla began to carve up Yamato's foothold in Mimana, and in 562 Mimana fell to the steadily improving forces of Silla. Yet leaders of the archipelago were strong enough to cause Silla to pay tribute until 646.

In essence, this standard view in the first two decades of the postwar era was only a modification of Tsuda's prewar position. Although most Japanese scholars maintained a critical attitude toward *The Chronicles* and denied the historicity of figures such as Jingū, they still saw their country as united and strong enough to control southern Korea from A.D. 350 to 562. The postwar consensus soon found its way into English, where it became the basis for summaries in textbooks in the United States.[16]

Detailed analyses of written and material sources done in the early postwar years tended to reinforce the conventional view. Most historians did not entertain Tsuda's doubts about how accurately the editors of *The Chronicles* had used the Paekche records cited there; they simply added 120 years to the stories of conquest in Jingū's annals to conclude that Yamato had ruled southern Korea from about 350. At the same time, Japanese scholars learned how to read the seven-branched sword and concluded that the inscription indicated Paekche was subservient to Japan and that the weapon's date of manufacture was probably 369, which corresponded neatly to the adjusted chronology for Jingū's reign.

Chinese dynastic histories added the weight of their authority to the standard interpretation. According to the annals and "the account of the Eastern Barbarians" in *The History of the Liu Sung Dynasty*, five kings of the Wa had dispatched ten missions to the southern kingdom (capital at Nanking). Other chronicles revealed that one ambassador each had also gone to the Eastern Jin, Liang, and Southern Qi. These trips to Nanking had taken place between 413 and 502, and historians rushed to equate the five kings with emperors listed in *The Chronicles.* Furthermore, the Wa kings called themselves by titles that asserted their right to rule southern Korea: in 451 and 478, Chinese emperors confirmed them in the title of "General Who Maintains Peace in the East Commanding with Battle-Ax All Military Affairs in the Six Countries of Wa, Silla, Mimana, Kaya, Qin-han, and Mu-han." Surely the ordinarily reliable Chinese histories were right.[17]

Everything had fallen into place perfectly—too perfectly. Japanese historians and archaeologists had operated until the early 1960s without noticing a growing community of scholars in North and South Korea. Koreans had been silent about their own history in the twentieth century because of Japanese colonization and the outbreak of their civil war from 1950 to 1953, but in 1963 a North Korean historian named Kim Sŏk-hyŏng put forth a thesis that sent shock waves through Japanese scholarly circles.[18] This interpretation argued that from the beginning of the Yayoi era (about 300 B.C.) through the fifth century, peninsular immigrants had streamed into Japan. They formed a large part of the population in three regions: northern Kyushu, Izumo-Kibi, and the Kinai, where their considerable skills made them invaluable. These immigrants soon formed their own "countries" and looked to their advanced native lands for guidance. In northern Kyushu, Paekche and Kaya peoples were ascendant; in Izumo-Kibi, Silla was dominant; and in the Kinai, where the original Japanese residents were still powerful, at first Silla immigrants flowed in from Izumo and Kibi, whereas in the fifth and early sixth centuries Paekche and Kaya émigrés increased.

Kim further asserted that the mother countries of these immigrants maintained control over their erstwhile residents as colonists until the fifth century. Peninsular kings ruled the three regions of Japan as satellites, thus the Japanese title of this thesis, "Korean satellite theory" (*Chōsen kei bunkoku ron*). In about the year 500, the five kings of the Wa united the three Korean states in Japan and began the first real Japanese dynasty. The passages of *The Chronicles* that contained Korean geographical names were a memory of Korean colonists in Japan. Japanese claims of control over Kaya, Paekche, and Silla were really empty attempts to bring their colonies in Japan under their sway, while Mimana was the location of the ancestral government of Kaya immigrants. This new view of early Japanese-Korean relations derived from different readings of the inscriptions on the seven-branched sword and the stele in southern Manchuria. Kim held that the writing on the weapon did not indicate that Paekche was subservient to Japan, but quite the opposite. In particular, he pointed to the use of the term "enfeoffed lord" (*kōō*) to refer to the Wa king, which he said put the Japanese beneath the Paekche ruler.

Kim's satellite theory had a salutary effect on South Korean scholars. Until the publication of his work, South Korean educators avoided dealing with the complex and sensitive topic of early Japanese relations with the states of the southern peninsula. Perhaps South Koreans were hesitant to offend the Japanese, or perhaps recent memories were too painful. When Kim's thesis appeared, South Koreans began to investigate ancient Japan-Korea ties in detail. By the late 1960s, South Korean scholarship was well under way. Many wrote that the North Koreans were advocates of narrow-minded nationalism and underestimated the power of the southern states.[19]

While not agreeing on much else, scholars of both South and North Korea claimed that the traditional Japanese interpretation of the monument was in error. The Japanese consensus was that "the Wa [Japanese] crossed the ocean, destroyed Paekche and [either Silla or Kaya] and considered them their subjects." Many Koreans read the same inscription as "because the Wa [Japanese] had invaded [Korea], Koguryŏ crossed the ocean and destroyed them. Paekche attacked Silla while leading the Wa and considered them [Silla] their subjects." By altering the subject from Wa to Koguryŏ, the Koreans had turned a monument that supposedly told of Japanese battles in Korea into a tale of a Korean invasion of the archipelago.[20]

The Japanese reaction to the Korean interpretations was mixed. Not many scholars believed that Japan had been a colony of Korean immigrants under the sway of their home governments. Historians pointed out that there was no attempt to prove that Kaya, Silla, and Paekche had each controlled a different region in Japan. Furthermore, Kim rejected the authenticity of the Japanese classics, including the Paekche annals cited in *The Chronicles,* and never tried to show why he held that position. As one Japanese historian has noted, the evidence for this interesting theory was weak.[21] Some Japanese were willing to see that the Korean readings of the inscriptions on the seven-branched sword and stele on the north bank of the Yalu River were possible.[22]

Yet the Korean satellite theory performed a valuable service to scholars committed to illuminating the ancient history of Korea and Japan by challenging the comfortable consensus in Japan in two important ways. First, even though the evidence for the new hypothesis was slim, Kim's disdain for *The*

Chronicles again raised the question of Japanese reliance on this source. Was any assertion credible in a work that had not been finished until the early eighth century (when because of self-doubt the Japanese court nurtured the twin myths of its own divinity and the barbarity of Silla)? Second, the Korean satellite theory emphasized the role of Korean immigrants in early Japan. Japanese had also started looking into the same topic, although the term used for immigrants, *kikajin,* implied that Koreans had moved to the archipelago to bask in the civilizing influence of the court.[23] In which direction was the cultural flow: from Japan to Korea or Korea to Japan? This question was one for the rising science of archaeology.

In 1972, South Korean historian Yi Chin-hŭi added fuel to the debate by pointing out that an officer of the Japanese Imperial Army, and not a scholar, had publicized the stele in southern Manchuria and controlled access to the first rubbing.[24] The Korean argued that the soldier, who was on a spy mission for the Meiji government, had altered the words on the monument to support the ideological basis for colonization of Korea. Since its discovery, the monument had supplied crucial evidence confirming Yamato suzerainty over southern Korea; if it was a forgery, the entire foundation for the Japanese consensus disappeared. In 1973, leading South Korean scholars of the ancient period convened and most agreed that the inscription had probably been altered, as evidenced by a lime coating over the stele.

Japanese historians rejected the South Korean claims. In particular, Japanese wondered why the army officer had chosen to alter many phrases but left intact the statement that Koguryŏ had inflicted a decisive defeat against the arms of Japan. Would not a nationalistic Japanese military spy bent on glorifying his country have first eliminated any reference to a humiliating Japanese loss? The Korean attack on the credibility of the monument soon brought calls for an international inspection and renewed attempts at interpretation.

Throughout the 1970s and 1980s, the Japanese consensus began to unravel as it underwent assault from four directions. First, historians started to reread all written sources—Chinese, Japanese, and Korean—to find out how East Asian leaders conducted international politics in the period from 300 to 700.

Second, Japanese historians commenced critiquing the court's ideology of the early eighth century when editors had compiled *The Chronicles.* Many postwar scholars, troubled by their government's treatment of Korean residents in Japan, sought to promote greater appreciation of peninsular civilization through the publication of the popular journal *Korean Culture Within Japan (Nihon no naka no Chōsen bunka).*

Third, Korean and Chinese historians and archaeologists made themselves heard in the Japanese academic community, and many Japanese scholars lent an ear to their interpretations.[25] In 1984, for example, the Chinese archaeologist Wang Jian-qun published a new and superior version of the inscription on the Yalu monument based on extensive investigation of the original.[26] Wang read more than one hundred characters that had previously been illegible. In the mid-1980s, a series of symposia dedicated to rereading the inscription took place in China, North Korea, and Japan. Soon Korean, Chinese, and Japanese scholars were traveling to each other's countries, publishing in each other's journals, and training each other's graduate students. At last scholars from East Asia had agreed to cooperate in joint research, although interpretations continued to differ from author to author.

Fourth, archaeologists in South Korea and Japan excavated new and exciting materials that provided background for an analysis of the slim textual evidence. By the 1990s, there was a spectrum of views among those who studied ancient relations among the peoples of the Korean peninsula and the Japanese archipelago, ranging from a few who still adhered to the 1960s Japanese consensus to some who endorsed their own version of the horserider theory or Kim's satellite hypothesis. Scholars came forth with many novel interpretations, utilizing innovative approaches in the process. Chief among these approaches was the increasingly critical and sophisticated field of archaeology.

THE ARCHAEOLOGICAL RECORD

The following list summarizes the current international scholarly consensus regarding the materials, technologies, and religious and political systems that flowed from the Korean peninsula to the Japanese islands between 300 and 700. The items noted here are particularly striking because they embrace all social classes, including things that common people would have used and consumed—such as blades for iron farming tools, household ovens, and pond-digging techniques—right along with methods of statecraft, religion, and aristocratic fineries. Entering the archipelago in the wake of the imports of the Yayoi age, these borrowings helped to define a material culture that lasted as long as a thousand years. The items are listed in order of their appearance in ancient Japan and may be grouped as follows:

1. Iron and ironworking techniques, including riveting:
   a. Scissors
   b. Iron attack weapons like swords, spearpoints, and arrowheads
   c. Iron defensive armaments like cuirasses, lamellar armor, and helmets

      d. Horse trappings (bridles, saddles, stirrups, and decorations)

      e. Iron fittings for hoes and spades as well as blades for sickles

2. Pond and canal-digging technology

3. Wheel-thrown, kiln-fired stoneware

4. Ovens for households

5. Stone-fitting technology:

      a. Stone corridor and chamber tombs

      b. Decorated tombs

6. Aristocratic accoutrements:

      a. Gold and silver jewelry and techniques such as gilding, open-work carving, and inlaying

      b. Bronze bells

      c. Glass vessels

      d. Silk weaving

      e. Writing

7. Methods of statecraft:

      a. Court titles (*kabane*)

      b. Aristocratic surnames (*uji*)

      c. Buddhism and its architecture

      d. Chinese-style law codes (*ritsuryō*)

      e. The district (*hyō; kohori*)

      f. Measurements for the checkerboard field pattern (*jōri sei*)

      g. Mountain fortifications

      h. The crossbow

And possibly:

8. Keyhole tumuli

9. Court ranking systems

10. Units (*be*) producing goods and services for the court

11. Stamped-earth building techniques

The next three sections describe these various technologies and materials as they passed from Korea to Japan. Many crucial details about this list are missing, of necessity, because archaeologists have just begun working in South Korea and remain hampered in their activities in both Japan and North Korea for several reasons.[27] In particular, little is known about the dating and routes of entry into Korea, thus obscuring the ways in which peninsular peoples may have adapted these objects to their own societies.

Despite great gaps in scholarly knowledge, it is possible to arrange these items into three categories. First, several of them essentially originated in the peninsula, such as iron and ironworking techniques, the cuirass, the oven, bronze bells, court titles and surnames, the district, measurements for the field pattern system, and mountain fortifications. Second, inhabitants of ancient Korea transmitted some items from China long after their invention, such as the ring-pommeled sword, iron attachments for agricultural tools, pond- and canal-digging technology, stoneware, silk weaving, the idea for service and producer units, law codes, and writing. Because of the long interval between the invention of these items in China and their transmission to the archipelago through Korea, natives of the peninsula are liable to have altered or refined them. Third, many items were invented elsewhere but were transferred virtually unchanged (lamellar armor, horse trappings, stone-fitting methods and tombs, gold and silver jewelry, Buddhism, and the crossbow). Taken together, these three modes of transmission reflect the seminal role played by peninsular peoples in the formation of Japan's Tomb-age culture.

Iron and Ironworking

To understand the development of iron tools and weapons in the archipelago, one needs some knowledge of the ferrous industries in the rest of the world. In the Mediterranean and Middle East, technicians smelted ore in a small furnace called a bloomery and formed the product through smithing methods on an anvil. The advantage of this technology was that it was simple and required little input of labor. This mode of ironworking diffused into the Central Asian steppe, where the nomadic Scythians carried the knowledge into eastern Siberia by 700 B.C.

The Chinese invented ferrous techniques later on their own.[28] While they may have experimented with iron casting and forging techniques as early as 800 or 900 B.C., artisans of the Middle Kingdom became proficient at making iron blades and tools from mined ore only centuries later, about 500 B.C. Unlike Mediterranean and Middle Eastern peoples, the Chinese of this period cast nearly all ferrous products using huge blast furnaces. Although such a method required a large input of labor and more sophisticated heating technology, it had the advantage of greater efficiency due to the big scale of production.

By 400 B.C., both the Scythian and Chinese methods were probably available to residents of northern Korea. However, no one has yet traced the precise routes of the spread of ironworking into Korea and down the peninsula.[29] Moreover, South Korean archaeologists have not uncovered furnaces for these early dates. Despite these problems, later evidence suggests that the peninsula's inhabitants preferred the simpler bloomery method.[30] Residents of Korea may have adopted the Scythian techniques in toto, but because of the dearth of evidence, many questions remain. Another alternative is that peninsular peoples invented bloomeries and smithing on their own in response to local conditions.

It is tempting to envision three periods of iron production in Korea. During the first stage, which started in 400 B.C. and lasted to 100 B.C., iron products entered the north and gradually flowed southward; evidence of mining and ironworking is still slim for southern Korea during these times. The second era, from 100 B.C. to A.D. 300, saw major expansion of iron extraction and ironworking in southern Korea, with the region supplying Chinese outposts and even parts of Japan.[31] The third epoch, which began in A.D. 300 with state formation, encompassed the mass manufacture of heavy iron armor, weapons, and tools.[32]

The three-stage peninsular pattern of ironmaking correlates well with the story of the same technology in Japan. As noted in Chapter 1, cast-iron ax blades made in China first entered Japan about 300 B.C. via the peninsula. For most of the Yayoi epoch, however, wood, stone, and bronze were the materials of choice for utilitarian as well as ritual implements. The amount of iron began to increase dramatically in the archipelago in the second and third centuries A.D., an era that corresponds with the establishment of the Chinese district Daifang near modern Seoul. Recall that Chen Shou wrote in A.D. 280 that the territory soon to be inhabited by the peoples of Kaya and Silla "produces iron; the Han, the Hui, and the Wa all pursue and take it. All markets use iron like the Chinese use cash. Also they supply iron to the two [Chinese] districts."[33] Perhaps the demand of the Chinese elite stimulated the growth of ferrous industries in southern Korea, where residents of Yayoi Japan received products and ore through trade.

During the ensuing Tomb period, the number of objects made of iron seems to have grown somewhat as production expanded in southern Korea. At Tsubai Ōtsukayama, a tomb of the late third century located between Kyoto and Nara, archaeologists found one suit of iron armor, more than twenty iron swords, and over two hundred iron arrowheads. Yukinoyama Tomb, which is situated in Shiga prefecture and dated to the middle of the fourth century, contained no armor, but its occupant possessed one iron helmet, seven iron swords, one point for a pike, and ten iron arrowheads. Although artisans at the end of the Yayoi epoch had forged iron arrowheads, it is doubtful that they made them in these quantities, and Yayoi ironworkers made no armor and fewer swords than smiths of the early Tomb age.[34] The greater quantity of iron in early Tomb-age Japan suggests either better access to iron in Korea or expansion of the peninsular industry.[35]

In the fifth century, perhaps beginning between A.D. 425 and 450, the quantity of iron from sites of all types in Japan grew dramatically. At Nonaka, for example, an outlier mound of the giant 225-meter-long, moated Hakayama Tumulus in Osaka, archaeologists have uncovered ten suits of iron armor complete with helmets buried in a wooden box; another receptacle hid one more suit. In addition, the deceased had been interred with 169 iron swords, 3 iron spearpoints, and about 300 iron arrowheads. At Ariyama Tomb of the same era (also in Osaka), scientists found 85 swords, 8 pike points, 1,542 arrowheads, 134 ax blades, 201 sickles, 49 U-shaped shovel fittings, and 90 chisels.[36] Other excavated tombs dated from the fifth century repeat the same story. It is little wonder that a leading Japanese scholar calls the 400s "the century of armor."[37]

What is more, the source for almost all this iron must have been continental, and most likely Korea, not iron-poor Japan. Recently scientists have discovered Enjo site north of Kyoto where craftsmen smelted into tools and ingots Japanese iron sand collected from river bottoms.[38] In addition to holes containing rusted pieces of iron and slag, there were remains of furnaces for refining the sand, foundries for forging tools, and kilns for manufacturing charcoal. At present, Enjo is considered the oldest iron-smelting site in Japan, but it dates from no earlier than the late fifth century. The implication is clear: nearly all the iron to make the first Japanese weapons and tools—from the primitive iron shoes of the late Yayoi period to the suits of fifth-century lamellar armor—came from Korea.[39]

Other archaeological evidence supports the view that inhabitants of the archipelago developed their ironworking capabilities with the aid of peninsular artisans and techniques during the early and mid-fifth century. Along with armor, spear points, and blades for hoes and spades, tools that smiths used to forge other iron implements commonly appear in Japanese tombs of the mid-fifth century. Instruments of the smithy's trade (large pliers, mallets, chisels, anvils) turn up in Japanese tombs and are identical to examples found in southern Korea, especially Silla and Kaya.[40] The resemblance between these sets of tools suggests that artisans of the archipelago followed the southern Korean tradition of bloomery technology; indeed, later Japanese furnaces (tatara) seem to have been a variant of the bloomery. Ancient Japanese thus preferred the southern Korean version of ironworking to the Chinese approach.

Artifacts also indicate that Silla and Kaya carried on a vigorous trade in iron ingots (tettei) with the Wa.[41] Measuring from 10 to 50 centimeters in length and weighing from 30 to several hundred grams, these pieces of iron appear in tombs stretching from northern Kyushu (50 ingots) to the Kanto (2) but are concentrated in Nara (200) and Osaka (137) prefectures. Sites on Okinoshima, an island off the northern coast of Kyushu that served as an anchorage and shrine for travelers going to Korea, have revealed twenty-two ingots.[42] In addition to the twenty-eight caches found in Japanese tombs that date from 425 to 550, archaeologists have uncovered seventy-seven piles of ingots with as many as a thousand ingots per pile, mostly around modern Pusan and elsewhere in ancient Silla or Kaya territory. The oldest ingots in southern Korea predate Japanese examples by about seventy-five years, suggesting that the idea may have been peninsular in origin.

Ferrous technology had many spin-offs that rippled through early Japanese society. With the making of iron came the use of bloomeries that could heat metal to as much as 1,200 degrees centigrade; the same capability might come in handy making pottery or firing glass. Secondary industries such as the manufacture of iron agricultural and fishing tools, horse gear, and weapons all became possible. Moreover, the implications of early Japan's near-total reliance on the southern Korea states for iron, iron tools and weapons, and ironworkers are profound.[43] The technological boost that the Wa received from the polities of southern Korea meant that state formation in the two regions would be intimately intertwined. All would-be rulers wanted iron and artisans from southern Korea to fashion weapons for gaining victories over their rivals at home and across the sea. Wa meddling in peninsular politics had less to do with any kinship among peoples of southern Korea and the archipelago than it did with the Wa chieftains' need for peninsular iron and ferrous technology.[44]

Iron Weapons

Because they were made of iron, most armaments used by Japanese soldiers, including arrowheads, spear and pike points, swords, and armor, had a link to Korea. The iron for many arrowheads probably came from Korea, at least until iron sand was discovered in Japan in the sixth century. Spearheads and pikeblades used by foot soldiers and modeled after Korean designs appear in some quantity in fourth-century Japanese tombs, and spears became more widely dispersed after 425 during "the century of armor." But spears and pikes eventually disappeared altogether because the occupants of later tumuli were horse-riding officers and not ground troops and because mass tactics utilizing these weapons never became widespread in ancient Japan.[45]

One weapon that had ties to southern Korea was the ring-pommeled sword (*kantō tachi*) wielded by foot soldiers and horsemen alike. It began as a Chinese invention of the Former Han dynasty, and eventually the idea made its way slowly down the Korean peninsula to Japan. At first all three civilizations forged prototypes of about 60 or 70 centimeters in length with plain pommels, which tended to become more elaborate as time passed. The early unadorned variety of ring-pommeled swords that dated to the fourth century and before has come to light in Paekche, but archaeologists have usually uncovered that type from Kaya and Silla. A South Korean scholar has argued that Paekche first imported the swords from China (even though few are extant) and later Kaya and Silla took up the custom.[46]

In Japan, archaeologists have discovered a few Han-dynasty ring-pommeled swords as early as the late Yayoi period. Although fourth-century tombs contained these swords, their number increased greatly in tumuli of the fifth century.[47] Until 500 or so, styles varied widely by region, but beginning in the sixth century there are signs of a nationwide standardization of design just as this type of sword was losing its value as a fighting instrument and becoming ornamental.[48] When Silla conquered Kaya and began to unify the peninsula about 550, Wa leaders lost access to imports, and so artisans crafted the swords in the archipelago, most likely in the Kinai.[49] Handle designs were elaborate, usually with dragon or phoenix patterns copied from Paekche. Many swords uncovered in Japan are exact replicas of Silla or Kaya artifacts. During the latter half of the sixth and seventh centuries, low-level court bureaucrats and local notables in service of the Yamato king wore the dragon and phoenix ring-pommeled swords as symbols of their rank and title.[50]

The most critical and controversial piece of military hardware that seems to have traveled from southern Korea to Japan was armor: the cuirass (tankō, close-fitting gear protecting both the back and breast and worn by foot soldiers), lamellar armor (keikō, sheets of thin plates attached with leather thongs or rivets and donned by horsemen), and the helmet (kabuto). (See Figure 2.1.) Japanese and South Korean archaeologists agree that lamellar armor and one type of helmet entered Japan from the peninsula. Generally, throughout their history the Chinese and nomads of Central Asia wore lamellar or scale armor, and these items fit into the category of technologies transferred from the continent via Korea with little change. But the cuirass is a design virtually unknown outside of southern Korea and Japan and therefore was probably a neither Chinese nor nomadic invention. Scholars of Japan and South Korea have long disagreed about who made these cuirasses. In essence, prewar Japanese scholars claimed that pieces found in Kaya territory were Wa imports whereas South Korean archaeologists recently have asserted that not just the patterns, iron, and technology for making Japanese cuirasses but the completed armor itself came from the peninsula.[51]

South Korean archaeologists have argued that cuirasses and helmets found in Japan had their origins in southern Korea. Their argument rests on two points. First, until recently the distribution of cuirasses—a disproportionate percentage has appeared in Japanese tombs—favored the Japanese position. During the 1980s, however, South Korean archaeologists began to discover many more in what would have been Kaya territory, thus bolstering South Korean claims to be the source of the cuirass.[52] Second, the earliest Japanese cuirasses of the fourth century showed strong regional variations, just at a time when Kaya pieces were uniform. According to one South Korean archaeologist, the uniformity of Kaya cuirasses suggests production by a central power that exported the idea to the archipelago, where various chieftains made their own versions.[53] This same South Korean archaeologist has also examined the fifth-century "Japanese" cuirasses found in Kaya territory. Although he agrees they resemble Japanese models of the same period, he argues that the Wa could not possibly have dominated Kaya and Silla because the Korean kings preferred lamellar armor, which was not yet found in the archipelago. The cuirasses found in Kaya may have been constructed in the archipelago and even worn by Wa troops, but the owners were people of lowly status controlled by Kaya rulers.[54]

Japanese archaeologists divide the years 300–500 into three periods.[55] (See Figure 2.1.) In the first era (300–380), Japanese tombs contained a limited number of cuirasses made of either vertical or square plates and a few helmets formed of iron slats, in both cases tied together with leather thongs. The second period began about 380 with the appearance of a new, uniform type of cuirass made of rectangular plates sewn together horizontally with leather thongs. After a few years, triangular-plated cuirasses joined the armor with horizontal pieces. There also appeared a new type of helmet made of triangular parts of iron; it had no visor but had flaps to protect the cheeks. Most scholars interpret the rise in uniform cuirasses, together with a concurrent increase in artifacts in the Kinai, as signs that the Yamato state had begun to direct the manufacture of armor.

From 425 to 500 (the second half of the second period), when the amount of iron found in Japanese tombs grew exponentially, armor production underwent an important technological improvement. Riveting replaced leather binding as a means of fastening the pieces of a cuirass or helmet together at the same time that a new type of visored helmet became popular. It is generally conceded that both technologies came from southern Korea. Also in the second half of the fifth century, the number of new uniform cuirasses discovered in northern Kyushu grew dramatically; one authority ties this trend to Wa expeditions to southern Korea.[56]

The third period of Japanese armor production commenced about 500, when the visored helmet and cuirasses of all types virtually disappeared. In their place leather-bound lamellar armor became widespread, especially in the Kanto. A few examples of lamellar armor have come to light from sites in western Japan that date to the mid-fifth century. More and more Japanese archaeologists view the growth in manufacture of lamellar armor as a sign of the rising popularity of horsemanship.

The evidence relating to armor merits three observations. First, both sides admit that Japanese armor owed a great debt to Kaya and Silla and ultimately Koguryŏ. Lamellar armor, the visored helmet, and riveting all came from the peninsula. Second, the exponential growth of artifacts in Japan once again indicates that the era 425–450 was an important epoch, just as it was for iron-making. Third, similarities between Japanese and southern Korean cuirasses, which constitute a design unique in East Asia, underline how close Kaya–

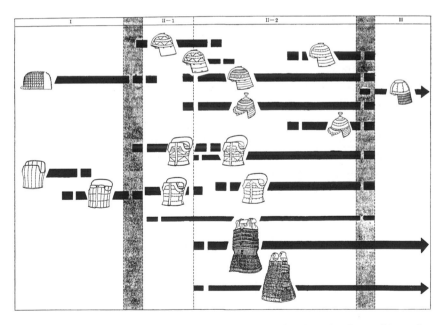

FIGURE 2.1   Armor in Ancient Japan. *Source:* Tanaka Shinsaku, "Bugu," in *Kofun jidai no kenkyū* 8: *Kofun* II: *Fukusōhin*, pp. 44–45. *Note:* From top, helmets, cuirasses, and lamellar armor.

Silla–Wa relations were. It would not be surprising to find that chieftains in the archipelago imported much of their armor from Kaya and Silla, or to discover that some of the cuirasses found in southern Korean sites belonged to Wa soldiers.[57]

Horse Trappings

In contrast to the heated disagreement over cuirasses, all scholars concur that equestrian gear and skills entered the archipelago from southern Korea. It is uncertain just how the technology came to Japan, and it is difficult to construct a firm chronology because of the sparse finds to date in South Korea. Surprisingly, however, many Korean archaeologists agree with their Japanese counterparts that the evidence on both sides of the Korean Straits fails to fit Egami's horserider theory.

It is best to see equestrian developments in Korea and Japan as part of the invention and worldwide dispersion of horse trappings.[58] The earliest equipment for riding a horse was simple: a cushion resting on the mount's back and a two-piece metal bit with straps of leather running to the rider's hands. Nomadic forces of Central Asia, perhaps the Scythians, created this simple but difficult-to-master gear. Qin and Han forces also used this technique about 200 B.C. Around A.D. 200, a sequence of incremental improvements overtook the equestrian arts. Inventors added two metal cheek pieces (or shanks) to either side of the bit to prevent it from sliding around in the horse's mouth, and they further ensured the stability of the rider by developing the saddle. The first saddles were basically two vertical boards, pressing the rider from front and back, connected by a horizontal seat that rested on the mount. Around 300 the Xian-bi, a Mongolian people then ruling northern China, learned to use the stirrup, at first slung over only the left side of the animal. By 400, the Xian-bi were dangling footrests from both sides of the saddle; these early stirrups were circular and composed of wood in the middle surrounded by riveted iron. Around the beginning of the sixth century, the form of saddle with which Westerners are familiar came into being. It later entered Europe, where it was a component of medieval society, courtesy of the nomads who overthrew the Roman Empire.

The first Koreans to use the horse in combat were soldiers of Koguryŏ doing battle with the Xian-bi. Wall paintings from tombs and other artifacts indicate that commanders of Koguryŏ's army preferred to armor both rider and horse.[59] Heavily armored cavalry was probably the most deadly military technology in the world before the advent of gunpowder, because it combined mobility with invulnerability. Most Japanese scholars, as well as many South Korean archaeologists, believe that Wa, Kaya, Paekche, and Silla foot soldiers first encountered this terrible new weapon during the war fought against Koguryŏ in southern Korea between 390 and 410, the war described in the inscription on the stele near the Yalu River.[60]

Interpretation of the southern Korea artifacts is still open to question, but most scholars acknowledge that horse gear was not placed in tombs until the end of the fourth or beginning of the fifth century.[61] The presence in excavations in all three southern Korean states of wood and iron stirrups, a technology that dated from around 400, would seem to support this view. One South Korean archaeologist has argued that Koguryŏ mounted troops introduced the simple bridle and wooden-centered, iron-covered stirrups forged from ingots to Silla and Kaya about 410. This authority further asserts that there is a strong affinity between Kaya, Silla, and Wa horse trappings; many typologies used in Japan, he argues, also apply to the equipment of southern Korea.[62]

Although at least one prominent Japanese archaeologist believes that horse paraphernalia entered the archipelago as early as the late fourth century, most regard this technology as appearing on the Japanese scene in the first half of the fifth century, perhaps during the era 425–450.[63] The earliest examples are simple, two-piece bits and stirrups of iron and wood, both of which were recovered in northern Kyushu, a sure sign of Korean import. Along with a few saddle parts, these primitive trappings predominated in the first half of the fifth century; many were probably peninsular products. From 450, about the time that horse raising commenced in Japan, artisans there began to produce simple gear. After 500, horse decorations like metal flowers (*gyōyō*) and bells, a more sophisticated bridle (with f-shaped iron cheek pieces called *kagami ita*), and pouch stirrups made their appearance.

Japanese scholars have not yet reached a consensus on which of the three southern Korean states sent horse trappings to the archipelago. One archaeologist argues that Japanese paraphernalia is most like that from Kaya and Silla; he states that Paekche has few examples akin to Japanese artifacts.[64] Others favor Kaya and Paekche.[65] The only certainty is that the Japanese could not or would not adopt the Koguryŏ custom of heavily armoring their mounts. Only one complete example of horse armor has appeared in Japan—in the tomb of a local strongman responsible for ferrying Wa troops to southern Korea.[66]

Japanese archaeologists have traced the dispersion of horse trappings. Only 1 percent of tombs constructed before 425 yielded these artifacts, almost all in the Kinai; only 10 percent of tumuli constructed before 500 contained horse-related artifacts.[67] Archaeologists have uncovered horse paraphernalia from

121 tumuli in eastern Japan, while only 74 tombs in western Japan have offered up these trappings.[68] These facts suggest the gradual spread of horse gear and riding skills throughout Japan over the fifth and sixth centuries, not a sudden explosion.[69] Moreover, the existence of horse trappings in a tomb may not always mean that the occupant rode a horse. To be sure, the earliest artifacts were all functional, but these pieces came from Korea, where a trader or soldier could have picked them up without the animal. One expert believes that local strongmen commonly hoarded the otherwise useless equipment.[70]

While there is no doubt that horse gear and riding skills entered Japan from southern Korea, the evidence does not fit Egami's horserider theory. Trappings appeared too late to have been associated with an invasion in the mid- or late fourth century; moreover, their spread across Japan was too gradual.[71] There are at least two other important reasons for rejecting the horserider theory: Japanese did not practice castration of livestock as in the Asian steppe, and Egami's characterizations of agricultural peoples as pacific and equestrians as warlike are inaccurate stereotypes.[72] Nomads did not gallop through Korea and Japan founding kingdoms, but inhabitants of Korea did play an essential role in transferring horse-riding technology to Japan.

Farm Tools and Irrigation

The iron and improved ferrous industries that entered Japan from southern Korea about 425–450 also had an effect on toolmaking. Although prototypes for some iron implements dated to the middle and late Yayoi period, the overall quantity of iron tools was still small even in Himiko's age. In the fifth century, the number of iron utensils of all kinds grew greatly. Simple iron tools that had been used in Japan since Yayoi times but increased markedly at this time include chisels, awls, saws, and blades for sickles and axes. One scholar has written that the new saws, chisels, and awls promoted woodworking in Japan; for the first time residents were able to produce not only finely detailed luxury goods but also large wooden structures such as boats and houses.[73] Also in the fifth century, newly designed axes came to Japan from southern Korea. The improved ax blade had a hole for a wooden handle, like axes of today; previously artisans had forged flaps to fold around the handle. (See Figure 2.2.) One expert has argued that craftsmen inhabiting the archipelago still lacked the sophisticated techniques necessary to forge the improved instruments.[74] Many examples of the more advanced ax head have come to light from tombs in Kaya territory.

By far the most critical new technology that entered Japan from southern

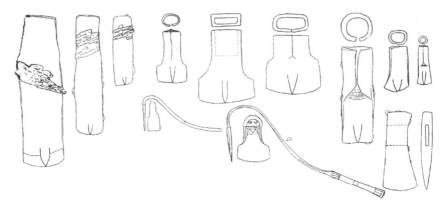

FIGURE 2.2   Ax Heads of the Tomb Period. *Source:* Furuse Kiyohide, "Nō kōgu,"
in *Kofun jidai no kenkyū* 8: *Kofun* II: *Fukusōhin*, p. 79.

Korea during the fifth century related to farming, and once again it is important to see developments in an East Asian context.[75] After learning to forge
and cast iron by 500 B.C., Chinese artisans soon turned their talents to manufacturing iron agricultural tools, perhaps as early as the third century B.C.
Archaeologists have recovered molds for cast-iron hoe blades from this time,
and by the Han period craftsmen were producing square iron fittings for
spades.[76] Two further advances went hand in hand with the invention of iron
digging tools: the construction of massive canals and irrigation works, such as
those at Zhengguo and Guanxian, and the utilization of draft animals to pull
plows.[77] By the Former Han dynasty, these three elements had combined to
create the most intensive and productive agricultural regime in the world,
centering on millet in North China and rice in the south.

About the time the Chinese first learned to make iron digging tools, wet-
rice agriculture entered Japan from southern China via the Korean peninsula.
In this first form of Japanese rice cultivation, tillers tended to plant in low-lying
areas with access to water. They mostly used wooden and stone tools, and
while they may have in some cases transplanted seedlings from prepared beds,
they usually sowed seed directly on the paddy and then painstakingly harvested each ear of rice by hand. (See Chapter 1.) Although this technique
required much labor, no iron tools or sophisticated irrigation facilities such as
ponds or long ditches for river-diverted water were necessary. Yields were not
good by modern standards, but so long as rain fell, rice would normally provide a living.[78]

By the third century A.D., the idea of using iron in agricultural tools had come to Japan from southern Korea, as witnessed by straight blades for sickles as well as iron shoes folding around wooden blades of hoes and spades uncovered in northern Kyushu sites of that date. But as elements of the Chinese agricultural regime came to the peninsula, the peoples of southern Korea made important refinements, probably starting in the fourth century.[79] The best-documented aspect of this refined farming technology is the dispersion of improved hoes and spades with U-shaped edges, which have been recovered from fourth- and fifth-century tombs in Paekche and Silla.[80] (See Figure 2.3.) The idea for U-shaped fittings was probably peninsular in origin; spades and hoes with these edges are still common in South Korea today.[81] The new tools represented an advance because they could bite more deeply into the earth and allow the clearance of land with heavy soil formerly closed to cultivators.

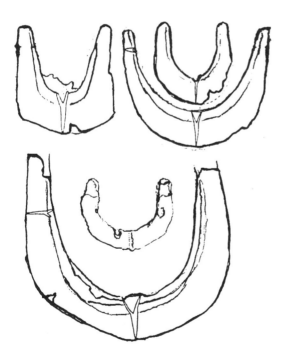

FIGURE 2.3
U-Shaped Shovel Fittings.
Source: Furuse Kiyohide,
"Nō kōgu," in *Kofun jidai
no kenkyū* 8: *Kofun* II:
Fukusōhin, p. 75.

The U-shaped hoes and spades also enabled Korean rice croppers to dig deeper ditches and pile up more earth for dams. As a result, peninsular peoples could concentrate their efforts on building irrigation ponds, a second refinement in the Chinese regime.[82] These reservoirs for watering rice had been less important in China, where rivers kept millet fields and rice paddies moist the year round. Irrigation ponds and improved ditches were beneficial because they permitted farmers access to more fertile soils at elevations higher than those exploited by previous cultivators.[83] The last element of the Chinese farming regime, the ox-drawn plow, also came to the southern peninsula about the fourth century, as indicated by iron plowshares found in former Paekche and Koguryŏ territory.[84]

Archaeological evidence suggests that beginning in the early to mid-fifth century inhabitants of the Japanese archipelago began to adapt all these new ideas to their environment. The two peninsular refinements, U-shaped iron edges for hoes and spades and improved ditch and pond-digging technology, were especially important.[85] Most iron hoes and spades have appeared in tombs in northern Kyushu, Okayama, and especially the Kinai and are nearly indistinguishable from southern Korean prototypes. Their importation completed the evolution of Japan's basic agricultural tools: similar models would be in use even during the Edo period.

Scholars have also noted signs of canal digging at the Furuichi site in Osaka on a scale unimaginable to Yayoi tillers. Between 8.5 and 9.5 meters wide, 4 and 5 meters deep, and 10 kilometers long, the Furuichi Canal was designed for either irrigation or navigation. It ran in a direct line among the giant tumuli of the Osaka plain, a fact which indicates to many that excavation may have first taken place in the late fifth century.[86] Written sources also support the view that the idea of pond construction was brought to Japan by immigrants from the southern Korean states.[87]

Of course, one must not exaggerate the immediate impact of the new inventions. Dispersion of technology is never smooth in a premodern society, especially in mountainous islands like Japan. The recovery of iron farm tools in tombs for elite leaders in the late 400s suggests that these implements may not yet have been used by most cultivators. Many peasants did not have iron parts for their hoes and spades even as late as the ninth century.[88] The technology for irrigation ponds was slow to spread in Japan, as well, and the animal-drawn plow may never have been widely employed among Japanese farmers.[89] Despite the slow rate of dispersion for these technologies, the Tomb-age population explosion seems to have continued the late Yayoi expansion. It is unclear which century saw the greatest increase after A.D. 300, but if one estimates the population of Japan at 2 million in 300 and 5 or 6 million at the end of the seventh century, then growth over the Tomb period would have been about 250 or 300 percent. Because of high mortality from foreign-borne epidemics beginning around A.D. 700, it seems likely that the bulk of demographic gains to 1200 had taken place by the end of the Tomb age.[90]

CERAMICS, TOMBS, AND GOLD: MORE BORROWINGS FROM KOREA

The importation of iron and ferrous technology, weapons, horse gear, and farming tools and methods suggests the fundamental impact that the peninsular peoples had on ancient Japan's economic and political development. In the cultural realm, too, the Korean states influenced the archipelago, as witnessed by the introduction of improved pottery techniques, novel burial customs, and various aristocratic fineries.

Stoneware

The English term "pottery" covers a world of differences in technology and products.[91] The simplest and oldest form of pottery is earthenware, which in ancient times was often built by hand and fired at 700 to 850 degrees centigrade in an open space where oxygen could combine with hot metals in the clay. Bowls and jars made of earthenware must have been a great advance over stone or wooden utensils, but because they were made without the benefit of a potter's wheel, they were hard to mass produce. Since makers baked their earthenware at relatively low temperatures, moreover, the resulting pieces were porous and unsatisfactory for holding liquid.

Another kind of pottery—the crucial one here—is stoneware. Fired at a minimum of 1,100–1,200 degrees centigrade in a closed kiln resembling a tunnel running up the side of a hill, the copper and iron in the clays making up stoneware are not oxidized but chemically reduced by cooking with moist foliage near the end of firing. This process sometimes gives bowls and jars a gray or black hue. Stoneware is nonporous and opaque, and artisans could manufacture this ware in large quantities since it was customarily shaped on a potter's wheel or in molds.

There can be little doubt that North China was the home of the first stoneware in East Asia. One Japanese archaeologist pushes the date for the earliest ancestor of Chinese stoneware back to 4400–3000 B.C.[92] The Chinese also introduced the use of the potter's wheel to the region between 2600 and 2300 B.C. For the next several centuries the new technologies diffused throughout China, making their way south across the Yang-tze River and northeast to Manchuria.

Although the route that stoneware technology took from China into southern Korea is open to dispute, all South Korean and Japanese archaeologists agree that emigrants from the peninsula brought the tunnel kiln (*anagama*) and perhaps the potter's wheel to Japan in the first half of the fifth century.[93] The three major types of Japanese ceramics that had existed prior to A.D. 450— Jōmon, Yayoi, and Haji—were all hand-built earthenware fired in the open at a low temperature. Sue pots, as the new stoneware came to be called when makers had adapted the techniques to Japan, were too sophisticated for householders to make, unlike earthenware bowls and jars. Highborn consumers required specialized stoneware makers to throw and bake their ceramics.

Archaeologists have recovered Korean stoneware (in Japanese, *tōshitsu doki*; in Korean, *kyŏngjil togi*), as distinct from the Japanese Sue pots, in many parts of Japan, especially in northern Kyushu and the Kinai.[94] Specialists can usually tell a Kaya or Silla pot from Sue ware because the shape or pattern incised on the piece is similar to examples unearthed in South Korea. In some cases, archaeologists have submitted the suspected peninsular stoneware to chemical analysis to determine the provenance of the clay. Still, in many instances it is difficult to distinguish between products of the peninsula and the archipelago, especially for the first half of the fifth century when the technology was first imported.[95]

Scholars are gradually piecing together evidence revealing how stoneware came to Japan and became a native industry. Most archaeologists now believe that the first gray stoneware came from Kaya, although some see similarities with Paekche and even Silla ceramics.[96] One South Korean archaeologist has traced the evolution of Kaya stoneware from A.D. 300 until 500 through four stages; in the last stage Silla and Kaya potteries became distinct from each other and about then the technology crossed the Korean Straits to Japan.[97] This same author ties the exportation of stoneware to the invasion of southern Korea by Koguryŏ troops in the early 400s.

The new pottery, which entered Japan between 425 and 450, closely resembled Silla and especially Kaya prototypes during most of the fifth century. Potters created jars and bowls that looked like Korean pieces, only to have them go out of production quickly as the needs and tastes of the ruling elite changed. Stoneware design differed somewhat in northern Kyushu and the Kinai in the early decades, possibly because local artisans modeled their creations on pieces from different regions of Korea. After 530 and the decline of Kaya, stoneware made in Japan resembled Kaya models less and less. A distinctive Japanese Sue ware—characterized by fewer and simpler incisions and much smaller handles—came into existence.

Once peninsular models had been adapted to Japanese tastes, the manufacture of Sue ware became a major industry. Sanuki, Mino, Owari, Harima, and Izumi sheltered the first artisans; in Izumi, Sue village was a large center 9 by 15 kilometers in size and equipped with some five hundred kilns that produced pieces for the elite of Japanese society. Stoneware technology spread slowly from these centers and did not reach northeastern Honshu until the eighth century. Artisans fired Sue pottery in large quantities until the middle of the Heian era in the Kinai; in less advanced areas, the gray ceramic was still in use until the fifteenth century. Sue pots were the ancestors of such renowned products as Bizen and Shigaraki ware.

Apart from its durability and beauty, this new style of ceramic is significant for two other reasons. First, it is no accident that stoneware entered Japan approximately when iron goods and the ferrous industries became more widespread. Each technology required heating and working materials at high temperatures; indeed archaeologists have uncovered large amounts of Korean-style stoneware in buildings presumed to have been blacksmith's forges.[98] Second, the recovery of so much Korean pottery in Japan may signify immigration from the peninsula on a grand scale. It is usually assumed that the first stoneware potters in Japan came from Korea. The peninsula did not just contribute technologies and material culture to early Japan: it sent many people as well.

The oven (*kamado*) eventually had a profound effect on daily life in ancient Japan.[99] (See Figure 2.4.) Made of clay or even terra cotta, it was a hollow cylinder with a semicircular hole cut out on one side to allow the user to tend the fire. The cook could place dishes in the upper end of the cylinder, directly above the flame. Most ovens were situated against one wall of the owner's house where an opening permitted smoke to exit. The oven represented a major advance for residents of Japan's pit dwellings because the Japanese had previously cooked their meals and warmed their houses with just a hearth (*ro*). These hearths usually had only a dirt firebreak around the outside; the cook placed pots right in the fire. One archaeologist has argued that hearths varied by region: in western Japan occupants located their fire on top of a hole

FIGURE 2.4
The Oven.
Source: Hayashi
Hiromichi, "Kamado
shutsugen ni kansuru
ni san mondai," in
*Mizu to tsuchi no
kōkogaku,* p. 105.

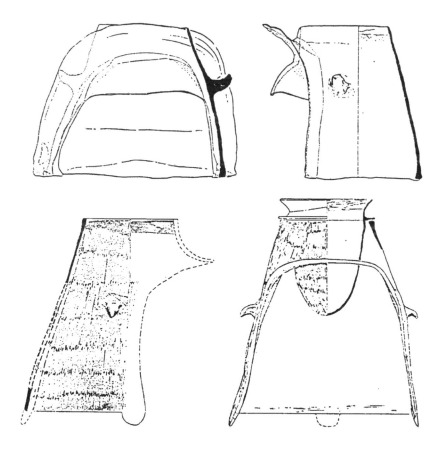

filled with ashes in the middle of the dwelling while eastern Japanese put the hearth flat on the ground somewhat off-center within the home.[100] Compared with either the eastern or western version of the Yayoi fireplace, the oven of the fifth century contained heat more effectively and safely, produced less smoking, and was easier to cook with.

The Chinese may have invented this oven, but the version that came to the Japanese archipelago during the fifth century had the peculiar imprint of the peninsular peoples. Writing in *The History of the Wei Dynasty,* Chen Shou noted that third-century ancestors of the peoples of Kaya and Silla were fond of ovens.[101] Scientists have uncovered an example from a dwelling near Kimhae in former Kaya territory and have dated the artifact to around 300.[102] The discovery that Japan's first ovens in northern Kyushu and the Kinai are associated with early stoneware also lends support to the idea of Korean origin. From these two areas the new technology spread slowly throughout Japan and was in common use by the seventh century. In the eighth and ninth centuries, these appliances were so closely associated with southern Korea that the Japanese called them "Korean ovens" (*Kara kamado*).

Tombs

The gigantic keyhole tumulus (*zenpō kōen fun*) serves as the universal symbol of the Tomb age. The largest monument, the great Nintoku mausoleum, is 486 meters long, 30 meters high, and 249 meters in diameter. Because workers constructed it on a plain, the tomb required a huge volume of earth and daunting inputs of labor. One Japanese archaeology journal has estimated the labor necessary to build a large imperial tomb at about 4 million worker-days; another archaeologist claims it would take the equivalent of a thousand laborers a day for four years.[103] Surely scholars have been correct to interpret the construction of such large monuments as signifying both an increase in population and the appearance of an organization strong enough to utilize the growing labor supply.

To the average Japanese, as well as most archaeologists and historians, the keyhole tumulus has become a unique symbol of native culture. It is perhaps for this reason that many Japanese are upset to think that the design of these tombs too could have come from southern Korea. In 1983, a South Korean archaeologist claimed to have found several keyhole tombs in what would have been Kaya territory.[104] Although the assertion set off a furor in Japan, not all the opinions were hostile: in fact, Mori Kōichi stated his agreement with the

Korean in a lecture program broadcast over Japanese educational television.

The idea of massive monuments to dead kings and chieftains is a Chinese concoction, at least in East Asia, but this does not mean that the keyhole tumulus, like so many other technologies and materials, originated there and then spread eastward. Even though the Korean archaeologist who first reported the "Japanese-style" monuments in southern Korea published his findings, most Japanese scholars have pointed out serious flaws in his research. First, the Korean drew his models of the tombs in question freehand and did not use scientific measurements. Second, the archaeologist did not account for the possibility that wind and rain may have destroyed the original shape of the tombs over the past millennium and a half. Many Japanese archaeologists have looked at the same tombs and concluded they were just two round mounds that eroded.[105]

Subsequent to this initial claim, however, South Koreans have pointed out other candidates, and Japanese archaeologists have accepted their arguments.[106] As in the earlier description, these Korean keyhole tombs are indeed found in erstwhile Kaya territory, but they are similar in shape to fifth-century Japanese tumuli. Some peninsular tombs are surrounded by Korean-made terra cotta cylinders, in the same way that *haniwa* were used in Japan.

Japanese scholars have been reticent in drawing conclusions. Given the dating and location of these tombs, it seems likely that the Japanese originated the design for keyhole tombs and then saw it transplanted to southern Korea. Such an argument could be used to bolster the view that Yamato rulers controlled Kaya, but these monuments may simply indicate cultural influence. At present, the evidence seems to show that the idea of keyhole tombs surrounded by terra cotta figures moved against the general cultural flow—from the archipelago to the peninsula.

Although Koreans cannot lay claim to having created the keyhole tomb, it is fairly certain that other elements of Japanese monumental architecture did originate in Korea. The first keyhole tumuli of the late third and fourth centuries were technologically rather simple: laborers moved tons of earth and constructed a circular mound that they connected to a raised, rectangular, flat area. The finished tomb usually had three or four tiers covered with stones. (See Figure 2.5.) Planners placed a trench near the center of the round portion of the tumulus. The rectangular surface probably served as a platform where ceremonies were conducted for interring the dead chief and perhaps naming his or her successor. Before the deceased could be buried, however, builders of Japan's first keyhole tombs needed to fashion a rock-lined chamber to hold the wooden coffin. In many cases, engineers put the coffin in place at the time of the chamber's construction and then piled up flat rocks to form walls. At the upper portion, the chamber was occasionally corbeled (*mochiokuri gihō*) inward, so that the ceiling could be covered with relatively small slabs and eventually with earth.[107] Giant though they were, each of the earliest monuments held only one individual per trench. The expenditure of immense amounts of energy for a single burial was a sign of the deceased's status. If it was necessary to inter more persons, a maximum of three separate vertical chambers (*tateana shiki sekishitsu*) were built. Most important, once the chambers were sealed over they were expected to remain that way forever.

All this began to change in northern Kyushu in the late fourth century. At Rōji Tomb in Fukuoka prefecture, a keyhole tumulus about 80 meters long, there were four interments, three of which upon first inspection appeared to be ordinary vertical-entrance chambers. As archaeologists excavated Rōji more carefully, however, they uncovered evidence of a pathway that linked the largest burial chamber to an opening on one side, through which mourners could enter and add coffins later.[108] The other three graves also showed signs of repeated horizontal entrance. In other words, onto the basic structure of a vertical-entrance chamber engineers had evidently grafted a side door (*tateana kei yokoguchi shiki sekishitsu*).

Rōji Tomb and others like Sukizaki Tumulus, also in Fukuoka, foreshadowed a significant shift in tomb-building techniques in Japan. The new stone corridor and chamber (*yokoana shiki sekishitsu*) tombs could all be entered from the side, allowing mourners to reopen the tomb in order to add more coffins. To accomplish this feat, stone corridor and chamber tumuli employed corbels more extensively than vertical-entrance tombs. The gently arching walls led up to large flat stones forming the roof. (See Figure 2.6.) Construction workers could then safely cover the stone burial chamber with earth.

While not all archaeologists agree, and there are problems with the dating of tombs in Japan and Korea, most scholars insist that the stone corridor and chamber tomb is another Chinese invention that made its way to the archipelago via the peninsula.[109] There can be little doubt that the Chinese began to build elaborate stone corridor and chamber tombs before anyone else in East Asia, probably as early as the Former Han dynasty. Chinese archaeologists have excavated several rectangular brick tumuli that date from the third and fourth centuries in southern China.[110] The route by which the idea for these Chinese-style monuments reached Japan is a matter of debate: some archaeologists in Japan and Korea argue that Koguryŏ was the first kingdom on the periphery of China to copy the design; others opt for Paekche.[111] Proponents of the Koguryŏ route believe that Chinese colonists introduced their burial practices to northern Korea with the establishment of the Le-lang district; a tomb of this sort in Pyŏngyang, which the Japanese excavated before World War II, contained a brick with the date 353.[112] From Koguryŏ these archaeologists presume that the idea for stone corridor and chamber tombs was transmitted to Paekche, in the area around modern Seoul.

One scholar has suggested that the earliest Chinese-style tumuli found in the region around Seoul date to the late fourth century, about the same time that stone corridor and chamber tombs appeared in northern Kyushu.[113] This early example is not in good condition, however, and the best evidence of a Paekche stone corridor and chamber tumuli occurs much later in the middle of the fifth century.[114] The later dates for Paekche stone corridor and chamber tombs leave open the possibility that Japanese chieftains may have hit upon this concept through direct communication with Koguryŏ or China or even invented the new form of interment on their own.

FIGURE 2.5   A Keyhole Tomb. *Source:* Tsude Hiroshi, ed., *Kodai shi fukugen* 6: *Kofun jidai no ō to minshū,* p. 1. © Kōdansha 1989.

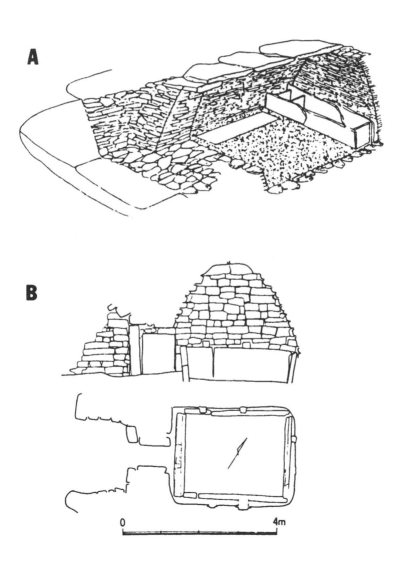

FIGURE 2.6
Stone Corridor and Chamber Tombs.
Source: (A) Yanagisawa Kazuo, "Kofun no henshitsu," in Shiraishi Taichirō, ed., *Kodai o kangaeru kofun,* p. 113; (B) Shiraishi Taichirō, "Kōki kofun no seiritsu to tenkai," in Kishi Toshio, ed., *Nihon no kodai 6: Ōken o meguru tatakai,* p. 214.

A

B

0   4m

However, the fact that the oldest known such tumuli are located in northern Kyushu argues strongly for a foreign source, probably southern Korea. And here it is important to note that the other two Korean states, Silla and Kaya, did not adopt the Chinese-style construction until later, possibly not until the sixth century.[115] Therefore it seems most reasonable to assume that the stone corridor and chamber tomb was an import from Paekche, a product of the intimate political tie with the Wa.

The dispersion of this new technique of elite burial within Japan was slower than one might imagine. Perhaps adopted in Kyushu about A.D. 400, these tombs were not constructed anywhere else in the archipelago until 450. Around then the other areas of Japan in closest contact with southern Korea began to utilize the new style of interment. The Kinai was one of these regions, and analyses of stone corridor and chamber tombs in the Kyoto-Osaka area suggest to one archaeologist that rulers of the rising Yamato state borrowed their technology directly from China rather than via Kyushu.[116] Subsequently, the technique spread to the rest of Japan, reaching intermediate lands around the Inland Sea between 450 and 500, the Japan Sea littoral by 550, and regions further east, notably the Kanto, no earlier than 600.[117]

The slow spread of the stone corridor and chamber technique went hand in hand with a gradual improvement in the tools and abilities of masons.[118] Stonecutting technology entered Japan from southern Korea in two waves, the first toward the end of the fourth century and the second in the latter half of the sixth. In the initial stage, masons worked soft, small rocks and concentrated their efforts on the production of coffins. After 550, however, stonecutters learned to use hard rocks such as granite, to shape and move large stones, and to work designs into blocks. The advances of the sixth century were probably linked to the arrival of more immigrants and the introduction of Buddhism from Paekche.

The sixth-century improvement in stonecutting techniques had an important impact on the spread of the stone corridor and chamber tomb. The earliest tumuli had been built with myriads of small, flat stones laid on top of each other, such as Rōji or Sukizaki tombs. But as masons learned to cut, move, and shape huge boulders, the stones in burial chambers became correspondingly larger and more finely fitted. The result was magnificent stone passageways and chambers made of rectangular slabs of rock weighing several tons, such as Ishibutai Tomb in Nara and Yata Ōtsuka Tumulus in Okayama. (See Figures 2.7 and 2.8.)

The utilization of large blocks of stone opened the way for further changes

FIGURE 2.7
The Ishibutai Tomb.
*Source: Asuka shiryō
kan: annai,* p. 35.
© Nara Kokuritsu
Bunkazai Kenkyūjo.

FIGURE 2.8   Interior of Yata Ōtsuka Tumulus in Kibi. *Source: Kibi no kyofun,* p. 18.

in tomb design. Japanese archaeologists have long held that both decorated tombs (*sōshoku kofun*) and tumuli with wall paintings (*hekiga kofun*), most of which are located in northern Kyushu and date from the fifth century and later, were imports from Korea.[119] The brilliantly painted tombs of Koguryŏ found in modern-day Manchuria certainly support such a position. The most famous Japanese tumulus with frescoes, the Takamatsuzuka Tomb of Nara, contains painted figures that are even dressed in Korean-looking garb.[120]

Jewelry, Bells, and Glass _____

The manufacture of earrings, crowns, caps, shoes, belt buckles, and plaques (flat metal pins) fashioned from precious metals was probably a Middle Eastern or Greek practice, but once again the Chinese were the first settled people in East Asia to wear these ornaments, having learned of the techniques over the Silk Route. Belts fastened by gold and silver buckles, as well as gilt earrings, were in use before 200 B.C.[121] In the third century A.D., the collapse of the Later Han dynasty encouraged further distribution of this technology because nomads gained access to talented Chinese artisans. Most bodily ornaments (*obi kanagu*) that archaeologists have recovered from Korea and Japan belong to typologies that scholars can ultimately trace to Jin models.[122]

The first peninsular people to acquire gold jewelry lived in Koguryŏ, where warfare and exchange with the Xian-bi and other peoples of Inner Asia were common. Strong likenesses between Silla and Koguryŏ artifacts suggest that Koguryŏ could have been responsible for introducing the adornments into this southern Korean land as early as 300.[123] Paekche and Kaya jewelry appeared somewhat later, perhaps by the early or middle fifth century, although in number and workmanship the Kaya and Paekche pieces are certainly the equal of items from Silla.

Even though the earliest belt buckle in Japan dates from the late fourth century, other gold and silver adornments have come to light only for the mid-fifth century and later. One expert has suggested that at first belt buckles and plaques entered the archipelago; these ornaments were all made by artisans residing in southern Korea and could be obtained only by members of the Wa elite with connections in Korea. Although the sample is small, distribution favors the Kinai: of forty-three pendant earrings (*mimikazari*) recovered in Japan, nineteen have come to light in the Kinai and another fourteen from northern Kyushu. Nine of seventeen gilt shoes (*shokuri*) had owners in the Kinai.[124]

By 450 or so, the know-how for fashioning pieces for belts, two types of crowns (*kanmuri*), caps (*kanbō*), earrings, and shoes began to take root in several parts of Japan from eastern Honshu to southern Kyushu. Many artisans were probably Koreans, but other inhabitants of the archipelago also began to master the sophisticated techniques of gilding, inlaying, and openwork carving (*sukashi-bori*). In the early to mid-sixth century workers stopped making belt buckles and concentrated instead on crowns, shoes, and earrings. At this time methods of manufacture spread to metalworkers in local regions, and the quality of products declined. The personal ornaments that appear most frequently in the late sixth and early seventh centuries are crowns, belts, and shoes.[125]

Just which Korean kingdom was responsible for exporting the idea for these bodily adornments to Japan is not yet clear. At one time, Silla seemed the logical source because it also had the lion's share of artifacts. But South Korean archaeologists are uncovering these prestigious ornaments in increasing numbers from Paekche and Kaya territory.[126] One Japanese archaeologist has argued that belt pieces found in Shin'yama Tumulus in Nara prefecture resemble Paekche artifacts stylistically and that their introduction is tied to stone corridor and chamber tomb technology.[127] Most Japanese authorities regard both Paekche and Kaya as probable sources.[128]

The Japanese elite did not simply import Korean-style jewelry at this time. Along with the gold and silver, the techniques of gilding, inlaying, and openwork carving also entered Japan in the fifth century. Once again it seems apparent that master metalworkers from the peninsula taught the natives of the islands their advanced skills. In addition to a steadily expanding jewelry industry, natives of the archipelago also found new products to cast in bronze, a metal that had been popular in the Yayoi period. A common item in the fifth century and after was the small bell (*suzu* in Japanese), which the Japanese attached to armor and horse gear with strings. Archaeologists have found about 70 percent of these Korean-style bells in the Kanto, home of Japan's equestrian fighters.[129]

Not all aristocratic fineries entering Japan from the peninsula were made of metal. A few glass saucers and cups are among finds from Japanese tombs and other excavations of the fifth century and later. The idea for these pieces originated in distant Iran or even Italy and traveled over the Silk Route to China and then on to Korea and Japan. Like bronze, glass had first come to Japan in the Yayoi era, but all the highly prized glass of that epoch was produced by Chinese and Korean artisans in the form of beads and then exported to the archipelago. From the early Tomb age the manufacture of glass beads in Japan increased rapidly. But the Japanese used earthenware and stoneware for their dishes, so glass remained a less important technology than it might otherwise have been, being limited primarily to beadwork.[130]

Silk Weaving

The Hata were one of the most famous peninsular families to make Japan their home in the ancient period. As recounted in *The Chronicles* and other sources, their ancestor came to the archipelago in the reign of the Emperor Ōjin bringing 127 villages of kin. According to *A Record of Titles and Surnames Newly Selected (Shinsen shōjiroku)*, Emperor Nintoku gave the immigrants the surname Hata because "they presented thread and silk cloth as tribute, and when the emperor donned the clothes they were soft and warm to the skin."[131] Some Japanese scholars believe that the story of the Hata's prowess in weaving silk was a myth invented by the authors of Japan's genealogies. ("Hata" is a homophone for loom.)[132] But the name Hata appears on a tapestry made for Prince Shōtoku now kept at Hōryūji, suggesting that the Hata might have specialized in weaving techniques after all.

There still may have been a link between silk weaving and southern Korea, even if not through the Hata. The Japanese had known silk during the Yayoi era, centuries before the beginning of the Tomb age, but Japan's foremost expert on ancient cloth believes that the production of fine-figured silk twill increased markedly after the fifth century. He links this growth with the other technological improvements that came from Korea at the same time.[133] It seems reasonable to place silk weaving in the same category as glassmaking or the ferrous industries—that is, crafts which the Japanese had some knowledge of from olden times but only began to exploit more fully with the wave of Korean influence that occurred in the mid- to late fifth century.

MORE IMPORTS FROM KOREA: THE HISTORICAL RECORD

Archaeologists have not been alone in pointing out peninsular influence on the ancient Japanese archipelago, although their findings have dominated scholarly attention recently. Some historians in Japan and the two Koreas have been making similar arguments for several decades. In combination, the experts in these two disciplines are beginning to establish an international consensus.

Writing _____

A Record of Ancient Matters contains the following story that purports to explain the origin of books in Japan during the reign of Ōjin:

> Again the Emperor commanded the land of Paekche: "If there be a wise man, present him!" Therefore, in response to this command, he presented a man named Wani-Kishi. *The Confucian Analects,* ten volumes, and *The Thousand-Character Classic,* one volume, altogether eleven volumes, he presented along with this man. This Wani-Kishi is the ancestor of the Obito of Fumi.[134]

The Chronicles also includes an interesting tale of an especially literate Korean for the year 572:

> The Emperor took the Koguryŏ memorial, and passing it on to the Ō-omi [an official], assembled all the scribes and directed them to read and explain it. At this time all the scribes for the space of three days were unable to read it. Now there was one Wang Chin-ni, founder of the family of the Funa no Fubito, who was able to read it and explain its meaning to the Emperor. Consequently the Emperor and the Ō-omi, both together, complimented him. . . .
>
> Nor was this all. The memorial presented by Koguryŏ was written on crow's feathers, and the characters, like the feathers, being black, nobody had been able to read them. Chin-ni accordingly steamed the feathers in the vapor from boiled rice, and took an impression of them on a piece of silk, whereupon all the characters were transferred to it, to the wonder of the Court.[135]

Along with other technologies described so far, Japan's earliest system of writing was another art originating in China that entered the archipelago through Korea. One may choose not to believe the particular renditions of the Japanese classics, but at least one reputable Japanese historian accepts the story of Paekche and Wani-Kishi as authentic to the late fourth century.[136]

Other evidence points to the peninsula as a seat of learning for the ancient Japanese, too. The few samples of Chinese writing that are extant from the Tomb age, for instance, mostly have a Korean connection.[137] The first example, the seven-branched sword discovered in Isonokami Shrine in Nara in 1873, has a message of goodwill from the king of Paekche to a Wa ruler. Most

experts believe that inscribers used an Eastern Jin reign period equivalent to
A.D. 369. A mirror that Sumida Hachiman Shrine in Wakayama has preserved
for generations contains the Chinese cyclical calendar signs most likely for 443.
It has an engraving that reads in part: "The king . . . while he was at the Oshi-
saka Palace sent Kawachi no Atai and Ayahito Konsuri to take two hundred
measures of bronze and make this mirror." Most historians believe that Ayahito, and probably Kawachi no Atai as well, were surnames used by peninsular émigrés to Japan.[138]

One of the most famous inscribed swords comes from Eta Funayama Tumulus in Kumamoto, a grave that has produced golden shoes, belts, and a cap
that strongly resemble Korean prototypes. The inscription discusses one
Murite, who served King Wakatakeru (probably Emperor Yūryaku of the late
fifth century). The engraving states that "the name of the one who made this
sword was Itaka; the one who wrote this was Chang An." While the appellation Itaka could refer to a native of the archipelago, Chang An was probably a
Korean working in the employ of the local lord for whom the sword was
made.[139]

The writing style of several other inscriptions also betrays Korean
influence. In 1984 archaeologists discovered the surname "Nukatabe no Omi"
on a sword from Shimane; the way in which the author had abbreviated the
character "be" resembled examples found in Paekche and Koguryŏ.
Researchers discovered the longest inscription to date, the 115-character
engraving on the Inariyama sword, in Saitama in the Kanto, seemingly far
away from any Korean émigrés. The style that the author chose for the inscription, however, was highly popular in Paekche. At least two other writings, one
etched on Tako stone monument in the northern Kanto and another appearing on a Buddhist statue at Hōryūji, contain characters similar to Paekche
prototypes.[140]

Like other technologies, the art of writing was all-important to the growing
kingdom of Yamato. It has long been known that nearly all Yamato scribes
(fumihito) and accountants (kurahito) had peninsular ancestors.[141] Historians
date the first wave of these immigrant scribes and accountants to no later than
450 or so, a time that corresponds well to the influx of other skilled immigrants. Indeed, The Chronicles states that Emperor Yūryaku saw to the establishment of the initial government organizations for secretaries in 458.[142] More
immigrant writers came to Japan in the sixth and seventh centuries. The story
of Wang Chin-ni shows that the advanced skills of newcomers sometimes put
those with obsolete abilities to shame.

Titles, Surnames, and Ranking Systems ————————————————————

Names of nobles at the ancient Japanese court had a set form with a special meaning. Consider the case of Mononobe no Ōmuraji Arakabi, a particularly influential general of the early sixth century. Mononobe was the functional surname (*uji*) and indicated a person's job at court (in Mononobe's instance, weapons bearer). Ōmuraji (Great Village Headman) was Mononobe's status title (*kabane*) and showed where he ranked at court. Arakabi was the personal name. Until the decline of the imperial court after the Kamakura period, every aristocrat possessed a three-part name that designated his or her function and rank in elite society.

Japanese historians have expended great effort analyzing the system of functional surnames and status titles used to distinguish members of the ancient aristocracy. Although the research is speculative because of the dearth of evidence, the standard view in Japan holds that the idea for both aristocratic surnames and titles originated during the late fifth century and came from the southern peninsula, probably Paekche.[143] Cornelius Kiley, an American scholar who studied the evolution of the Yamato court, has also tied Japan's adoption of surnames and titles to Paekche models of the 400s.[144] Some titles, such as *kishi* and *suguri,* and surnames, like Aya and Hata, probably derive directly from words in the languages of the southern Korean kingdoms.

Like many other technologies and materials discussed thus far, both surnames and titles were Chinese inventions, first applied to the nobility during the Zhou dynasty. The custom of granting surnames to commoners began only in the Chin and Han dynasties. Nomadic peoples in the surrounding regions undoubtedly learned the idea from China: when the Xian-bi founded the Northern Wei dynasty in the fourth century, they adopted surnames and titles to distinguish aristocratic families. Paekche and Koguryŏ royalty first used surnames in the late fourth and early fifth centuries, respectively, as their countries opened diplomatic relations with the Eastern Jin dynasty.[145]

Compared to surnames and titles, ranking systems were far more precise because the court granted a rank to an individual, not to an entire family. Moreover, because ranks were usually not hereditary, the court could reward merit. If an individual's labors on behalf of the ruler were fruitful, the court might raise the industrious person's rank while keeping less meritorious courtiers in place. Japan's first known system of ranking, the twelve-grade Confucian-based institution supposedly invented by Shōtoku Taishi in 603, utilized caps of various colors and designs to distinguish bearers of differing status. Inoue Mitsusada has noted several similarities between Shōtoku Taishi's system and ranking institutions in Silla, Paekche, and Koguryŏ. These like-nesses include the design and colors of the caps and the number of grades. Cap ranks may therefore, like other ideas of the Soga kinsman and Buddhist saint, have been inspired by Korean precedents.[146] It should be noted, however, that recently many Japanese historians have dissented from Inoue's view, arguing instead that the Yamato court imported this essential technology directly from China.[147]

Artisan Groups under Government Control

Peasants and technically skilled men and women paid goods and services as tribute to the Yamato court through regional or craft units known as *be*. Because the evidence is thin, little is known about how these organizations actually functioned or where they came from. Here I offer a brief sketch of current research, especially on the question of origins. At one time it seemed safe to conclude that these units were a late fifth-century import from south-ern Korea, probably from Paekche.[148] None other than Tsuda Sōkichi argued that the word "*be*" was derived from the Paekche language.[149] The reliable *His-tory of the Northern Zhou Dynasty* (556–581) listed several types of these Paekche organizations, many of which, like the medicine *be* and sword *be*, seemed to be similar to Yamato groups.

The notion that the idea for Yamato tribute units originated in Paekche took shape during the 1960s and 1970s, but recently this view has come under attack. First, scholars began finding Chinese origins for the *be*. Kitō Kiyoaki argued that when Paekche formed its units, it modeled them on a Chinese tra-dition that dated back to *The Rites of Zhou*, a text describing the governmen-tal structure of the Zhou dynasty (1122?–403 B.C.).[150] Other historians also linked the Paekche service organizations to Chinese precedents.[151] Second, another more "nativist" opinion was based on the inscription found on the Inariyama sword.[152] The sword, which dates from 471 or later, discusses one local powerholder's service to the court (probably to Emperor Yūryaku), but it does not use the word "*be*" to describe the military unit called to duty. The first scholar to form this interpretation argued that there was a service organi-zation called the *tomo* that preceded the *be* and dated from the origins of the Yamato king as one of many local magnates scattered around Japan in the early fourth or even late third century. The leaders of these initial tribute groups (the *tomo*) were officials known as *tomo no miyatsuko*, a term used in the sources as late as the seventh century. In this view, the alteration of the term "*tomo*" to "*be*" to reflect current Korean usage did not occur until the early sixth century and was merely a name change—the organization had been there from the inception of the Yamato chiefdom as a native invention.

At present, written sources are too few and scholarly opinions too diverse to enable one to formulate an ironclad hypothesis. But with all the new technologies entering the archipelago from southern Korea in the Tomb era, it seems likely that the Korean organization to provide tribute to the ruler would have been influential with the Yamato king as well. To be sure, the Korean model may have harked back to Chinese examples. Moreover, there may have been a form of service in Japan that predated the Korean *be,* and it may have shaped how the growing Yamato kingdom organized later units.[153] But the influx of Korean immigrants and their advanced skills, which were essential to early Japanese statecraft, must have had a significant impact on the fledgling Yamato court.

Buddhism and the Arts _____

It almost goes without saying that Japan's earliest version of Buddhism, which defined thought and the arts into the ninth century, came to the archipelago from Korea. To be specific, according to *The Chronicles* the year was 552 (a more reliable source says 538) and the benefactor was King Sŏng-myŏng of Paekche, who sent a gilt bronze statue, flags and umbrellas, and sutras. As many scholars have pointed out, some Japanese had likely learned of Buddhism earlier than 552 through the efforts of peninsular immigrants, some of whose countries had permitted worship of the Buddha long before the mid-sixth century.

It is important to be clear about what the Japanese were importing when the court eventually decided to support Buddhism in the late sixth century. In addition to one of the world's great religions with its own ethics and cosmology, the Yamato court received a ruling ideology that promised to protect believers in return for propagation. "Profit in this world" (*genze riyaku*) was the watchword of early Buddhism in Japan as late as the ninth century. Proper behavior by a true believer could protect him or her from disease, ensure prosperity, and defeat personal and political enemies.

Buddhism also served as a vehicle for Chinese culture, of course, especially that of the Southern Dynasties then popular in Paekche. In 553, the year after King Sŏng-myŏng's offer of Buddhist items, Paekche sent medicine, doctors, scholars, a calendar, and diviners to its ally across the Korean Straits. In 577 and again in 588, the gifts were temple architects and sculptors of Buddhist statues. In the early seventh century astronomers, geographers, exorcists, and calendar makers came to the archipelago. The pattern in which peninsular peoples introduced continental civilization to their island neighbors had been established by at least the fifth century, but by no means did it come to a halt after the initial wave.

Architecture was one art that changed forever with the importation of Buddhism. Native Japanese building techniques and materials were simple: a builder set four or five wooden posts in holes and thatched the structure with grass. But Buddhist temples required more: posts needed foundation stones to support heavy roofs made of tile. This new style of architecture was also used for government offices, beginning with the capitals of the seventh century and including provincial and district buildings in the countryside later.

One technique of layering and solidifying soil came in particularly handy. In the stamped-earth method (*hanchiku hō*), workers spread soil to a depth of about 10 centimeters and then tamped it down before spreading and tamping the subsequent layer.[154] After several repetitions, planners had a solid earthen base useful for walls and foundations. The stamped-earth technique was originally a Chinese invention that came into use perhaps as early as the Neolithic era (3000 B.C.). Scholars have uncovered this same construction method in Korea, where laborers on Paekche fortifications used the technique.[155] Workers also employed the same artifice for the foundations of pagodas in Paekche. It is therefore possible that the stamped-earth method was another Chinese technology introduced to Japan from Korea, but the evidence is meager. Some archaeologists believe that the Japanese knew of the method as early as the Yayoi era, others see the technique in use in keyhole tombs, and still others argue that pounded-earth construction came in the seventh century directly from China.[156]

Building temples soon became a popular endeavor for the Japanese. By 623, after great encouragement by the Soga, *The Chronicles* noted that Japan possessed 46 temples, 816 priests, and 569 nuns.[157] As J. Edward Kidder pointed out over twenty years ago, Koreans provided plans, materials, and even workers for many of Japan's famous early temples, including Asukadera, Shitennōji, and Ikarugadera.[158] The original layout of buildings and pagodas within temple precincts came directly from Paekche or Koguryŏ; several temples, like Hinokumadera and Kudaradera, were exclusively for the use of peninsular immigrants.[159]

The Asuka Century and Korea _____

From 592, when Emperor Suiko moved her residence to Toyura Palace until
the relocation to Nara in 710, the Asuka basin was the hothouse in which a
burgeoning Japanese civilization thrived. In addition to the propagation of the
newly arrived Buddhism, Asuka was the focus of politics in the archipelago: it
is well to remember that the Taika coup, the civil war of 672, and the compilation of the early compendia of Chinese-style law all took place in Asuka.
Increasingly, Japanese historians are realizing that the "origins of Asuka" lay
not only in China, but also in Korea.[160]

Consider the Chinese-style law codes put together in the second half of the
seventh century. Japanese chronicles reveal that there may have been as many
as three different collections: the doubtful Ōmi Code of 668, the Asuka Kiyomihara Code of 689, and Taihō Code of 701. Most studies of Chinese-style
institutions in Japan have looked to the origin of the idea and compared Japan
with the Middle Kingdom, arguing that systems of statecraft molded for China
never did work in Japan, searching for the ways in which the Japanese adapted
Chinese law to fit their own society, or seeing Japan as a carbon copy of the
mighty Tang.

But like most of the ideas and technologies discussed thus far, Chinese-style
institutions in Japan have a distinctive peninsular aspect. One should realize
that the Korean states adopted Chinese law much earlier than Japan did;
Koguryŏ may have used the institutions of the Middle Kingdom as early as the
late fourth century, while even latecomer Silla had recognized the wonders of
Chinese law by 520.[161] The experience of the Koreans came in handy, because
in 663 Japan fought a battle against Tang China and Silla trying to prevent the
destruction of Paekche and the unification of the peninsula. Yamato's utter
defeat supplied the motivation for more borrowing of Chinese civilization
while at the same time straining Japanese-Chinese relations.

For thirty-two years, from 669 until 701, Japan sent no emissaries to Tang
China. Despite the assertion of Inoue Mitsusada to the contrary, I think that,
in effect, the two countries had broken off diplomatic relations.[162] To be sure,
the Japanese court had sent at least seven emissaries to China from 600 to 659
prior to the beginning of hostilities, and the mission of 653 arrived just in time
to watch the promulgation of the Yung-hui Code in 652. Yet during the crucial period in which the Japanese court was drafting its three sets of Chinese-
style law, there was virtually no official communication with Tang China. How
did the Japanese manage?

They went to Korea. During the three decades when Japan had poor relations with the Tang, the court dispatched eleven emissaries to Silla. Moreover, Korean immigrants served on the committees that drew up the law codes. Of the nineteen members of the committee that drafted the Taihō Code, eight were from Korean immigrant families. There were no Chinese. If one excludes the high aristocrats such as Fujiwara no Fubito and Prince Osakabe, who probably did little of the actual writing, then about half of the authors of Japan's most comprehensive set of Chinese laws were from Korea.[163]

The Korean connection may have given the Japanese law codes their distinctive character. The Taihō Code reflected an idealized vision of China constructed from several periods of Chinese history, not just the Tang Dynasty; the statutes on land, taxes, and census taking look more like those of the Northern Wei than the Tang.[164] The authors of these compilations, unable to see the latest Tang institutions in action, looked back to the Chinese past, and here the Koreans, who had centuries of experience in administering Chinese-style law, must have been invaluable.

It is impossible to list all the aspects of "Chinese-style civilization" of the Asuka century that have ties to Korea, but certain elements, such as letters and court music, are beyond doubt.[165] The lowest level of local administration, the district (*hyō, kohori*), originated in a Korean model, as did the tribute tax.[166] Military strategists took the ideas of mountain fortifications (like those found in northern Kyushu, Okayama, and Nara) and the crossbow from Korea.[167] Even the system by which farmers divided arable land into uniform parcels (*jōri sei*) used the Korean foot (*Koma jaku*) as its basic unit of measurement.[168] Written sources confirm that the pattern of peninsular peoples' introducing continental civilization to Japan continued even into the late seventh and early eighth centuries.

TIES BETWEEN STATES IN ARCHAEOLOGICAL CONTEXT

The archaeological and historical records show that for over three hundred years, from 375 until 700, wave after wave of ideas, institutions, technologies, and materials originating on the Asian continent flowed into Japan. Items poured into all regions, particularly western Japan, and they affected members of every social class and most occupations. While the Chinese invented most articles, inhabitants of the Korean peninsula served as middlemen, placing their distinctive stamp on many ideas and materials. Historical works may give some clues about this great influx of Korean-borne culture, but Japanese and South Korean archaeologists are the scholars who have uncovered the true extent of the "invasion." How does the notion that peninsular peoples played a crucial role in introducing continental civilization to Japan shed light on the controversial historical record of relations among the ancient states of Japan and Korea?

The Alternatives

The easiest way to deal with this complex and sensitive issue is to envision a broad spectrum of current views. At one extreme, older Japanese interpretations based on *The Chronicles* emphasize native development of the Yamato state and argue that Yamato dominated southern Korea from the fourth century until 663. At the other extreme, a few nationalistic North and South Koreans hold that their homeland was the fount of all ancient Japanese civilization and once ruled the archipelago. Between these extremes, other historians and archaeologists from Japan, the two Koreas, Western Europe, and the United States have recently begun to offer new and interesting interpretations. Using the archaeological evidence presented earlier, one can evaluate all these perspectives, narrowing the range of plausible interpretations considerably.

By now it should be apparent that the older Japanese perspective garnered from *The Chronicles* contradicts the archaeological record. If one agrees with the growing consensus of Japanese, South Korean, and Western archaeologists that ancient Koreans carried invaluable technologies and ideas into Japan, there is little doubt that all the states of the peninsula were more advanced than the Wa. One is left with a conundrum: how could a society as technologically and institutionally unsophisticated as the Wa have dominated three of its four more advanced Korean neighbors—Silla, Paekche, and Kaya—for three centuries? Moreover, the skills that peninsular peoples introduced comprised such fundamentals of political and economic power as ironworking, weapons, horse gear, gold and silver metallurgy, stonemasonry, and writing. These facts make it seem doubtful that the Yamato court or even a Wa confederation could have subjugated southern Korea.

One can ask why *A Record* and *The Chronicles* portray Yamato as dominating the southern peninsula beginning in Jingū's mythological reign. In my view, such assertions of control are merely reflections of the current ideology of the Japanese court.[169] According to commentaries on the Yōrō Code of 717, the ruling elite maintained that Japan (Nihon) was the "Middle Kingdom" (*chūka*) of its East Asian world; the Tang was simply "the country next door" (*rinkoku*). Silla, the unifier of the peninsula, was deemed to be "the barbarian country" (*bankoku*).[170] As Japan's reputed inferior, Silla owed obeisance and tribute items, both of which the Korean kingdom refused after 700. Throughout the eighth century, Silla asserted its equality with Japan, a view that led to imminent hostilities on more than one occasion.

In essence, the Japanese court tried to turn Chinese concepts of civilization and barbarism to its own advantage. This ideology transformed the imperial court into East Asia's seat of civilization and granted legitimacy to other peoples only when they recognized Japan's superiority. It required that Koreans and other immigrants to Japan be given the perjorative title *kikajin,* which implied that they could be redeemed exclusively by the civilizing influence (*kika*) of Japan's divine dynasty. The court's hauteur toward Silla (and even China) was thus intertwined with the myth of imperial divinity (called *bansei ikkei,* "one lineage for ten thousand generations"), as expressed in the sacred texts.

One can press the inquiry a step further and seek the origins of the court's contempt for Silla. There are several pieces of evidence to consider, many deriving from questionable passages in the eighth-century records. *The Chronicles* usually describes Wa-Silla relations as poor, even as early as the fourth century. In a more reliable entry dated to the early sixth century, *The Chronicles* asserts that Silla interfered in Wa domestic politics, bribing the Kyushu chieftain Iwai to rebel against Yamato. Perhaps making Silla into a bogeyman was a ploy to remind local contenders for power that they had better submit to Yamato or face disorder and even invasion. More likely, the eighth-century court's antipathy toward Silla derived from Silla's destruction of Japan's long-time allies on the peninsula. In 562, Silla conquered Kaya; almost exactly one century later in 663, Silla subdued Paekche. Both actions were bitter blows to Japan's ruling class, and the archaeological evidence presented earlier helps explain why. Kaya, Paekche, and even Silla—all more culturally and technologically advanced than Japan—were like precious jewels. They were rich in their own right and provided the Wa with a continuing stream of continental innovations, occasionally listed in *The Chronicles* as rare and marvelous tribute items.[171] When Silla destroyed first Kaya and then Paekche, the Japanese court lost its easy access to advanced technologies, resources, and ideas. The self-centered ideology of the early eighth century was one expression of the court's increased vulnerability.

On the other extreme, there is a nationalistic Korean view that emphasizes the Japanese debt to the southern peninsula. With wave after wave of advanced Korean-filtered culture coming into the archipelago, one may be inclined to agree with those experts, Korean and Japanese, who see Korea as the wellspring of Japanese culture before 700. In particular, the importation of iron and the ferrous industries must have been a great boon to Japan and the desire for iron a prime motivation for involvement on the peninsula. But as argued earlier, Egami's horserider theory—in whatever variation—does not fit the archaeological facts. The dating of artifacts is too late for Egami's invasion of the mid- to late fourth century, and the distribution of horse gear indicates a slow spread over the archipelago, not a sudden incursion. Besides, many other monuments and artifacts in Japan, from the characteristic keyhole shape of tombs to the size, material, and structure of coffins, show strong continuities over the period when horseriders were supposed to have been radically transforming culture in the islands.

If one rejects Japanese claims of control over southern Korea and dismisses the horserider theory in its strictest sense, then what was the mechanism by which so much Korean-borne culture entered the archipelago? One alternative that immediately leaps to mind is trade. Undoubtedly peoples of the islands and the neighboring peninsula must have engaged in exchange, which archaeologists have proved existed beginning in Yayoi times. Yet there are problems because South Koreans have not yet excavated enough sites to allow them to generalize about an influx of Japanese goods into southern Korea. Moreover, as one might imagine, South Korean and Japanese archaeologists often disagree about the origins of artifacts: Japanese scholars claim items as being of Japanese provenance that South Koreans do not recognize.

But even if one sides with Japanese archaeologists and accepts all the artifacts uncovered in southern Korea that they maintain originated in the archipelago, the list is not impressive.[172] Scholars have found small bronze mirrors and cylinders, beads, earthenware and terra cotta cylinders, and perhaps cuirasses (debated earlier). Although items have been discovered all over southern Korea and indicate extensive contacts between the two peoples, the quantity and value of Japanese artifacts found in Korea cannot possibly compare to the volume of materials coming into Japan. One must either assume that the Wa exported perishable products like grains, horses, lumber, or cloth to the peninsular states, an unlikely prospect, or look for another answer.[173]

Trade does not seem to have been solely responsible for the dramatic influx of Korean-borne culture into Japan. Immigration was surely part of the reason. All evidence, archaeological and historical, shows a nearly constant inmigration of peninsular peoples into Japan ever since the Yayoi period.[174] The frequent wars on the Korean peninsula that began in the second half of the fourth century and raged on and off until the end of the seventh undoubtedly created a recurring flow of refugees.

How many persons went from Korea to Japan? No one has any way of knowing precisely, but one can make estimates. For the six centuries of the Yayoi period, one Japanese anthropologist has argued that as many as 3,000 people per annum, or about 1,800,000 immigrants, entered Japan.[175] An archaeologist who specializes in the Tomb era notes that *A Record of Titles and Surnames Newly Selected*, the ninth-century official compilation of aristocratic lineages, contains three divisions: imperial (*kōbetsu*), divine (*shinbetsu*), and barbaric (*shoban*). If one assumes that "barbaric" meant Korean, as argued earlier, then perhaps one-third of the ruling elite could trace their recent (post-Yayoi) ancestry back to peninsular roots.[176] Of course extrapolating from the aristocratic court to a commoner population involves many assumptions about the motivations and composition of migrant groups. No matter what the percentage, Korean immigrants of the period 400 to 700 were the bearers of many ideas and technologies discussed previously. Specifically, iron agricultural tools, pond and ditch-digging methods, household ovens, stoneware, and stone corridor and chamber tombs all could have been ideas carried to Japan by refugees. Many ironworkers, gold and silver engravers, clerks and scribes, masons, potters, and other craftsmen and women came to Japan to escape the turmoil in southern Korea.

It is plausible, therefore, to ascribe a large proportion of newly arrived ideas and technologies to immigration.[177] Moreover, items came as political gifts. Reliable historical sources disclose that Paekche shipped Buddhist materials to Yamato in 538 and Koguryŏ sent the crossbow in 618. Scholars also know that Paekche's elite dispatched artisans, scrolls, and other stores continuously for Yamato's use beginning about 500. The stoneware makers, ironworkers, and weavers who reported to the Yamato court in the late fifth century all came as donations from Korean courts.[178] It seems reasonable that other items also found their way to the archipelago as "tribute gifts" from the courts of Paekche, Koguryŏ, Silla, and even Kaya.

What was the quid pro quo for these shipments of valuable technologies and material culture? One reasonable hypothesis contends that the peninsular states wanted and received Wa military aid in their wars.[179] No matter how one reads the written sources, it is clear that the Wa sent troops to join in the recurrent strife in Korea between 390 and 663. This fact is corroborated not only by the controversial stele on the banks of the Yalu River but even by Korean histories, which repeatedly write of the Wa's dispatching men to attack Silla and Koguryŏ. Of course, it may not have been technologically sophisticated military aid. Paekche and Kaya may have sent advanced military technology to allies in Japan, who in turn armed their men and shipped them back to Korea to help the friendly regimes.

Given the nature of the historical records, it is difficult to establish a point-to-point correlation between peninsular "gifts" and Wa military aid. Yet if one filters out the biases of *The Chronicles,* it provides occasional glimpses of such a trade-off. In the late fifth century, for instance, a Yamato general sent to defend Paekche against Silla returned home with numerous groups of skilled artisans. During Keitai's era (early 500s), Paekche emissaries gave presents to Japanese generals dispatched to that country; later that same annal writes that one of the gifts was "a scholar acquainted with the Five Classics."[180] One must be careful with these entries because chroniclers always portray the Korean kingdoms as paying tribute to a superior Yamato monarch, as required by the court's eighth-century ideology. But leaving aside the phraseology, one may infer the reciprocal relationship.

The donation of cultural and technological aid in return for soldiers was sensible foreign policy for both sides.[181] In the Koreans' favor, Wa's shipments of troops would have helped them to maintain their independence, albeit with an occasional foreign military presence. The same relationship found support in Japan because it kept the continental culture flowing. A divided peninsula may have been in the Wa's favor, too, although written sources do not disclose Japanese thinking on this point.

Therefore it is best to see the influx of Korean-borne goods and services from the late fourth to the late seventh centuries as a result of at least four factors. Trade undoubtedly brought some items to the archipelago. Immigration was probably responsible for a substantial percentage of materials and technologies entering Japan. The foreign policies of the peninsular states, especially Paekche, sent more ideas and goods to the islands. And perhaps plundering by Wa soldiers fighting in Korea resulted in some technology transfer. Whatever the method, the cultural waves from the peninsula were crucial to Japan's political development, just as the intervention of Wa troops affected the conflict on the peninsula.

Korean-Borne Culture and Domestic Politics in Japan

Niiro Izumi, an archaeologist specializing in the Tomb age, has argued that there was a relationship between Japan's political organization and the influx of continental materials and technologies. He envisions competition among the regional Wa lords in the fifth and sixth centuries for foreign goods and services, just as Japanese companies today compete for the most advanced technology and information from abroad. The more successful a Wa strongman was in obtaining these items, the more secure his hold on power. This interpretation helps to explain the distribution of such items scattered throughout the archipelago.[182]

Ōtani Tomb in Wakayama is one example of an outlying area yielding Korean-borne goods.[183] Containing a wealth of artifacts such as iron armor, swords and arrowheads, iron farming tools, golden earrings and belt buckles, Sue ware, and horse gear, the monument may be dated to the fifth century. The identity of the tomb's occupant is an open question, but most agree that it was probably a powerful leader of the Ki, who operated naval expeditions down the Inland Sea to Korea. Whatever this lord's activities, they evidently allowed the Ki strongman to come into contact with the advanced civilization of southern Korea. Historical sources suggest that Kibi, an early rival of Yamato, also had intimate links to southern Korea.

Northern Kyushu was nearest to the southern peninsula, and archaeological evidence also indicates close ties between these two regions. Mausoleums such as Ikenoue, Eta Funayama, and Oda Chausuzuka, all in northern Kyushu, possess artifacts that show extensive ties with the states of southern Korea.[184] Relics uncovered from Okinoshima, the island shrine off northern Kyushu, indicate that the Munakata no Kimi, the local lord in charge of the shrine, received gifts from both Yamato and Silla as late as the fifth century. Along with other regional strongmen of northern Kyushu, the Munakata no Kimi maintained a "semi-independent" existence into the sixth century.[185]

Of course, one may also interpret the continental artifacts uncovered in local areas as Yamato gifts signifying official recognition. Some may have been gifts of this sort, but in my view attributing all items to Yamato largesse overstates the court's control of political affairs in the archipelago, at least until the mid-sixth century. It was not until 528 that Yamato could punish the Kyushu lord Iwai who allied himself with Silla and rebelled against the Japanese court.[186]

The waves of peninsular goods and services flowing into Japan played a critical role in the archipelago's gradual unification under Yamato from 500 to 700. It is no accident that the Soga, the strongest family at the Yamato court from 550 to 645, had intimate ties to Korea and Korean immigrants in Japan.[187] Yamato eventually gained hegemony in Japan by reducing regional lords' access to continental culture while simultaneously securing the court's own resources with the help of Paekche until 663 and numerous émigrés thereafter.

REREADING THE HISTORICAL SOURCES

We turn now to an outline of relations among Japanese and Korean states until Silla's unification of the peninsula in 676.[188] I have tried to examine all primary written sources—Korean, Japanese, and Chinese—and have assumed that when these sources agree on events, there is a high probability that an element of truth exists in their descriptions. This interpretation draws mostly on Japanese and English-language scholarship of the last twenty years but includes Korean and even Chinese perspectives.

Relations among the polities of the peninsula and archipelago fall into three periods: stage one, origins to A.D. 407, when Yamato cemented its alliance with Paekche, the Wa garnered iron from southern Korea, and the Wa confederation suffered a crushing defeat at the hands of Koguryŏ; stage two, 407 to 562, when all five Korean and Japanese states curried favor with one or another Chinese dynasty, and Silla and Paekche destroyed Kaya; and stage three, 562 to 676, when Yamato's last attempt to revive Paekche's fortunes in the face of the Tang-Silla alliance failed miserably, and both China and Korea became unified under able leaders hostile to Yamato.

Stage One: To A.D. *407* ⎯⎯⎯⎯⎯⎯⎯⎯⎯⎯⎯⎯⎯⎯⎯⎯⎯⎯⎯⎯⎯⎯⎯⎯⎯

Southern Korea and western Japan were intimately bound together during the Yayoi era even before state formation took place. The large-scale immigration from Korea into western Japan, the importation of basic technologies such as rice agriculture and metallurgy through the peninsula, and Himiko's relations with the Chinese districts of Dai-fang and Le-lang all underline this proposition. Archaeological artifacts suggest that the terms "Korean" and "Japanese" have little meaning for border regions such as Tsushima. Thus the involvement of the Wa with peninsular peoples in the Tomb era rested on prehistoric foundations.

The earliest Korean state to come into existence was Koguryŏ during the first century A.D.[189] It fought both the Later Han empire and numerous nomadic tribes of Northeast Asia (especially the Xian-bi), but from A.D. 100 Koguryŏ began to lose its wars in Manchuria and turn southward. About 310 the former Chinese colonies of Dai-fang and Le-lang collapsed, probably due to a Koguryŏ attack. The northern Korean kingdom was unable, however, to gain control of the territories once held by the Chinese, and an independent government of émigré Chinese may have ruled central Korea for the next fifty years.[190] The southward advance of Koguryŏ's troops resumed in the second half of the fourth century, and military pressure encouraged the evolution of more centralized governments in southern Korea.

Scholars may never ascertain exactly when state formation occurred in either Japan or among the most prominent ethnic groups in southern Korea (the Ma-han, Chin-han, and Pyŏn-chin), but Chinese histories provide a clue.[191] The last references in Chinese sources to the Ma-han and Chin-han peoples appeared in 290 and 286, respectively; the first mention of the states formed in the regions inhabited by these peoples, the kingdoms of Paekche and Silla, was 345 and 377, respectively. Chinese historians noted kings for these two states in 372 and 382, respectively. Thus it seems likely that the development of centralized, kingly governments in southern Korea took place somewhere between the last two decades of the third century and the first half of the fourth century, about the time that keyhole tombs were initially built in the Kinai.

State formation in Japan is an especially relevant consideration at this point, because of the implications for relative power relationships both within and outside the archipelago. Most Japanese archaeologists would argue for a powerful state in the archipelago by the late fourth century in light of the stylistic uniformity of keyhole tombs stretching from Kyushu to northern Honshu.[192] Since tombs represented the most visible sign of kingly authority, the argument goes, autonomous local chiefs would have wished to express their independence by building a different style of tombs. The size of the keyhole tombs must surely imply centralized control over huge numbers of workers.

While granting that much labor went into the fifth-century monuments, it is a leap of faith to read the spread of keyhole tombs as directly indexing the extension of Yamato political control. The widespread geographic distribution of similar tombs might be explained by many nonpolitical factors, including cultural predispositions. Moreover, the thousands of Japanese tombs show an astonishing variety, and most are not keyhole-shaped. It seems prudent to assign at least equal weight to Chinese historical accounts, which write of numerous "countries" (*guo*) in Japan as late as the early sixth century. Later Japanese political history also cautions against investing the center with too much power.

It is therefore best not to think of the initial polities of Japan or southern Korea as too powerful. There must have been some territory that lay beyond any ruler's control and thus was disputed regularly. One such contested area existed between Silla and Paekche in south-central Korea west of the Naktŏng River on the tip of southern Korea along the Pacific coast, formerly the habitat of the Pyŏn-chin peoples who had traded with the Wa in iron and other items in Yayoi times. This land soon came to be known as Kaya, a loose federation of at least six principalities.

Scholars differ on the degree of Wa's initial involvement in Kaya. One older Japanese historian believes that in the second half of the fourth century the Wa maintained a "foothold" (*ashiba*) in the Aya and Kimgwan areas, along the coast west of modern Pusan, but Chinese and Korean texts do not corroborate this point.[193] Most Japanese writers see the fourth-century Wa as dispatching troops and seeking allies in Kaya.

Part of the problem with interpreting the written sources from both China and Korea is the vague term "Wa." Not only is it unclear which region of Japan is meant, but some writers argue that Wa included territory along the southern coast of Korea. One scholar asserts that the area called Mimana in *The Chronicles* was composed of local notables in Kaya sympathetic to the Wa.[194] It seems likely that Wa residing in Aya and Kimgwan, Kaya chieftains sympathetic to the Wa, and people of mixed descent all played a role in Kaya's development.

For early Japanese and southern Korean leaders, Kaya must have been even more important than its geographical position would imply. Along with Silla and Paekche, Kaya had a wealth of iron, a mineral the Japanese had not yet uncovered in their homeland; competition for influence in Kaya may well have centered on its iron resources. Iron was crucial to an advanced military, which could secure a king's place atop a political hierarchy in either Japan or Korea.

By the middle of the fourth century, Paekche felt the brunt of a Koguryŏ assault and sought an alliance with the Wa by sending a seven-branched sword to the Wa in 372. The Paekche royal house was forced to look beyond the peninsula for an alliance, since Silla was a rival in Kaya. As a Japanese scholar has pointed out, dating the opening of friendly relations between Paekche and the Wa to the year 372 fits a Korean source (*The Basic Records of Paekche; Paekche pongi*) contained in *The Chronicles* as well as the Korean histories and the inscription on the sword itself.[195] Furthermore, the sword's inscription does not imply that either country had submitted to the other; Paekche's gift merely indicated that the Wa and the Korean state were allies. Judging from later ties with the Paekche ruling house and from the location of the seven-branched sword in Isonokami Shrine, I think that Yamato, a more powerful Wa state located in the Kinai, probably received the sword and may even have been the leader of a Wa confederation. Soon after receipt of the weapon, Yamato shipped one hundred troops to Paekche, which dispatched a royal hostage to Yamato. Perhaps as a result of the new alliance, Paekche did surprisingly well against the fierce warriors of Koguryŏ, driving them back north with a reported army of forty thousand men in 377.[196]

Japan's early relations with Silla are more problematic. Both Japanese and Korean sources describe Wa-Silla ties as hostile from the outset, with the Japanese frequently attacking Silla from the eastern seas and the south. "Wa" may well refer to northern Kyushu regional chieftains who assaulted Silla from Tsushima. Silla in turn invaded Tsushima from time to time. *The Chronicles* emphasizes Japanese aggression from the southwest, which meant Kaya, but as one historian has suggested, the editors were probably trying to legitimize Yamato claims to rule Kaya.[197]

In the late fourth century, the king of Silla had a change of heart and sent a royal hostage to the Yamato court.[198] The cause for Silla's turnabout was pressure from Koguryŏ; Silla also sent tribute to the king of Koguryŏ, thus appeasing both sides. By the end of the fourth century, Koguryŏ's aggression had succeeded in uniting Paekche, Wa, Silla, and Kaya in an unlikely alliance against the ferocious northern kingdom. Seven emissaries went back and forth between Paekche and Yamato at the end of the fourth and beginning of the fifth centuries.

At this point, the monument on the banks of the Yalu River becomes a critical source. Composed in 414 to commemorate the meritorious achievements of King Kwanggaet'o of Koguryŏ (r. 391–412), the inscription is an authentic but exaggerated account of events on the Korean peninsula. I endorse the authenticity of the stele because the description corresponds closely to the version supplied by a Korean source, *The History of the Three Kingdoms*.[199] In my view, the stele states that the Wa began a buildup of troops in southern Korea in 391 to engage Koguryŏ. In 396, Koguryŏ dealt a harsh blow to Paekche, compelling the Paekche king to swear allegiance to his erstwhile enemy, but by 399 Paekche was once again allying itself with the Wa. In the meantime, Wa leaders used the alliance to send troops against Silla, which had tried to appease both Japan and Koguryŏ; the Japanese destroyed many Silla fortifications. Silla requested aid of Koguryŏ and in the year 400 Koguryŏ reportedly sent fifty thousand horseriders and foot soldiers south against the alliance and won a smashing victory.

Following on its victories in Silla, Koguryŏ turned on Kaya, where it repulsed both Wa and allied Korean soldiers. In 404 the defeated Wa forces tried once again, advancing to Dai-fang, but the Koguryŏ king quickly put another army in the field and routed them. Once again in 407, according to one possible reading of the monument, another 50,000-man host of Koguryŏ foot soldiers and horseriders gave aid to Silla and drove the Wa back home, where they may have forsaken the search for a military solution in Korea for the time being.[200]

The archaeological evidence presented earlier also corresponds in general terms to the story on the Yalu monument. The first wave of Korean-borne continental material culture—iron, weapons, horse gear, stoneware, and other technologies—probably came into Japan not long after the Koguryŏ victories. Undoubtedly immigration in the face of the Koguryŏ invasion was the chief agent of this influx, but one should not discount the possibility that Paekche or Kaya dispatched goods such as iron and other technology. In the late fourth and early fifth centuries, however, the Tomb-age flood of continental culture was just beginning.

This endorsement of the general thrust of the words on the monument does not, however, mean that every phrase in the inscription must be taken as literally true. For instance, it is doubtful that Paekche and Silla were submissive to the Wa or even Koguryŏ, as the boastful author of the stele asserts. Moreover, the author may have exaggerated the extent of Wa military involvement in Silla to emphasize the impressive degree of assistance rendered by Koguryŏ to its ally. In A.D. 400, it is better to see the Wa and the three major states of Korea as near-equals quarreling with each other; with its victories, Koguryŏ had merely secured its southern front.[201]

Stage Two: 407–562

As Koguryŏ located its new capital at modern Pyŏngyang, Wa leaders hit upon a new strategy to ensure the friendship of its allies Paekche and Kaya, subjugate Silla, resist Koguryŏ, and impress their competitors domestically: ask the Chinese for help. Sixteen times from 413 to 502, the Wa sent emissaries to Nanking, the capital of southern Chinese dynasties, to pay tribute and receive political titles. Five times the Chinese emperor invested the Wa leader with the phrase "King of Wa and Generalissimo Who Maintains Peace in the East"; twice the Chinese added the pedigree "Commanding with Battle-Ax All Military Affairs in the Six Countries of Wa, Silla, Mimana, Kaya, Chin-han, and Mok-han."

Most Japanese historians equate the Five Kings of Wa mentioned in the Chinese sources with specific persons described in *The Chronicles* as Japanese emperors. While there is some disagreement about precisely which individuals best fit the Chinese names, the consensus that the Yamato court represented the Wa at Nanking seems plausible. From this point on, the Wa king mentioned in the Chinese dynastic histories probably refers to Yamato, the rising leader of a Wa confederation. Yet the archipelago was a long way from being unified, for the lineage that produced the Five Kings died out late in the fifth century and several decades of internal conflict ensued.

How is one to interpret the sweeping grants of authority from the Chinese? The difficulty with equating such grandiloquent statements with reality is that both Koguryŏ and Paekche had asked for Chinese recognition earlier, in 336 and 372 respectively, and the Chinese confirmed both countries in titles that were more impressive than the Wa's. Koguryŏ was granted command of the two former Chinese districts of Le-lang and Dai-fang, and Paekche was recognized as an independent military power. Furthermore, Yamato twice requested recognition of control over Paekche, but the Chinese rejected its request.[202] According to Suzuki Yasutami, if Silla had not waited until 508 to open relations with the Chinese, the Chinese would have removed Silla from Yamato's sphere of influence as well. Even Kaya dispatched a mission to China in 479, when its leader inherited a title as "King of Kaya and Generalissimo Who Assists the Country."[203] The investment occurred too late, however, to delete Kaya from the Yamato king's titles.

Meanwhile, the war between Paekche and Koguryŏ revived. In 472, Paekche sent an envoy requesting aid to the Northern Wei dynasty, which had recently unified northern China, complaining of over thirty years of warfare. Paekche also put aside its differences with Silla and asked for an alliance against Koguryŏ. Three years later, however, Paekche suffered another humiliating defeat at the hands of Koguryŏ. The army of the northern kingdom captured the Paekche capital of Han (near Seoul) and killed Paekche aristocrats. At that juncture, the alliance with the Wa again proved its value, for Yamato sent a royal heir in the company of five hundred troops to the new Paekche capital at Ungjin, which lay over a hundred miles south of Han. Both the Paekche-Yamato friendship and Paekche's losses to Koguryŏ appear in Japanese and Korean histories.[204]

The Koguryŏ victory had an added dimension: it cut the Wa off from easy access to China. The Wa King Wu described the hostility between Koguryŏ and himself as "defiance of the law," in which Koguryŏ committed murder and pillage. Wu's father became so incensed with Koguryŏ, according to the narrative in the Chinese history, that he "gathered together a million archers and was about to launch a great campaign." Wu's father's death probably foreclosed what would have been another bloody conflict in Korea.

The repeated convulsions in Korea are the context in which historians should place the archaeological evidence of the influx of Korean-borne technologies and material culture. Again, Korean immigration to Japan was undoubtedly responsible for much of the influx, and it is important to remember that all during the fifth century Paekche and Yamato were close allies, so intimate that Paekche sent its royal heirs to Japan for safety. Furthermore,

Paekche was a crucial way station on the route to southern China; many Wa envoys must have stopped in Paekche at Han to wonder at the southern Korean state's imported Chinese culture, as attested by archaeological excavations such as King Muryŏng's tomb.

With the importation of more continental culture, the latter half of the fifth century became a period of great growth for Japanese society and the Yamato polity.[205] The arts of writing, ironworking, gold and silver metallurgy, and stoneware manufacture all entered Japan in the middle of the fifth century. The shipment of Korean artisans by Paekche and Kaya led to the elaboration of a court bureaucracy (*uji/kabane*) and mechanisms for control such as the *be*. Yamato's growing power is visible in the swords inscribed with words of homage to Yūryaku from as far away as northern Kyushu and the Kanto dating to this period.

The late fifth and early sixth centuries were also periods of rapid development for Silla.[206] After losses to Koguryŏ in the north, Paekche and Silla turned against Kaya, which by this time was marching toward greater unity. The Wa replied by attacking Silla from 459 to 463, again in 465, and in 476–477, according the Silla annals of *The History of the Three Kingdoms*. At the same time, the Wa attempted to assist Paekche in its expansion against Kaya, and in return Paekche sent scholars to Yamato.[207] Paekche shipments to Yamato reached an all-time high, symbolized by the gift of Buddhist materials in the mid-sixth century. Paekche was Yamato's window on the southern Chinese dynasties and their elegant Buddhist culture.

But the exchange of Paekche gifts for Yamato troops was to no avail. Pressured continually by Koguryŏ armies in the north, the Paekche royal house was forced once again to move its capital further south in the early sixth century. Silla's military gradually conquered more and more of Kaya. In 532 Kimgwan Kaya fell, in 544 Aya's leaders adopted Silla court clothing, and in 562 Great Kaya became a province of Silla. Later Chinese histories noting the fall of Kaya discuss the event as a war between Silla and Paekche and never mention Yamato.[208]

Yamato's response to Silla's aggression was to send military expeditions on five occasions. If *The Chronicles* is to be believed, in 511, 527, 532, 554, and 562 court-backed troops crossed the Korean Straits to battle the advancing Silla host. It was also in the early sixth century that *The Chronicles* claims that Yamato established the Japanese Military Government of Mimana (Mimana Nihon fu) as a temporary base for its actions. Some Japanese historians believe they can infer a structure for this organization, but everything rides on how seriously one takes *The Chronicles*. One Japanese historian cautions that

Yamato never divided Kaya territory into administrative units or collected taxes. The Wa received aid from sympathizers and dispatched troops to Kaya, but that was all.[209]

Stage Three: 562–676

With one ally gone and its lands in the hands of the enemy, Yamato's position on the peninsula became desperate. Paekche was facing an even more treacherous pincer movement, caught between the advancing hordes of Koguryŏ to the north and Silla to the east. During the second half of the sixth century, Paekche continued to send Yamato its culture and technologies, and Japanese courtiers discussed the option of sending expeditions to revive Kaya's fortunes even as the flow of refugees from Kaya and Paekche grew.

In 589 the Sui dynasty made the situation even worse for Yamato by unifying China and pursuing an aggressive foreign policy.[210] Paekche, Koguryŏ, Silla, and Yamato all paid court to the mighty Sui, but there was a decided difference in their attitudes. Although the Korean states asked for and received titles of investment such as they had gotten from earlier southern Chinese dynasties, Yamato asked for and received none. The upstart Japanese court even had the temerity to insult the Sui emperor as "the Son of Heaven in the land where the sun sets." This policy suggests that Yamato may have been unhappy about its increasingly peripheral status in a China-centered world.

During this time, *The Chronicles* records that Yamato received missions from Silla bearing "tribute" for the Japanese court from conquered Kimgwan Kaya.[211] Boats laden with goods supposedly entered Yamato's harbors at Naniwa in 575, 600, 610, 611, 623, and 638. Why would Silla have presented the Japanese court with tribute from Kaya if Yamato had never ruled the territory? One interpretation is that Silla was hoping to discourage Japanese military intervention on either Paekche's or Kaya's behalf. These shipments to Yamato may lie behind the statement in *The History of the Sui Dynasty* that "both Silla and Paekche consider Wa to be a great country, replete with precious things, and they pay it homage."

In 621, Silla dispatched its first emissary to the Tang dynasty, which had replaced the Sui in 617. For the next thirty years, Silla maneuvered until it was able to strike up an alliance with Tang in 650 and cease its tribute to Yamato. Yamato continued its support of Paekche and allied itself with Koguryŏ in Koguryŏ's continuing war against the Chinese. In 663, Silla and Tang destroyed Paekche, and the last wave of Korean immigration into the archipelago commenced. Koguryŏ fell to the allied armies and navies in 668, and in 676, after a clash, Tang recognized Silla as sole ruler of the Korean peninsula. By the late seventh century, Yamato and its regional lords faced united and hostile powers in Korea and China.

RECAPITULATION

The interpretation of ancient ties among the peoples of the Japanese islands and the Korean peninsula has been a major focus of scholarly controversy, especially during the twentieth century. During the decades before 1945, many Japanese accepted an official state ideology that justified their imperialism in East Asia and claimed that Japan had ruled southern Korea as its colony from time immemorial. After 1910, Koreans were defined as Japanese subjects and forced to keep their nationalistic sentiments to themselves. Some iconoclasts, like Tsuda, questioned the chauvinistic descriptions of *The Chronicles,* but they met with doubt and even jail terms.

In the early postwar era, the old ideology quickly faded and critics of Japanese sources were abundant. Some, like Egami Namio, built upon suggestions by prewar archaeologists that the political and cultural flow was in the opposite direction—from the continent into Japan. Egami said that nomadic horseriders migrated down the Korean peninsula, crossed the straits, and founded Korean and Japanese states as they went. Nevertheless, the comfortable consensus among Japanese historians still saw the Yamato court as powerful enough to control southern Korea from the late fourth century until 663.

This consensus was shattered initially by Korean scholars. In 1963, Kim Sŏk-hyŏng presented a thesis that emphasized the role of peninsular immigrants in the archipelago; in 1972, Yi Chin-hŭi pointed out that the Japanese Imperial Army had procured and possibly altered a rubbing of the inscription on the monument near the Yalu. Through the work of Koreans and Japanese scholars sympathetic to the plight of Koreans living in Japan, the answers of the early and mid-1960s began to undergo increasing scrutiny. By the 1990s, scholars from around the world were cooperating to unravel the mysteries of ancient Japan's ties to Korea.

Archaeology contributed more to the growing consciousness of early Japan's debt to Korea than any other discipline. Together South Korean and Japanese archaeologists have been able to show that from the late fourth through the late seventh centuries Korean-borne continental ideas, technologies, and materials streamed into the archipelago. Influence from the peninsula hit peaks in the mid-fifth, mid-sixth, and late seventh centuries and played a crucial role in population growth, economic and cultural development, and the rise of a centralized Yamato state.

A chronological list of Korean contributions includes iron, iron goods, and the ferrous industries, which really matured in the fifth century although known earlier. Horse use and equipment gave rise to mounted warfare. Ditch- and pond-digging technology gave peasants access to more fertile, higher grounds for the first time. Ovens became available for households, and Japan's initial wheel-thrown, kiln-fired gray stoneware was used by the aristocracy. Techniques for stone corridor and chamber tombs, more sophisticated stone fitting, and decorated grave walls entered the archipelago from Korea, as well as gold and silver jewelry. New silk-weaving methods; writing and mathematics; more advanced methods of bureaucratic elaboration such as the surname, title, and eventually ranking; a system to supply the court with services and craft goods; Buddhism and its architecture; Chinese-style law; mountain fortifications and the crossbow—these were other peninsular contributions.

Two points about this list of imports stand out. First, they affected every class—rulers, artisans, and farmers. Second, even though most of the ideas, technologies, and materials described in the list were of Chinese origin (at least in East Asia), Korea played the all-important role of experimental way station along the road to Japan. Peninsular peoples fulfilled this role especially in the cases of the ferrous industries, the cuirass, ovens, bronze bells, court titles and surnames, artisan organization, the district, and mountain fortifications. They also left their distinctive imprint on several Chinese inventions, such as stoneware, agricultural techniques, and the law codes of the early eighth century.

There were four mechanisms by which peninsular culture and technologies progressed to the archipelago. First, although archaeological evidence for Japanese items in southern Korea is not impressive, some trade in goods undoubtedly took place. Second, immigration of Koreans fleeing the constant turmoil on the peninsula must have been a major factor in the influx of Korean material culture during these centuries. Perhaps as much as a third of eighth-century aristocrats could trace their origins to Korea since A.D. 300. Third, plundering by Wa troops involved in battles on the peninsula was also a conduit. And fourth, because all four peninsular states were technologically and culturally more advanced than the Wa, their sophistication and resources gave them value in the eyes of Yamato and lesser Wa lords. The polities in Korea, especially Paekche, carried out a policy of granting critical goods and services to the Wa in return for troops to battle enemies on the peninsula. Competition among Japan's regional lords for Korean-borne culture helped drive the importation of continental items. Yamato's eventual unification of the archipelago by 700 was a direct result of its increasing control over the cultural flow from the continent.

Viewed in the context of the archaeological record, early ties among the polities of the peninsula and archipelago become somewhat clearer. It is doubtful that Yamato ever controlled any territory in southern Korea; the only basis for such an opinion is the inventive *Chronicles*. The nature of Yamato power in the archipelago—written sources suggest it was probably a federation of local notables supporting each other's authority—reinforces the likelihood that Yamato never directly ruled southern Korea. But the Wa did send expeditions to southern Korea, support Kaya sympathizers, and intermarry with residents of all the Korean states.

While accepting that Korea was more advanced than the Wa, I simultaneously reject the horserider theory for reasons elaborated several times: it fits neither the archaeological nor the written record. But this does not mean that the horserider theory should be ignored or, as two Japanese archaeologists wrote recently, relegated to the realm of "amateur historians and foreigners."[212] Instead, I prefer the formulation of a more sensitive Japanese historian who said that while Koreans may not have founded the Japanese imperial line, peninsular culture influenced early Japan "intensely" (*mōretsu ni*). Call this version the "cultural horserider theory," if you will. Egami's thesis has helped to put ancient Japanese history into a comparative context, just as Henri Pirenne's hypothesis did for early medieval Europe.[213]

The various technologies, materials, and ideas that entered Japan between 400 and 700 played a fundamental role in the development of ancient Japan and built upon the growth of the Yayoi age. Imports of the fifth century like iron, weapons, horse gear, gray stoneware, iron farming tools, and new irrigation techniques were particularly noteworthy. Because most had been tested in the Korean kingdoms, they were more readily adaptable to Japan. The direct introduction of Chinese civilization that increased markedly after 650 thus met a society that had already developed a basic structure and material culture and was better able to "digest" the added new influences of the Middle Kingdom.

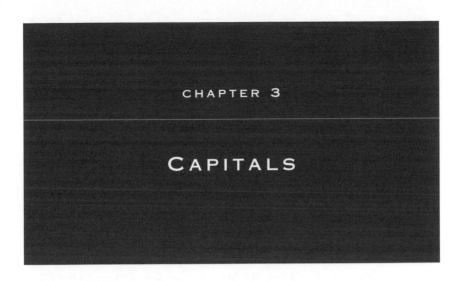

CHAPTER 3

CAPITALS

The spring of 701 was a momentous time for the Japanese court. In the first month, after a hiatus of thirty-two years, the government reaffirmed an earlier decision to learn directly from China by sending an embassy to the Tang dynasty. Ten more official missions traveled to Chinese capitals during the next 150 years to report on East Asia's most advanced civilization. Then, in the third month of 701, aristocrats finished compiling the Taihō Code, Japan's initial comprehensive edition of Chinese law. Anxious to increase its power at home and fearful of invasion from abroad, the court sought more thorough control of the archipelago's land and people through the institutions of Taihō.

From 710 to 784, the grand new capital at Nara served as a symbol of the court's emulation of Chinese civilization. Measuring about 5.5 kilometers east to west and 4.5 kilometers north to south, Heijō (as Nara was also known) seemed like a fitting monument to the majesty and grandeur of the new imperial institution. Nara was hardly alone, however. Before it was constructed, there had been Fujiwara (694–710), Naniwa, and Ōtsu; Kuni and Shigaraki were capitals for a brief interlude (740–745); and both Nagaoka (784–794) and Heian (794–1868) were home to the ruling family after Nara. If anything epitomized the elite's indebtedness to Chinese civilization and statecraft during the late seventh and eighth centuries, it was these magnificent cities.

Japanese historians have long grappled with two related questions concerning the archipelago's Chinese-style capitals. First, how did planners and politicians adapt the thousand-year-old Chinese idea of a large, symmetrical capital to their land? Second, how completely was the government able to construct these giant urban centers? The sustained efforts of Japan's archaeologists have made it possible to examine these important problems in greater detail than ever before.

OUTLINE OF PREVIOUS RESEARCH

Unlike the study of Yamatai or early Korea-Japan relations, writing on the archipelago's palaces and Chinese-style capitals has lacked any single overarching argument and has been free of major controversy.[1] Historians and geographers working in the Edo period were the first to turn their attention to this subject, and usually they concentrated on such problems as the location and plan for a palace or city. Before the Meiji Restoration, Kitaura Sadamasa, a scholar of National Learning, used old records in an effort to infer the size and layout of Nara; he actually walked the area of Heijō and proposed the existence of the Northern Grid (*hoppen*) to the northwest of the palace.[2] Two Neo-Confucians debated the exact placement of Naniwa and Ōtsu, while National Learning devotees Kamo no Mabuchi and Motoori Norinaga studied Fujiwara.[3]

Capitals received little attention from historians and other specialists before 1900. The exception was Kyoto, which had served as home to the emperor during the Edo period and held a wealth of primary sources, including maps surviving from earlier epochs. For the first time a historian queried why the court had moved to Heian from Nara in the late eighth century. On the eleven hundredth anniversary of the founding of Heian in 1894, architects reconstructed the imperial palace from plans and other materials in Kyoto and oversaw the erection of Heian Shrine based on their model.[4]

Between 1900 and 1920, the study of Japan's ancient capitals and palaces became a major scholarly undertaking. Kita Sadakichi (1871–1939) was most responsible for this heightened interest. In 1915, he published *August Capitals* (*Teito*), which rose above narrow antiquarian concerns to look into larger problems arising from Japan's borrowing of Chinese civilization. Among Kita's lasting accomplishments were these: his assertion that Naniwa under Emperor Kōtoku (645–654) was Japan's first Chinese-style palace; his discovery that Japan, like China, had had more than one capital at a time; his detailed comparisons of Heian and Heijō with the Chinese cities of Chang-an and Luo-yang; and his discussion of why Japan's political centers had had no outer walls.[5]

Kita followed Japanese tradition by using historical geography to describe each capital, and his inferences proved invaluable to later scholars. In research on Emperor Tenji's palace at Ōtsu, Kita correctly proposed that discovery of the remains of the temple Sūfukuji would provide a key in locating the capital. In a study on Fujiwara, Kita stated that all previous opinions on the palace were wrong and that three ancient roads had set limits on the grid layout for the metropolis.[6] Kita also compared the layouts and size of Heijō and Heian and noted the remnants of an outer wall around Heian's southern gate (rashō mon).[7] Kita's greatest mistake was his opposition to the fashionable thesis that Nara had had a sizable eastern extension known as the Outer Capital (gekyō).[8]

Other factors increased interest in Japan's Chinese-style capitals during these decades. In 1913, some workers accidentally uncovered elaborate roof tiles while digging the foundation for a modern military warehouse in downtown Osaka. The discovery raised the possibility that Naniwa had been located there.[9] Scholars began to apply new approaches, such as economic and cultural analyses, to their research on Heian, the best-documented of ancient Japan's political centers.

In the midst of modern Japan's first economic transformation, the public voiced concern for the preservation of these buried treasures. Beginning in 1899, Nara resident Tanada Kajūrō led efforts to preserve what was then considered to have been Japan's first permanent capital at Nara. He placed signs advertising the path to Heijō Palace from Japan Railways' Nara station and began to buy up land for a modern reconstruction like Heian Shrine in Kyoto. The Japanese government, however, refused to help. Nevertheless, in 1906, Tanada organized the Society for the Preservation of the Ruins at Heijō Palace, and in 1916 he utilized donations to buy about 10 hectares (25 acres) thought to include remnants of the main structures. Finally in 1923, after Tanada's suicide because of financial ruin, the government made Nara a national historical monument. Preservationists presented their land to the government. But only Nara among Japan's ancient capitals had the advantage of government recognition.[10]

Surprisingly, the period from 1920 through 1945 saw a major new activity: the first archaeological excavations. Work commenced at Heijō, where roof tiles and foundation stones had already been recovered. A local man led the first excavation in 1924, discovering that the audience halls (daigoku den) of Heijō and Heian had different layouts. In 1928–1929, Kishi Kumakichi, an engineer working for Nara prefecture, found pottery with the names of eighth-century offices in a ditch about 300 meters northeast of the audience hall. Because of this find, the government bought more land in Nara.[11]

Archaeologists soon started excavating other sites. At Ōtsu, a historian led a team of archaeologists looking for the capital in 1928 and again in 1938–1939.

The search failed to find any remains of Ōtsu, but it did uncover the foundation of Sūfukuji in the mountains not far from Lake Biwa.[12] Archaeologists also recovered foundation stones for Yoshino Detached Palace deep in the mountains of Nara prefecture. Two palaces, one possibly being Asuka Kiyomihara of Emperor Temmu and the other Ikaruga Palace of Prince Shōtoku, also came to light. Meanwhile geographers, architects, and Marxist historians dominated study of Heian.[13]

The most exciting work, however, proceeded at a site that had been unexamined so far. Fujiwara was located in a rural district of Nara prefecture, and except for Kita few had paid it much attention. In 1934, Kishi Kumakichi and other scholars of the Japanese Ancient Culture Research Institute (Nihon ko bunka kenkyū jo) excavated Fujiwara and uncovered foundation stones. Despite the primitive excavation method, which included inserting a metal pole into the ground until the wielder struck a stone, archaeologists continued their work intermittently until 1943; by that year they knew the layout of the audience hall and official compound (chōdōin). Few could doubt that Fujiwara was the site of an important political center.[14]

In the first five years after World War II, scholars had little money for excavations of early capitals. But by the mid-1950s the Japanese economy was entering a period of phenomenal growth and economic development had begun to present both problems and opportunities. The first and most significant site that archaeologists excavated was Heijō, where the Japanese government had established the Nara National Cultural Properties Research Institute in 1952. The following year the U.S. Army, which had a base in downtown Nara, requested that an east-west road through the northern edge of the palace be broadened. While digging ditches at the government-designated special historical landmark, workers uncovered postholes and archaeologists began an excavation that revealed the plan of a 100-meter-long building. Archaeologists soon realized from further investigations that they had discovered the southeast corner of the gallery (kairō) around the audience hall. (See Figure 3.1.) Beginning in 1959, excavations became an annual event.[15]

In 1960 the government owned only the eastern two-thirds of the palace area.[16] Kintetsu Railway wanted to buy the western one-third to build Saidaiji Station, which would provide express service to Kyoto or Osaka. Then in 1959 and 1960, archaeologists uncovered wooden tablets at the site, making it clear that the imperial kitchen (daizen shiki) was situated nearby. Newspapers quickly informed the public of the danger that Kintetsu's plans posed to a national treasure, and soon a broad-based public movement to "Protect Heijō Palace" was under way. A proposal to buy the threatened parcel went to the National Diet and members finally agreed to buy the additional land in 1965.

As this danger subsided, planners decided to construct a new highway from Kyoto to Wakayama, running it near the eastern border of the palace. In an excavation prior to construction, archaeologists discovered many wooden tablets indicating that the office for brewing rice wine (*zōshū shi*) had stood in the area. They also found a huge well. Eventually scholars learned that an area they named the Eastern Grounds (*tōin*) of the palace bounded Hokkeji, which once had been Fujiwara property and later the residence for the heir apparent. The very existence of these Eastern Grounds had been unknown before the excavation because historians had wrongly believed that Nara Palace was a perfect square. Now they knew better, and in 1970 the government purchased the additional land.[17] An area as large as the imperial residence in Tokyo (124 hectares, or 310 acres) was under state control by 1979.

Although Heijō was clearly the most important palace site, archaeologists also dug elsewhere. In 1953, while searching for remnants of seventeenth-century Osaka Castle, they found a piece of roof for what could only have been a royal structure. In 1954, workers discovered that the site was indeed the location of Naniwa Palace and that it consisted of two levels of debris.[18] The lower level seemed to be either the palace of Kōtoku (645–654) or Emperor Temmu (672–686). These choices were suggested by charred remains which may have been those of the treasury ministry that burned in 686 in a fire recorded in *The Chronicles*. The upper layer was the palace built by Emperor Shōmu of the early to mid-eighth century. Scholars concluded from their excavations that Shōmu's Naniwa and Heijō had much in common architecturally. In 1960, the Osaka Prefectural Board of Education established a preservation society for Naniwa. The government began to buy small sections of downtown Osaka to preserve the ruins of Naniwa despite the proliferation of new highways and hospitals. By 1976, over 3 hectares (about 7.5 acres) were in public hands; landscape architects had shrubs planted to evoke a sense of the ancient palaces and the entire area became a pleasant city park.

Archaeologists have had little success in interpreting remains in Asuka, the main home of the royal family from 593 to 694. Beginning in 1951, the Nara Prefectural Board of Education oversaw an excavation that uncovered a line of postholes in the shape of a rectangle laid out along the points of a compass. Stones used in a giant well and remnants of a raised aristocratic residence lay within the rectangle. Nearby there was an even more magnificent palace with an outer wall. Edo-period scholars had speculated that this vicinity was the site of Itabuki Palace (643–645), but Kita had argued for Temmu's Kiyomihara Palace (672–694). Other finds at Asuka included a structure that may have been Toyura Palace of Emperor Suiko and remains of a water clock that may have been the one reported in 660 in *The Chronicles*.[19]

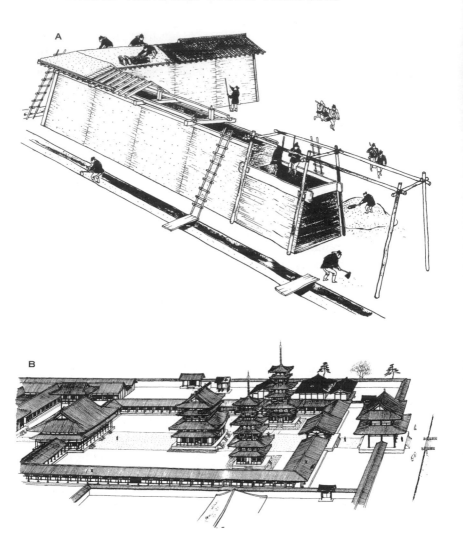

Just north of Asuka, digging at Fujiwara resumed in 1966 after a hiatus of more than twenty years. The immediate impetus was a plan to build a highway running northeast to southwest through what was thought to have been the imperial residence (*dairi*). Workers brought to light dozens of wooden tablets and clarified the northern boundary and eastern and western corners of Fujiwara Palace. As a consequence, planners altered the route of the proposed highway and the government named Fujiwara Palace a special historical monument and bought suitable land. In 1970, the Asuka-Fujiwara branch of the Nara National Cultural Properties Research Institute began operation. To date,

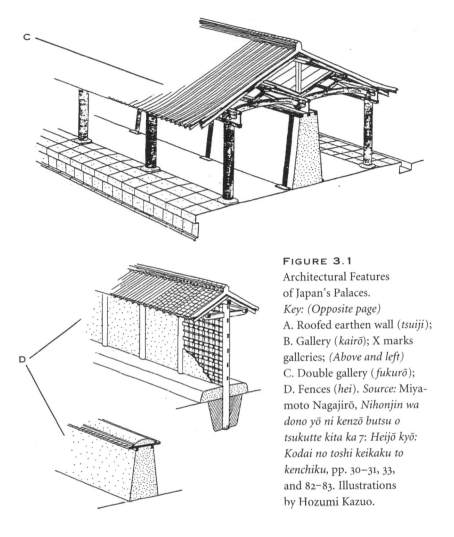

FIGURE 3.1
Architectural Features
of Japan's Palaces.
Key: (Opposite page)
A. Roofed earthen wall (*tsuiji*);
B. Gallery (*kairō*); X marks
galleries; *(Above and left)*
C. Double gallery (*fukurō*);
D. Fences (*hei*). *Source:* Miyamoto Nagajirō, *Nihonjin wa
dono yō ni kenzō butsu o
tsukutte kita ka 7: Heijō kyō:
Kodai no toshi keikaku to
kenchiku,* pp. 30–31, 33,
and 82–83. Illustrations
by Hozumi Kazuo.

archaeologists have excavated only about 10 percent of the palace area, but they have located the sites of the gates to the palace grounds, the audience hall, government offices, and the Suzaku Great Road, which divided the capital into eastern and western halves.[20]

In the meantime, the only monument to Nagaoka, which had served as capital from 784 to 794, was a single stele erected in the modern period. Digging at Nagaoka commenced in 1954, when archaeologists uncovered the southern gate to the official compound. They found ruins of the audience hall and an imperial residence in 1961 and 1969, respectively. By the 1970s, scholars had inferred the existence of a grid plan for Nagaoka, and one excavation in the old city recovered wooden tablets. Nagaoka has become a thriving suburb of Kyoto, but sites such as the audience hall, two imperial residences, domiciles for two heirs apparent, and the fence around the council of state (*dajō kan*) have been preserved.[21]

Research on Japan's most famous capital causes even more headaches for scholars because the modern city of Kyoto is directly on top of Heian. Much has undoubtedly been destroyed. Beginning in the 1920s, scientists carried out small excavations (the only kind possible in Kyoto) that recovered tiles from the audience hall and remnants of the official festivities hall (*buraku den*). In the postwar period, notable discoveries included the detached palace of Emperor Toba (1103–1156) and the foundations for the temple Saiji, but little of the original city has come to light. The construction of a subway occasioned more digging in the 1980s, and at present archaeologists conduct about one hundred investigations a year.[22]

Scientists have begun to study the short-term capitals only recently. In 1957, archaeologists uncovered the foundations of Shōmu's audience hall at Kuni in southern Kyoto prefecture; in 1973, the local government established an organization to excavate there. In 1974, scholars found postholes for what may have been Tenji's palace at Ōtsu; subsequent digging uncovered more remnants. Archaeologists have exposed several base stones and platforms at Shigaraki, but much more excavation is necessary before scholars know very much about this site.[23]

By the early 1980s, the National Diet and prefectural governments had authorized teams of archaeologists to excavate and study each of Japan's Chinese-style capitals. During succeeding years, scientists made many exciting discoveries that have sharpened the queries of previous scholars and begun to supply some answers. To understand recent work on Japan's ancient capitals, it is necessary to examine the origins of the idea on the continent.

THE MAKING OF JAPAN'S CAPITALS: AN OVERVIEW

As normally conceived for ancient Japan, the Chinese-style capital (*tojō; miyako*) was a giant, unwalled rectangle laid out along the points of a compass. (See Figures 3.2 and 3.3.) A square known as the imperial palace—composed of the royal family's residential buildings and grounds (*dairi*), an audience hall, and official compound—was located in the north central portion of the rectangle. A symmetrical grid of streets running east-west and north-south and

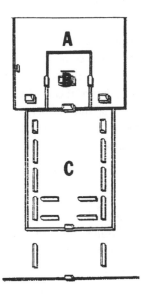

FIGURE 3.2
Fujiwara Palace.
Key: A. Imperial residence (*dairi*); B. Audience hall (*daigoku den*); C. Official compound (*chōdōin*).
Source: Machida Akira and Kitō Kiyoaki, eds., *Shinpan kodai no Nihon 6: Kinki* II, p. 392.

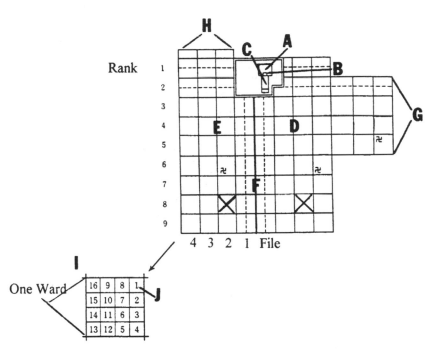

FIGURE 3.3 The Capital at Nara. *Key:* A. Imperial residence; B. Audience hall; C. Official compound; D. Left Capital; E. Right Capital; F. Suzaku Great Road; G. Outer Capital; H. Northern Grid; I. Right Capital, Ninth Rank, Fourth File; J. First residential lot; X. Markets. *Source:* Kishi Toshio, "Nihon no tojō sei sōron," in Kishi, ed., *Nihon no kodai 9: Tojō no seitai*, p. 33.

dividing the city into ranks and files (*jōbō sei*) lay outside the walls of the palace. A ward (*bō; machi*) was the name for the square produced by the intersection of each rank and file. Usually partitions surrounded the wards and alleys crossed inside the unit to form residential lots (*chō*). Officials determined a subject's general area of residence according to social status. There was also one market each in the eastern and western halves of the city. This urban configuration reflected Chinese, Korean, and earlier indigenous influences.

China

Ho Ping-ti has written that "the Chinese were a nation of walled-city builders par excellence."[24] One source records that from the beginning of their history until 1644, residents of the Middle Kingdom constructed about 4,500 walled cities; the earliest ones date back more than three thousand years to the Shang period. Chang-an of the seventh and eighth centuries was probably the most populous (1 million inhabitants) and most extensive (50 square kilometers) walled city of all time.

Japanese courtiers eager to learn about Chinese civilization probably had some knowledge of most capitals that predated the late seventh century, including Chang-an and Luo-yang of the Han, Northern Wei, Sui, and Tang eras as well as Jian-kang (Nanking) of the Southern Dynasties. Between 600 and 701, Japanese envoys visited both the Sui and Tang capitals five and seven times, respectively. Many, if not most, elements of the plan for Japan's capitals came from the Middle Kingdom: the rectangular shape laid out along points of the compass; the location of the monarch's palace in the north and the adoption of an audience hall; the symmetrical grid of avenues and partitioned wards arranging homes of dwellers by social status; and the placement of markets in the eastern and western halves of the metropolis. Given the general resemblance between Chinese and Japanese political centers, there can be no doubt that the inspiration for Japan's capitals came from China.[25]

Moreover, it is evident that Japanese engineers and politicians understood that the ideas underlying the Chinese capital had evolved, and they wanted to borrow the most up-to-date concepts. Japanese capitals all resemble Northern Wei or Sui Chang-an more closely than earlier Chinese models. The location of markets, the uniformity in the size of wards, the settlement of the population according to social status, the placement of the palace and government offices in one walled area—all these ideas came from the long Chinese experience with capital building.

Yet planners adapted the Chinese concept to their particular conditions.

John Hall has argued that one difference between Japan's and China's capital cities, the lack of a massive wall surrounding the archipelago's capitals, may have derived from the court's lack of foreign enemies and its style of warfare.[26] Yet one has only to consider the history of the seventh and eighth centuries, when the Japanese government outfitted several expeditions to intervene in Korean politics and suffered serious domestic challenges to the throne in virtually every reign, to question Hall's interpretation. While the absence of a defensive wall probably originated from conditions unique to Japan, other factors may also have played a role.

Another Japanese adaptation in capital building was the omission of shrines to the ancestors of the ruling family and to the gods of the earth, as prescribed by *The Rites of Zhou*.[27] Neither religious concept entered Japan before workers had constructed the first capitals in the middle of the eighth century. Apparently Chinese ancestor worship and deities of the earth had no counterparts in the beliefs of the elite of the archipelago because planners did not add shrines at Nagaoka or Heian even after the thought systems had been introduced.

Korea

Koguryŏ, Silla, and Paekche all had capitals that predated Japan's by centuries.[28] Koguryŏ's capitals were often made up of two parts: a walled city on a plain and a mountain citadel. In 586, when the Koguryŏ king moved his residence to Changan (modern Pyŏngyang), he encircled it with an oval wall, placed his palace and court inside, and planned and built a grid of streets, though the plan was not symmetrical. The Silla capital Kyŏngju also comprised a flat area where palaces and offices stood surrounded by mountain fortresses. The part of the city that was located on the plain had a grid plan, but like the Koguryŏ example it was not symmetrical. Kyŏngju also lacked an encircling wall.

Paekche had three capitals: Han (Seoul), Ungjin, and Puyŏ. Information is available only for Ungjin (475–538) and Puyŏ (538–660), both of which were at least partly encompassed by a wall. Mountain forts ringed both capitals, and the Paekche aristocracy lived on the plains, as did Silla nobles. Yet there is no mention of a grid layout for either Ungjin or Puyŏ. Based on this knowledge, Kishi Toshio, Japan's leading authority on capitals, has concluded that Korean examples had little connection with the political cities of the Kinai.

Before completely rejecting the possibility of a Korean tie, however, one should note two further facts. First, Korean engineers and carpenters served on the committees that planned and built both Nara and Kōtoku's Naniwa.

Second, while it is difficult to perceive a Korean influence in Japanese capital building, the plan of the northern Kyushu administrative and trade center at Dazaifu strongly suggests Korean ideas of capital design. The adjacent mountain fortresses and the lack of a grid plan indicate Korean origins. Even the engineers themselves came from Paekche.[29] Korean exiles were constructing Dazaifu in 664; thus the Japanese concept of a city may have switched from a Korean to a Chinese model during the course of the late seventh century.

Indigenous Palaces _____

Foreign prototypes may have been essential to the design of Japanese capitals, but one should not overlook the native tradition of palace building before 600. There is little reliable information on this topic: *A Record* and *The Chronicles* note only locations in a general way and are of doubtful veracity, and Japanese archaeologists have done less digging on pre-600 royal residences.[30] The one exception might be the excavation at Wakimoto, which some archaeologists believe was the site of Yūryaku's palace of the late fifth century. It was a small structure housing only the monarch, his family, and personal servants. Easily disassembled, this edifice was from an era before a large officialdom had evolved to gather at court and serve a ruler.[31]

Long after Yūryaku's time, Suiko occupied Oharida Palace from 603 to 628.[32] According to *The Chronicles,* foreign ambassadors came to Oharida in 608 and again in 610, and descriptions of receptions given to the visitors touch briefly on the layout of the palace. The emissaries entered through a gate that opened onto a courtyard immediately to the north; in that space Suiko's workers had built an indeterminate number of government offices. To the north of these offices was a wall with another large portal to the monarch's residence and grounds. The two-part layout of Suiko's palace suggests that by the early seventh century the court employed many officials who worked in a compound directly to the south of Suiko's living quarters.

It is uncertain how accurately *The Chronicles* recorded Oharida's layout. After all, compilers were writing over one hundred years after Suiko's time when engineers had designed Chinese-style capitals such as Fujiwara and Nara. The Chinese concept of the north-south orientation of the palace could easily have influenced the way editors described Oharida.[33] But other sources also suggest that later Yamato monarchs and their royal families lived in quarters that opened onto a courtyard of office buildings. In *The History of the Sui Dynasty,* a Japanese envoy to the Chinese court in 600 reported his ruler's customs as follows:

The King of the Wa deems heaven to be his elder brother and the sun, his younger. Before break of dawn he attends the Court, and, sitting cross-legged, listens to appeals. Just as soon as the sun rises, he ceases these duties, saying that he hands them over to his brother.[34]

The emissaries' remarks undoubtedly referred to the fourth-century origins of the Yamato state, whose chieftains probably worshiped the Sun Goddess every day at the break of dawn. As the story implies, however, by the early seventh century the sunrise rites for Yamato's progenitrix had evolved into the habit of carrying out administrative chores early in the morning. The buildings where officials and the Yamato ruler did their daybreak work later came to be known as "morning halls" (*chōdōin*). Both the name for the halls and the work schedule were an irreplaceable element of every Japanese capital from Naniwa to Heian.

It seems wisest, therefore, to regard Japan's Chinese-style capitals as representing three different strands of urban history. The general outline of the imperial capital came from China, while Korea contributed engineers and carpenters. The division between royal residence and morning halls was probably a product of political evolution within the archipelago. Indeed this domestic factor merits special emphasis. Consideration of the historical record together with the most recent archaeological evidence for each capital site shows just how much conditions within ancient Japan impinged on the implementation of these schemes.

FUJIWARA AND ITS ANTECEDENTS

Even though Fujiwara served as the capital from 694 to 710 and is manifestly Japan's first Chinese-style city, English-language textbooks almost always give the credit to Nara. Certainly Nara deserves attention for its size (over three times larger than the Fujiwara plan most widely accepted as late as 1990). Nara also served as the court's home nearly five times longer than Fujiwara and was the capital during the apogee of Japan's apprenticeship to Chinese civilization. But Fujiwara merits analysis because it speaks to the all-important question of origins.

The problem of origins is illuminated by Naniwa and Ōtsu, as well, political centers antedating Fujiwara in the mid-seventh century. Unlike Fujiwara, these two capitals have not revealed striking finds or been the subjects of inter-

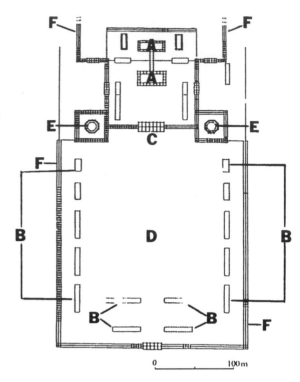

FIGURE 3.4
The Earliest Palace at
Naniwa. *Key:* A. Imperial
residence; B. Morning
halls; C. Gate; D. Official
compound; E. Octagonal
turrets; F. Double gallery.
Source: Ueki Hisashi,
"Yamato e no genkan,"
in Machida Akira and
Kitō Kiyoaki, eds.,
*Shinpan kodai no
Nihon 6: Kinki* II,
p. 23.

esting theorizing, but they are significant nonetheless. The Asuka region outside of Fujiwara, too, has its share of secrets to divulge, especially regarding the mysterious Wa Capital (Wa-kyō) referred to in *The Chronicles.*

The First Palace at Naniwa

As mentioned earlier, there are two layers at the Naniwa site: the lower probably predates 686 while the upper suggests habitation several decades thereafter. The major controversy that has enveloped the lower site is whether the remnants represent Kōtoku's Nagara Toyosaki Palace (645–653) or Temmu's efforts at capital building between 679 and 686. As there are few artifacts by which to date the ruins, it is doubtful that archaeology alone can provide an answer. Here I will describe the archaeological "facts" and then refer to written evidence to present arguments for each possibility.

Three generalizations about Naniwa's first palace meet with the approval of all scholars. First, most postholes held ash, indicating that the structures at the lower level had burned down. The consensus is that the ashes were left over from the fire recorded in 686 in *The Chronicles* and therefore establish a terminus for occupation of the bottom layer. Second, the construction of all buildings followed native, not continental, traditions.[35] There is no surviving evidence of foundation stones or tiles for roofs; posts were set directly in the ground and roofs were thatched. Third, the standard measure for one "foot" (*shaku*) used at Naniwa was 29.2 centimeters, which is shorter than that employed for later palaces such as Nara.

Scholars also concur on the layout of the palace, which was arranged with the imperial residence in the north and the official compound of morning halls in the south.[36] (See Figure 3.4.) A roofed double gallery (*fukurō*) surrounded the entire complex of residence and offices, and a massive gate, larger than a comparable gate at Nara, divided the ruler's private quarters from government bureaus. The area for morning halls measured 230 by 263 meters with fourteen or more rectangular buildings forming a U shape and facing onto a large courtyard. The northernmost structures in the official compound were shorter and wider than the others, suggesting to scholars that these two halls had some special functions.

The monarch's residence grounds measured 113 by 123 meters, about half the area of the official compound. It included two palaces, one 37 by 19 meters and the other about 34 by 15 meters, aligned in tandem. A special passageway (*konrō*) linked the two edifices, which displayed extended eaves (*hisashi*). Early Naniwa's most unusual feature—two octagonal turrets surrounded by a square double gallery 32 meters to a side—was situated between the imperial residence and the official compound. Each tower was surrounded by three concentric rows of posts, perhaps to support fences. Outside the palace complex, archaeologists have found two rectangular halls in the south.[37] These buildings probably served as the "morning gathering halls" (*chōshū den*) where officials went before dawn and the opening of the official compound. To the northeast and northwest of the palace, scientists have discovered what they believe to have been more offices and warehouses, both of which give evidence of a fiery demise and thus may have been the location of the treasury ministry.[38]

There are two clear conclusions regarding this excavation. First, the earliest political center at Naniwa was meant to be impressive. The area covered by the palace, the large octagonal turrets, and the giant gate leading from the monarch's domicile to the official compound all reflect a desire to overwhelm. Second, this palace looked more like a native political center than a Chinese capital. Evidently there were no foundation stones or roof tiles. And there was no audience hall as such, although the front structure in the imperial residence may have served the same purpose of housing the throne. The arrangement of imperial residence and morning halls seems to follow the early-seventh-century prototype, Oharida, where builders also juxtaposed the two sections. The close proximity of the imperial residence to the official compound, where bureaucrats conducted their day-to-day business, suggests the monarch's personal involvement in governing.[39]

The facts presented so far might reasonably fit palaces constructed in either Kōtoku or Temmu's era. Because archaeologists have found few artifacts by which to date the lower level, the debate over its identity would seem to have no end.[40] Fortunately the historical record provides some clues, beginning with the reign of Kōtoku. Late in 645, after Prince Naka, Nakatomi (later Fujiwara) no Kamatari, and Kōtoku had killed most of the powerful Soga family, they announced that they would "remove the capital" to Nagara Toyosaki at Naniwa. Directed by the Korean engineer Aratai no Atai Hirafu, workers dug ditches, leveled hills, filled in swamps, made roads, raised walls, and erected palatial buildings for the next six years. Kōtoku took up first one temporary home and then another until the end of 651, when Buddhist monks burned 2,700 candles and intoned two sutras to celebrate his settlement at Nagara Toyosaki. Laborers continued their tasks for another year. In 652, the editors of The Chronicles wrote that "it is impossible adequately to describe the appearance of the Palace Halls."[41] Kōtoku resided at Naniwa until his death at the end of 653.

The description of Temmu's efforts at capital building at Naniwa, by contrast, never refers to the palace. In 679, Temmu ordered workers to raise a wall (rashō) around the city. Late in 683, Temmu declared Naniwa to be his choice for an alternate capital and ordered officials to go to Naniwa to receive residential lots. Therefore, while Temmu undoubtedly had laborers working on the palace at Naniwa, he seems to have expended most of his energy constructing the surrounding city. The remains at the lower level of Naniwa seem to correspond well to Kōtoku's impressive structures, and the lack of references in Temmu's age may imply that he simply refurbished Kōtoku's magnificent palace.

A further argument that the remnants are those of Kōtoku's Nagara Toyosaki can be made on the basis of design. Had Temmu built the palace at the lower level of Naniwa, it seems likely that he would have followed the same plan as at Fujiwara. In fact, the lower level has several unique features. First, the palace uncovered at Naniwa evidently had no foundation stones, roof tiles, or audience hall, whereas Fujiwara did. Second, although the official compounds at Naniwa and Fujiwara are almost the same size, the lower level of Naniwa contains at least fourteen halls (and maybe more) while Fujiwara had twelve, the usual number for a Japanese capital. Third, two structures—the octagonal turrets—had no analogs at any other political center discovered to date. These towers may have had a Buddhist meaning and may have been modeled on capitals in Korea.[42] Other aspects of the lower level of Naniwa also echo Korean designs.[43] These points suggest that the palace at the lower level of Naniwa was a unique mixture of native and Korean elements, a fact that fits Nagara Toyosaki better than Temmu's palace at Fujiwara. Remember that Aratai no Atai Hirafu, the engineer for Nagara Toyosaki, was Korean.

Still, not everyone agrees that the remains at the lower stratum of Naniwa were Nagara Toyosaki. J. Edward Kidder thinks that the lower level belongs to Temmu's age because it is so close to the debris of the upper level that a century could not have elapsed between the two layers. Moreover, the official compounds at Naniwa and Fujiwara are virtually the same size, and the two-to-one ratio of that area to the grounds of the imperial residence nearly matches that of Fujiwara.[44] Therefore, although most experts see the lower level of Naniwa as Nagara Toyosaki, there is still room for further debate.

No matter which age the lower stratum of Naniwa belongs to, the huge official compound with fourteen halls has engendered some imaginative interpretations. One advocate of Nagara Toyosaki has proposed that the number of bureaucrats during Kōtoku's reign was so large that the court had to assemble many officials in the oversized compound and numerous morning halls for ceremonies and document shuffling.[45] Another historian has asserted that official business at that time relied heavily on word-of-mouth transmission rather than written records, encouraging the need for more space: presumably Kōtoku would gather his subordinates and announce his will to them verbally. This same author also believes that Kotoku and his court required the huge area to entertain local notables who came to the new capital to participate in official ceremonies and negotiations.[46]

One can plausibly argue that Kōtoku constructed a magnificent palace at Naniwa, but did he try to construct a capital? Although the written record is no help on this issue—the oldest mention of municipal construction at Naniwa comes in 679—several historians and geographers think there may have been a grid layout for a symmetrical Chinese-style capital as early as Kōtoku's reign. (See Figure 3.5.) Three points provide supporting evidence for Kōtoku's Naniwa as Japan's first real capital. First, The Chronicles indicates that road building went on during Kōtoku's reign, and some of that construc-

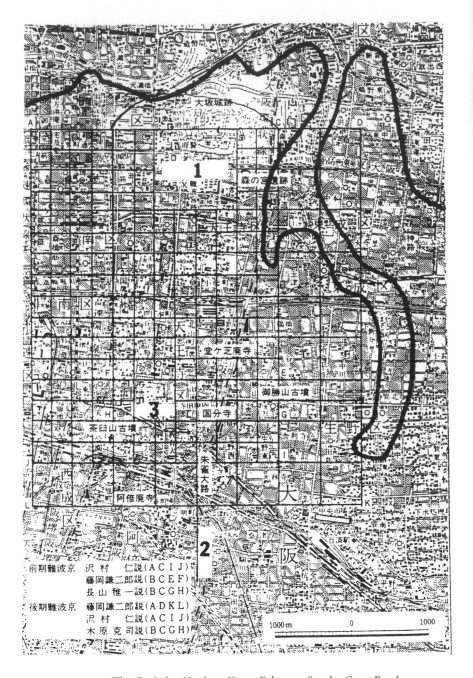

FIGURE 3.5 The Capital at Naniwa. *Key:* 1. Palace; 2. Suzaku Great Road; 3. Shitennōji. Plans for Early Naniwa: Sawamura Masashi ACIJ; Fujioka Kenjirō BCEF; Nagayama Masakazu BCGH. Plans for Later Naniwa: Sawamura Masashi ACIJ; Fujioka Kenjirō ADKL; Kihara Atsushi BCGH. *Source:* Yagi Hisae, "Naniwa no miya," in Tsuboi Kiyotari, ed., *Kodai o kangaeru kyūto hakkutsu,* p. 78.

tion may have been at Naniwa. Second, a center line drawn from north to south through the palace exactly matches a road still in use today; near the palace, moreover, archaeologists have uncovered a small, unpaved stretch of flat pounded earth that might well have been the chief north-south thoroughfare, Suzaku Great Road. Third, Shitennōji, a temple constructed early in the seventh century, decades before Nagara Toyosaki, sits neatly within the grid, and at the southern border of the temple there is even the place-name "Great Road," which could indicate the southern extremity of the capital.[47]

All this evidence notwithstanding, it seems wise to be cautious about the existence of a full-blown capital at Naniwa prior to 679. After all, archaeologists have yet to excavate any roads or ditches that fit a Chinese-style grid layout.[48] Furthermore, reconstructions of Osaka Bay for the seventh century indicate that some portions of a city at Naniwa would have been submerged. While the palace at the lower stratum of Naniwa is probably Nagara Toyosaki, there is only the slimmest possibility that Kōtoku built a Chinese-style capital at Naniwa.

Ōtsu

During the last year of Kōtoku's life, Prince Naka, the heir apparent and chief power broker of the group that had ousted the Soga, split with his fellow conspirator and moved the royal family back to Asuka. Reasons for this enmity are unclear, but even as Kōtoku drew his last breath in the palace of his dreams at Nagara Toyosaki, his family and consort were already making their homes in Asuka. For the next fourteen years, from 653 to 667, Naka and his coterie followed the older tradition of moving from palace to palace in Asuka. These years were tumultuous ones for the court. In 663, it mounted an expedition to revive Paekche and met with a humiliating defeat at the hands of Silla and Tang China. Naka began to exert strong efforts to centralize rule along Chinese lines, even as the court prepared for an invasion by the victorious powers.

According to *The Chronicles*, the prince had been named heir apparent early in Kōtoku's reign, and while his exact status is a matter of debate, his influence had always been great.[49] With the death of his mother, Emperor Saimei, in 661, he became an even more powerful leader. Yet he did not ascend the throne until 668, perhaps because of unpopularity due to the defeat in Korea or perhaps because he was better able to wield power behind the scenes.

In 667, Prince Naka decided to move to a new palace where he would assume the royal dignity. Known posthumously as Emperor Tenji, Naka chose Ōtsu on the shores of Lake Biwa in Ōmi, far from any other previous palace, especially Asuka. The choice was not a popular one:

> The capital was moved to Ōmi. At this time the people of the realm did not desire the removal of the capital. Many made satirical remonstrance, and there were also many popular songs. Every day and every night there were numerous conflagrations.[50]

The decision to dislodge the aristocracy from their long-standing home in Asuka made few friends for Naka.

The political center of Japan remained at Ōtsu until 672. *The Chronicles* gives the reader glimpses of the palace at Ōtsu, referring to treasury warehouses, the imperial kitchen, a water clock, a tower on the beach, buildings in the imperial residence, the courtyard for the official compound, a gate, and a Buddhist edifice.

After Tenji's death in the twelfth month of 671, his son Ōtomo and brother Ōama contested the throne in a major conflict, the Jinshin War of 672. Tenji's son Ōtomo lost and Ōama (Temmu) made Asuka his home. Losers both at home and abroad, Tenji's line in the imperial family retreated from the political scene, the court abandoned Ōtsu, and within a century the location of Tenji's capital became a matter of dispute.[51]

A recent excavation seems to have uncovered the short-lived palace.[52] The site reveals the usual two compartments: the imperial residence in the north and official compound in the south. (See Figure 3.6.) A simple fence (*hei*) surrounded what is believed to have been the imperial residence; a short double gallery and a small gate marked the boundary and entrance to the official compound. This excavation also recovered portions of two structures that may have been morning halls, and there may have been two small granaries north of the palace. No remnants of the palace wall dividing official quarters from other homes have come to light.

Archaeologists have thus had little luck finding many details of Ōtsu Palace, and they have not even tried looking for a capital city. Modern Ōtsu is squeezed between steep mountains to the immediate west and Lake Biwa to the east; in the seventh century Biwa extended 600 or 700 meters inland into what is today dry, so there was even less space for Tenji to plan a Chinese-style capital.[53] One historical geographer has reconstructed what he thinks a capital at Ōtsu would have looked like: his plan is 1,090 meters east-west by 1,635 meters north-south, only about half the size of Naniwa.[54] The grounds for a proposed palace measure a mere 545 square meters.

It is doubtful that Tenji had the resources or room to construct a large palace at Ōtsu, much less a Chinese-style capital. But the scantiness of findings

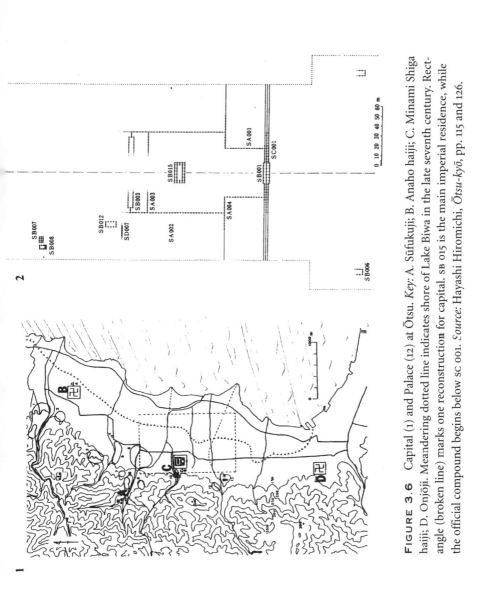

FIGURE 3.6 Capital (1) and Palace (12) at Ōtsu. *Key*: A. Sūfukuji; B. Anaho haiji; C. Minami Shiga haiji; D. Onjōji. Meandering dotted line indicates shore of Lake Biwa in the late seventh century. Rectangle (broken line) marks one reconstruction for capital. SB 015 is the main imperial residence, while the official compound begins below SC 001. *Source*: Hayashi Hiromichi, *Ōtsu-kyō*, pp. 115 and 126.

does not mean that Ōtsu is devoid of interest for those inquiring into Japan's early political centers. Four major temples were located around Tenji's Ōtsu—Sūfukuji to the northwest, Anaho haiji to the northeast, and Onjōji (Miidera) and Minami Shiga haiji to the south.[55] Directly to the east was Lake Biwa and routes to eastern Honshu, while immediately to the west were high mountains. It is almost as if Tenji was seeking protection from continental dangers. A leading authority on Ōtsu argues that the mountainous terrain around Tenji's palace is strongly reminiscent of Kyŏngju and other Korean capitals, where defense was an important consideration.[56]

What Was the Wa Capital?

According to The Chronicles, when Prince Naka decided to move most of the royal family to Asuka in 653, he did not name the palace where he wanted to go but simply said that his band was leaving for the "Wa (or Yamato) Capital."[57] In addition to the prince's imputed usage of this term, The Chronicles makes six other references to the Wa Capital as a concrete destination: twice at the end of Kōtoku's reign and four more times during the civil war of 672. It seems likely that the "Wa Capital" referred to a real entity, whatever its origin. What and where could it have been?

Japanese historians interested in locating Japan's first Chinese-style political center have spent the past twenty-five years debating the existence and character of the Wa Capital.[58] Although many points are still unclear, scholars now believe that during the time that the court made its home in the Asuka region in the seventh century, engineers built three parallel pounded-earth roads (called Lower, Middle, and Upper Ways in The Chronicles), which ran north and south across Nara basin, and two east-west highways leading from the basin to Osaka Bay. (See Map 3.1.) Historians and archaeologists propose that as each new ruler had more palaces and temples constructed near these roads, the area bounded by Upper and Lower Way, Great Crossing Avenue, and Tachibanadera came to be known as the Wa Capital.[59]

The Wa Capital was not planned, but grew up naturally, and scholars differ on when it came into being. Recently one expert asserted that the Wa Capital was a product of Saimei's era (655–661), during which time workers completed a water clock and a ground for political ceremonies. Laborers also attempted to build a large moat and a wall around Saimei's palace but failed to finish them.[60] The existence of a unifying grid layout for the Wa Capital is very much in doubt, and there was no Chinese-style capital administration until 685, late in Temmu's reign.[61]

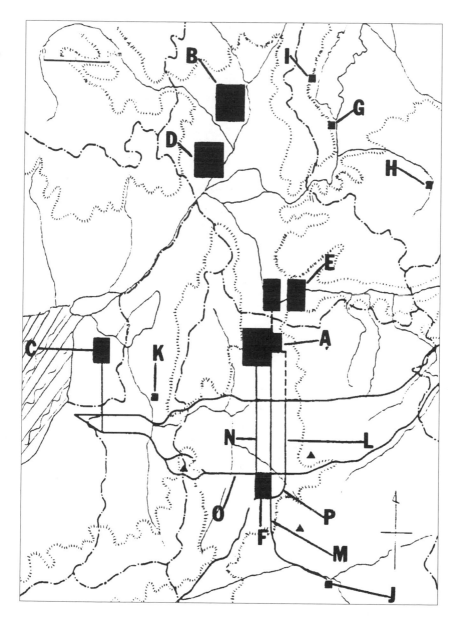

MAP 3.1 Road Map of the Kinai, ca. A.D. 700. *Key:* A. Nara; B. Heian; C. Naniwa; D. Nagaoka; E. Kuni; F. Fujiwara; G. Hora; H. Shigaraki; I. Ōtsu; J. Yoshino; K. Yuge; L. Upper Way; M. Middle Way; N. Lower Way; O. Great Crossing Avenue; P. Yamada Road. *Source:* Kishi Toshio, "Nihon no tojō sei sōron," p. 27.

To imagine what the Wa Capital may have looked like, one must reconstruct the palaces and temples in Asuka, a gigantic task that is just now beginning. During the years 593 to 694, Japanese rulers had seven main palaces erected in Asuka. (See Figure 3.7.) Although scholars have been excavating since the 1950s, even the locations of some monarchical residences remain controversial. There are only five for which we have significant archaeological information: Suiko's Toyura Palace (593–603); Jomei's Asuka Okamoto Palace

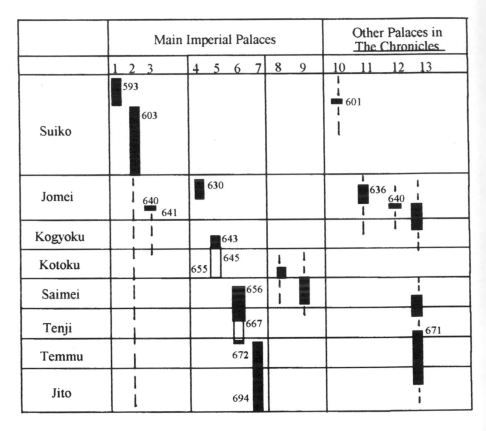

FIGURE 3.7   Palaces in Japan, 593–694. *Key:* 1. Toyura; 2. Oharida; 3. Kudara; 4. Asuka Okamoto; 5. Asuka Itabuki; 6. Later Asuka Okamoto; 7. Asuka Kiyomihara; 8. Asuka Kawabe; 9. Asuka Kawara; 10. Miminashi; 11. Tanaka; 12. Umayasaka; 13. Shima. *Source:* Ōwaki Kiyoshi, "Shin'yaku-kyō no kensetsu," in Machida Akira and Kitō Kiyoaki, eds., *Shinpan kodai no Nihon 6: Kinki* II, p. 66.

(630–636); Kōgyoku's Itabuki Palace (643–645); Saimei and Tenji's Later Asuka Okamoto Palace (656–667); and Temmu's Kiyomihara Palace (672–694).[62] Little or nothing is known about the archaeological record for Oharida or Jomei's Kudara Palace.

Archaeology can do little more than confirm the existence of Toyura, Asuka Okamoto, Itabuki, and Later Asuka Okamoto. Scientists have found what they believe was part of Toyura beneath remains of the temple of the same name. The small palace grounds measured only 200 by 80 meters and contained one small building, an earthen foundation, and a flagstone yard.

Archaeologists, having discovered three layers at a site situated on a slope between Asuka Niimasu Shrine and Okadera, are coming to the conclusion that Asuka Okamoto, Itabuki, Later Asuka Okamoto, and Kiyomihara palaces were all in the same basic location. At the bottom level (Layer I), which may be Asuka Okamoto, archaeologists have discerned that the buildings were, like Toyura, 20 degrees off a north-south axis. They have also found evidence of fire, which matches The Chronicles' description of Asuka Okamoto's end. Layer II, probably Itabuki, includes buildings within a 200-meter-square fence laid out on a north-south axis. The uppermost layer (Layer III) had two substrata: III-A seems to have included remains from Later Asuka Okamoto Palace, although little else is known. Substratum III-B has laid bare the most complete picture of any of Asuka's pre-Fujiwara palaces. This site, which many believe to be Kiyomihara, was composed of two walled compounds laid out on a north-south axis and surrounded with an outer wall. (See Figure 3.8.) The larger compound was 158 by 197 meters, while the smaller measured 100 by 98 meters.

Archaeologists have investigated only the northern and southern ends of the larger compound, but they have uncovered in the southern portion the foundation of a hall that strongly recalls the imperial residence at Nagara Toyosaki. Excavation has also revealed a sand-covered area perfect for imperial rites. The northern end of the compound consists of eastern and western sectors, with a symmetrical arrangement of structures that includes great wells. Some archaeologists now believe that this larger compound functioned as Temmu's private quarters. The smaller walled compound contained the largest building of all those so far brought to light, and it was complete with a fence and gate. Some believe that Temmu used it as his audience hall; if so, Kiyomihara represented a transitional arrangement between Nagara Toyosaki with no audience hall and the standard layout of Fujiwara and later capitals. No evidence of morning halls is yet visible at this site.

FIGURE 3.8
Kiyomihara Palace
Candidate. *Source:* Ōwaki
Kiyoshi, "Shin'yaku-kyō
no kensetsu," in Machida
Akira and Kitō Kiyoaki,
eds., *Shinpan kodai no
Nihon* 6: *Kinki* II, p. 76.

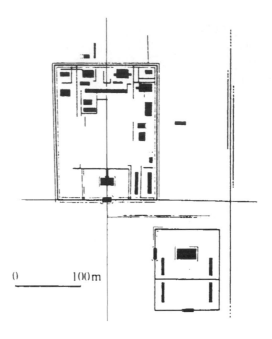

0   100m

Layer III-B may well mark where Temmu built his headquarters after the victory in 672, and *The Chronicles* speaks of Kiyomihara in grand terms.[63] It apparently possessed an imperial residence, morning halls and an associated courtyard, an audience hall, southern and western gates, and offices for the council of state and six major ministries. At the same time, the brevity of construction work implies that builders of Kiyomihara used parts of previous palaces. Temmu may have decided that Kiyomihara would be only a temporary home until he had designed a more magnificent, Chinese-style capital elsewhere.

With its many palaces, the Wa Capital of the second half of the seventh century must have been a focus of political activity, although clearly it did not fit the definition of a Chinese-style capital. Asuka was also home to most seventh-century temples. A 680 entry in *The Chronicles* states that there were twenty-four temples within the Wa Capital, and archaeologists have collected distinctive roof tiles for many Buddhist edifices in Asuka. Though it may have been asymmetrical and unplanned, the Wa Capital made adequate material from which Temmu and his consort Jitō could fashion Japan's first authentic Chinese-style capital.

Capital Building under Temmu and Jitō _____

Scholars generally agree that the drive to create a more centralized Chinese-style state in Japan accelerated under Temmu after 672. The capital was one facet of Chinese statecraft that Temmu and his heirs sought to adapt, and *The Chronicles* uses the Chinese word for capital more frequently beginning with Temmu's reign. For example: in 676, Temmu had the weapons of high aristocrats living in "the capital" inspected; the next year *The Chronicles* notes that drought had struck "the capital"; twice in 680 the court took pity on the poor and Buddhist temples within "the capital" and made donations of cloth and food; in 681, temples in "the capital" showed their gratitude by chanting sutras for Temmu's consort at a religious festival; court records for 685 note the death of a high aristocrat in charge of "capital" administration (*kyōshiki*), an office organized after the Chinese model. One should probably construe all these entries as referring to the Wa Capital, indicating that official consciousness of the city as a Chinese-style municipality was growing.

While it is clear that Temmu began planning a great new capital early in his reign, controversy surrounds the exact nature of his efforts.[64] The older view states that early on Temmu already had a specific site in mind. William Aston's translation of *The Chronicles* says that in 676 "it was intended to make the capital at Nihiki," possibly located at modern Kōriyama city.[65] Aston records that in 682 planners inspected Nihiki, and Temmu himself toured the area a few months thereafter.

Kishi Toshio, however, has argued that the characters Aston construed as "Nihiki" can also be read "*shinjō*" ("New Walled [City]"), which would refer to no specific site. Other records show that usage of the more general term was common. This new view implies that Temmu repeatedly searched for a location for his "New Walled City" from 676 to 682 but was unable to settle on a suitable place. To support this interpretation, scholars note that wooden tablets (*mokkan*) bearing writing and uncovered from a canal used in construction of Fujiwara Palace date back no earlier than 682.[66] Kishi's interpretation therefore seems to be closer to the truth and is widely accepted by Japanese historians.

Toward the end of his life, Temmu's statements took on a concreteness they previously lacked. In 683, *The Chronicles* reports that the emperor toured the capital; he did so again early in 684, but this time the purpose was to mark off land for a palace. He already had Kiyomihara, as described earlier, and the assumption is that he had found a place for a new, more magnificent, more authentically Chinese-type capital. References to the search for a site disappear at this point, implying that Temmu had begun building. The newly designated capital was probably Fujiwara, which was soon to become Japan's first authentic Chinese-style political center.

As he considered constructing a more magnificent capital in Asuka, Temmu turned his attention to long-neglected Naniwa. In 679, he ordered checkpoints placed on the two major east-west routes leading from Asuka to Naniwa; in the same proclamation Temmu ordered workers to raise a wall around Naniwa. This was the first time the court ordered such a barrier around a political center—an action that implies the existence of a full-fledged capital. Archaeologists have found nothing to indicate that such a wall ever came into being. Naniwa burned in 686, and it is possible that the wall was never built.

Late in 683, Temmu made his most comprehensive declaration on the topic of capitals:

> Capitals and palaces should not be in just one place, but without fail We ought to construct two or three. Thus We desire first of all to make Naniwa a capital. Based upon this, officials should each go and receive his or her residential plot.[67]

Temmu was, it appears, declaring his intention to follow the Chinese custom of dual capitals: instead of Chang-an and Luo-yang, it would be Asuka and Naniwa.

The edict about Naniwa raises the question of that port's condition since the death of Kōtoku in 654. Many scholars believe that, even in the 680s, Nagara Toyosaki Palace must have stood much as Kōtoku had constructed it, although thirty years was a long time for timbers to survive.[68] Most historians, including Kishi Toshio, also believe that a symmetrical grid layout came into existence for Naniwa during the last years of Temmu's reign.[69] There is some archaeological evidence that Temmu covered with sand the road leading north from Shitennōji to the palace and ordered construction of east-west earthen avenues and some ditches. At least one older historian argues, however, that there was no symmetrical capital at Naniwa in Temmu's day because the order cited here specified that officials had to go to Naniwa to receive their household lots, a trip that would have been unnecessary if a grid had already existed.[70]

Construction on dual capitals at Fujiwara and Naniwa probably continued from 683 to the middle of 686, although there is no written testimony to indicate that work was actually going on. Then in 686 disaster struck when Temmu died and Naniwa burned. All construction stopped.[71] Emperors continued to favor Naniwa with their presence even after the fire, but no one knows what remained at the site from 686 until Shōmu decided to rebuild it forty years later.[72] The court waited for Prince Kusakabe, the heir apparent and son of Temmu and Jitō, to assume the throne, but he died in 689. Jitō herself took up the imperial dignity in 690 and continued her husband's policy of rapidly adopting elements of Chinese civilization. Almost immediately, the project in Asuka became a top priority.

In the tenth month of 690, officials inspected the site for a palace, now called Fujiwara; Jitō herself toured Fujiwara about a month later. Construction must have gone well, for in 691 the court dispatched envoys to perform a service for the tranquility of the new capital, and within six weeks Jitō had reviewed road construction near the palace and the government was assigning residential lots to aristocrats. This poem is attributed to workmen assembling logs for the palace:

> Then the gods of heaven and earth,
> Gracious to serve,
> Float the cypress timbers
> From Mount Tanakami of Ōmi
> Down the stream of Uji;
> We people throng into the river—
> Splashing in the water like so many mallards,
> Never thinking of our homes,
> And forgetful of ourselves—
> To gather and turn those timbers
> Into the river of Izumi; . . .
> And there the logs are roped into rafts
> Which we vie in poling
> Against Izumi's stream;
> Looking on these labors well we know,
> All is done by her divinity! [73]

In the early summer of 692, religious officials conducted another rite to ensure a peaceful metropolis, while other priests went to Shinto shrines to announce the erection of the palace to the gods. Soon Jitō herself examined her new home. Late in 694, the eighth year of her reign and a full ten years since Temmu had laid plans for a new palace, Jitō and her court took up residence in Fujiwara.

Archaeologists have been at work on Fujiwara since before World War II, and there is a fair degree of certainty about Temmu and Jitō's palace, which served their descendants until the move to Nara in 710.[74] (See Figure 3.2.) The great wall (*ōgaki*) that surrounded the palace was 925.4 by 906.8 meters, denoting a court that was much larger than its predecessors. The use of tile roofs and large foundation stones for the great wall and its gates also indicates a new level of permanence in capital building: previously only Buddhist temples had employed these continental construction techniques. The arrangement of buildings within Fujiwara Palace also established a tradition. The imperial residence stood in the north, the audience hall in the center, and twelve halls of the official compound in the south. Of these three segments, the audience hall was a new addition. Jitō and Temmu meant for their headquarters to symbolize lasting imperial rule.[75]

One of the most impressive structures of Fujiwara Palace was the tile-covered great wall, which circled the entire complex. An inner moat 3 meters wide and 0.5 meter deep paralleled the wall on the inside, while an even wider moat 4 to 5 meters wide and 1.5 meters deep encircled it on the outside. Between the outer moat and the roads and ditches of the capital proper lay 40 meters of open area (*senchi*) for which scholars have as yet ascertained no precedent or function. Scholars assume there were three tile-covered gates on each side of the rectangular great wall, and so far three of the twelve gates have come to light.[76] Immediately within the great wall were blocks of office buildings where bureaucrats carried out the daily business of government. So far archaeologists have discovered three groups of offices, and none had surrounding fences or ditches. The halls themselves tended to be narrow, rectangular structures. Neither these offices nor the two morning gathering halls to the south of the official compound had tile roofs or foundation stones.

The imperial residence lay deep in the heart of Fujiwara Palace. It too was constructed according to traditional posthole techniques and was encircled by a wall at some points and a fence at others. Edo-period farmers dug a large irrigation pond over most of the imperial residence and destroyed the site, but archaeologists estimate that Jitō lived in an area measuring about 305 by 350 meters. They also believe that workers rebuilt the living quarters once. Some think that laborers erected towers in the northeast and northwest corners and along the southern border. Excavations also reveal that peasant dwellings occupied the site before Jitō moved there.

The greatest innovation of the Fujiwara Palace was the construction of Japan's first authentic audience hall (or Hall of the Great Ultimate). There the monarch could sit on his or her throne and gaze upon the courtyard of the official compound during ceremonies and receptions. Archaeologists have uncovered a great moat 6 meters wide running north-south and linking up with the eastern ditch alongside Suzaku Great Road. They have argued that it served to transport construction materials to the palace. Wooden tablets— many with dates from Temmu's time—suggest that this canal was in use from the early stages of building.[77] Most tiles recovered from the sites of the audience hall and the twelve morning halls are newer and simpler, however, than those used for the great wall and its gates, suggesting that workers had not yet finished the former edifices when Jitō moved to Fujiwara in 694. Using continental architecture, these buildings may have been difficult to erect or perhaps were less vital to Jitō's welfare.[78]

Until the mid-1980s, most scholars believed that the plan of the capital city was as predictable and straightforward as that of the palace proper. Kishi Toshio set forth what became the conventional interpretation.[79] (See Figure 3.9.) According to Kishi, Temmu and Jitō laid out the checkerboard plan for Fujiwara by using the old roads of the Wa Capital. Great Crossing Avenue (*yoko ōji*) became the northern boundary for Fujiwara; the Lower Way (*shimotsu michi*) became its farthest western extent; and the Middle Way (*nakatsu michi*) was the eastern border. Only in the south was it necessary to make the last thoroughfare more narrow so that it would coincide with the previously laid Yamada Road.

Viewed in this way, Fujiwara looked like the quintessential Chinese-style capital. East to west it measured 2.12 kilometers, while north to south it was 3.18 kilometers (4 by 6 "leagues," or *ri*). Planners, thought Kishi, had divided the rectangle into twelve east-west ranks (*jō*) and eight north-south files. Two alleys intersected in the middle of each ward (*bō*), making four residential lots. Fujiwara Palace itself, the complex of the imperial residence, offices, and ceremonial grounds, fit neatly into the grid just north of the city center. Several other considerations seemed to corroborate Kishi's hypothetical design for Fujiwara. First, four major temples (Kiidera, Daikan daiji, Hinokumadera, and Yakushiji) rested exactly within his proposed grid plan. Second, placenames like "Horikawa" and "Nakagawa" (ditches) corresponded to boundaries between wards. Third, if one extended the center line for the palace due south, it intersected the burial mounds for Temmu and Jitō, the imperial planners of Fujiwara.

Archaeological findings tended to support Kishi's theory at first. Two north-south ditches each 5 meters wide were discovered at a location about 150 meters south of the south central gate of the palace; the distance between

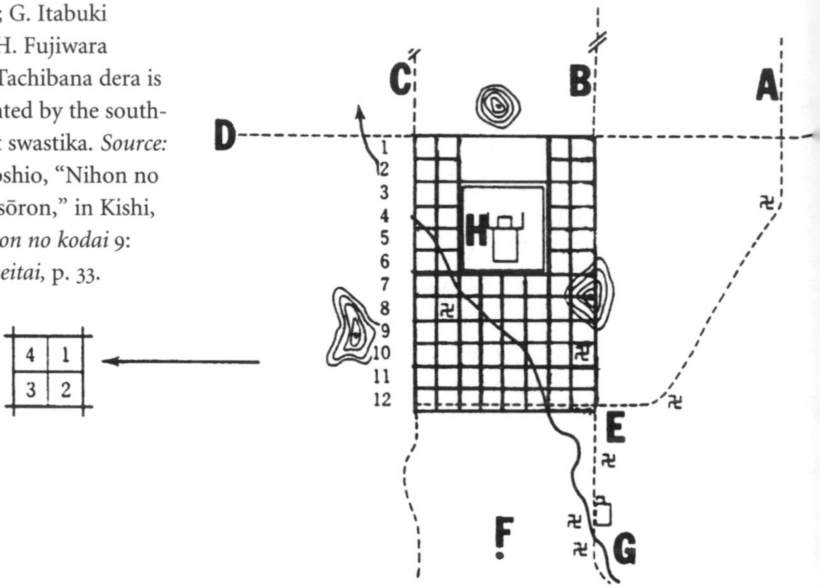

FIGURE 3.9
Kishi's Plan for a
Capital at Fujiwara.
Key: A. Upper Way;
B. Middle Way; C. Lower
Way; D. Great Crossing
Way; E. Yamada Road;
F. Tombs of Jitō and
Temmu; G. Itabuki
Palace; H. Fujiwara
Palace. Tachibana dera is
represented by the south-
ernmost swastika. *Source:*
Kishi Toshio, "Nihon no
tojō sei sōron," in Kishi,
ed., *Nihon no kodai* 9:
tojō no seitai, p. 33.

the two ditches was 19 meters, probably the breadth of Suzaku Great Road. Moreover, scientists who conducted small excavations throughout the grid area of Fujiwara found unpaved, pounded-earth surfaces that looked like lengths of roads. Excavations indicated that the Second Way (*nijō*) was 15.2 meters wide, the Third (*sanjō*) 9 meters, the Fourth (*shijō*) 16 meters, the Sixth (*rokujō*) 21 meters, and the Eighth (*hachijō*) 15 meters wide.[80] Unlike Naniwa, roads and ditches were turning up exactly where predicted.

Kishi thought his discovery of the street grid for Fujiwara had two major implications. First, he argued that Fujiwara resembled pre-600 Chinese capitals (such as Northern Wei Luo-yang or Jian-kang [Nanking]) more closely than Sui or Tang Chang-an. Like Luo-yang, Fujiwara was longer north-to-south than east-to-west; Chang-an was the opposite. Unlike Chang-an, Fuji-wara had no outer wall and no walls separating government offices from the imperial residence within the palace complex. The location of the palace com-pound in Fujiwara was closer to the center of the capital than in Tang Chang-an; Fujiwara was like Northern Wei Luo-yang in this respect. Kishi suggested that Japan was too backward to have copied Tang Chang-an, the world's largest city, in one fell swoop. A Chinese archaeologist challenged Kishi's reconstruction, however, asserting that it still looked more like Tang Chang-an than any other Chinese city.[81]

The second implication of Kishi's work on Fujiwara had to do with Nara and the development of later cities in Japan. (See Map 3.1.) Kishi believed that when engineers designed Nara in 710 they used Fujiwara as the model, not Tang Chang-an. Noting that the east-west breadth of Fujiwara was exactly one-half the width of Nara, he proposed that designers followed the Asuka roads straight north to a large flat plain, where they doubled the width of Fuji-wara to obtain that dimension for Nara. Deriving the length was a bit more complicated, since Fujiwara had twelve ranks and Nara only nine, but basi-cally planners also doubled that dimension. Thus when one excluded the Outer Capital (*gekyō*), Nara was about four times as large as Fujiwara.

Kishi thought the reliance on Fujiwara to plan Nara explained many previ-ously misunderstood points.[82] First, the remnant of grid arrangements (*hop-pen*) to the northeast of Nara Palace reflected the Fujiwara layout, which had a sizable checkerboard arrangement north of the palace. Second, each ward (*bō*) at Nara had four times as many residential lots (*chō*) as Fujiwara, a figure that planners had derived by squaring Fujiwara's four *chō* to allow for Nara's doubled length and width. Third, the greater width of roads around Nara Palace was another result of using Fujiwara to plan Nara. Finally, Kishi thought that the homologous location of temples such as Daianji and Yakushiji in Nara and Fujiwara was another sign that Fujiwara had served as the model. Kishi stressed that he was not arguing Japan's capitals had no Chinese antecedents, as they obviously did; but when it came time to design Nara, the lessons learned from Fujiwara were more relevant than those of the giant Tang Chang-an.

As so often happens in archaeology, however, new finds in the late 1980s raised substantial doubts about Kishi's hypotheses.[83] Archaeologists found earthen streets and ditches where Kishi had predicted, but they began uncov-ering them elsewhere as well. Roads were excavated underneath Jitō's palace and at regular intervals outside the area Kishi had designated for Fujiwara. Furthermore, no avenues came to light south of Kishi's predicted Tenth Rank

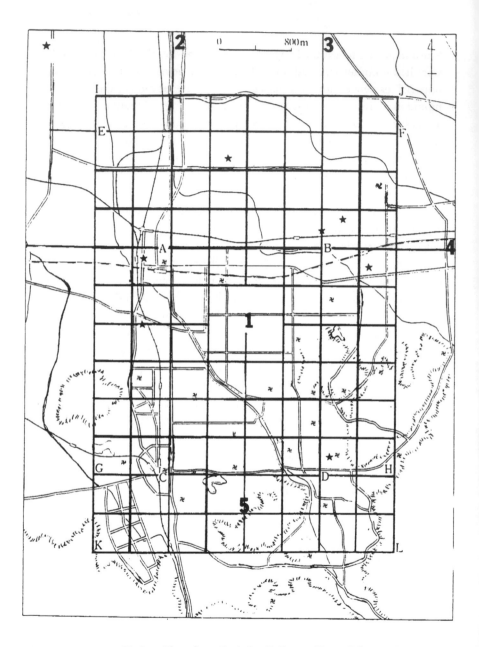

FIGURE 3.10   Various Plans for a Capital at Fujiwara. *Key:* 1. Palace; 2. Lower Way; 3. Middle Way; 4. Great Crossing Avenue; 5. Suzaku Great Road. ABCD: Kishi Toshio; EFGH: Akiyama Hideo; IJKL: Abe Yoshihira/Oshibe Keishū. *Source:* Ōwaki Kiyoshi, "Shin'yaku-kyō no kensetsu," in Machida Akira and Kitō Kiyoaki, eds., *Shinpan kodai no Nihon* 6: *Kinki* II, p. 83.

(*jūjō*), even though he called for two more. He countered by arguing that the unpredicted roads were part of the Wa Capital, but doubts have lingered.

Currently most scholars accept Kishi's measurements for individual units within Fujiwara's grid, but they differ on the capital's extent. (See Figure 3.10.) The most popular idea is that Fujiwara was really much larger than Kishi imagined, overflowing all the nearby roads of the Asuka plain.[84] There is some historical evidence for this view: in places *The Chronicles* calls Fujiwara "the newly expanded capital" (*shin'yaku-kyō*). The newer versions of Fujiwara are as large as Nara or larger. Perhaps Temmu planned a small capital within the old thoroughfares of Asuka, but after his death Jitō built a giant city in her husband's memory. Or maybe Temmu designed a greater Fujiwara but Jitō, becoming more realistic after Temmu's demise, scaled down construction.

The new concept of a Greater Fujiwara as spacious as Nara does not necessarily negate all of Kishi's theories, however. His point that the Japanese were unlikely to copy contemporary prototypes exactly remains valid. All recent predictions about Fujiwara put the palace right in the middle of the capital, not at the northern edge as at Tang or Sui Chang-an. These hypotheses look more like the idealized Chinese-style capital described in *The Rites of Zhou* than anything from seventh-century China, much as Kishi argued.

Whichever reconstruction of Fujiwara one accepts, everyone agrees that the work necessary to make the metropolis livable—filling in bogs, leveling hills, digging ditches, erecting walls, raising mansions—would have been a mind-boggling task.[85] One historian has estimated that it would have required 30,000 worker-days to complete just the 3.2 kilometers of a moat as large as the one that supplied building materials to the palace. Plans required 200 kilometers of smaller ditches in Fujiwara, too. There were many other backbreaking jobs as well. The main structures of the palace required at least four thousand posts 50 centimeters in diameter and 7 meters tall—and the source for timbers by Lake Biwa was 54 kilometers away by water. The Chinese-style offices of the palace needed two thousand foundation stones of several hundred kilograms each. Kilns for fragile roof tiles weighing 7 or 8 kilograms apiece were 8.5 kilometers from the construction site. The project would have required years of time; Fujiwara was occupied only sixteen years. Understandably, some Japanese scholars doubt that the city was ever finished, despite the decade of planning and the existence of many temples and palaces near the site in Asuka from earlier times.

About Jitō's palace few mysteries remain, but for the city it will take years of excavation to answer the riddle of Fujiwara. So far archaeologists have laid bare only a few wards with alleys, wells, homes, and even a kiln.[86] The 18 percent of Kishi's proposed Fujiwara that archaeologists have excavated (most of that in the palace) only scratches the surface. *The Man'yōshū* contains a poem about Temmu and his capitals:

> *Our Sovereign, a god,*
> *Has made his Imperial City*
> *Out of the stretch of swamps,*
> *Where chestnut horses sank*
> *To their bellies.*[87]

Converting a marsh into a thriving metropolis was undoubtedly a heroic feat worthy of the ambitious Temmu.

To Nara, to Kuni, and to Nara Again

Nara (also called Heijō) is commonly known as Japan's first permanent capital, but this simple proposition belies the city's varying fortunes during the seventy-four years and eight reigns of the Nara era. After the transfer of the capital from Fujiwara to Heijō in 710, the government refurbished Naniwa again in 724 and reconstructed Nara Palace in a grander manner. Only sixteen years later in 740, Emperor Shōmu made the decision to move first to Kuni, then to Shigaraki, and back to Naniwa in the wake of a serious rebellion. Even after the return to Heijō in 745, monarchs continued to maintain residences at other locations and to renovate the imperial domicile at Heijō. The multiple capitals and rebuilding have guaranteed that Nara, specifically the palace, remains the center of controversy. The two main issues debated by Japanese scholars are the plan of Heijō Palace and the chronology of its construction.

Building Nara the First Time: The Historical Record _____

By the early years of the eighth century, Fujiwara was a decade old. The desire to escape the influences of Asuka's entrenched aristocratic families and religious institutions, the hope that a new capital would exorcise the demons of famine and pestilence, the dream of building a city appropriate to the recently promulgated Taihō edition of Chinese-style laws—all these elements no doubt played a role in the decision to change. Most important, the new capital would be a monument to Temmu's great-grandson and heir apparent Prince Obito, later known as Shōmu.[88]

High aristocrats first discussed the possibility of leaving Fujiwara early in 707, while Temmu's grandson Mommu was still on the throne. The court deferred its decision after his death later that year; it was not until the second month of 708 that the government officially announced in a most Chinese declaration that there was need for a new capital. Scribes modeled their edict on that issued by the founder of Sui Chang-an, indicating the intention to erect a truly magnificent metropolis. Planners had chosen Nara as the site because, in the words of the proclamation, "three mountains establish a bastion and the divining rod and tortoise shells both follow [Our desire]."[89] The actual construction of roads and bridges, however, would have to wait until after the harvest.

In the meantime, the government hastily assembled a team of seventeen officials to oversee the project. Of the two chiefs-of-operations, one had helped plan the great wall for Fujiwara Palace and was good at mathematics; the other specialized in economics. A second-in-command had held religious posts previously, while another was a scion of a local Nara family. The chief carpenter was Korean. Fujiwara no Fubito, the strongest aristocrat at court and maternal grandfather of Obito, had arranged the appointments.[90] The recently enthroned Gemmei (Mommu's consort) toured Nara at about the same time officials took their posts. Late in 708 an imperial prince announced the project to the gods at Ise Shrine. By the end of the year, the government had removed about ninety commoner houses from the site and held a rite to guarantee a pacific new capital, both signs that construction was starting.

For all of 709 there are only three entries in official annals, *The Chronicles of Japan Continued* (*Shoku Nihongi*), directly stating that construction was proceeding. The first entry concerns awards given to the foremen of labor gangs early in the fall; the second is an order to the project leaders to reinter any cadavers accidentally disturbed by the digging; the third entry refers to tax relief given to householders whom the government had displaced. Throughout the autumn of 709, the imperial palanquin continued its visits to the site of the new palace. Late in 709, however, there was a sign that all was not well. The court issued an order to the governors of Ōmi and the Kinai to prevent concealment of runaway laborers (*shichō*).[91] The problem was that unnamed persons (presumably provincial governors and the wealthy) were assigning such laborers to tasks for their own purposes, and in the end the laborers stayed with the concealing parties and did not proceed to Nara or return to their homes. The law mandated a search for six weeks, during which time both hiding workers and their employers could come forth without punishment. Harsh measures awaited those who did not comply within the specified time. This regulation suggests two points. First, commoner resistance to labor at Nara was sufficiently widespread to hamper the building of the new capital. Second, high aristocrats and local magnates desired to use laborers themselves and assisted those wishing to avoid work at the new capital. A further implication may be that the supply of labor was inadequate to meet the demands of the government and other parties simultaneously.

On the tenth day of the third month of 710, *The Chronicles of Japan Continued* observes that the court removed to Heijō "for the first time." The ministry for construction of palaces (*zōgū shō*) continued to exist and carry out repairs intermittently for the rest of the eighth century.[92] There can be little doubt that the Nara to which Gemmei relocated in 710 was unfinished.[93]

As a law issued in the fall of 711 states, the resistance of unskilled laborers was a severe problem and one of the major reasons that sounds of construction reverberated throughout the palace even after occupancy: "Recently many corvée laborers (*ekimin*) working on the palace still flee. Even though the court has proscribed such behavior it does not stop." Furthermore, even the great wall around the palace was incomplete, and protection of the imperial family was impossible.[94] There could be no returning to Fujiwara, however, because sometime in 711 it burned, along with Daikan daiji and several other temples.

Prohibitions alone could not stem the tide of runaway laborers. In the first month of 712, another edict suggests a reason that many avoided labor at Heijō: "As corvée laborers return to their native villages, their provisions run out and many starve by the side of the road; there are not a few corpses filling up ditches." The court directed governors to take pity on laborers and feed them, or at least see that their bodies were buried.[95] In the fall of 712 the government addressed the problem again, advocating that workers use their wages, which consisted of newly minted copper cash, to buy grain on the way home. This latter proclamation was as much an attempt to encourage the circulation of cash as it was a policy to aid suffering laborers.

From 713, entries directly reflecting conditions of construction at Heijō disappear. Late in that year the minister for palace building died in his post, having advanced only one degree in court rank during his tenure. In the autumn of 714 the government added six more scribes to the same ministry; it was not until the spring of 715 according to contemporary records that the audience hall and the main gate linking the palace to the city (*Suzaku mon*) were completed. Certainly living conditions at Nara Palace had improved, but in the spring of 715 the court appointed a new minister for palace building, perhaps indicating that work was still ongoing.

The Archaeology of Nara City _____

Although it was not as convenient to Osaka Bay as Fujiwara, the engineers who designed Heijō kept transportation routes in mind. (See Map 3.1.) As noted previously, the Lower Way (which may have formed the western boundary of Fujiwara) ran almost due north and became Suzaku Great Road, leading through the center of Heijō City to the front door of Nara Palace. Archaeologists have dug up this main street, discovering that its 74-meter width overlays the older Lower Way.[96] In addition, Middle Way (which may have defined the eastern edge of Fujiwara) took a similar northward path and became the easternmost road at Nara. In this way the court at Nara could maintain its overland contacts with both Asuka and Naniwa; to the north of Nara Palace the Kizu River provided water transportation to Osaka Bay (via the Yodo River) or Lake Biwa (via the Uji River).

The capital was essentially symmetrical and divided into a left and right half (2 kilometers east to west) on each side of Suzaku Great Road. (See Figure 3.3.) There were nine ranks (*jō*) and eight files, and planners further subdivided each ward (*bō*) into sixteen lots, normally of one *tsubo* (or one *chō*; 1.69 hectares). Two additional areas gave Nara its distinctive appearance: the Northern Grid (*hoppen*) north of the western half of the capital and the Outer Capital (*gekyō*), an eastern addition to the left half of Heijō. The Outer Capital was a sizable four ranks and three files in area (2.1 by 1.6 kilometers). Given that from the beginning designers allowed for Gangōji and the Fujiwara family temple Kōfukuji, which are situated in that area, it seems likely that the Outer Capital was part of the original plan for Nara.[97] Heijō measured 5.5 kilometers east-west, including the Outer Capital, and 4.5 kilometers north-south.

Archaeologists have proved that the checkerboard layout predicted by historical geographers from aerial photographs was fairly accurate.[98] The roads around the palace were the widest; especially important was the Great Avenue of the Second Rank (*nijō ōji*), an east-west thoroughfare that was 37 meters wide in front of the palace. Kishi Toshio determined that engineers of the mid-eighth century erected the main entrance for Tōdaiji at the end of this thoroughfare, and he has called Tōdaiji's gate the "eastern terminus for the Silk Road" because of all the exotic items found in Tōdaiji's storehouse.[99] Other streets in Heijō ranged from 5 to 25 meters in width; the lanes dividing files into lots were the narrowest. Most streets had ditches of varying breadths located on each side; wooden bridges usually spanned the ditches.

One interesting excavation project focused on the main south entrance into Nara and the Gate of the Encircling Wall (*rashō mon*). Archaeologists dis-

FIGURE 3.11

Prince Nagaya's residence.
Key: A. Princess Kibi's residence;
B. Prince Nagaya's residence;
C. Buddhist chapel; D. Kitchen;
E. Garden; F. Administrative offices;
G. Work stations; H. Second Rank
Great Avenue. *Source:* Machida Akira,
"Heijō-kyō," in Machida Akira and
Kitō Kiyoaki, eds., *Shinpan kodai
no Nihon* 6: *Kinki* II, p. 121.

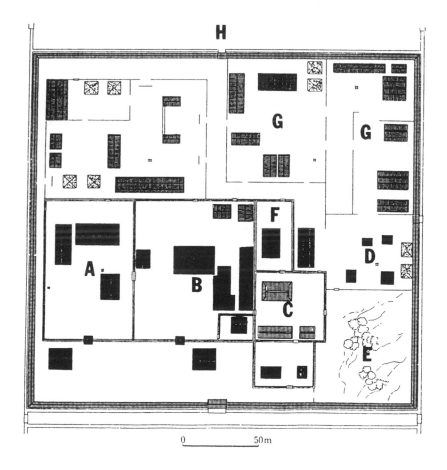

0   50m

covered the gate's foundation and concluded that workers built it anew at Nara rather than moving the old one from Fujiwara. Parts of a great wall, as well as a 28-meter-wide moat, came to light next to the gate, but it is believed that only a simple earthen embankment surrounded most of the city.

Archaeologists have conducted many excavations on aristocratic and commoner dwellings within Nara.[100] The builders of Heijō followed the practice first established in Northern Wei Luo-yang and set both location and size of residence according to social status. High-ranking bureaucrats, of whom there were about 120 in the early eighth century, lived in mansions situated north of the Fifth Rank, occupying at least one lot (one chō) apiece. The typical noble estate had a main residence building of about 100 square meters in the center of his or her lot, with several smaller Japanese-style buildings and a well placed nearby. A fence or gallery encircled this inner estate. Outside this inner estate were buildings for storage, kitchens, and the like, with a second or outer wall (gaikaku), sometimes tiled, and a ditch. Only about 7 percent of a noble's plot was occupied by buildings; the rest was for gardens and ponds.

The highest aristocrats, such as Prince Nagaya (four chō) and Fujiwara no Nakamaro (eight chō), were especially blessed.[101] Archaeologists have uncovered most of what is believed to have been Prince Nagaya's estate at the Third Rank and Second File. He was of imperial blood and held his highest appointment as minister of the left from 724 to 729, when his Fujiwara enemies forced him to commit suicide. Nagaya's land was surrounded by a roofed mud wall (tsuiji), rather than a simple fence; the inner estate was in the southwestern part of his lot and surrounded by a wooden fence. (See Figure 3.11.) Seven buildings and a well occupied Nagaya's inner estate, and the largest edifice, used as the prince's sleeping quarters, covered 354 square meters, being nearly as large as the emperor's sleeping quarters at Nara (593 square meters). The other buildings within this area may have been for concubines and servants.

Around Nagaya's inner estate were three other important compounds, each encircled by a roofed wall. To the southeast was a tiled structure that archaeologists suspect functioned as the prince's Buddhist altar. Just to its north was a smaller enclosure with a single building; most scholars believe that Nagaya's household administration oversaw the prince's lands, buildings, workers, guards, and other possessions from offices located there. Immediately to the west of Nagaya's central dwelling may have stood the residence of his wife, Princess Kibi, who occupied three buildings, including one large living unit. Outside Nagaya's and Kibi's personal quarters, in the northern and eastern parts of the lot were kitchens, storehouses, sleeping quarters for servants, and a place for transcribing sutras. In the southeastern corner of his lot, the prince even had his own pond where he could host parties for friends.

The luxurious accommodations of men such as Nagaya and Nakamaro contrast with the commoner's lot. In the first half of the eighth century, ordinary people received plots of one-sixteenth of a *chō* (about 900 square meters), about 1.5 percent of Nagaya's lot. Even commoners, however, usually demarcated their lots with a wooden fence or shrubbery. Typical residences included two to five buildings, one larger than the others, with a well. Gardens and other functional areas were also part of the typical commoner residence. One authority has pointed out that after 750, aristocratic lots became more expansive even as commoner plots decreased in size.[102]

The issue of sanitation has received much attention lately. In 1992, archaeologists at Fujiwara discovered the remains of an ancient toilet, which consisted of a hole in the ground with two boards across it for the user to squat on. The toilet was right next to a ditch, but there were no means for the waste to empty into it. Presumably residents and servants at Fujiwara simply collected human waste at each residence and disposed of it in one of the many ditches that meandered through each lot or near each road. It seems likely that human excrement accumulated within the city, where it was a source of infection. The egg cases of several human parasites survived in the toilet dug up at Fujiwara.[103] Archaeologists recovered what may have been the remnants of a late-eighth-century toilet over 60 meters northeast of Nagaya's mansion. Unlike the one at Fujiwara, this latrine siphoned water from a nearby ditch, continually washing away the droppings. A flushing latrine would have been a big improvement over the Fujiwara version. A similar facility has also been discovered at Heian, but written sources note that one Heian toilet backed up and flooded a nearby street, causing pedestrians endless trouble.[104]

The problem of sewage at Nara is related to its population. Sawada Goichi, renowned statistician of the 1920s, estimated that as many as 200,000 people lived in Nara, but the trend among contemporary historians is to doubt Sawada's calculation and favor a smaller number. One of Sawada's techniques was to compare Nara to a modern city of comparable area, but eighth-century Nara was not nearly so densely settled as twentieth-century urban centers. The ratio of buildings to total space at Nara ranged from 5 to 15 percent, while current standards are between 60 and 80 percent. A count of between 50,000 and 100,000 people seems a more reasonable estimate for Heijō's total population.[105]

In addition to elite and commoner residences, roads, walls, and ditches, Nara contained many temples and the eastern and western markets. A record from 720 states that the city already had forty-eight Buddhist temples within its precincts, and they rested on lots ranging in size from one to sixteen *chō*, or 1.69 to 27.04 hectares. Few excavations have focused on Nara's temples, many of which are located in the center of the modern municipality. More information is available on the eastern and western markets, which operated within four 250-square-meter sectors situated within the Left Capital (Eighth Rank, Third File) and Right Capital (Eighth Rank, Second File), respectively. (See Figure 3.3.) At the eastern market, archaeologists have uncovered a fenced-in area with a gate in the middle of one side and roads dividing the area into four parts. A canal 10 meters wide and 4 meters deep aided transportation to the market. The Japanese-style buildings found in the market area and a bridge over the canal continued to be used even after the court left Nara in 784. Offices for market overseers may have come to light in a central open space; locations for artisans shops are easily imagined.[106]

Heijō's Palaces

Even though archaeologists have dug only about 1 percent of Heijō, the picture of the city is relatively clear. Yet the more scientists excavate the palace, the more controversial its portrait becomes. Overarching generalizations about Heijō Palace (Heijō-kyū) are easy: it occupied the north central portion of the city as at Tang Chang-an; the palace compound was about 1.3 by 1 kilometer with an eastern extension; and there were twelve gates through its great wall (*ōgaki*). The details, however, are not easy. To make the scholarly debates about Nara Palace as comprehensible as possible, let us begin with the points of agreement and proceed from there to the most hotly debated questions.

Like Fujiwara, Heijō had a great wall encircling the palace. Archaeologists have found the barrier, which was 5 meters high and 2.7 meters wide at the base. The foundations for six of the twelve gates have also come to light: each was 10 by 25 meters. The wall was constructed using the pounded-earth technique that may possibly have been imported from Korea. Interestingly, scientists recovered a wooden tablet containing the date 728 from the bottom of the southern portion of the great wall, suggesting that problems delayed its completion until well into the Nara period.[107]

Also like Fujiwara, office buildings lay at the periphery of the palace immediately within the great wall. (See Figure 3.12.) Archaeologists recently uncovered an office compound just to the northwest of Mibu Gate in the southeastern corner of the palace; from the written evidence unearthed there most scholars have concluded that the buildings housed the war ministry. The compound was a square surrounded by a roofed mud wall 74.5 meters to a side; seven buildings stood at the north, east, and west edges of the square and there was an open area in the center. The larger structures measured 6 by 21 meters and had stone foundations and tiled roofs. In addition to the war ministry, archaeologists have located the ministry of rites (on the northeastern side of Mibu Gate), as well as the government and imperial kitchens (*daizen shiki; naizen shi*) with their giant wells; the office for the brewing of rice wine (*zōshū shi*) and its pure spring and large vessels; and the bureau of horses (*meryō*) complete with barns.[108]

Ponds and gardens for relaxing and entertaining were also situated near the great wall. The largest pond was in the northwestern corner of the palace, while in the southeastern corner engineers designed another complex called the "eastern gardens" (*tōen*).[109] The largest of all aristocratic preserves, the pine grove garden (*shōrin'en*), rested 240 meters outside the great wall to the north and occupied half a square kilometer in area. Around parts of its perimeter the

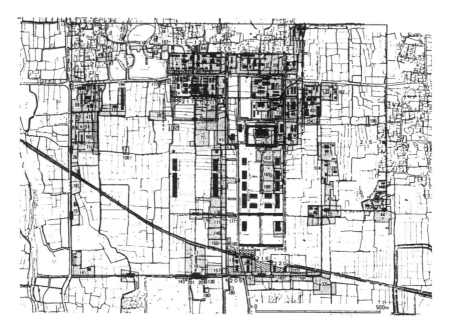

FIGURE 3.12 Excavations of Offices at Heijō Palace. *Key:* 205 and 214. Ministry of war; 220. Ministry of rites; 215-13. Great kitchen; 50 and 71. Horse stables; 40. Office for brewing rice wine. *Source: Heijō-kyūseki hakkutsu chōsa bu: Hakkutsu chōsa gaihō*, p. 2. © Nara Kokuritsu Bunkazai Kenkyūjo.

pine grove garden had an earthern wall with a base 2.7 meters wide. Tiles from the wall may be dated prior to 710 and came from Fujiwara. The pine grove garden was probably modeled after a similar preserve north of Tang Chang-an.[110]

Turning to the central palace and the domicile of the emperor, one notes the great efforts expended to build Heijō. Archaeologists have discovered the outlines of a large keyhole tomb beneath the imperial residence, and they have concluded that laborers tore down the tumulus and removed the earth. Scholars have located the source of the foundation stones used at Nara in mountains in Asuka and Osaka prefecture. Timbers for the palace came from near Lake Biwa and what would later become Kyoto; workmen bound them into rafts and shipped them by river to the construction site. Pillars ranged from 20 to 50 centimeters in diameter, and the largest posts came from trees estimated at three hundred years old. Tiles manufactured for Heijō originated in kilns at nearby Mount Nara on the Yamashiro-Yamato border.[111]

The layout of Heijō Palace becomes considerably more complicated as one enters the central area: there are eastern and western halves, each with two layers. (See Figure 3.13.) Until recently archaeologists and historians believed that

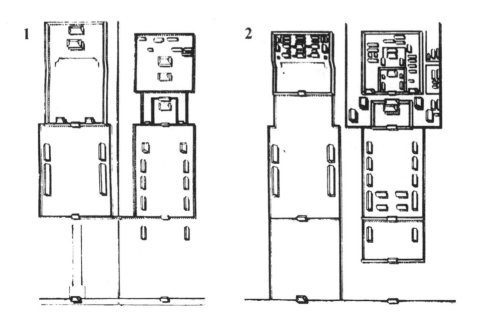

FIGURE 3.13   Heijō Palace: Early (1) and Late (2). *Source:* Machida Akira and Kitō Kiyoaki, eds., *Shinpan kodai no Nihon 6: Kinki* II, p. 393.

each half was a palace unto itself and thought that the imperial family moved from the eastern half to the western half at some point during the Nara period. The discovery in 1985 of a lower level for the eastern half showed the inadequacies of this older theory, however. Scholars have now rejected it, even though much published material still reflects the old theory.[112] Today there are two overarching questions about Heijō Palace: why did the court construct both an eastern and western half, and when did workers rebuild the palace to produce two strata?

To examine the current state of knowledge, let us begin with the lower layer. The western half, which officials entered through Suzaku Gate in the early Nara era, was divided into north and south sections.[113] A roofed wall surrounded the northern part, which contained two tiled edifices aligned in tandem and resting on raised bricklike foundations. A gate led from the northern section to the south, and on either side of the gate were two turrets built not long after Nara became the capital. Scholars are unanimous in the opinion that the main building in the northern section housed Nara's first audience hall, which workers probably did not construct anew but moved from Fujiwara when the court first occupied Nara in 710. This structure was dismantled and hauled to Kuni when Shōmu transferred the capital there in 740, and it remained there when the government renamed Heijō the capital in 745.

The character of the southern section of the western half is still a mystery.[114] In 710 this large open space may have been vacant, but by the 720s it contained long continental-style structures that stood end-to-end, two each along the walls of the east and west flanks.[115] At first a wooden fence, and later a roofed wall, encircled the entire section. The southern section probably functioned as an adjunct to the audience hall, but it had too few halls to have been the official compound. Some believe that it was a ceremonial ground where official receptions took place; others think it was a copy of an edifice within the palace of Tang Chang-an (Hanyuan dian).[116]

Whereas the western half of the lower layer had two sections, the eastern half had three: north, central, and south. A wooden fence with a gate facing north encircled the southern part; the twelve halls that have turned up in this section confirm that it was the official compound, built in the Japanese style (no tiles or foundation stones) when Nara became the capital in 710. Excavations of the north end of the southern section have revealed remains suggesting that it was the site of ceremonies performed by either Gemmei or Shōmu.[117]

The central section had two wooden fences, one surrounding the perimeter and the other demarcating the main building. This building occupied the center; one authority thinks it may have been the living quarters for the heir apparent, but this is only speculation. The northern section served as the imperial residence, complete with a wooden fence around the perimeter, and it contained several Japanese-style structures. By the time of Emperor Shōmu, around 730, planners had divided the imperial residence into four clusters of buildings, the postholes of which archaeologists have laid bare.[118]

Early Nara Palace looked different from any imperial enclosure ever devised in Japan. There was an audience hall, as in Fujiwara, but it was not located between the imperial residence and the official compound; it was off to the side north of a magnificent open space of indeterminate function. Several theories have emerged to explain the arrangement of edifices at early Nara. One states that designers built the western half to impress upon foreigners the wonder of the imperial institution; another suggests that accession to the imperial dignity took place in this half. Yet another argues that the eastern half was a Japanese-style counter to the Chinese western half and says that the eastern section was what written sources called the emperor's Palace of Refuge (*daian den*).[119] The historical record for the early Nara period adds further complications. *The Chronicles of Japan Continued* notes that by the 720s the palace contained an area called the "middle palace" (*chūgū*); most experts believe that this term refers to the eastern half of Heijō Palace, perhaps even the imperial residence in its northern section. But this point is still speculative, another uncertainty among many.

Additional problems arise when one examines the upper level of Heijō Palace. (See Figure 3.13.) Once again there are two halves, but it is clear that the eastern half had become the focus of court activity. Builders expanded the Mibu Gate linking Nara city to the palace, and they shut off the formerly all-important Suzaku Gate to its west. Although it had lost its central function as home to a magnificent audience hall, the western half continued to exist in the later Nara era. The southern section of the western half—the area of greatest controversy in the lower layer—looked much as it had before, with two long halls end-to-end in the east and west flanks. There was a gallery enclosing three sides of the southern section, which was actually somewhat smaller. The northern section of the western half (occupied by the audience hall in the early Nara period) was crowded with twenty-seven regularly arranged wooden-shingled, Japanese-style edifices.[120] Some believe that this section was a replica of a palace layout in Tang Chang-an, a product of Fujiwara no Nakamaro's sinophilic dreams, although sources do not refer to the edifices until after Nakamaro's demise. Most think that this section was Emperor Shōtoku's "Western Palace," where she entertained her reputed lover the monk Dōkyō.[121]

The eastern half maintained the general spatial arrangement of the early Nara period but added a fourth section in the far south where two new, continental-style "morning gathering halls" were located. To the immediate north stood the standard twelve morning halls of the official compound, also built in continental style. Despite the new architectural style, the morning halls of Heijō were smaller than their counterparts at Fujiwara. To the north of the official compound was the audience hall, surrounded by a double gallery in an area much smaller than the audience hall in the western half of the lower level.[122] Due north of the audience hall through two gates was the imperial residence and its four clusters of Japanese-style structures—in the same place as in the early Nara period but encircled by a gallery and not just a fence. A second gallery surrounded both the audience hall and imperial residence. In sum, the eastern half of the upper layer at Heijō Palace fit the customary scholarly model with its imperial residence, audience hall, and official compound aligned north to south.

One authority on Nara Palace has summarized the overall appearance of the two levels as follows:

> Although the remains from the early layer give forth a stirring yet simple impression, they were immature and unfinished. In contrast to this, the remains of the upper stratum show a delicate but regular design, even though each edifice is somewhat undersized [in comparison with the lower level].[123]

Scholars have surmised that designers planned Nara in two halves because they wanted Heijō to look more like Tang Chang-an, which had one palace apiece in the north and south. No one has made a detailed argument, however, to flesh out this general theory.[124] The idea that the Japanese court may have tried to copy Tang Chang-an more closely than it did at Fujiwara fits the general pattern of the adaptation of Chinese-style institutions to Japan.

The issue of Heijō's eastern and western halves is intimately bound up with the hotly debated problem of the upper stratum's date. The dating problem is so controversial that archaeologists at the Nara National Cultural Properties Research Institute, which is responsible for the excavation, disagree among themselves. Those in charge of writing archaeological reports contend that the upper level should be dated to the years immediately after Shōmu returned to Nara in 745. This conclusion rests upon two archaeological foundations: first, that the design for the tiles of the morning halls and audience hall of the upper layer dates back no farther than the mid-eighth century; and second, that two wooden tablets recovered from a posthole of the lower stratum contained the dates 729 and 731, suggesting that the upper level was built somewhat after those years.[125]

But neither of these pieces of evidence is altogether convincing. Archaeologists are hesitant to give absolute dates for tiles. The proposed age of each tile design depends on its relation to others' age, so if one dates "later" tiles differently, the dating of an entire range of designs may be pushed backward or forward. If one dismisses the tile evidence, then there are only the wooden tablets, a flimsy foundation on which to build an entire theory. Another problem with the hypothesis that workers built the upper level of Nara Palace in 745 is the implication for the imperial family. After the court decided to leave for Kuni, it ordered the audience hall transferred to Kuni from the western half of the lower level. In 743, the emperor declared the need for branch temples throughout Japan and soon thereafter donated the materials from his old audience hall to Yamashiro province. As of 745, then, there was no audience hall for several years until workers raised the new smaller version in the eastern half of the upper layer sometime later.

The absence of an audience hall may seem like a small point, but to the court it was the "Hall of the Great Ultimate," analogous to the North Star in the heavens. Just as there is only one Pole Star around which all else revolves, there could be only one emperor. If there was no audience hall, politics lost its orientation. More concretely, the audience hall was where the imperial throne resided; another less appropriate building would have had to serve as home for Shōmu when he reviewed his bureaucrats or met with foreign ambassadors. Having no official throne room was tantamount to having no emperor—for as long as a decade. Advocates of the post-Kuni facelift for Heijō have a difficult time explaining the vacuum.

Another major weakness of the post-745 dating is that written sources make no mention of it. Would the court have undertaken so major a project and remained silent about it? Surely such a serious undertaking would have received attention from chroniclers interested in the fate of the imperial family.

There are two viable alternatives to the post-745 date. Many historians and archaeologists choose the period from about 720 to 730 or so and assert that the palace was being rebuilt in preparation for Shōmu's accession. Politically this hypothesis makes good sense, for Gemmei had planned and constructed Heijō as the symbol of her descendant, Emperor Shōmu. Nara was Shōmu's city. There is strong written evidence to support this claim. After 717, building at Nara Palace seems to have quieted for a few years, although the palace was unfinished. But *The Biography of Fujiwara no Muchimaro*, which pertains to a prominent aristocrat, states that in 721 the court appointed Muchimaro the minister for construction of palaces (*zōgū kyō*): "He led forth engineers and carpenters, guided them through the palace, and they rebuilt it as of old; as a result the palace became extremely beautiful, and people learned respect for the emperor."[126] Muchimaro continued to head palace construction until at least 726.[127]

Apart from the dating of tiles and the two wooden tablets, there are two major problems with the notion of rebuilding Nara in the years right after 721. First, even if workers did not finish the structures in the upper level until 730, it is doubtful that timbers used in posthole construction would have lasted from 730 to the end of the Nara era. Of course, the buildings may have undergone repairs over those fifty years, as the longevity of the ministry for construction of palaces suggests. Second, a difficulty again arises from the audience hall. If workers refurbished Heijō Palace at this date, there would have been two "Halls of the Great Ultimate." When one recalls that the audience hall symbolized the Pole Star and the emperor himself, then having two audience halls was analogous to asserting that there were two Pole Stars or two emperors, an impossibility. There could no more be two audience halls than there could be none.

In addition to 745 and 721, there is a third alternative for the raising of a new Nara Palace: the time around 760, the heyday of the sinophile Fujiwara no Nakamaro. According to *The Chronicles of Japan Continued,* in 757 Nakamaro invited his sister the Emperor Kōken to his spacious Tamura Estate situated at the Fourth Rank, Second File (due south of Hokkeji) while workers reconstructed the palace. Then in 760 the court named a new minister for construction of palaces, and in 761 the government canceled New Year's Day business because the palace was still in an unfinished state. In the tenth month of the same year, the annal asserts, Emperor Junnin went to his erstwhile residence at Hora while laborers refurbished Nara. Two months later the government omitted traditional New Year's Day ceremonies because of the rebuilding of Heijō Palace. Although the court returned to Nara by midyear, it continued to appoint officials to oversee construction until Nakamaro's death in 764.[128] This third alternative for the dating of the upper layer of Nara Palace has both good and bad points. On the positive side, it fits with the image of Nakamaro as a sinophile as well as the archaeological testimony from roof tiles and the 729 and 731 wooden tablets. As might be expected, however, the 760 date once again presents the problem of no audience hall, only in a more extreme form—a fifteen-year gap, not just five to ten as in the 745 scenario.

Pending conclusive evidence, which is unlikely to appear, Japanese archaeologists and historians will continue to argue about the dating and plan of

Heijō Palace. Those who emphasize archaeological evidence will weigh the tile designs and wooden tablets as paramount and date the building of the upper layer at 745; those who rely mainly on written sources will envision a refurbishing of Heijō Palace in the 720s by Muchimaro or else in the 760s by Nakamaro, which date also accommodates the archaeological data. The archaeology of Naniwa and Kuni shows that information about other capitals can help scholars resolve this problem.

The Second Palace at Naniwa

In 725, the ambitious, newly crowned Emperor Shōmu decided to revive the idea of dual capitals by building a palace at Naniwa for a third time. He named Fujiwara no Umakai the leader of the project. In 732 Isokawa no Hirafu took Umakai's place and the court awarded gifts to all those responsible for the construction efforts. In 734 the project seems to have been near completion, at least the court doled out residential lots to lucky aristocrats. Apart from these brief notices, documents of the early 730s describe activities at Naniwa such as the provisioning of laborers from nearby provinces with food and rice wine; the substitution of new workers for runaways; and the dispatch and payment of carpenters from as far away as northern Kyushu and the Kanto. One jurist of the early 730s even defined a laborer as one who toiled at Naniwa.[129]

Archaeologists have discovered Shōmu's palace in the upper level of the Naniwa site, above the ashes from the fire of the late seventh century.[130] (See Figure 3.14.) Later Naniwa had three sections: an imperial residence in the north, audience hall in the middle, and official compound in the south. The imperial residence possessed a double gallery of 180 meters along its east-west perimeter; an inner fence surrounded the living quarters. The grounds containing the audience hall were 108 by 80 meters with a main tiled edifice. The official compound was 161 by 178 meters encircled by a gallery; inside were eight long, continental-style structures arranged around a courtyard that opened northward.

As even a casual glance at the plan for Shōmu's Naniwa suggests, it had much in common with the eastern half of the upper layer of Heijō Palace. Both layouts contained the imperial residence–audience hall–official compound on a north-south axis, but Naniwa Palace was somewhat smaller than Nara. Both audience halls were the same size. The similarity between Shōmu's palace at Naniwa and the eastern half of the upper stratum of Nara Palace has led many archaeologists and historians to conclude that they were erected at the same time. It makes sense that the court would refurbish Nara Palace, as attested to by historical records, and then turn to the secondary capital at

1

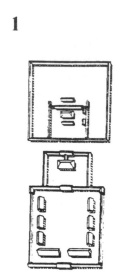

2

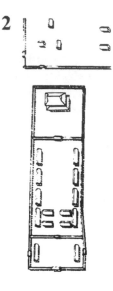

FIGURE 3.14
Naniwa Palace (1),
Kuni Palace (2), and
Kuni Capital (3).
Key: A. Kizu River;
B. Kuni Palace;
C. Mount Kase.
Sources: Naniwa and
Kuni palaces: Machida
Akira and Kitō Kiyoaki,
eds., *Shinpan kodai no
Nihon* 6: *Kinki* II, p. 392;
Capital at Kuni: Nakatani
Masaharu, "Kuni-kyō,"
in Tsuboi Kiyotari, ed.,
*Kodai o kangaeru kyūto
hakkutsu*, pp. 176–177.

3

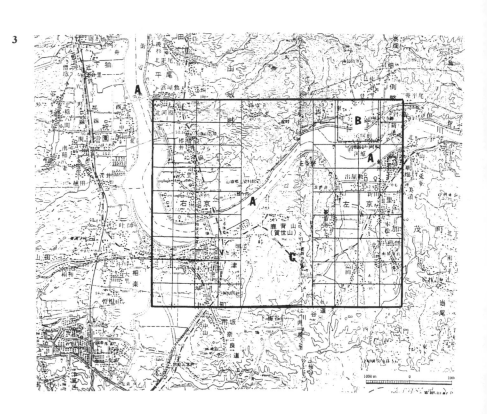

Naniwa and remake it in a similar image. Some have noted, however, that instead of using Nara as the model for Naniwa, the opposite could also have been true, though it does not seem in character for the ambitious Shōmu to have modeled his main residence on his secondary capital. To the extent that the upper level of Naniwa Palace is a relevant consideration, it suggests that workers rebuilt Heijō Palace in the late 720s and early 730s, not after 745.

Kuni

Shōmu was perhaps the pivotal figure of the eighth century. For decades statesmen planned the future of the Chinese-style state on his accession to the throne. His government spent massive amounts of wealth constructing portions of Nara and rejuvenating the burnt-out ruins of Naniwa. All of this planning could do the court no good, however, when in 735 Japan imported a smallpox virus that racked Shōmu's kingdom for three years and brought him to contrition. To deepen the emperor's heartache, in 740 Fujiwara no Hirotsugu raised the standard of revolt. Shōmu was so alarmed that he fled to Ise Shrine and thought about going all the way to eastern Honshu (*tōgoku*).

While Shōmu lingered at Ise late in 740, the most influential aristocrat at court, Tachibana no Moroe, made a visit to the administrative village of Kuni in Yamashiro province, a short distance overland from Nara.[131] Probably at the suggestion of Moroe, Shōmu proceeded to Kuni and announced that he was moving the capital there. Shōmu held court there on the first day of 741 even though there was no great wall to protect him. The audience hall was transferred to Kuni from Nara and the annals of Shōmu's reign place it at the new capital by the sixteenth day of the first month. Three months later, Shōmu commanded that the weapons used to guard the court be moved from Heijō to Kuni. Shortly thereafter he banned aristocrats from living in Nara.

By the autumn of 741, workers moved the eastern and western markets from Nara to Kuni. Sources state that to raise a capital at Kuni, officials conscripted 5,500 laborers (*ekifu*) from the four provinces of Yamato, Kawachi, Settsu, and Yamashiro and employed them as workers. Residents received lots there. The Kizu River flowed through the precincts of Kuni, but no laborers willing to construct bridges came forward, and so the court drafted youthful Buddhist acolytes (*ubasoku*), probably led by the well-known monk Gyōki.[132] The government promised them the tonsure if they would construct a bridge; seven hundred and fifty received rewards.

On the first day of 742, Shōmu bestowed gifts from a half-finished audience hall. Later in the first month he praised twenty commoners who had come to take up their residence in Kuni. A year and a half after the decision to move, laborers still had not finished the great wall, so Shōmu began to bestow court ranks to encourage them. The court requested monetary payments from provincial governors to recompense laborers erecting bridges and laying out roads. At the end of 743, *The Chronicle of Japan Continued* asserts: "Since [Shōmu] transferred to Kuni, it is now the fourth year; the effect has been little, but the exhaustion of resources has been beyond calculation."[133]

Shōmu soon decamped to Shigaraki, another village in Ōmi province, and stopped all construction on Kuni.[134] But Kuni remained popular, as revealed by two facts: officials split evenly when he polled them about whether they preferred Kuni or Naniwa as a capital, while nonofficial merchants favored Kuni. Six weeks later, however, the court shipped the throne and court weapons to Naniwa and allowed persons to move freely from Kuni. Shōmu made one more trip to Kuni, and when peasants saw his palanquin they greeted it with shouts: "Long live (*banzai*) Shōmu!"[135] In the fifth month of 745, Shōmu renamed Heijō his capital, probably to save resources and return stability to the government.

The court's flirtation with Kuni lasted only three years, making it one of Japan's least important Chinese-style capitals, and archaeologists paid it little attention until about twenty years ago. Since then, however, their findings have suggested that engineers planned Kuni on a much smaller scale than either Heijō or Naniwa. (See Figure 3.14.) There are widespread doubts that the city at Kuni was ever much more than a plan on paper; excavations completed thus far have not uncovered any roads or ditches confirming the existence of a metropolitan grid outside the palace. According to most scholars, even if workers completed some parts of the checkerboard layout, Kuni would have been one of the world's strangest capitals with its sizable hill and the Kizu River in a central "no-man's-land" and the palace in the northern area of the left half of the city.[136]

Recent excavations have revealed more about Kuni Palace. At one time scholars thought it was about the same size as Nara, but digging in 1991 showed that Kuni Palace was only about half as wide. (See Figure 3.14.) Scientists have also found that laborers never finished leveling the earth, so important in hilly terrain like Kuni's, although it is thought that diggers removed one tumulus near the audience hall. This hall came from Heijō, as confirmed by tiles and measurements, and it is plausible that other structures were transferred to Kuni from nearby Mikahara Detached Palace. A few postholes have come to light where one might expect the imperial residence to have been, but the holes are not aligned with the north-south axis of the audience hall. Archaeologists have also laid bare the remains of a fence for the imperial residence, complete with postholes that were filled with broken tiles, probably because the posts had been removed for use elsewhere. Remains of buildings where one might anticipate the official compound also suggest later recycling as residences.[137]

Altogether Kuni is poor in artifacts and other evidence of structures, showing that the impulsive move, short span of construction, and mountainous terrain took their toll. Future excavations will probably make the picture clearer, but still Kuni will be best known as Japan's most short-lived Chinese-style capital. This conclusion also has an impact on the debate about when the upper stratum at Nara Palace came into being. For if the court could not muster the wealth and labor force to complete Kuni, then one must wonder if it could have done so at Heijō in 745. Several facts—the drafting of Buddhist acolytes to do hard labor, the recycling of old timbers and tiles, the constant flight of workers, and, not least, the very unfinished nature of Kuni itself—imply that the government lacked the resources to bring major projects to completion. The history of the last two major Chinese-style capitals, Nagaoka and Heian, reinforces this impression.

NAGAOKA AND HEIAN

The construction of two new Chinese-style capitals at the end of the eighth century calls up an image of a vigorous imperial government operating from a growing economic and demographic base. After all, planners designed the cities of Nagaoka and Heian to be big, and their palace enclosures were impressive as well, as large as Heijō's and filled with awe-inspiring continental-style edifices.[138] Digging through old documents and the layers of earth under Kyoto has shown, however, how very superficial is the impression of continued expansion.

The Historical Record on Nagaoka

Historians have advanced many reasons for the removal of the capital from Nara to Nagaoka: the alleged desire of newly ascended Emperor Kammu (r. 781–806) to distance himself from Temmu and emphasize his heritage as a descendant of Tenji's line; the wish to be free of defilement resulting from the death of the preceding emperor at Nara; and the need to escape forces that opposed a reinvigorated imperial institution, notably Buddhist temples and jealous aristocrats. To explain the choice of Nagaoka, scholars have noted its convenient central location within the road and river network of the Kinai as well as Kammu's ties with immigrant Korean families living in the vicinity.[139]

Some historians believe that Kammu's intent to move from Nara became clear as early as 782, when he abolished the ministry for construction of palaces, an office that oversaw the refurbishing of Heijō.[140] They argue that the ministry's supplies were sufficient for the short period that Kammu wanted to stay at Heijō. About two years later, in the spring of 784, the court sent officials to examine Nagaoka village in Yamashiro province as a possible site for a new capital; within a month of their dispatch Kammu had named emissaries for the building of Nagaoka Palace and construction had begun.

If written sources are to be believed, the raising of the essential edifices at Nagaoka Palace took place in record time. By the sixth month of 784, the government had assembled provisions and wages for the workforce. When people who were living on the hill where engineers planned to build the palace objected to the project, the court paid them 43,000 sheaves of rice to leave. Kammu spent 680,000 sheaves to persuade aristocrats to settle in Nagaoka. After three provinces provided the wood to build Yamasaki Bridge at a strategic point south of Nagaoka, Kammu appointed emissaries to calm the populace at Heijō and in the eleventh month he moved to Nagaoka. Through the end of 784 the court busily awarded court ranks and prizes to officials and commoners who had given gifts of lumber, food, and other supplies, and Kammu celebrated the first day of 785 in his new imperial residence and audience hall.

The undertaking at Nagaoka proceeded under the watchful gaze of the emperor, as records from the summer and fall of 785 show. In midsummer of that year, according to *The Chronicles of Japan Continued*, Kammu employed 314,000 people to build the new palace. As the leading expert on labor in ancient Japan has argued, this tabulation referred not to the total number of laborers but rather to worker-days; the number could reflect about 3,500 workers hired for a season of ninety days, for example.[141] In any case, within a month the wall around the offices for the council of state had gone up. Most buildings were still unfinished, however, and workmen were laboring day and night even a month later.

Archaeologists excavating Nagaoka have found plentiful evidence of the feverish pitch of construction at the new capital, including requests written on wooden tablets for nails, workers, and lumber. Roof tiles recovered in the palace area show that Kammu's determination to finish Nagaoka led him to employ agencies for the building of Tōdaiji and Saidaiji, temples located in Nara. Like his predecessor Shōmu, Kammu impressed Buddhist acolytes (*ubasoku*) as construction workers with promises of elevation to the priesthood.[142]

When construction at Nagaoka was at its zenith, assassins murdered Fuji-wara no Tanetsugu, Kammu's confidant and overseer of the project. A con-spiracy against Tanetsugu came to light and those responsible received pun-ishment. But Prince Sawara, the heir apparent, was among the suspects, and he soon died after a hunger strike. This incident cast a pall over the entire attempt to move to Nagaoka, and it eventually appears to have resulted in another transfer of the capital.[143]

Building at Nagaoka continued for the next few years. In 786, the court gave rewards to merchants settling in the city, and also in that year laborers completed structures for the council of state and officials took their seats at work. In 788, tax relief was issued to provinces sending workers to Nagaoka; in 789, Kammu moved from the original imperial residence to a new domicile named the Eastern Palace, for reasons that will become clear as this chapter proceeds. Later that year, officials in charge of construction donated rice wine and food to needy workers, and the government awarded high court ranks and other gifts to its patrons. As late as 791, eight provincial headquarters car-ried out an order to move gates from Heijō Palace to Nagaoka.

By 793, however, Kammu had decided that Nagaoka was dangerously inauspicious, based on several relatives' unexpected deaths and the outbreak of famines and epidemics. He also seems to have desired to establish a grander, more imperial city. Early in that year he had officials investigate Uda village a little to the north as a possible imperial home, and by the tenth month of 794 he had moved to his new domicile of "Peace and Tranquility" (Heian). Building had proceeded at Nagaoka throughout the ten years it was the capi-tal, and although it was "even in the end unfinished," its essential structures had come into existence in about one-quarter of the time required at Nara.[144] How had Kammu done it?

The City at Nagaoka

Archaeologists have conducted a surprising number of excavations within the old city of Nagaoka. They have ascertained that in most important respects its plan resembled Nara's, with the palace located in the north central portion of the city and nine ranks ($jō$) and four files in each half of the grid. (See Figure 3.15.) Also like Nara, Suzaku Great Road and Second Rank Great Avenue were wider than other streets, but engineers had arranged Nagaoka's checkerboard layout so that most residential lots were the same size, usually about 1.4 hec-tares (3.5 acres). The only exception to the rule came in lots fronting on Naga-oka Palace, which were slightly smaller. Since lots at Heian were uniformly 1.4

FIGURE 3.15
The Capital at Nagaoka.
Key: A. Nagaoka Palace;
B. Markets; C. Katsura River;
D. Suzaku Great Road.
Source: Satō Makoto,
"Nagaoka-kyō kara
Heian-kyō e," in Sasayama
Haruo, ed., *Kodai o kangaeru
Heian no miyako*, p. 55.

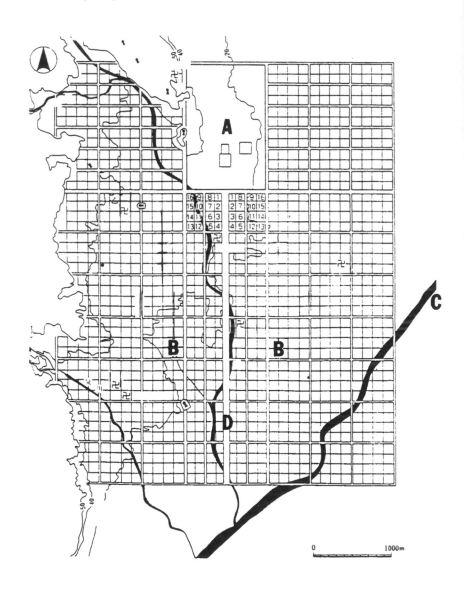

hectares, Nagaoka represents a transitional plan from Nara to Heian and demonstrates that trial and error played an important role in the development of Japan's first cities.[145]

While excavating throughout old Nagaoka over the last fifty years, archaeologists have found ditches, roads, and walls whose measurements were characteristic of other Chinese-style capitals in Japan. There was a distance of 70.9 meters between the walls flanking Suzaku Great Road; other roads vary from 4 to 24 meters in width.[146] It should be noted, however, that no remains have come to light for the Eighth and Ninth Ranks of the city, and many areas south of the Fifth Rank exhibit a layout different from areas to the north.[147] There is considerable evidence of commoner occupation, including postholes for soldiers' huts containing wooden tablets requesting rice wine.[148]

Nagaoka Palace

The secret behind Kammu's ability to build a new capital so rapidly despite his many political enemies and financial woes lay buried beneath the earth until recently.[149] At first glance, the original Nagaoka Palace looks like a scaled-down version of Fujiwara or the eastern half of the upper stratum of Heijō, since it has an imperial residence, audience hall, and official compound on a north-south axis in the center of the palace grounds. (See Figure 3.16.) Archaeologists have also uncovered a later imperial residence to the southeast of the first. The audience hall had an encircling double gallery, but the buildings of the hall were not connected to the gallery, a characteristic Nagaoka shared with Heian. The official compound contained eight morning halls, fewer than Fujiwara, Nara, or Heian, and measured 159 square meters.

In addition to this central complex, archaeologists have excavated five other areas thought to hold offices. To the south of the later imperial residence, they have found what many believe to have been the foundations for the buildings that housed the council of state; in another 120-square-meter section west of the official compound some think they have discovered the remains of the horse bureau (*meryō*). To the northwest of the official compound excavators have laid bare the remnants of buildings both with and without foundation stones. Other areas north of the audience hall and southeast of the official compound could have housed the treasury ministry and the palace for Heir Apparent Sawara (*tōgū*), respectively.[150]

The clue to Kammu's rapid success, however, comes from the roof tiles of the continental-style structures. (See Figure 3.16.) About 90 percent of the roof

FIGURE 3.16

Tiles Used for Nagaoka Palace.
Key: 1. Audience hall; 2. Official
compound; 3. Offices west of the
official compound (western section);
4. Offices west of official compound
(eastern section); 5. Offices south of
official compound; 6. Offices south of
second imperial residence; 7. Second
imperial residence; 8. Northern offices.
Source: Yamanaka Akira and Shimizu
Miki, "Nagaoka-kyō," in Tsuboi
Kiyotari, ed., *Kodai o kangaeru
kyūto hakkutsu,* p. 201.

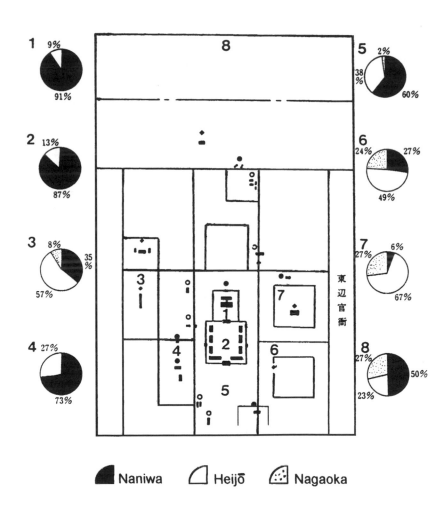

tiles for the edifices of the official compound and the audience hall are identical to tiles used for Shōmu's palace at Naniwa; those not coming from Naniwa originated at Heijō Palace. Workers baked no special Nagaoka-style tiles for either the audience hall or the official compound, which were almost precisely the same size as comparable structures at Naniwa. Of the eight blocks of office buildings for which significant amounts of data are available, only five utilized tiles freshly baked for Nagaoka. In most cases the percentage of Nagaoka tiles was small; Figure 3.16 shows that the highest proportion of new tiles used for any structure was about one-fourth.

Thus scholars are now unanimous in thinking that the secret to the rapid construction of Nagaoka Palace lay in Kammu's near-total utilization of preexisting structures from Naniwa and later Heijō.[151] This strategy was probably forced on Kammu by at least four factors: he needed to minimize the political resistance to the move from Nara; to conserve on outlays from the treasury; to reduce further deforestation around the new capitals; and to save labor. To be sure, Kammu's use of recycled structures was not a new practice. When the court moved from Fujiwara to Nara, for example, workers were ordered to hollow out pillars used in the great wall at the old capital and employ them as troughs at the new.[152] At Kuni, the court moved and reassembled the audience hall used at Heijō. But these efforts at recycling were small in scale; Kammu's nearly total reliance on the preexisting structures of Naniwa and Nara was unprecedented.

Eventually, as resistance to the move lessened and more people left Nara, the project also borrowed tiles, timbers, and stones from there. Of the eight sections of Nagaoka Palace for which information has come to light, on average about a third of the tiles came from Nara. The reliance on materials from that capital is particularly conspicuous at the second imperial residence, which was raised in 788 and 789 due east of the audience hall. Only 6 percent of the tiles for the later imperial residence were originally from Naniwa. This building also included the highest percentage of new materials made at Nagaoka. The mixture of Nagaoka, Heijō, and Naniwa elements resulted in a unique structure that was the direct ancestor of the imperial residence at Heian in terms of spatial design, location, and size.[153] The move from the original residence to the southeastern domicile probably signaled Kammu's tiring of the older Naniwa residence as well as his desire to create a new precedent.

Far from representing another grandiose Chinese-style capital, Nagaoka symbolized the political and economic constraints that tethered the ambitious Kammu. Not only was the palace smaller and made from recycled materials,

Nagaoka epitomized retrenchment in yet another way. When Kammu utilized the timbers and tiles from Naniwa and Nara to build Nagaoka, he in effect abolished Japan's on-again, off-again system of dual capitals.[154] Maintaining two political centers in the Kinai cost too much in men and materials. The era when each new emperor could construct a new palace was over, but Kammu would try once more.

The Building of Heian

Kammu probably considered Heian as a possible site for a new capital a year before investigators actually examined Uda village in the first month of 793.[155] A local family, the Hata of Sagano, appears to have played a crucial role in determining the location. Once Kammu had made the decision, events moved rapidly; within a week he had left Nagaoka Palace so that workers could begin to tear down buildings. Emissaries from the court announced the transfer of the capital at Ise and Kamo shrines, and in the third month Kammu himself toured the site. Also in the third month, the court ordered bureaucrats above the fourth tier (*sakan*) and all aristocrats to provide laborers. This command may have marked the start of construction, and it was a significant departure from the state-run corvée system previously used to obtain workers. By summer the government had directed several provinces to raise new gates for the palace. Kammu visited the site, bestowing gifts of clothing on 139 officials and foremen. By that fall a grid layout for the city must have existed because the court specified lots for residents.

Officials canceled New Year's Day ceremonies at Nagaoka in 794 because offices there had been dismantled, and in the fourth month Kammu toured the building site once more. By that summer the government had overseen the moving of the eastern and western markets from Nagaoka and had hired five thousand cleaners to wash the palace. Soon provinces presented eleven thousand sheaves of rice to women of the consort's office as a start-up fund so they could erect new homes; in the tenth month a commoner donated another thousand bushels (*koku*) of rice to the project. By the end of that month, after receiving further donations from courtiers and the headquarters of Yamashiro province, Kammu had moved into the new palace. In the eleventh month Kammu sanctioned the use of new characters for Yamashiro, changing their meaning from "the other side of the mountains" to "mountain fortress," and named his new capital Heian, "Peace and Tranquility."

The audience hall at Heian was still incomplete on the first day of 795; later that year Kammu watched carpenters working on the morning halls of the official compound. By New Year's Day of 796 laborers seem to have finished the audience hall, and later that year specifications appeared for houses in the city. Construction must have continued, because in 796 new officials received appointments as engineers for the construction of the palace. That year the government also dedicated grounds for two new temples, Tōji and Saiji, which were to flank Suzaku Great Road in the Ninth Rank.

Despite four years of labor, Heian was only partly complete. Most written sources for the next few years have not survived, but one record states that in 797 four provinces sent 20,040 workers to Heian; it is unclear whether this figure refers to actual persons or worker-days or why they were sent. In the first month of 799, the court had not yet been able to finish a major festivities courtyard (*buraku in*). In the sixth month Kammu toured the city, and in the twelfth month eleven provinces, almost all of them adjoining Yamashiro, sent workers to raise new portions of Heian Palace.

Annals make little mention of construction between 800 and 805, until Kammu's trusted advisers Fujiwara no Otsugu and Sugano no Mamichi protested to him that "at present all under heaven suffer from military expeditions and construction; if the court stops these two things, then the people will take comfort from it."[156] Early in the twelfth month of 805, the government sent 1,281 laborers (*shichō*) back to their homes and excused twenty-one provinces from forwarding revenues, which usually defrayed the cost of wages. Two months later, the court abolished the bureau for construction of the palace (*zōgū shiki*), implying that the age of large-scale building, regardless of Heian's state, was over.

Construction did not cease totally, however. By 808 artisans had finally finished the main festivities hall (*buraku den*). In the same year, a consolidation of ten offices occurred, perhaps because the incomplete palace could not house them separately. In 810, the newly retired Emperor Heizei plotted a move back to Nara, employing 2,500 workers and engineers until his subterfuge failed at the end of the year.[157] In 815, historical annals state that the government hired 19,800 laborers to refurbish the morning halls of the official compound. In 816 when strong winds ravaged the city and overturned the gate of the encircling wall (*rashō mon*) at the southern entrance to the capital, no official repairs took place. Material and demographic constraints had put an end to imperial dreams of constructing new Chinese-style capitals.

FIGURE 3.17

The Capital at Heian.
Key: A. Heian Palace; B. Imperial
residence; C. Official compound;
D. Festivities hall; E. Shinsen'en;
F. Markets; G. Suzaku Great Road;
H. Tōji; I. Saiji; J. Kamo River;
K. Katsura River. *Source:* Kishi Toshio,
"Nihon no tojō sei sōron," in Kishi,
ed., *Nihon no kodai 9: Tojō no seitai,*
p. 57.

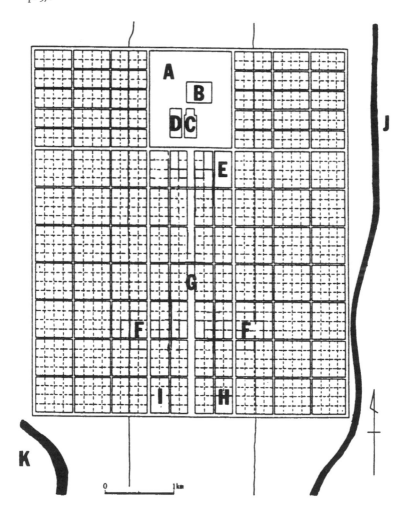

The Archaeological Record for Heian _____

Scholars who want to know what Heian looked like in A.D. 800 confront the inescapable problem of excavating below Kyoto, a vibrant modern city of 3 million residents. Apart from the destruction wrought by modern urban contractors, Kyoto was the capital of Japan and one of its most important metropolises for almost twelve hundred years, which means that remains of other eras lie above those of the ninth century. For these reasons, archaeologists have been digging Kyoto seriously for only about the last twenty years, and many of the hundred sites excavated each year are only the size of a "cat's forehead."[158]

Nevertheless, significant gains in knowledge have occurred. (See Figure 3.17.) Scientists have confirmed the existence of the anticipated checkerboard plan by uncovering ditches, roads, and walls exactly where predicted at over 150 sites. Remains indicate that some roads in Heian were covered with a light carpet of gravel, unlike the earthen thoroughfares of Nara or Naniwa. A small section of Suzaku Great Road revealed a parallel ditch 2 meters wide that was reinforced with wooden planks and spanned by a bridge. Archaeologists attempted to locate the gate of the encircling wall, but neither the gate nor the wall has come to light. An area associated with the western market in the Seventh Rank has revealed ditches, buildings, and other signs of regular land division; a well has yielded coins, pottery, and measuring sticks.[159]

From a planner's point of view, the uniform residential lots of Heian (about 120 meters on each side) represented a perfection achieved after the trial and error of Fujiwara, Nara, Naniwa, and Nagaoka. Although restricted in the area they can excavate, archaeologists have discovered several examples of residences in the metropolis. Aristocratic dwellings of one *chō* or more occupied the eastern half of the capital north of the Fifth Rank; in the western part of the city, one aristocrat's residence consisted of a main building in the center of the lot flanked by two smaller posthole structures. One scholar has seen in this arrangement the origins of the noble architectural form known as *shinden zukuri*.[160] A few commoner homes, usually no more than one-thirty-second of a *chō*, have also come to light. Historians have voiced doubts about how densely settled ninth-century Heian was. A tenth-century record states that the western half of the capital was nearly empty of people or houses; excavations have demonstrated that the comment is not literally correct.[161] A more credible ninth-century annal says that only about half the city was fit for residents in 828, suggesting that Kammu skimped on leveling hills and filling in swamps for large sections of Heian.[162]

Like the city proper, Heian Palace has been the object of sustained archaeological activity only for about twenty-five years and even that is on a small scale. A diagram from the twelfth century shows the palace in great detail, but it is unclear how well it conforms to ninth-century arrangements. Another little-used, badly damaged diagram from the early ninth century seems to reveal a somewhat different layout of offices.[163] (See Figure 3.18.) Scholars agree that the central complex of Heian Palace included a twelve-hall official compound due north of Suzaku Gate, with a small audience hall connected to the north. Directly to the west of the official compound was the difficult-to-finish festivities hall; the imperial residence followed the precedent of Nagaoka and lay northeast of the audience hall. On its northern border Heian Palace resembled Fujiwara.

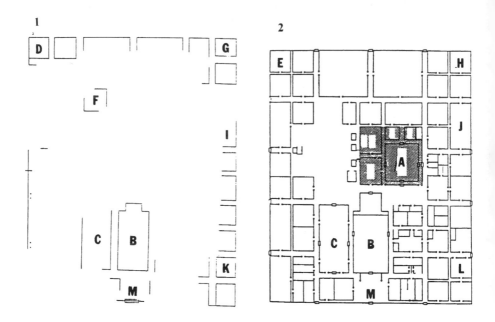

FIGURE 3.18   Two Plans for Heian Palace: Ninth Century (1) and Twelfth Century (2). *Key:* A. Imperial residence; B. Official compound; C. Festivities hall; D. Office of drums and flutes; E. Lacquer-making shop; F. Office of government slaves; G. Offices of blacksmith; H. Tea garden; I. Falconry; J. Office of Left Palace guards; K. Office for unemployed bureaucrats; L. Office of deities; M. Suzaku Gate. *Source:* Tōno Haruyuki, "Nanto shoden kyūjō zu zanketsu ni tsuite," *Komonjo kenkyū* 20 (February 1983):2–3.

Archaeologists have gleaned bits and pieces of information to add to this picture. The audience hall rested on a stone platform; the morning halls of the official compound were wider than either Nagaoka's or Nara's. Part of the foundation for the festivities hall has appeared where expected. Scientists have also recovered some postholes and stones for both the central ministry (*nakatsukasa shō*) and the population ministry (*minbu shō*).[164]

By far the most interesting discovery at Heian Palace, however, comes as it did at Nagaoka—from roof tiles. Although excavation has just started and statistics are not available, a large number of tiles at Heian originated in Nagaoka, Naniwa, and Nara.[165] Some even came from Fujiwara. Several Heian aristocrats also utilized old tiles for their mansions. These findings suggest that workers often moved structures from previous capitals when they raised Heian, just as they did at Nagaoka. Only between 796 and 799, when the festivities hall came into being, was the government able to afford to construct new buildings.[166]

Thus construction at Heian suffered considerable limitations. Certainly Kammu was unhappy with the scaled-down Nagaoka Palace, and he tried to rectify that shortcoming by making Heian especially grand. Witness the twelve morning halls, instead of Nagaoka's eight, in the official compound. The plan for Heian may have been the most perfect of all those tried by the Japanese court in its age of apprenticeship to Chinese civilization, but adverse economic and demographic conditions plagued the last magnificent project. Among these restrictions was a shrinking labor supply.

CAPITAL BUILDING AND LABOR

Scholars usually analyze Japan's Chinese-style capitals from either a political or cultural perspective. Both approaches have been employed in this book to explain the archaeological evidence. But in addition to being political and cultural expressions, the new capitals were reflections of ancient Japanese society and economy. There is one crucial question that no one has examined in English: where and how did the court obtain a supply of labor to carry out these projects?

As scholars of medieval Europe and other civilizations have suggested, two major factors influence the availability of labor in a premodern society: the general health of the populace and the rate of demographic increase. If people are reasonably healthy and bear numerous offspring who survive to adulthood, the pool of unskilled workers expands and major construction becomes possible. But if men and women suffer from scourges such as disease, war, or famine and do not reproduce themselves, the labor supply shrinks and large-scale undertakings such as Japan's capitals become difficult or even impossible.

Various data suggest that eighth-century Japan witnessed a transition from the first condition to the second.[167] Vital statistics from population records of 702 indicate annual growth of more than 1 percent per annum, and in 715 the government organized a new layer of village administration to accommodate the additional peasants. In 735–737, however, a major smallpox epidemic struck the archipelago, killing between a quarter and a third of all inhabitants. Numerous government retrenchment policies show that the sharp reduction in population reverberated throughout society. Famine was a recurrent threat, and between 774 and 812 the court fought a war against residents of north-eastern Honshu.

Moreover, the repeated efforts at monumental construction seem to have contributed to ecological degradation in the Kinai, the home of most labor-ers.[168] Not only did the requirements for buildings gobble up timber stands, but the baking of roof tiles and Sue ware consumed enormous amounts of fuel in comparison with the low-fired earthenwares utilized exclusively until the mid-fifth century. Through the examination of charcoal remains found in ancient kilns, archaeologists have determined that by the eighth century the broadleaf and evergreen forests of the Kinai were gone, to be replaced here and there by Japanese red pine, a secondary forest cover that typically grows in nutrient-poor soil.

The stifling effects of deadly foreign-borne pestilence combined with these other factors to make survival increasingly difficult over the period from 680 to 900. By the early tenth century, courtier Miyoshi Kiyoyuki complained of depopulation in Bingo; archaeological excavations show that fields cultivated in the Nara period were abandoned in the ensuing Heian era.[169] I contend that over these centuries the demographic trajectory showed short-term rises and falls, but essentially remained flat, or even began to fall somewhat.

The rhythms of demographic ebb and flow help to explain the timing, methods, and results of city building in ancient Japan. While the fragmentary evidence makes it impossible to draw incontrovertible conclusions, in my view a shortage of workers and materials was a growing problem after 737 and a major reason for the shortcuts at Nagaoka and Heian and the near-abandon-ment of great construction schemes thereafter.[170] This section examines one of these input factors, the ancient Japanese labor market, and suggests how the archaeological and historical evidence for capital building fits into that context.

During the heyday of capital building in the 700s, the government obtained workers from three sources. The first type of laborer was called a "service adult" (*shichō*).[171] These toilers supplied between 20 and 80 percent of the heavy, unskilled labor the government needed in the eighth century, depending on the task and locality. According to pre-645 custom, local notables (*kuni no miya-tsuko*) periodically presented two such service adults per thirty households to the Yamato court, but the Taihō Code of 701 reduced the rate to two persons per fifty households. Originally the two functioned as a unit, one performing hard labor while the other served as his cook (*kashiwade*). The court provided them with rations (usually salt and brown rice) but did not pay them; the pair's home village sent the rest of their essentials. As an added enticement, the court reduced their taxes, but the burden must have been onerous because the pair toiled every day from dawn to dusk with only a two-hour midday break. The government limited service terms to three years, but some laborers stayed longer in exchange for court ranks. Many absconded.

By the middle of the eighth century the system of service adults was already undergoing two important changes. First, not long after the smallpox epidemic of 735–737, the distinction between the toiler and his cook began to disappear; in other words, the government impressed cooks to labor at construction projects, too. A wooden tablet unearthed from Nara Palace showing eight cooks gathering firewood for the emperor's kitchen is an example of such a trend.[172] Second, beginning in the ninth century, the court allowed these workers to pay cash or cloth in lieu of coming to work. In one example, only eleven of a total of seventy-six service adults actually appeared; the rest made the payment.[173] In a labor-short economy, why did the government not try even harder to enforce labor dues? Two factors encouraged commutation: prohibitive enforcement costs and the attraction of cash and cloth for use in local commerce. As in the Edo period after 1720, or the fourteenth and fifteenth centuries in Western Europe after the Black Death, the commutation of labor services generally takes place when unskilled workers are unavailable or too expensive.

The history of a second type of toil—unpaid miscellaneous corvée (*zōyō*) duty that was restricted to sixty days per year—is much less understood than the institution of service adults.[174] Nevertheless, it may suggest a growing dearth of workers. This duty may have had pre-645 roots as service (*kusagusa no miyuki*) to the Yamato monarch when he or she traveled, but this point is as yet conjectural. A statute based on Chinese precedent was probably a part of Japanese law as early as the 689 Kiyomihara Code, but even eighth-century sources are mostly silent on this form of toil. Fujiwara no Nakamaro reduced the limit from sixty to thirty days in 757 to lighten the burden on a populace suffering from crop failures.

One legal commentator (*koki*) on the Taihō Code writing around 730 made elaborate distinctions between nine jobs listed in the statutes that he believed lay within the sixty-day limit of miscellaneous corvée and fourteen that did not. The author argued, for example, that tasks such as sending medicinal plants or straw to the capital should employ workers on miscellaneous corvée while repairing broken walls or shipping taxes should not. Japanese scholars have not yet determined how to interpret the jurist's remarks. Some believe that he was making a real distinction between those tasks that were under the authority of the provincial governor (and therefore subject to miscellaneous corvée) and those that were not; others argue that the jurist was merely playing a game of abstract, legalistic reasoning. In any case, miscellaneous corvée does not appear to have been a widely used form of labor in the eighth century. The court did not even keep records on it.

In the ninth century, the miscellaneous corvée duty began to undergo changes. After a return to the sixty-day limit with Nakamaro's demise, in 795 the number of service days fell from sixty to thirty by government fiat; in 864 the requirement dropped further to twenty. Lawgivers reasoned that these reductions were necessary to ease the burden on people and to counter local abuses. Both reasons are consistent with a shrinking labor pool. One may also interpret the reduction of the maximum length of miscellaneous corvée in other ways. One might argue that the government had either less need for workers or more satisfactory ways of obtaining them after 795. The first assertion seems implausible, however, because the government still required laborers to raise Heian and to send large military expeditions to northeastern Honshu. There is no evidence to support the second statement. Instead of viewing the reductions as implying growth in the labor supply, Yoshida Takashi contends that the court was reducing the limit on miscellaneous corvée from sixty days, which had never been approached in the 700s, in exchange for a lower maximum (twenty or thirty days) that would be fully enforced.[175]

Moreover, descriptions of the labor market found in ninth-century orders imply that even this marginal source of labor came under increasing pressure due to shortages. In 808, as the construction of Heian was winding down, a regulation states that "emergency conscriptions [of workers] are many, while corvée adults are few."[176] An order of 823 states that "people are few although deterioration [of government facilities] is increasingly widespread"; a command of 864 reads: "In some cases provincial governors in a biased fashion say that corvée workers are insufficient and enjoy using up wages and provisions."[177] The first two quotations directly state the labor shortage while the third shows that this condition allowed corrupt local officials to line their own pockets.

The third and most important form of work was short-term, paid corvée (*koeki*).[178] Documents of the eighth century indicate that 54 percent of all toilers were short-term paid corvée workers. Most members of the labor gangs that built Japan's capitals fell into this category. It appears that Japan possessed a system of seasonal, unpaid corvée (*edachi*) prior to 701.[179] This institution was undoubtedly responsible for recruiting the workers who raised mansions and government offices such as Kōtoku's Nagara Toyosaki Palace. After 701, however, even though the Taihō Code referred to ten days of unreimbursed corvée labor, in reality the court collected hemp cloth or other items from every adult male liable for service and used the proceeds to hire the required laborers in the Kinai and vicinity.[180]

The government employed paid corvée workers throughout the eighth century, and the fact of doing so highlights the problem of securing enough toilers for the court's magnificent projects. Tang China's reliance on wage labor rather than unpaid corvée may have influenced Japanese lawmakers, but the arrangements of the two societies were basically dissimilar. The real reason for Japan's strange, hybrid category of government-conscripted wage labor was to obtain sufficent workers by the carrot-and-stick policy of combining payments in cash or cloth with government sanctions. Even with reimbursement, officials could not be certain of enough workers, and thus lawgivers included an element of coercion by making appearance at government-sponsored projects a duty and part of the tax structure.[181] Such a policy is reminiscent of fourteenth-century European attempts to enforce artificially lowered wages on a sparse and resistant populace.[182]

One trend of the eighth century is particularly suggestive of the growing shortage of laborers even with the use of paid corvée: the impressment of non-workers. Shōmu began this practice by using Buddhist acolytes to build Kuni, and it is no coincidence that this method of obtaining laborers started after the smallpox epidemic of 735–737. Soldiers (*heishi*) were another group of coerced laborers. The habit of compelling soldiers to do unrelated, unskilled labor was probably an old one, but it is especially notable after the pestilence. Five wooden tablets uncovered from Nara Palace in 1971 note that the court employed soldiers to do various menial tasks "because of the deficiency of numbers" in the years immediately following the epidemic.[183] In 763, the government rewarded soldiers from Ōmi and the Kinai for work on the new imperial palace at Hora.[184]

Japan's attempts to construct Chinese-style capitals, the largest building projects before the 1500s, are consistent with a shrinking labor market, as even a cursory examination of population trends suggests. The erection of mid-seventh-century palaces such as Nagara Toyosaki took place in what appears to have been an era of population growth. Greater Fujiwara also arose while demographic conditions were still favorable, but the builders decided not to raise a massive wall encircling the entire city, even though that was the custom in China. The difficulties of acquiring a sufficient labor force may well explain why no wall was built.

The first grandiose attempt to construct Nara took place in 710, but the project was incomplete because of peasant resistance to government work demands (documented earlier). Localized plagues struck the archipelago in fifteen of the sixteen years from 698 to 713, and famines were frequent from 705 through 715. It seems reasonable that worker resistance would become more effective when the labor supply was unstable. Between 713 and 735, however, there were only four years of pestilence, and two of those do not appear to have been severe. Famine was also less common. It is no accident that Shōmu was able to rebuild Nara and finish Naniwa during this period. The upper layer of Nara Palace also probably belongs to this era of resumed population growth, rather than to the decades after the population dropped.

After the harsh famine of 733 and the smallpox outbreak of 735–737, mobilization of labor became more difficult. Despite the impressment of unqualified persons, Kuni was unfinished and Shigaraki no more than a temporary lodging. When Shōmu and the court returned to Nara in 745, they may have done a few renovations, but large-scale construction seems improbable until the population could recover somewhat. Judging from the incidence of plagues and famines, one might conclude that the effects of this small recovery were felt in the 750s, or just when the planning and building of Tōdaiji and Nakamaro's refurbishing of Heijō Palace were proceeding.

Famines and epidemics were again severe in the 760s and early 770s, but between 775 and 784 there were only two recorded outbreaks of plagues. The threat of famine also receded somewhat, suggesting that the population may have begun to grow again. Yet even with the renewed increase, a partially finished Nagaoka was not an easy accomplishment. Kammu was forced to rely almost completely on recycled materials because they saved him labor and outlays from the treasury, some of which went to pay increasingly scarce unskilled toilers.

Kammu and his court were too ambitious, however, to make do with a second-rate palace, and so he attempted Heian, once again using leftover tiles and timbers from previous imperial domiciles. By the first decade of the ninth century, not only had construction on Heian slowed to a stop, but the court wisely decided to cease all large-scale building projects. This cessation reflected population trends, for the ninth century was an era of even harsher epidemics and famines, especially from 800 until 850.[185] Emperors may have desired new capitals, but demography was a major factor hindering the realization of imperial plans.

The growing deficits in workers and materials affected all forms of construction in eighth-century Japan. For example, workers began Nara's most famous temple, Tōdaiji, at Shigaraki and then transferred the plans to Nara in 745. Work proceeded, but despite Shōmu's visit to see the finished statue of the Great Buddha in 749, the lecture hall was incomplete until 756, the building for the statue until 758, the eastern pagoda until 760, the mess hall until after 762, the golden backdrop (kōhai) for the statue until 771, and the monks' quarters until 782.[186] The government had created an office for the construction of Tōdaiji to build the temple, and the office's continuation throughout the eighth century suggests that the project may have still been unfinished even forty years after its initiation. Of course, the office's prolonged existence may also be explained by its responsibility for building other temples, notably Akishinodera, Saidaiji, and Shin'yakushiji.

The court may also have delayed or been unable to finish Tōdaiji's branch temples (kokubunji) located throughout the provinces. Initiated in 741, the plan to erect branch temples in the sixty-odd provinces of Japan ran into trouble almost from the start. In 747, Shōmu complained that "lazy provincial governors" had chosen poor locations or failed to begin building on their projects.[187] In 756, when memorial services for the deceased Shōmu were held, twenty-six provinces—almost all of them in western Japan where the smallpox epidemic was most lethal—had to do so in temporary edifices because their branch temples were still under construction.[188] In many cases, including Yamashiro, governors may have used recycled materials or designated preexisting temples to serve the purpose. Archaeological excavations on the numerous sites for branch temples may reveal how many were actually finished, but at this stage it is difficult to tell.[189]

The best-documented temple raising was that of Ishiyamadera in Ōmi in

762. Officials at the site complained to the office for the construction of Tōda-iji about their need for more provisions—vegetables, salt, seaweed, and rice—for their workforce and worried that "if you do not grant the items requested previously and the workmen here scatter, we fear they will be difficult to rehire."[190] It is doubtful that officials at the work site who oversaw this project would have worried so about rehiring toilers in an overpopulated labor market. A senior Japanese historian who studied the Ishiyamadera project concluded that enticement of workers by wages alone had proved inadequate: the scarcity of hands had required resort to paid corvée.[191]

All the construction analyzed here was official government work. What was happening in the private sector? There is almost no information on this topic. Proof for the growing shortage of workers would come in the form of increasingly higher wages, but such figures are impossible to find for the ancient period. Part of the reason is that the distinction between "state" and "private," although proclaimed in records, was vague in reality. Aristocrats used government-made tiles for their own mansions, even as private subjects received official rewards for contributions to government building projects. Yet it is hard to believe that the private sector had no problems when the court was suffering so from the growing labor shortage. Examination of the difficulties in securing labor for big aristocratic and religious land clearance projects suggests that a labor deficit did afflict such endeavors.[192]

From the ninth century, the court came to rely on contributions, forced and otherwise, from well-heeled politicians and wealthy temples. The imperial treasury was empty, and labor was just too scarce to raise another Nara or Heian. Even maintaining the existing city proved to be a challenge. The court continued to impose labor obligations, but these were often commuted into payments of rice or cloth.[193]

RECAPITULATION

Geographers and antiquarians of the Edo period showed early interest in Japan's Chinese-style capitals, but research did not really become serious until after 1900. With the publication of Kita Sadakichi's *August Capitals* in 1915, new theories became popular just as excavations uncovered tiles at Naniwa and the public became aroused about the dangers that economic development posed for the remains at Nara Palace. Despite Japan's slide toward militarism after 1930, digging at Ōtsu and Fujiwara brought more information to light.

Study of Japan's monumental capitals expanded dramatically after 1945. The government established the Nara National Cultural Properties Research Institute in 1952 to oversee excavations at Nara and later Asuka, and it gradually bought all the land now believed to have lain within the great wall of Nara Palace. Work at Naniwa revealed palaces on two levels: the lower many believe to have been Kōtoku's Nagara Toyosaki Palace of the 650s; the upper was undoubtedly Shōmu's creation of the late 720s. Digging has also proceeded at Fujiwara and Asuka, while Nagaoka and Heian have become objects of the archaeologist's spade since the 1970s.

There can be little doubt that Japan's first capitals drew their inspiration from Chinese models. The Middle Kingdom has a long history of constructing walled metropolises, and from the unification of the empire in 221 B.C. onward, each dynasty built capitals to symbolize its moral and political authority. The first capitals to influence the Japanese were those of the Northern and Southern dynasties. Northern Wei Luo-yang, the earliest capital to place the imperial palace in the northern city, plan regular wards, and settle citizens according to status, was especially important. Sui Chang-an, the largest city in the world in its day, added the conventions of a separate audience hall and markets in each half of the city. Despite the adherence of the Japanese court to the Chinese model in a general way, it was not slavish in its emulation. It did not adopt the Chinese idea of an encircling wall and omitted shrines to the ruler's ancestors and the gods of the earth. The court evidently felt free to use the latest concepts from Tang Chang-an even as it retained features of the Zhou period. Korean capitals too served as models for the layout of Japan's cities, especially Dazaifu.

But Japan had its own native tradition of kingly residences as well. The earliest sites were no larger than those of many local chieftains and consisted of wooden buildings with thatched or shingled roofs but no foundations. By 603, however, builders located a courtyard with attached offices (morning halls) to the south of a walled or fenced-in royal residence at Oharida. The court may have invented or stumbled on the north-south arrangement of imperial residence and official compound or borrowed it from China. In any case, this arrangement was already well established when the heavy influx of Chinese institutions began after 700.

The oldest imperial residence for which archaeologists have provided much information is the lower level at Naniwa, which may have been occupied from 651 to 653. Although Naniwa had only traditional Japanese-style edifices lined up with the imperial residence in the north and the official compound in the south, it had some unique features, notably the two octagonal turrets and the large number of morning halls (fourteen) in the official compound. It is now doubtful that a full-fledged capital with uniform thoroughfares and symmetrical wards existed at early Naniwa or Tenji's palace at Ōtsu.

The date for Japan's first Chinese-style capital is a matter of dispute. By the late seventh century, the Asuka region had been home to the imperial family for nearly a century and had acquired its share of palaces and temples. The term "Wa Capital" that appears in the written sources probably refers to the asymmetrical, unplanned city that had grown up in Asuka by then.

Temmu wanted to construct a more authentic Chinese-style capital during his lifetime. He died before finishing either Naniwa or Fujiwara, however, which he seems to have hoped would serve like Luo-yang and Chang-an in China as dual capitals for his government. Naniwa burned, but perhaps not before the court had completed its symmetrical layout. Temmu's consort Jitō finished Fujiwara. It had the standard imperial residence in the north, a brandnew Chinese audience hall in the middle, and a twelve-hall official compound in the south. Many edifices were continental-style, with tile-roofed structures resting on foundation stones. The scholarly agreement regarding the layout of the palace at Fujiwara contrasts with the controversy surrounding the larger city. Kishi Toshio proposed that Fujiwara was relatively small and bounded by four ancient roads, two that ran west to Naniwa and two northward through Asuka. Kishi thought that Fujiwara had taken its inspiration from Jian-kang (modern Nanking) or Northern Wei Luo-yang rather than Tang or Sui prototypes, and he argued that Fujiwara had provided the model for Nara. Recent digging, however, has shown that Fujiwara extended beyond the ancient boundary roads posited by Kishi, and more and more archaeologists now believe that Fujiwara was as large as Nara or Heian or larger. It is unclear, however, how far Japanese planners actually went toward making Fujiwara a functional city.

The imperial family moved to Nara in 710, but the construction was difficult owing to worker resistance. The two-part palace, which featured the transplanted large audience hall from Fujiwara placed north of another indeterminate section in the west and the imperial residence and Japanese-style morning halls in the east, was of heroic proportions but probably incomplete. A scaled-down version of this first Nara Palace was built atop it. This upper stratum of Heijō also had east and west divisions—with Shōtoku's western compound replacing the former great audience hall—and a new, smaller audience hall was erected north of continental-style morning halls in the east. The date of Nara's refurbishing is one of the most hotly debated topics in Japanese archaeology. Historical sources suggest either the 720s under Shōmu or the late 750s under Fujiwara no Nakamaro. Relying on tile patterns and a few wooden tablets, however, leading archaeologists of the Nara National Cultural Properties Research Institute believe that workers rebuilt Nara Palace around 745. A shortage of laborers after the famine of 733 and the epidemic of 735–737 seems to militate against the 745 thesis. Nara was also home to commoners, of course, but excavations indicate that Nara's population was probably only about half the long-standing estimate of 200,000. With its asymmetrical northern edge and Outer Capital, Nara's configuration was unique, but it began the Japanese capital tradition of nine ranks and eight files, with sixteen residential lots per ward. Archaeologists have unearthed dwellings ranging from the grandiose aristocratic estate of Prince Nagaya to the humble abodes of peasants.

Archaeological finds at both Kuni and the upper level of Naniwa feed into the debate over the date of Nara's upper layer. There can be no doubt that the later Naniwa Palace came into existence in the reign of Shōmu as his secondary capital, and its layout resembles the eastern half of the upper level of Nara Palace, which may suggest that workers built both after 725, when population was growing and labor relatively abundant. Kuni, located north of Nara and begun in 740, was never completed despite the use of recycled materials and the impressment of Buddhist acolytes for construction. Its small dimensions and poverty of relics undercut the hypothesis that any great new building took place at Nara in the years immediately following 745.

Nagaoka (784–794) foreshadowed Heian in its placement of the imperial residence and layout of residential lots. But it probably was incomplete, as archaeologists can find no ditches or walls in the Eighth or Ninth Ranks. Nagaoka Palace was less ambitious than either Nara or Heian, and laborers constructed it almost entirely of recycled materials from Naniwa and Nara— presumably to save on labor, retard deforestation, and reduce the drain on the imperial fisc. In some respects, Heian represented the perfection of court dreams of a Chinese-style capital in Japan. It had regular residential lots, a festivities hall, and a twelve-edifice official compound. Yet like Nagaoka, Heian used recycled timbers and tiles liberally, even from dilapidated Fujiwara. In 805, Emperor Kammu called off construction on Heian even as buildings were still going up.

Evidence regarding the labor market in the period between 645 and 900 is spotty and subject to diverse interpretations. But cumulatively it supports the contention that able-bodied workers were increasingly difficult to mobilize, from which one may infer a growing shortage. This dearth was an important impediment hindering construction of Japan's Chinese-style capitals and religious monuments. A system of service adults evolved during the pre-645 era, whereby each village sent two persons acting as a laborer and a cook to the palace to build for the monarch. As depopulation occurred in the eighth century, however, officials impressed the cooks and eventually allowed service adults to commute workdays into payments of goods. The sixty-day unpaid corvée of the Taihō Code probably never operated on the scale envisioned in the statutes. By the ninth century, lawgivers tried reducing the number of days first to thirty and then to twenty, even as they complained of the lack of suitable toilers. Short-term paid corvée was the central pillar of the court's labor policy; commoners remitted hemp cloth or rice that was in turn used to pay and provision laborers, mostly conscripted from the Kinai. The government continued to utilize paid corvée in the ninth century, albeit on a small scale.

Japanese scholars and citizens have been wont to see an expression of the power and grandeur of the Japanese emperor in the great capitals of the eighth century. Just as occupants of the imperial throne were immortal gods, so the cities they built had transformed swamps into magnificent abodes for the celestial court. The undying imperial ideology created in the late seventh and early eighth centuries bolstered such a vision.

An examination of historical sources and the archaeological record, however, has challenged this vision. Surveying the development of Japanese political centers over three hundred years from 500 to 800, one can see that almost all the growth in size and sophistication came during the first two hundred and thirty years. In this sense, the building of Fujiwara and Nara represented the pinnacle of imperial power, but it created an infrastructure that depended on continuing economic and demographic vitality. By the late 700s, the court was operating in a tight labor market with limited resources, and it constructed Nagaoka and Heian only with the greatest difficulty. After the epidemic, it is doubtful that any of the Chinese-style cities built came to completion. The contribution of historical archaeology has been to distinguish the ideology of imperial glory from the reality of its limitations and to emphasize the eighth century as a transitional era from expansion to contraction.

In another sense, however, Heian was the acme of capital building in Japan. Even though it may never have been completed, Heian possessed a more perfect urban plan than any other city ever erected in the archipelago. Heian showed that the Japanese court and its engineers understood the basic lessons of Chinese civilization well.

CHAPTER 4

WOODEN TABLETS

The year 1961 was one of the most memorable dates in the study of ancient Japan. As Kishi Toshio describes it:

> The time was January 1961 and the falling snow danced above the excavation site at Heijō Palace. To think that, even in Japan, just like China, wooden tablets (*mokkan*) with writing on them were used in place of paper. Furthermore, they appeared in large numbers from the earth. This was something that we researchers had never imagined in our wildest dreams. . . .
>
> The importance of these wooden tablets . . . was that they rejuvenated the study of ancient Japanese history, which had reached its limit because of sparse sources. For us, it was as if a light had suddenly shone on the future; nothing could equal our gratitude and joy.[1]

Kishi wrote this in 1978 when about 30,000 tablets were known to exist—and the nearly 140,000 (and counting) that have subsequently come to light all over Japan have amply demonstrated the truth of his observation.

This chapter examines the role of these new written sources in research on late seventh- and eighth-century Japan. Because of the huge number of wooden tablets that archaeologists have recovered, this inquiry will focus on a few selected problems: the authenticity of the Taika Reform, especially as it pertains to local government; the workings of the bureaucracy; the origins of the tax system; and the daily life of the high aristocracy. Once again archaeologists have provided valuable data that supplement and redefine older historical debates.

ABOUT WOODEN TABLETS

These new sources of information vary considerably in size, shape, material, and function.[2] Most tablets are no more than 5 by 20 centimeters, some reaching as much as 40 centimeters in length, and only 3 to 5 centimeters thick when new. A giant specimen uncovered near Fujiwara Palace measured nearly a meter in length. Usually officials carved suitable strips from Japanese cypress (*hinoki*), but some also used Japanese cedar (*sugi*). One archaeologist at Nagaoka inferred a three-step process for mass-producing tablets in which officials split long uniform strips from boards, cut them in two across the width, and then whittled individual *mokkan*.[3] Even with this manufacturing process, however, Japanese artifacts come in various sizes and shapes, betraying a diversity not apparent in similar finds in China.[4] In terms of their contents, historians classify wooden tablets into two major types: documents (*monjo mokkan*) and labels or tags (*tsukefuda; nifuda*). Where paper was scarce, these tablets performed all the functions of official records, conveying orders to subordinates, requests from superiors, summons, reports, work evaluations, and dispatches of men and materials. They served as transit passes and even as doodling pads to practice brushmanship (*shūsho; rakugaki*). Almost all labels came attached to tax goods, which might be dried fish or seaweed, bales of rice, iron, cloth, or other items.

Wooden tablets have been recovered from five hundred sites all over Japan and from many different periods. Ancient finds range from Akita in the north to Fukuoka in the south, but as of 1992 about three-quarters had come from Nara. Archaeologists have recovered about seven thousand from Fujiwara and over a thousand apiece at Asuka, Nagaoka, Dazaifu, and Shimotsuke provincial headquarters in the Kanto. Ancient *mokkan* survive in greatest number for the years from 700 to 800, but a few have been discovered that date to the middle decades of the seventh century. Others reveal fascinating details about life in the middle and late Heian, medieval, Edo, and even Meiji periods.

Once tablets are unearthed, preservation becomes a top priority.[5] As soon as a site yields a *mokkan,* archaeologists wash it so that trained assistants may record its contents. After a thorough but gentle rinse, technicians wrap the specimen in a special type of gauze and place it in a plastic tub filled with water and preservatives. As soon as feasible, employees of archaeological agencies such as the Nara National Cultural Properties Research Institute photograph and copy the tablet by hand, on occasion using infrared television cameras to aid in reading it. Long-term storage has been difficult, because these items have tended to darken in time and become illegible. To solve this problem, impregnating with polyethylene glycol, setting in plastic, and freeze-drying have been tried.

The variety in writing style is one characteristic of wooden tablets that is difficult to demonstrate in English.[6] Relics from Fujiwara and Nara differ fundamentally in brush-stroke technique and forms of official address: the Fujiwara tablets utilize customs of China's Six Dynasties period (A.D. 222–589); those from Nara exhibit later Tang (618–907) style. The updated Tang-inspired brushwork probably came into vogue with the implementation of the Taihō Code in 702, but it may have dated from the transfer to Nara in 710. When one compares the technique of Fujiwara tablets with samples of Korean writing, moreover, the Japanese indebtedness to Silla and Paekche models is clear. With handwriting, as with capital building and other activities, the Japanese court seems to have relied on Korea for its initial borrowings of civilization and then adopted Chinese precepts.[7] Even then, the court was not nearly so punctilious about documentary forms as were scholar-officials of the Middle Kingdom.

While the year 1961 inaugurated the real hunt for wooden tablets in Japan, archaeologists had been aware of them in the prewar period. The Treasure House (Shōsōin) of Tōdaiji holds about 350 *mokkan*. Yui in Mie prefecture yielded a single tax label in 1928, and three tablets relating to military matters were found at Hotta Palisade in Akita in 1930. One widely respected scholar argued that the artifacts from Hotta suggested that Japan had copied this Chinese custom of the Han dynasty, but no one at that time realized how correct he was.[8] In 1978, Japanese scholars formed the Society for the Study of Wooden Tablets (*mokkan gakkai*) under Kishi's leadership. The society still flourishes: its annual journal lists almost all tablets discovered in the previous year together with photographs, descriptions of sites, interpretations, and pertinent articles. By the early 1990s, the membership numbered several hundred and included scholars from around the world.

THE TAIKA REFORM

According to *The Chronicles,* Kōtoku announced the four-part Taika Reform edict on New Year's Day of 646. This proclamation purportedly abolished landholdings and artisan and peasant communities that hitherto had made payments to aristocratic families. It established a Chinese-style capital in the Kinai, along with districts (*gun*) and a system of post-horses for the entire archipelago. It ordered a regular census for officially administered villages. And it set taxes on land and local products, contributions to the military, and arrangements for sending maidens-in-waiting to the palace. It is difficult to find a more sweeping imperial pronouncement in Japanese history. Indeed, the edict is commonly pictured as marking the start of Japan's transformation from a "backward" kingdom into a civilized, Chinese-style state.

Throughout most subsequent Japanese history, few have questioned the importance of the Taika Reform. Arai Hakuseki thought the year 646 marked a watershed in Japan's past, and he shares responsibility for the lofty position that the Taika Reform enjoyed among scholars of the nineteenth and early twentieth centuries.[9] Following as it did the assassination of the usurper Soga family, who attempted to seize the prerogatives of Yamato royalty, the edict seemingly inaugurated an era of edifying direct monarchical rule. Japan's first family had set the country on its upward path toward civilization and enlightenment; over a millennium later the Meiji period would echo this accomplishment.

The iconoclastic Tsuda Sōkichi was the first scholar to raise doubts about the authenticity of the 646 edict.[10] Writing in 1930, he noted that many of its phrases exactly reproduced statutes that appear in later legal compilations such as the Yōrō Code of 717. He argued that it was highly unlikely that the 646 plan had served as the model for the eighth-century statutes. Rather, he suggested, in the year 720 editors of The Chronicles merely copied more recent laws when they put together the chapter that covered the Taika Reform. Tsuda proposed that authors of The Chronicles had probably used the now-lost Ōmi Statutes of 668 most extensively in preparing their Taika chapter. Tsuda did not, however, believe that the 646 edict was a complete fabrication. He noted, for example, that certain parts differed from later legal compendia and those parts tended to appear at the beginning of each of the four articles. The longer explanatory sections following the opening summaries were, in contrast, almost always verbatim quotations from later codes. Tsuda argued that there had indeed been a Taika Reform edict on New Year's Day of 646, but he contended that editors of The Chronicles had added long explanatory notes based on law codes of their own times. Tsuda thus created what might be called the "kernel of truth" interpretation of the 646 edict.

Until 1945 few dared pursue Tsuda's line of thought. But in the liberated atmosphere of the postwar period, other scholars quickly expanded on his work.[11] Soon there were almost as many views on the Taika Reform edict as there were historians of the period, but basically all perspectives fell into one of three camps. A dwindling number of writers held that the edict had appeared just as annalists of The Chronicles reported it. Officials had announced the edict and the court had moved speedily to implement it. Most who held this position were senior scholars (such as Sakamoto Tarō) educated in the prewar era.[12]

A second large group followed Tsuda's "kernel of truth" theory.[13] The most prominent historian maintaining this view was Inoue Mitsusada, who wrote extensively on the topic. Essentially he argued that there was a Taika Reform edict, primarily limited to the introductions (*shubun*) of each article; that the court began to move seriously toward centralizing reforms after 646; and that the prime movers behind the edict were the royal family (notably Kōtoku and Prince Naka) and its ally Fujiwara no Kamatari. This interpretation enjoyed its greatest popularity among graduates of Tokyo University.

A third, vociferous, Kyoto-based group led by Hara Hidesaburō and Kado-waki Teiji regarded the Taika Reform edict as a hoax, a concoction of the compilers of *The Chronicles*.[14] They claimed that court chroniclers of the early eighth century were determined to paint Japan as an enlightened, civilized country ahead of the "barbaric" kingdom of Silla. To do this, the editors needed to show that the Japanese court, particularly the royal family, had seen the need for Chinese-style reforms before the military defeat at the hands of Silla and the Tang during the Battle of the Paekch'ŏn River in 663. The period after the 645 coup d'état made a perfect place in *The Chronicles* to insert a sweeping policy change such as the 646 edict, because it preceded the Paekch'ŏn disaster and transformed the soon-to-be imperial leaders into heroes.

The Kyoto scholars also showed that a careful, entry-by-entry examination of *The Chronicles* raised more doubts about the authenticity of the reform edict. Not only was the the edict clearly doctored, but later seventh-century laws seemed pointlessly to duplicate its tenets. For instance, one of the central goals of the Taika Reform was, purportedly, to do away with independent units (*be*) producing goods and services for aristocrats and local notables and put all Japan's land and people under authority of a divine emperor. But in 664, under the very same Prince Naka who had supposedly helped to write the reform edict, the court "set up retainers" (*kakibe o sadamu*), a type of *be* or labor source for noble families. Why would Naka establish separate bases in 664 if he had been instrumental in abolishing them nearly twenty years earlier? Was the Taika edict ever carried out? Or did the textual contradiction mean that the 646 edict had been a later fabrication of the editors of *The Chronicles*?

Another area of contention advanced by many doubters was the supposed establishment of Chinese-style districts (*gun*) by Prince Naka and his clique. Tsuda had clearly shown that this term came from the law codes. Later scholars revealed that seventh and early-eighth-century materials such as *The Hitachi Gazetteer,* the inscription on Nasu Monument in Ibaraki in the Kanto, and *The Chronicles of Japan Continued* showed that current usage favored the Korean-style unit of local control called *hyō* or *kohori*.[15] Debate over Chinese-style versus Korean-style local administration, called the *gunpyō ronsō* by Japanese experts, soon became a hot topic. Even young Inoue Mitsusada expressed grave reservations about the reform edict because of the many sources listing Korean-style units of local control scattered from Satsuma to northeastern Honshu.[16]

The argument over the Taika Reform and Korean-style as opposed to Chinese-style local government seemed likely to continue unresolved, as have many historical debates in Japan. Then in 1968, archaeologists at Fujiwara Palace uncovered eighty-three wooden tablets, of which twenty-three were tax labels (*nifuda*) that specified their point of origin by administrative village, district, and province. Twenty labels used the Korean-style designation for district (*hyō*); only three used the Chinese-style term.[17] Moreover, these tablets showed that local officials applied the Korean-style appellation in places all over Japan—in the Kinai, in the Kanto, and in western Honshu. Most lacked dates, but one specimen with the Korean-style local unit name contained the year 699. As archaeologists continued to dig at Fujiwara, more tax labels with the Korean term appeared and the debate shifted in favor of regarding the Korean-style nomenclature as normative for all the post-645 period. A 1978 book listing wooden tablets recovered at Fujiwara between 1969 and 1977 reported that thirty-four relics referred to local units of administration: twenty-six used Korean-style terms and eight Chinese-style. Like the 1968 finds, these tablets reflected usage all over Japan during the late seventh and early eighth centuries.[18] Those skeptical of the authenticity of the Taika Reform edict became even more certain of their doubts.

As *mokkan* accumulated, a pattern emerged. Few tax labels included dates, but of those that did, tablets with the Korean-style local unit had dates ranging from 691 to 700, while those using Chinese-style district units (*gun*) were dated 702, 703, and 709. It appeared to scholars that Japanese local officials had preferred the Korean-style name for their bailiwicks until the central government authorized the change with the implementation of the Taihō Code in 702.

This interpretation had two implications. First, it confirmed the significance of the Taihō Code for institutional historians interested in tracing the evolution of Japan's early apprenticeship to Chinese-style arrangements. Of Japan's three verifiable compilations of Chinese-style laws—the Kiyomihara Administrative Statutes of 681, the Taihō Code, and the Yōrō Code—only the last is extant. Some fragments of the Taihō Code have survived, but it is generally assumed that it was similar to the Yōrō Code. The tablet dating seemed to confirm that the Taihō Code marked a watershed in Japanese institutional history. One could agree with one early eighth-century epitaph which stated that Taihō was "the first time a Chinese-style law code (*ritsuryō*) had been established" in Japan.[19] Second, the transition from Korean-style to Chinese-style terms as late as 702 indicated that during the seventh century the Japanese court still looked to Korea as its model. Despite the sinicized pronouncements of the 646 Taika Reform edict, the direct borrowing of Chinese-style civilization by the Japanese did not begin until about half a century later. Reform of local administration may have been particularly slow in coming because the court relied on indigenous local families to administer their own jurisdictions and was neither willing nor able to force rapid change there.

Following the 1968 discovery at Fujiwara, the Taika Reform edict looked even less reliable and significant than before. Most historians still cited *The Chronicles*, but almost always with the proviso that "at least this is what it says in *The Chronicles of Japan*." None would say that *The Chronicles* "proved" anything, least of all the existence of the comprehensive Taika Reform initiated by the royal family, if it was not listed somewhere else.

Yet archaeology in Japan has a way of wreaking its revenge on those who are too certain of themselves. Just as critics of the Taika Reform edict were feeling most fully vindicated, a single wooden tablet unearthed from the Asuka basin revived the beleaguered supporters of the edict. In 1975, archaeologists were excavating an ancient ditch that ran north-south outside the eastern wall of the traditional site for Itabuki Palace, the spot where Prince Naka and his conspirators had supposedly murdered the Soga in 645. In the process they came upon fourteen *mokkan*, some of which plainly referred to mid-seventh-century court ranks. Among them was a tax label that read simply: "Shiragabe 50 households."[20] Inoue Mitsusada, a supporter of the "kernel of truth" theory of the Taika Reform edict, was overjoyed. The 646 edict and the Taihō and Yōrō codes all specified that every administrative village was to consist of fifty households. The tax label reading "Shiragabe 50 households" seemed to confirm that reform of local government had indeed taken place around 646. A short but crucial phrase in the sweeping explanatory section, rather than merely the opening summary, of Prince Naka and Kōtoku seemed to be authentic, despite textual critics such as Tsuda and others.

Archaeologists came to the defense of those claiming the wooden tablet's validity. Excavators had discovered it in a layer of soil that held a specimen noting the court rank "Great Flower, lower grade" (*daika-ge*). According to *The Chronicles*, the cap rank system that contained this status was in effect from 649 until 664. Therefore "Shiragabe 50 households" must belong to the mid-seventh century as well, possibly as early as 646. At the time, these were the oldest wooden tablets known for Japan and seemed to bolster proponents of the authenticity of the Taika Reform edict.[21] The new evidence, like the debate over Korean-style versus Chinese-style units of local control, pertained to local administration. It showed that in at least one area, and most probably in more, reformers had achieved their goal of instituting Chinese-style village administration at an early date. Perhaps Shiragabe, wherever it was, had been located on land already controlled by the monarchical family and therefore was easy to rearrange into units of fifty households. Doubters of the 646 edict argued that Shiragabe was exceptional, and that the tax label specified fifty households precisely because it was not the norm for most of Japan, but generally they mounted no effective rebuttal. Kishi Toshio, a quiet skeptic of Taika but above all loyal to the evidence wherever it led, offered his opinion in a collection of essays dedicated to his archrival Inoue Mitsusada when the latter retired from Tokyo University in 1978: the wooden tablet supported the authenticity of the 646 edict.

Since the discovery of "Shiragabe 50 households," archaeological testimony pertaining to the 646 edict has continued to flow in. At Fujiwara Palace, ten more tax labels, mostly undated but listing point of origin, came to light in 1977–1978 alone. Of the ten, eight use the Korean-style term (one with the date 683), while two employ the Chinese-style unit.[22] In one informal tabulation of tax labels uncovered from 1980 through 1993 at Fujiwara Palace, thirty-eight items use the Chinese term while twenty-one contain its Korean alternative.[23] Significantly, the rule that Korean-style units preceded the Taihō Code and Chinese-style units followed it continued to hold true.[24]

The archaeological finds relating to district and administrative village have encouraged scholars to come to a new consensus on the Taika Reform and the nature of the changes that occurred in Japan between 645 and 702. Most scholars have now come to embrace a modified version of Tsuda's "kernel of truth" interpretation, although there are still many disagreements on particulars. Archaeologists have managed to discredit those adhering to either of the two extremes: those who saw Japan as quickly implementing a Chinese-style centralized government after 645 as well as those who totally denied the existence of the Taika Reform edict.

Thus the period between the coup d'état in 645 and the implementation of the Taihō Code in 702 has become a transitional stage during which some members of the court and their allies gradually forced the country to accept their idea of Chinese-style civilization and the state.[25] It has also become clear through the work of Japanese, Korean, and Chinese historians that the stimulus for the slow changes was more foreign (especially Korean) than domestic, as skeptics of Taika had long argued. Scholars have shown that the 645 coup was similar to contemporary centralizing revolts in the three Korean kingdoms as the leaders of Yamato, Silla, Paekche, and Koguryŏ reacted to aggressive Tang expeditions into Manchuria and the peninsula between 644 and 648.

Refugees from the wars in Korea poured into Japan in the 640s as they had during times of turmoil over the previous three centuries. Émigrés helped the court learn about Chinese and Korean models and even about Tang military strategy on the continent. Prince Naka and his conspirators may well have been able to issue a précis of their plans on New Year's Day of 646 as the Taika Reform edict, although not in the form preserved in *The Chronicles*. As demonstrated by Japanese scholars, Korean-style units of local administration were common throughout the archipelago between 645 and 702.[26] Their widespread existence shows the centralizing clique's continuing indebtedness to Korean institutions.

As of midcentury, the Taika Reform was still only a plan, and for the next seventeen years centralizing actions were slow, patchy, and not very successful. The reform clique could not overcome considerable local resistance to a Chinese-style state until the Tang dynasty demonstrated its superiority by destroying a Japanese fleet at the Battle of the Paekch'ŏn River in 663. This decisive defeat gave rise to a fear of invasion, for which the discredited Tenji feverishly prepared. Yet true centralization along Chinese lines had to wait until Temmu won the throne in the civil war of 672. Then the court moved rapidly to borrow Chinese models, producing three Chinese-style law codes in just thirty-seven years.

TALENT AND HEREDITY IN ANCIENT OFFICIALDOM

Organizing a large bureaucracy was a crucial task that lay before government leaders in the late seventh and early eighth centuries. Founders of the new Chinese-style state envisioned an emperor controlling all the realm's land and population, and the reigning family needed help to accomplish this basic goal. Tax accountants, military officers, university professors, experts in divination and medicine, scribes and secretaries, imperial servants, local officials, religious overseers, prison wardens—all were necessary to a well-run, centralized government. The Yōrō Code listed over six thousand offices, and by 750 as many as ten thousand bureaucrats worked for the emperor. With so many government employees, the emperor needed a way to keep track of his servants: he required a system of ranking, evaluation, promotion, payment, and dismissal. As the Japanese court was located next door to one of the world's greatest bureaucratic empires, the court of the late seventh and early eighth centuries quite naturally turned to China for guidelines.

The Yōrō Statutes contained chapters that explained office and rank (*kan'i-*

ryō), learning (*gaku-ryō*), selection and promotion (*senjo-ryō*), evaluation and testing (*kōka-ryō*), stipends (*roku-ryō*), dress (*ifuku-ryō*), and documentary forms (*kushiki-ryō*). These laws hardly make for exciting reading. Until the late 1960s, few Japanese scholars understood the esoterica of ancient bureaucratic rules and regulations, and because the subject was so abstract and legalistic, there existed no cogent explanation of how officialdom actually functioned. Then in 1969 Nomura Tadao published *The World of the Ancient Bureaucrat* (*Kodai kanryō no sekai*), a fascinating guide to the intricacies of the bureaucracy, and with its appearance a difficult field of study became comprehensible to nonspecialists.[27] Other scholars soon followed his lead, and well-documented and colorful descriptions of the lives of eighth-century officials, especially low-ranking ones, have become common tales.[28]

The work of Nomura and others came on the heels of the discovery in 1966 of a large cache of wooden tablets pertaining to official evaluation and promotion.[29] Numbering over twelve thousand, these artifacts came to light in the northeastern portion of the ditch that lay just outside the great wall (*ōgaki*) of Nara Palace. Further to the east lay the estate of Fujiwara no Fubito, chairman of the committees that wrote the Taihō and Yōrō codes and the most influential courtier of the early Nara period.[30] Although few tablets contained dates, most seemed to belong to the latter half of the eighth century.[31] Archaeologists classified the majority of these relics as shaved pieces (*kezuri kuzu*). They were remnants of tablets the government had used over and over again, shaving them down until little was left. Many had only one or two legible characters, but historians quickly developed theories about them based on what they knew from the law codes. A few examples will suggest how these scholars combined tablet data with other information to illuminate the process of adapting Chinese government practice to their own situation.[32]

The first example is a rare complete tablet. On the front it reads:

> Lesser Initial Rank, Lower Grade   Takaya no Muraji Yakamaro
> Age: 50   Right Capital
> Total Days for Six Work Evaluations: 1,099
> Six Years: Middle Level

On the back it says:

> Bureau of Divination (*on'yō-ryō*)

The first line of the artifact clearly listed an official and his rank. Takaya's status followed the Taihō Code under which there were thirty grades and nine numbered ranks; Takaya's Lesser Initial Rank was at the very bottom. The second line mentions Takaya's age (fifty) and his place of registration in the government census, the right half of the capital, Heijō. About two-thirds of the 215 officials named in tablets from the 1966 exacavation hailed from Heijō or the five adjoining provinces. Thus Takaya no Muraji Yakamaro was a low-ranking bureaucrat who lived in Nara in the latter half of the eighth century. The third line needs more explanation. Takaya had probably been working for the government for many years; at least he had received annual evaluations (kō) by his superiors for the last six years. By surviving six consecutive annual reviews, the law codes state that he now had a chance for a promotion. Furthermore, the tablet reveals that over the course of those six years Takaya had come to the office on 1,099 days, an average of 183 days a year. Was Takaya qualified for a promotion in rank?

To answer that question, a little background is helpful. The Taihō Code designated two categories of officials: salarymen (chōjō), who were required to come to the office every day, and shift workers (bunpan), who served in rotations. A year for either kind of official began on the first day of the eighth month. Salarymen had to come to the office at least 240 days a year; shift workers were required to work 140 days to be eligible for a yearly work evaluation and advancement. This requirement, which was established by the Taihō Code, undoubtedly was designed to discourage absenteeism. Takaya's average of 183 days at the office per year qualified him for a series of six annual reviews, which indicates that he was a shift worker. Scholars also know that he was deemed a satisfactory worker. The law codes required responsible superiors to evaluate every eligible subordinate shift worker in terms of three performance levels: Good (jōtō), Average (chūtō), or Poor (getō). Takaya's job was probably in the bureau of divination, as written on the reverse side of the tablet, and for each of the six years he worked there his superior rated him as Average.

The Taihō and Yōrō codes specified how a shift worker earned this rating.[33] Takaya's mark meant that he "came for his shift without fail and accomplished the work requested of him"; for a Good evaluation Takaya would have had to "have few desires, been respectfully wise, and his management of affairs been capable." A Poor rating went to those who "ran away and did not appear for rotation" or whose "management of affairs was lacking." Thus it might appear that Takaya was an average bureaucrat doing his job. But the wooden tablets unearthed in 1966 suggest that Takaya either had a strict superior or was an inferior worker. For while Takaya earned an Average assessment, the overwhelming majority of tablets that showed marks for shift workers recorded Good ratings.[34] Perhaps favorable evaluations reflected well on a superior or, as some Japanese scholars hold, evaluating a subordinate might ordinarily have been a mechanical exercise.[35]

The law codes allowed the ministry of rites (*shikibu shō*), which was charged with evaluating and promoting officials, to calculate how far up the ladder of thirty grades Takaya's performance would take him. In his case it was simple: the law stated that an Average rating would enable the worker to advance a single grade.[36] Therefore Takaya no Muraji Yakamaro, aged fifty, had managed after six years of supervised work at his shift position in the bureau of divination to go from the Lesser Initial Rank, lower grade, to the Lesser Initial Rank, upper grade.

Takaya's experience may have been common.[37] Other wooden tablets show more about how the system functioned:

TABLET 1
Last Year: Good Rating
Rank Child
Junior Eighth Rank, upper grade   Hirone no Hiroji
Age: 32   Asukabe District, Kawachi Province

TABLET 2
Last Year: Came Out
Rank Child
Unranked   Hinooki no Miyatsuko.............................
Age: 34

TABLET 3
Shadow Grandson
Unranked...........................[38]

The first tablet was complete and begins with the rank holder's evaluation from last year, in this case a Good rating. His name was Hirone no Hiroji, and he held the Junior Eighth Rank, upper grade, which put him four grades above Takaya even though he was eighteen years younger. Hirone appeared for the census in Asukabe district of Kawachi province, not far from a river leading to Nara. The basis for Hirone's higher rank was probably his status as a "rank child" (*ishi*). According to the Taihō Code, candidates for bureaucratic preferment fell into four categories: "shadow children" (*onshi*); "shadow grandchildren" (*onson*, as in Tablet 3); "rank children" (Tablets 1 and 2); and "plain adults" (*hakuchō*). The law guaranteed that the aristocracy (the Fifth Rank and above) was almost always restricted to offspring of the highest nobility; in practice, similar guarantees held for lower-ranking bureaucrats, who usually came from families of current jobholders.

To elaborate, the bureaucratic system could make such guarantees because it allowed aristocratic offspring to start their careers higher up in the bureaucracy, basing their enhanced rank on their father's or grandfather's rank. (See Table 4.1.) For example: if one was the male heir ("shadow child") of an aristocratic father holding the Third Rank (frequently attained by such great noble families as the Fujiwara or Ōtomo, for instance), then one could begin a career at age twenty-one at the Junior Sixth Rank, upper grade, only three grades from entrance into the aristocracy at the Junior Fifth Rank, lower grade. Nonheirs began one grade lower; nonheir grandchildren, two. With Good evaluations, the bright noble youth would be on the verge of entering the exclusive society of the Nara court after one evaluation period (age twenty-seven). Even Average ratings would place the heir to a good family in a similar position after three six-year evaluation periods, or by age thirty-nine.[39]

"Rank children" like Hirone were not as fortunate as "shadow children" or "grandchildren," but they still had some advantage in hiring and promotion by virtue of their father's position. By law, a "rank child" was the heir of a lower-level bureaucrat of the Sixth to Eighth Rank. Hirone's tablet does not state his father's status or how Hirone had managed to rise to the Junior Eighth Rank, lower grade, at the relatively young age of thirty-two. He fared much better than Takaya, perhaps due to better evaluations, more frequent promotions, or his father's influence, but Hirone no Hiroji was still very unlikely to reach the aristocracy.[40]

Thus the rules of the game determined who would be the primary beneficiaries even before anyone went to work. Nomura has compared the differential rates of promotion to nobles' traveling from Tokyo to Osaka by the bullet train while everybody else rode a local. Furthermore, although most "shadow sons" and "grandsons" went to the state-sponsored university or gained experience as chamberlains (*toneri*) for various government agencies, one can interpret the laws as meaning that a noble son could idly await his twenty-first birthday and automatically obtain the preordained high rank.

One can argue, as Robert Borgen has done in his excellent *Sugawara no Michizane and the Early Heian Court,* that Japan was merely adapting a Tang system that was itself neither fully open to talent nor egalitarian and thus gave a particularly prominent place to families with the proper bloodlines.[41] It is well to remember, however, that rather than merely borrowing the idea of "shadow sons" and "rank children" from the Chinese, authors of the Taihō Code made significant changes. Although the Japanese court did not permit the advantage of birth to extend to "shadow great-grandchildren," as was the case in China, this disadvantage was small so long as the same lineage consistently produced high rank holders. Moreover, Japanese "shadow sons" and

Table 4.1 Shadow Ranks in Ancient Japan and Tang China

A. Japan

Official's Rank	Heir	Nonheir	Heir-Grandson	Grandchildren
First	Junior 5, lower	Senior 6, upper	Same	Senior 6, lower
Second	Senior 6, lower	Junior 6, upper	Same	Junior 6, lower
Third	Junior 6, upper	Junior 6, lower	Same	Senior 7, upper
Senior Fourth	Senior 7, lower	Junior 7 upper		
Junior Fourth	Junior 7, upper	Junior 7, lower		
Senior Fifth	Senior 8, lower	Junior 8, upper		
Junior Fifth	Junior 8, upper	Junior 8, lower		

B. China

Official's Rank	Child	Grandchild	Great-Grandchild
First	Senior 7, upper	Senior 7, lower	Junior 7, upper
Second	Senior 7, lower	Junior 7, upper	Junior 7, lower
Senior Third	Junior 7, upper	Junior 7, lower	Senior 8, upper
Junior Third	Junior 7, lower	Senior 8, upper	Senior 8, lower
Senior Fourth	Senior 8, upper	Senior 8, lower	
Junior Fourth	Senior 8, lower	Junior 8, upper	
Senior Fifth	Junior 8, upper	Junior 8, lower	
Junior Fifth	Junior 8, lower	None	

Source: Nomura Tadao, *Kodai kanryō no sekai,* p. 26.

"grandsons" started at a considerably more elevated rank than did their peers under the Tang. Nomura has concluded that the Japanese court greatly expanded the opportunity given to those with proper blood ties over what was available to nobles in China.[42]

One could always go to the government university, as described in Borgen's book, but no one interested in gaining influence in the eighth century would have chosen this path, much less tried to graduate, because it was so difficult and took so long.[43] In theory anyone could become a university student, even as early as age thirteen, but the newly matriculated pupil would then face six or seven years of hard study and a grueling final exam that practically no one in ancient Japan ever passed. Even if one was successful on the exam, as Sugawara no Michizane just barely was, the university graduate of lesser family started out lower in rank than "shadow children" and usually at a more advanced age. In hiring, evaluating, and promoting the bureaucrats who served the emperor, the court determined that an aristocrat, often but not always talented, was a better risk than even a capable commoner.

Official emphasis on heredity in assigning rank was undoubtedly based on the long experience of the Yamato court. Initially the use of surnames (*uji*) and titles (*kabane*), probably related to those in Korea, signified hereditary membership and function in the aristocracy. The court of the fifth and sixth centuries further recognized the importance of bloodlines by naming several immigrant families to be hereditary scribes (*fuhito*). In an age when literacy was not widespread, select families tended to excel at the arts of composition and mathematics. In the early seventh century, cap ranks possibly adopted from Paekche or Silla allowed for the consideration of individual ability for the first time.[44] Political pressures within the court when the Taihō Code was written may have reinforced this trend. The Yōrō Code probably struck the correct balance by referring to talent (*keiseki*) six times while retaining the guiding principle that ability and the leisure to study ran in families.

The pattern of rule by an aristocratic elite remained entrenched throughout the 700s. Although a careful study of social mobility in the Nara aristocracy is beyond the scope of this book, familiarity with the political history of the eighth century suggests that the same noble lineages which dominated the Yamato period continued to hold sway. John Hall has characterized the Heian period as evincing a "return to familial authority," but most evidence suggests that the Japanese court of the eighth century never abandoned or even significantly curtailed its reliance on bloodlines.[45] If anything, more opportunities seemed to have opened up for university students in the ninth century, as devotion to Chinese cultural norms heightened at the court.[46] But even in the early Heian period heredity continued to be a sine qua non of membership in officialdom.

Wooden tablets unearthed from Nara have helped to show how the court put together a large bureaucracy by linking Chinese-style principles of evaluation and promotion to the earlier tradition of hereditary rule. They have also begun to show how the ancient bureaucracy evolved over the years. These artifacts suggest that work evaluations of subordinate officials were regularly carried out but were usually lax, fleshing out a procedure that the law codes only outlined.

TAXATION

In organizing and codifying the revenue system, as with the bureaucracy, the court of the late seventh century needed to take its own traditions into consideration. Yamato kings of the sixth and seventh centuries had been collecting taxes for many years, and despite the court's desire to use the best Chinese-style principles to enhance its power, these guidelines had to be adapted to fit Japan's history and customs. This section describes the origins and operation of Japan's tax system of the late seventh and eighth centuries, focusing on the numerous tax tags and labels (*nifuda* and *tsukefuda*) that archaeologists have unearthed from capitals at Fujiwara, Nara, and Nagaoka over the last thirty years.

In essence, the Nara court relied on head taxes paid in kind from three sources: a local products levy (*chō*); corvée exemption revenue normally submitted in hemp cloth (*yō*); and a land tax (*so*).[47] In actuality, the system was more complicated than these three terms convey. To begin with, there were four variants on the local products tax, including one paid exclusively in medicinal herbs. Moreover, in addition to the 3 percent land tax, most of which stayed at the provincial headquarters, peasants also contributed to the council of state 100 percent of the grain they harvested from the imperial demesne (*kanden*) and 20 percent of the crops they raised on certain other government lands (*kōden*).

The idea for these three major taxes came from the Tang dynasty.[48] The Chinese local products tax (*diao*) consisted solely of cloth, as did the corvée exemption levy (*yung*); the land tax (*zu*) comprised millet or rice and was not burdensome. The unit of taxation in China was the individual, whose name appeared in a census and who received a grant of land from the government. As numerous scholars have indicated, this system of taxes-in-kind fit a society, such as northern China around 500, where money was not yet in widespread use and where turmoil was common because of nomadic invasions and epidemic outbreaks. By making equal allocations of land and levying the same tax on each adult, the northern Chinese governments from the fall of the Later Han in 221 to the seventh-century Tang hoped to ensure a growing, or at least stable, tax base.

The Japanese court too desired maximum revenues from its own recalcitrant and disease-ridden populace and for this reason borrowed the sophisticated Chinese-style system. Wooden tablets unearthed from Nara and Fujiwara show, however, that a different Japanese reality lay behind the simple one-syllable terms *chō, yō,* and *so.* Consider first the local products tax (*chō*). According to Tang law, the levy was payable only in cloth, but the Japanese codes specified that it could be satisfied by submitting iron, salt, or any of several varieties of fish, game, or vegetables. The court was attempting to adapt a Chinese idea to domestic conditions, but in doing so it altered the Tang revenue in an important way.

A simple comparison of the Japanese and Chinese statutes had led some scholars to suspect that the Japanese court was incorporating native traditions of taxation into the Chinese-style system, but the 1963 discovery of wooden tablets at Heijō Palace clinched the argument because they listed a type of revenue not mentioned in the codes.[49] The little-known tax was called *nie* ("offering"), and wooden tablets using this term soon came to light at Fujiwara also. Scholars eventually noted that this word appeared in other sources: in *The Man'yōshū,* in tales from *The Chronicles,* and in eighth-century administrative documents written by provincial governors. Even the Taika Reform edict included the heretofore obscure levy in a rare variation of the wording of later law codes.

By 1993, archaeologists had discovered about 120 wooden tablets containing this term.[50] Here are some examples:

1. *Front:* One measure (*to*) of bean paste (*miso*)   Great offering (*ōnie*) from Chichibu district in Musashi province
    Back: Tenpyō 17 (745) . . .
2. *Front:* Seaweed (*wakame*) produced from Tsuno Island, Toyura district, Nagato province   Tenpyō 18/3/29 (746)
3. *Front:* Jellyfish (*kurage*) from Bizen province, especially submitted   Two measures (*to*) of *minie*
    Back: Tenpyō 18/9/25 (746)[51]

The tablets bearing this writing are all rectangles (*tansaku gata*) with indentations near the top where a string could attach the label to the product being contributed.

Japanese scholars studying the Nara tax system soon noted two character-istics shared by most tablets denoting *nie*. First, officials had tied the over-whelming majority to goods from the sea, most of which were defined as sub-ject to local products tax (*chō*) in the law codes. Second, although the statute specified that the local products levy was a head tax, tablets never referred to individual taxpayers but usually named a district, island, or producer group. Combining these two observations with references in *The Man'yōshū* and *The Chronicles*, historians pieced together the evolution of one-third of the Nara tax system. They concluded that the local products levy, and perhaps the entire tax system of the eighth century, originated in the practice of localities' sub-mitting "the riches of the sea" to the Yamato king as an "offering" (*nie*). This practice spread across the realm, presumably as different regions came under the court's domination in the centuries before 645. Eighth-century tablets retained the postulated custom of locality-based tribute despite introduction of the Tang system based on head taxes.

When the court adopted the Chinese local products tax in 701, it appears that lawgivers simply subsumed the goods that had formerly come as "offer-ings" (*nie*) under the heading of the local products tax, and the term for the Yamato-era levy dropped out of the Taihō Code. Local officials writing wooden tablets, however, continued to characterize their contribution as an offering (*ōnie; minie*). What looked like a straightforward borrowing of the Chinese idea of a cloth tax thus turned out to be in the case of many items a new name (*chō*) for an old Japanese practice (*nie*).[52]

Most surviving tablets tied to goods submitted as "offerings" came from the provinces of Awa, Izu, Wakasa, and Shima. Fourteen tablets from Awa province in the Kanto, which came to light at Nara, were all originally attached to abalone and used the Yamato-period term "*nie*."[53] One historian has sur-mised that in Awa offerings of abalone began as tribute from residents to that area's leading family. When Awa came under the control of Yamato in the late sixth century, abalone served as tribute to the Yamato monarch from the ser-vice groups (*be*) there. It is surely no accident that Awa was a base for the Kashiwade family, who were in charge of supplying the imperial larder. Sub-sequently the Taihō Code designated abalone as an item to be submitted as a local products levy. Izu province too sent a sea product (*bonito*) to Yamato. But in contrast to Awa, there had been no strong political leader in Izu before the Yamato court began setting up service groups (*be*) there after 500.[54] Eighth-century tablets from Izu contain many names using the character "*be*" in ways that suggest the collection of the bonito "offerings" was little changed from what it had been under Yamato control. Historians cite similar examples for the evolution of abalone, seaweed, and salt taxes in Shima and Wakasa.[55]

These tablets and other sources suggest that practically all items listed under the local products tax in Nara law codes had earlier been sent to the Yamato court. Some, notably sea products and other foods, had been known as "offerings" (*minie*); others, such as iron and salt, had been called "tribute" (*mitsuki*).[56] To date, no tablets listing cloth as *nie* have come to light, and such cloths as silk and hemp may not have been taxable items prior to the adoption of the Tang cloth tax. Indeed, Japanese lawgivers may have first included fabrics as part of the local products tax merely to copy the Chinese. The court had required hemp and silk prior to 645, however, so it seems plausible that even these items, which formed the heart of the Chinese cloth levy, were part of the Yamato tribute system.

Some Japanese scholars believe that the concept of a tribute tax was related to similar practices in Paekche and Silla.[57] According to Ishigami Eiichi, Japan's leading expert on the tribute tax in Japan and Korea, the Paekche king collected tribute from local areas as early as 498. The Japanese court may have learned much about this type of levy from Silla, as well, which collected various products from regional leaders as signs of their submission beginning in 512. Of course, the Yamato state could have invented the custom on its own. But given the close relations between Yamato and the southern Korean kingdoms, it seems more plausible that Yamato adapted the idea of tribute revenue from Paekche or Silla in the sixth century.

In fact, the origins of all three Nara-period taxes probably antedated the determination to borrow from China in the late seventh century. The light land tax (*so*), which constituted anywhere from 3 to 5 percent of a peasant's harvest, was handled in a manner fundamentally different from the Tang levy (*zu*): whereas Tang functionaries shipped all grain revenues to the capital, in Japan the lion's share of the land tax stayed at the provincial and district level, where officials stored it for use in emergencies.[58] As indicated in Chapter 3, the corvée exemption tax (*yō*) in Japan also operated differently from the Chinese levy (*yung*), because after 702 Japanese officials always collected hemp cloth and other staples from adult males to defray the wages of a hired labor force. In China, at least in the early Tang period, the corvée levy was often satisfied through twenty days of unremunerated labor under government supervision.[59]

Wooden tablets occasionally reveal other native practices that Japanese officials represented through Chinese terms. Consider the case of rice paid as the corvée exemption levy (*yōmai*). As of 1981, archaeologists had uncovered some thirty-nine examples of tablets attached to bales of rice that were meant for workers laboring at Heijō. For instance:

Front: Kawakami small administrative village (*ri*)
Yamano large administrative village (*gō*)
Ana district, Bingo province
Back: Yatabe Konu: 3 *to*
Yatabe Kimi: 3 *to*
The aforementioned corvée exemption rice (*yōmai*):
6 *to*[60]

A senior Japanese historian has observed that the amount of rice contained in a bale was standard at either 5 *to* (five examples), 6 *to* (seven examples), or 5 *to* 8 *shō* (two examples).[61] Scholars have suggested two ways of looking at the standardization of bale size. Several have pointed out that 5 to 6 *to* of rice was the quantity necessary to feed one laborer (*shichō*, "service adult") for one month. The variation between 5 and 6 *to* may have occurred because during some months (particularly cold ones) laborers would require more food than others. Another historian at Tokyo University has argued that standardization was for the convenience of the taxpayer; each male adult paid 3 *to* of rice and two payments were combined into a 6-*to* bale submitted to the government.[62]

The wooden tablets attached to rice paid in lieu of corvée (*yōmai*) reflect a pre-Taika labor custom. When service adults came to the capital to work before 645, the court also regarded them as tribute from their home village. In that spirit, the Yamato state required the village to provide a cook and pay the laborer's expenses. Tablets showing rice payments in exactly the amounts required to feed one service adult for a month indicate that even after the adoption of Chinese-style institutions, this Yamato practice changed little. It would not be at all surprising if the 6 *to* of rice submitted from Bingo province in the preceding tablet eventually found its way into the stomachs of workmen from the same province, as dictated by pre-Taika custom.

The evidence from tax tags relating to the local products and corvée exemption levies suggests a hypothesis about the nature of the changes the Japanese revenue system underwent in the late seventh and early eighth centuries. Even though the court compiled three new sets of statutes between 681 and 718, to a large degree they were simply codifications of earlier customs, like the "offering" levy or the "service adult," which continued with new Chinese names. To be sure, the adoption of Chinese-style institutions meant a reorganization for Japan and its court, and the reorganized tax system was probably more efficient and thorough than its Yamato predecessor. But the foundations for eighth-century practices had been laid during the Yamato period.

Apart from shedding light on the adaptation of Chinese-style tax institutions, tags and labels provide historians with another bit of valuable information. Thanks to the many dated tablets listing the tribute's province of origin, historians are beginning to gain insight into the vicissitudes of the eighth-century tax base. Tables 4.2 and 4.3, which enumerate tablets by place and year, have limited significance, since the uncovering of a large new cache of tablets could radically alter the evidence of tax receipts for particular years or areas—as happened with the "Second Rank Great Avenue" (*nijō ōji*) discoveries that accounted for the disproportionate number of tablets for the years 735–736 or for Izu or Oki provinces. Yet it is probably noteworthy, for example, that the court received no revenues from the Tohoku and very little from Kyushu, north central Honshu (the Tōsandō), or the northern Japan Sea littoral (Hokurikudō). Tax goods from Kyushu were consumed at Dazaifu, but there is at present no explanation for the other shortfalls. The tax base seemingly centered on central and western Honshu and coastal provinces west of Hakone (Tōkaidō). The eighth-century state was truly a "western Japanese" phenomenon.

The relative dearth of tablets for the last twenty years of the Nara period is also suggestive: only twelve tags dating after 764 have been recovered. Legal sources indicate that the government began to complain about the nonpayment, poor quality, or late submission of revenues such as the local products tax by 800. Archaeological evidence, however, hints that the problem may have started somewhat earlier:

> *Front:* 5 *to* of rice from Mino province in payment of
>   assessment for Hōki 11 (780)
> *Back:* Enryaku 8 (789)[63]

By the late eighth century, the tax system that had served aristocrats so well was beginning to change. To understand these changes and their causes, scholars must await further discoveries of tax tags and labels that will slowly clarify the picture of the eighth-century tax base's ups and downs.

ARISTOCRATIC HOUSEHOLDS

In the late 1980s, two massive finds of wooden tablets near Nara Palace revealed the power of these archaeological sources to enhance the study of ancient Japanese history. These two caches, known as the tablets of Prince Nagaya (*Nagaya ōke mokkan*) and those of the Second Rank Great Avenue (*nijō ōji mokkan*), amounted to about 35,000 and 70,000 respectively, effectively trip-

Table 4.2   Recovered *Mokkan* Used to Tag Tax
Payments, Listed by Five-Year Intervals

710–714	(23)
715–719	(8)
720–724	(22)
725–729	(27)
730–734	(36)
735–739	(202)
740–744	(2)
745–749	(72)
750–754	(4)
755–759	(12)
760–764	(14)
765–769	(5)
770–774	(5)
775–779	(1)
780–784	(1)

ling in one fell swoop the number of such relics available to scholars. Tablets from these finds were so numerous that even as late as 1995 archaeologists were still washing their precious artifacts and trying to assess their meaning.[64] In the view of one historian, the discoveries began a new era in research on *mokkan*.[65]

The two caches came to light about 300 meters south of the indented southeastern corner of the great wall (*ōgaki*) of Nara Palace. (See Figure 3.3.) Archaeologists recovered the tablets of Prince Nagaya from a ditch about 3 meters wide by 1 meter deep that lay within an aristocratic residence compound fronting on the south side of Second Rank Great Avenue. Because the compound was located so near the palace and the avenue, it was clear that the owners were highly placed aristocrats. The tablets bore dates from 711 to 716, and scholars believe that Nagaya's staff must have thrown them away soon after the latter date. The other batch of *mokkan* was unearthed atop a section of the avenue, and internal clues suggest that it had once belonged to Fujiwara no Maro, who could well have possessed a residence compound comparable to Nagaya's just across the street to the north. These tablets covered the years from 732 to 739; most were dated 735 and 736.

**Table 4.3　Recovered *Mokkan* Used to Tag Tax Payments,
Listed by Province of Origin**

Kinai and Adjacent Provinces	*Western Honshu*
Yamashiro (1)	Hōki (3)
Izumi (1)	Oki (37)
Kawachi (2)	Mimasaka (1)
Tanba (7)	Bizen (6)
Tajima (4)	Bitchū (3)
Ōmi (2)	Bingo (2)
Wakasa (24)	Izumo (3)
Ise (2)	Iwami (2)
Shima (14)	Awa (5)
Kii (15)	Suō (8)
Awaji (5)	Nagato (4)
Harima (2)	Sanuki (4)
Inaba (9)	
Kyushu	*Tōkaidō*
Buzen (3)	Owari (8)
Higo (6)	Mikawa (78)
Hizen (4)	Suruga (28)
Chikugo (3)	Izu (74)
Chikuzen (1)	Kai (3)
	Sagami (1)
Tōsandō	Musashi (4)
Mino (4)	Awa (24)
Shinano (1)	Kazusa (3)
	Tōtōmi (2)
Hokurikudō	Hitachi (4)
Noto (7)	
Echizen (5)	
Etchū (1)	

Sources: *Heijō-kyū mokkan* 1–4: *kaisetsu*; *Heijō-kyū hakkutsu chōsa shutsudo mokkan gaihō*, vols. 4–25; and *Mokkan kenkyū* 1–16 (1979–1994). Only those provinces for which there are data are listed.

If in fact the two aristocrats owned homes right across the street from each other, it would be one of the great ironies of Japanese history, for the two were bitter political rivals. Nagaya was the son of Prince Takechi, who in turn was the son of Temmu and also one of Temmu's right-hand men. During the years mentioned in his tablets, Nagaya was in his late twenties and held the lofty status of Junior Third Court Rank. Yet Nagaya's day in the sun was to come later, from 721 to 729, after the death of the powerful Fujiwara no Fubito. In 729, Nagaya was forced to commit suicide, victim of a plot by certain Fujiwara. The other aristocrat, Maro, was born in 695, son of Fubito and later founder of one of the four main branches of the Fujiwara. He served in many important positions, among them chief official of the Left Capital, and the Second Rank Great Avenue tablets contain many references to his service in that post. Maro was also the minister of war and as such led an expedition against the "barbarians" of northeastern Honshu. After ousting Nagaya in 729, Maro and his brothers controlled the court until 737, when the smallpox epidemic of 735–737 killed them all. Only a few tablets associated with Maro originate after 736.

Scholars consider the chief significance of these wooden tablets to be what they tell about aristocratic household organization. According to the law codes of the early eighth century, the government granted recognition and support for aristocrats of the very highest ranks. As siblings or first-generation offspring of an emperor, princes and princesses (*shinnō* and *nai shinnō*) had their own system of court ranks, graded from First to Fourth Degree (*hon*), and each was served by as many as seven state-ranked and state-salaried bureaucrats who oversaw the household. The top three court ranks (*i; kurai*) for all other aristocrats also included government support, though on a less lavish scale. An official of the Junior Third Rank, such as Nagaya, was supposed to have been served by two officially graded and stipended assistants. Nagaya did not qualify for support because of his princely standing but because of his rank, and even then he stood near the bottom of this small topmost slice of the aristocratic few.

Nagaya needed considerable help to manage the resources put at his disposal by the state. According to law, he should have been assigned sixty attendants (*shijin*) to run his messages and perform menial tasks; two hundred or more "sustenance" households (*fuko*) to pay directly to his household taxes otherwise remitted to the government; and forty *chō* of income-producing land based on his rank (*iden*). Indeed, even though he stood at the bottom of this small cluster of state-supported aristocrats, Nagaya would have had an estate as large as some of Japan's smallest provinces.[66]

Wooden tablets associated with Prince Nagaya show that he was even richer than one might imagine from a cursory reading of the codes.[67] The excavation covered six hectares (15 acres) and revealed the existence of about thirty buildings, where Nagaya's four wives, at least eighteen children and siblings, and their four wet nurses spent time.[68] Besides residences, the thirty buildings housed the main office (*keryō sho*) where state-supported bureaucrats did their jobs, as well as other administrative centers employing workers of every description. Various divisions of these centers handled Nagaya's enterprises. (See Figure 4.1.) Eight of them supervised the feeding and clothing of his family, employing cooks, rice wine brewers, yogurt makers, firewood collectors, seamstresses, dyers, potters, metal pot makers, movers, and many others. Nagaya's manufacturing division included plasterers, tanners, bronze casters, makers of swords, bows, arrows, belts, and harps (*koto*), and sculptors of Bud-

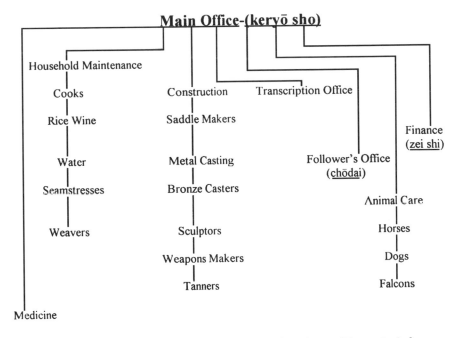

Main Office-(keryō sho)

Household Maintenance

Cooks   Construction   Transcription Office

Rice Wine   Saddle Makers

Water   Metal Casting   Follower's Office   Finance (*zei shi*)
                                   (*chōdai*)

Seamstresses   Bronze Casters

                                   Animal Care

Weavers   Sculptors   Horses

                 Weapons Makers   Dogs

                 Tanners   Falcons

Medicine

FIGURE 4.1   Prince Nagaya's Household Organization. *Source: Nagaya ō teitaku to mokkan*, p. 100. © Nara Kokuritsu Bunkazai Kenkyūjo.

dhist statues. A special division oversaw the transcription of Buddhist sutras. Other offices managed Nagaya's attendants, cared for his horses, dogs, and falcons, diagnosed his family's illnesses and prescribed medicines, and managed a system of rice loans that financed many enterprises.[69]

The economic base for Nagaya's household, as the reference to assigned households and lands suggests, was impressive. Tablets refer frequently to family fields and gardens in Yamato and Yamashiro, all worked by local peasants. Slaves cultivated some of Nagaya's lands. He had an ice storehouse at Tsuge in Yamato, lumberyards in the mountains of Tanba, and a charcoal-firing center and a salt bin at unknown sites. Moreover, more than thirty provinces shipped tribute items to his family, probably from sustenance households allotted him by the government. From Ōmi and Echizen, Nagaya received polished rice. Suō provided him with salt. Riches of the sea came to Nagaya as "offerings" (nie).[70]

While not as detailed as the Nagaya artifacts, tablets associated with Fujiwara no Maro also hint at an elaborate household administration. About four hundred tax tags have come to light, and they show that Maro probably consumed maritime "offerings" from Mikawa, Izu, Suruga, Awa, Wakasa, and Oki. Only sparse evidence of Maro's bureaucratic arrangements survives, but there are mentions of a bureau of the household at Okamoto (Okamoto taku no tsukasa), an office of gardens at Ikebe, Uda stables, and fields at O. Many tablets deal with guard duty at Nara Palace, as befits records of the minister of war. Ten tablets also pertain to Maro's administration of the Left Capital, mostly recording the donation of rats to be used as food for his falcons.[71]

Many questions surround these two caches, but none is more important than the most obvious: who owned and who was the primary resident at the great estate uncovered by the excavation? To be sure, archaeologists quickly named the batch of tablets found at the estate "the Prince Nagaya mokkan," but the phrase derived from the appearance of the prince's name on only eight artifacts. Scholars, the media, and the general public were so excited to think that archaeologists had actually found Nagaya's residence that the name stuck. In fact other tablets—including one for Princess Hidaka (later Emperor Genshō) and eleven for the "Northern Palace" (or "Mistress," kita no miya)—suggest that Nagaya may not have been the owner or primary occupant.

Moreover, historians soon realized that not one but two organizations oversaw household affairs.[72] One was suited to Nagaya's status rather well: it was small and included only two state-graded and state-salaried bureaucrats (keryō; shori).[73] The other unit was much larger, having four officials, as was appropriate for an imperial relative of the Second Degree (nihon). Scholars disagree over the identity of the patron of the second organization, but many, including archaeologists at the Nara National Cultural Properties Research Institute, think it belonged to Nagaya's chief wife, Princess Kibi.[74] Other records indicate that Kibi was known as the "Northern Mistress."[75]

The prince had a noble lineage, but Princess Kibi's was positively exalted. As Figure 4.2 shows, her father was Kusakabe, Temmu's favorite son who died tragically before ascending the throne. Her mother was Emperor Genmei, her brother Emperor Mommu, and her sister Emperor Genshō. Between 711 and 716, Kibi held the Third Degree, a stature that formally entitled her to a household bureaucracy more elaborate than her husband's.[76] Her economic resources, on the other hand, were slightly less, consisting of sixty attendants (chōdai), tax receipts from two hundred sustenance households, and thirty-four chō of land. Fields and gardens in Yamashiro probably belonged to Kibi, too. On balance, she was Nagaya's equal or better.

Kibi owed her considerable perquisites to authors of the codes. They, in turn, had altered Tang practice to guarantee that women who were close imperial relatives would have their own state-supported bureaucracy and an extensive economic base. The extant Tang codes do not contain the sentence

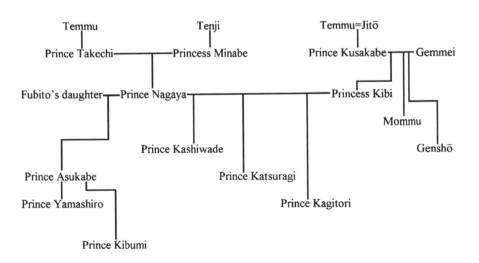

FIGURE 4.2   Nagaya's and Kibi's Lineages.

"princesses (*nai shinnō*) shall follow this" [precedent set for princes (*shinnō*)], a phrase found in the Yōrō Code.[77] The woman historian who first stressed this point believes that this establishment of state-recognized aristocratic households in the law codes merely legalized prevailing Japanese custom.[78] In revealing the state-sanctioned political and economic power of the highest aristocratic women, the Prince Nagaya tablets have once again shown a pragmatic Japanese court adapting Chinese institutions and laws to a different environment and social structure.

The character of Nagaya and Maro's economic bases is a second topic frequently analyzed by historians. Legal sources delineate the lands and taxes due such people as Nagaya and Maro, but tablets rarely reveal explicitly that the two aristocrats were living off grants from the court. The lack of direct reference to such institutions as sustenance households leads one to ask: which aristocratic possessions were hereditary and which had the Nara court granted to Nagaya and Maro recently as a result of their personal acquisition of particular ranks and offices? One can come closer to answering this query for Nagaya's land than for any other property. Tablets pertaining to plots of land sometimes state acreage in round numbers, which may indicate that the fields in question were "rank land" (*iden*) allocated by the state. The reason for this conclusion derives from the few documented cases of rank land allocation, which were in round numbers.[79] But in most cases, tablets did not give rounded-off figures denoting size of fields and gardens, thus giving the impression of odds and ends of holdings scattered throughout Yamato and Yamashiro. This sort of land, which composed most holdings discussed in the tablets, was probably acreage that had been in Nagaya's or Kibi's family for several generations.

Other properties may also have been inherited. The Tsuge ice storehouse probably was. Moreover, even though they were supposedly granted by the state, one also wonders about the prince's two hundred sustenance households. According to *The Chronicles*, Nagaya's father Prince Takechi held five thousand such households in 692. Rather than withdrawing all five thousand upon Takechi's death in 696, some portion may have continued in the family and eventually been allotted as Nagaya's share. As some scholars point out, Nagaya's sources of income included inherited family property as well as support from the state, and it is nearly impossible to distinguish the two.[80]

The Nagaya tablets give other hints about continuity and change over the late seventh and early eighth centuries. For example, one undated tablet probably composed between 712 and 716 contains the name of Nagaya's senior administrator (*keryō*), Akasome Toyoshima, who held the Junior Seventh Court Rank, upper grade. As one historian has indicated, Akasome no Miyatsuko Tokotari had followed Takechi in 672, thus aiding Temmu's cause in the civil war.[81] Another relative helped oversee sutra transcription for Nagaya in 728. One suspects that the Akasome were regular "retainers" of the prince's family. *A Record of Titles and Surnames Newly Selected* reveals that the Akasome were of Korean origin, lived in the Kinai, and before 645 served as officials (*tomo no miyatsuko*) managing a service group (*be*) that was responsible for dyeing cloth for courtiers. The Akasome seem to have been typical of lower-ranking families that formed alliances with powerful aristocrats; as other examples show, these ties often engendered strong feelings of loyalty.[82] The Akasome appear to have retained their tie to Prince Takechi and his family from the civil war of 672 to Nagaya's demise in 729, a point implying continuity in the composition of aristocratic household staff over this half-century.

Finally, the Nagaya *mokkan* have raised questions of legal terminology. Consider the following tablet in which Kibi summons a female servant:

> *Front:* Princess Kibi orders with a Great Command (*ōmikoto*):
> That the slave Hakoirime come forward
> *Back:* Fifth month, eighth day　　　Secretary (*shō shori*) Kunitari Administrators (*keryō; kafu*)[83]

Great Commands normally referred only to verbal orders given by the emperor, often as part of an oral edict (*senmyō*).[84] But in this tablet the author uses the term for words of a close imperial relative. As one senior scholar has pointed out, such usage departs from guidelines on state documentary forms (*kushiki-ryō*) in the Yōrō Code. There are also four other cases in which Prince Nagaya, who was merely an imperial grandchild, used the Great Command. Use of this term by imperial relatives could suggest that Princess Kibi and her husband approached the status of emperor.[85] But there is also another explanation for these terms: perhaps administrators were unfamiliar or unconcerned with precise legal meanings.[86] Throughout the Nagaya tablets, officials of his household often deviated from Taihō Code–style documentary conventions.[87] Officials rarely inserted their court rank when they made out wooden tablets making requests or giving orders, for example, although that was required by law. They also tended to confuse forms: when transmitting a command (*fu*), they sometimes used the document (*i*) intended for communication between offices of the same status; when writing to an equal, they sometimes used the form designed for a command. Administrators may have been unaware of the relevant Taihō statutes, or they may have been too hurried to care.

It will be some time before scholars have mined the wooden tablets of Prince Nagaya and Second Rank Great Avenue for all they will yield. Many discoveries undoubtedly await. But for the present, these tablets show the creative and careful adaptation of Chinese institutions to fit Japanese conditions.

RECAPITULATION

Wooden tablets have added fascinating detail to the study of ancient Japanese history. They touch on diverse aspects of life, but this chapter has concentrated on four areas. Regarding the Taika Reform, wooden tablets at first undermined the 646 edict. Nearly all tax labels and tags from before 702, the date when officials implemented the Taihō Code, contained the Korean word for district (*hyō; kohori*) rather than the Chinese term (*gun*) that one would expect. A discovery in 1975, however, made the Taika Reform edict seem more credible. Scholars came to believe a modified "kernel of truth" argument which held that while most of the edict was doctored, the four introductory statements were likely to be authentic. This reading of the edict suggests that Kōtoku and Prince Naka had been able to start a modest momentum toward a more centralized, Chinese-style state beginning in 645.

The bureaucracy is another facet of the system on which wooden tablets shed light. They have allowed historians to begin fleshing out the lives of the nameless bureaucrats who ran the new state, and they confirm that in fact as well as in law low-level bureaucrats had little chance to enter the higher levels of aristocracy. The pre-Taika emphasis on heredity remained, although by 702 lawgivers had fused it with Chinese principles of hiring, evaluation, and promotion.

The tax system adopted by founders of the Nara state also utilized pre-645 practices. In theory the court borrowed its head taxes from the Chinese, but in reality all three had antecedents in pre-Taika times. This was especially true for the local products revenue (*chō*), which developed out of a Yamato-era tribute system and may have been related to Korean institutions. Tax labels help scholars in defining the geographical base of the government and indicate how tax revenues fluctuated over the eighth century.

The inner working of aristocratic households is a fourth area that wooden tablets have brought to light as never before. Information on over 100,000 tablets from the Nara residences of Prince Nagaya and Fujiwara no Maro describes a state-ranked and state-paid officialdom as well as a substantial set of activities to clothe, feed, and maintain the household's high-ranking nobles and large staff of underlings. Tablets show that a woman, possibly Nagaya's chief wife Kibi, maintained a substantial household organization and economic base; the unusually strong position granted to the highest noblewomen by the codes was a pragmatic adaptation to fit native social structure.

Scholars have long debated the precise nature of Chinese-style institutions, arguing that a Chinese system could never have worked in Japan, searching for aspects adapted to native society, or seeing Japan as a carbon copy of the mighty Tang. In 1971, Yoshida Takashi designed two diagrams to explain his view of this problem.[88] (See Figures 4.3 and 4.4.) Figure 4.3 suggests that the percentage of Japanese society actually affected by Chinese-style institutions was small. In particular, the penal codes, which the ruling class adopted virtually verbatim from Chinese sources, had little to do with Japanese society. Figure 4.4 supports the hypothesis that the Taihō Code basically institutionalized practices of previous ages. Except in the relatively few cases where the court utilized a Chinese law unchanged, authors either rewrote Chinese statutes, altering their basic meaning to fit local customs; eliminated the Chinese law altogether because it was irrelevant or violated strictures of ancient Japan;

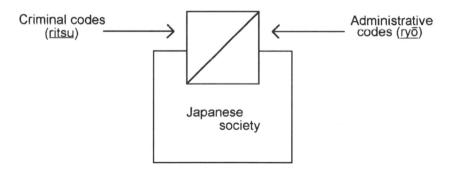

FIGURE 4.3   Law Codes and Japanese Society. *Source:* Yoshida Takashi, "Ritsuryō to kyaku," in Okazaki Takashi and Hirano Kunio, eds., *Kodai no Nihon 9: kenkyū shiryō*, p. 245.

Content of Law / Purpose of Law	(I) Same As Chinese Law	(II) Revise Chinese Law	(III) Newly Created In Japan; Not in Chinese Law	(IV) Cut Chinese Law
(a) Creation of a New Institution	●	●	○	
(b) Pre-existing Native Japanese Institution	○	●	●	
(c) No Need to Create a New Institution				●

FIGURE 4.4   Compiling the Chinese-Style Law Codes. *Source:* Yoshida Takashi, "Ritsuryō to kyaku," in Okazaki Takashi and Hirano Kunio, eds., *Kodai no Nihon 9: kenkyū shiryō,* p. 247. *Note:* Darkened dots indicate preponderance of cases.

or invented a law to justify a native custom that was not part of Chinese society. The statutes that functioned best in Nara Japan were those originating in the Yamato age with no analog in China. The least successful, unenforced sections were those that most closely resembled Chinese counterparts.

Wooden tablets have contributed to this debate by providing welcome evidence on the workings of government and society during the seventh and eighth centuries. They show clearly that a court, bureaucracy, and law codes were all operating then. At the same time, these invaluable new sources vindicate scholars who have asserted that the changes from 645 to 800 were "pragmatic compromises with existing institutions" and included "differences and innovations which were a product of the domestic realities of seventh century Japan."[89]

CONCLUSION

This book has combined both historical and archaeological sources to trace Japan's development from about A.D. 100 to 800. Chapter 1 examined the long-standing controversy over Yamatai as seen in Chen Shou's *History of the Wei Dynasty*. Historians framed the original debate, mining the "Account of the Wa" for clues as to the location and nature of the "queen's country" even as early as the Edo period. By the twentieth century, historians had divided into two camps: one postulated that Himiko was nothing more than a village shaman from northern Kyushu, while the other argued that Yamatai was located in the Kinai and encompassed most of western Japan. Although some historians analyzed other problems, such as the nature of the Wa confederation, most were consumed by this endless controversy.

Archaeologists began to address the Yamatai problem in the prewar era, but they made their greatest contributions beginning around 1960. Despite their best efforts, the site of Himiko's home and burial place remain unknown, but the framework established by historians has affected archaeological research. Many archaeologists maintain that Chen's account is a generally accurate portrayal of late Yayoi Japan, and they consequently see Yamatai as only one chiefdom among many. They may locate it in either Kyushu or the Kinai. Other archaeologists use data from mirrors and tombs to conclude that Himiko lived in a transitional era, and they usually side with historians arguing that Yamatai was based in the Kinai and controlled much of the western archipelago.

While archaeologists have achieved no consensus on Yamatai, their work has brought second- and third-century Japan to life as never before. The technologies of rice agriculture and metallurgy introduced around 300 B.C. encouraged dramatic population increase, perhaps by a factor of ten. Bilateral kinship was probably the rule for many families, who practiced age and gender discrimination. People learned to weave and wear hemp clothes and use tattoos to distinguish residents of different villages, while continuing Jōmon customs such as the application of cosmetics and the firing of earthenware. Inhabitants conducted trade in stone tools and bronze ceremonial bells, swords, and halberds. Cultivators accumulated enough surplus grain to carry out widespread warfare and support small chiefdoms scattered throughout western Japan.

Archaeologists have shown that the changes which overtook Japan during these centuries were impressive. Only a few things—pottery and lacquer techniques, the pit dwelling, and hunting and gathering—survived relatively unaffected from the Jōmon era. At the same time, archaeologists have pointed out that rice agriculture was still primitive and people relied heavily on other crops and Jōmon livelihoods. Natives of the archipelago also lacked livestock. Artisans casting bronze articles probably wandered from settlement to settlement, an indication that craft specialization was not advanced. Although imports from the continent resulted in the appearance of class distinctions, the elite was tiny and not very wealthy, as shown by the scant burial goods found in late Yayoi graves. The use of iron was still limited mostly to northern Kyushu, near the source in Korea.

Chapter 2 addressed the controversy over Korea-Japan ties from 350 to 700. Once again, historians initiated and set the terms for the debate. Relying on passages in *A Record* and *The Chronicles,* most prewar authors assumed that the Yamato court had dominated the southern Korean kingdoms. Only Tsuda Sōkichi dared to dispute the accepted view, and even he saw Yamato as a conqueror. Slowly over the postwar era, the comfortable consensus dissolved under assault from archaeologists, non-Japanese scholars, and Japanese historians upset by their government's treatment of Korean residents in Japan. By the 1990s, scholars of Japan, North and South Korea, China, Western Europe, and the United States were sharing material and textual evidence and theories with each other.

Archaeologists have shown that between 350 and 700 Japan was inundated by a flood of materials, technologies, ideas, and institutions from the continent. Although many items originated in China, peninsular peoples performed the invaluable role of cultural transmitters, in many cases inventing or altering objects to fit their own societies. Residents of Paekche, Silla, and Kaya sent the Japanese iron for tools, armor, swords, and arrowheads. Koguryŏ probably introduced the Wa army to the horse and its military uses, and immigrants brought stoneware, ovens, pond and ditch-digging techniques, and stone-fitting skills for application in constructing corridor and chamber tumuli and decorated tombs. Korean artisans taught the Japanese to fashion gold and silver jewelry.

Historical evidence bolsters the archaeological hypothesis. Peninsular scribes and accountants introduced their skills to the Yamato court and other chieftains. The Kinai kingdom's first institutions of control—surnames, titles, ranks, and producer groups (*be*)—may all have had Korean roots. Paekche kings told their Yamato counterparts of the benefits of new ideologies such as Buddhism and Confucianism. Peninsular peoples continued to place their distinctive stamp upon Japan, even in the early eighth century, through their work on law codes, mountain fortresses, crossbows, and local government.

These 350 years of Japanese learning from their Korean neighbors came about through four mechanisms: limited trade, large-scale immigration, some plundering, and the conscious foreign policy of states such as Paekche and Koguryŏ. In return for peninsular "gifts," Yamato and the other Wa chieftains sent troops to southern Korea to intervene in politics and support sympathetic rulers. Yamato was able to achieve paramountcy in the archipelago only as it shut off the flow of Korean-borne technologies and ideas to its rivals over the period from 500 to 700.

During the latter half of the seventh century, Japan entered a new stage in its relationship to the continent. Under military pressure from recently unified kingdoms in China and Korea, the court intensified efforts to borrow Chinese models to enhance its power. Chapter 3 examined one facet of the apprenticeship of the Japanese elite to Chinese cultural norms: the construction of capitals. Historians, geographers, and antiquarians began study of Japan's first large urban centers in the Edo period, and Kita Sadakichi discussed many important problems in the early twentieth century. But unlike the previous topics, archaeologists played a crucial role in research on these capitals almost from the beginning. Today archaeologists are constantly presenting new data that historians try to synthesize with the written record.

On the origins of these cities, scholars generally agree that the inspiration was Chinese, but one is impressed by the degree to which Japanese and immigrant planners felt free to alter Chinese patterns to fit Japan's own needs. There was no encircling wall, probably because the court could not secure labor for the project, and shrines typical of Chinese capitals were also omitted. The court used models from throughout Chinese history, especially the sixth-century Northern Wei. The north-south alignment of imperial residence–morning halls may have been a native tradition, however.

An overview of written and archaeological evidence shows how the court adapted continental ideas to its environment. The lower level at Naniwa, which may have been Kōtoku's Nagara Toyosaki Palace, had more in common with Japanese and Korean palaces than with Chinese. While the Asuka region was probably the site of Japan's first major urban center at Wa-kyō, it was not until Fujiwara in 694 that the court succeeded in constructing a more sinicized capital, with a palace grounds housing an imperial residence, audience hall, and official compound arranged from north to south. The boundaries of Fujiwara city are uncertain, but recent digging suggests that it was more like Northern Wei Luo-yang than Tang Chang-an.

In 710, the imperial family moved due north of Fujiwara to a heroically proportioned but incomplete Nara Palace. The second attempt at erecting Heijō Palace probably took place in the 720s or 760s, not in 745 as many believe. The new palace was a scaled-down version of the original. With its northern section and Outer Capital, Nara city was unlike any Chinese capital and may have served 50,000 to 100,000 residents. The three capitals built after Nara—Kuni, Nagaoka, and Heian—refined many traditions established at Heijō. But all three relied heavily on recycled timbers and tiles. Each was left in an unfinished state because of political infighting, the government's financial insolvency, and an increasingly tight labor market.

While archaeologists are providing information on how complete these great projects were, only historians can answer the question of where the labor came from and how it was organized. The court created three institutions to supply workers: the service adult, the sixty-day unreimbursed corvée, and paid forced labor. Although data are scanty, they suggest a growing labor scarcity over the course of the period from 645 to 810, as seen in the impressment of unqualified workers and the commutation of labor duties to fixed payments. The timing and results of these large-scale capital-building projects are intimately related to population trends.

Chapter 4 examined wooden tablets to illuminate governing techniques borrowed from China. Since most tablets contain writing referring to myriad aspects of ancient society and government, historians have been the ones most affected by their discovery. The role of archaeologists is limited primarily to preservation and contextual site analysis. Scholars were unaware of the existence of these sources before 1961 and have used the tablets to add exciting detail to established fields of study.

Wooden tablets have helped to resolve the debate about the authenticity of the 646 Taika Reform edict, lending support to a modified "kernel of truth" theory while showing the importance of the Korean example. Historians now suspect that Kōtoku and Prince Naka were able to initiate a modest momentum toward reforming the system after 645. In study of the ancient bureau-

cracy, tablets have demonstrated that the court adapted Chinese-style principles of hiring, promotion, and dismissal toward the greater purpose of preserving the pre-Taika emphasis on hereditary rule. Tax tags have revealed the
Yamato-era origins of the Nara revenue system and indicate details of the
reorganization of the tax structure between 645 and 702. They also refine
knowledge of the geographical origins of Nara levies and their year-to-year
fluctuations. The tablets of Prince Nagaya and the Second Rank Great Avenue
suggest continuities in the resources available to early Nara aristocratic families and indeed continuities in the composition and definition of that class.
Overall, tablets show the creative and pragmatic adjustment of Chinese-style
institutions to fit Japanese conditions.

The seven centuries described in this book cover the period in which Japan
went from a relatively simple hunter-gatherer culture to a more complex agricultural society forging metals and erecting monuments and great urban centers. Seen from the perspective of world history, Japan's evolution toward
complexity, which by no means was over in 800, was different from that of
most regions.[1] The accompanying table lists six characteristics of "civilization"
for eleven areas of the globe. Three generalizations seem reasonable from these
data. First, the constituent elements of complex society varied considerably
from region to region. Few people followed Mesopotamia's neat path from
farming to city-states, writing, and metallurgy. Timing for the invention or
introduction of various elements differed, and some regions did not even
invent or possess certain items. Second, several areas made a much later start
in the scramble toward complexity than did others. Korea and Japan were
especially late, and not surprisingly people in these regions did not invent
complexity from scratch but borrowed and adapted what they could, sometimes under threat of force. Both societies produced a unique culture fusing
local and foreign lifestyles. Third, once Japan and Korea began to evolve toward
complexity, they moved at breakneck speed.[2] In a little over a thousand years,
Japan went from the Jōmon hunter-gatherer populace to the Nara state. Korea
took about five hundred years longer, but it too moved rapidly toward what
Gordon Childe has termed "the urban revolution." Undoubtedly Japan and
Korea owed this unusual speed of development to their geographical position
on China's doorstep. Except for Han colonization of the northern peninsula,
these two regions did not face military pressure from a more complex society
until relatively late in their development. By that time (the 600s), they had
made large enough strides toward complexity to resist the invaders by adapting Chinese institutions to enhance indigenous patterns.

Careful examination of the Japanese case suggests there were two distinct

Characteristics of Complexity in Assorted Regions

Region	Farming	Metals	Monuments	Writing	Bureaucracy	Cities
Mesopotamia	9000 B.C.	b: 3000 i: 1400	2100	3300	3400	3500
Egypt	5000 B.C.	b: 2500 i: 800	2650	3000	2650	None
Indus	6500 B.C.	b: 2500 i: 1000	None	2500	2500	2500
China	6000 B.C.	b: 2000 i: 700	300	1200	1500	1900
Mediterranean	7000 B.C.	b: 2900 i: 1000	2000	1650	2000	700
Europe (N. Alps)	6500 B.C.	b: 2300 i: 200*	4500	500*	500*	800*
New World	4500 B.C.	None	1700 O: 1000 M: 400	M: 500*	O: 900 M: 500*	None
West Africa	3000 B.C.	i: 1000	None	None	500*	500*
SE Asia	7000 B.C.	b: 2500	800*	300*	100*	800*
Korea	1000 B.C.	b: 700 i: 400	300*	400*	500*	500*
Japan	400 B.C.	b: 300 i: 400	300*	450*	600*	650*

Key: * indicates A.D.; M = Maya; O = Olmec; b = bronze; i = iron

Sources: Gina Barnes, *China, Korea and Japan;* William McNeill, *A History of the Human Community;* Albert Craig et al., *The Heritage of World Civilizations;* William Duiker and Jackson Spielvogel, *World History;* Jiu-hwa Upshur et al., *World History;* and Chris Scarre, *Smithsonian Timelines of the Ancient World.*

phases in the "rise of civilization" there. First came the demographic, economic, and social changes of the Yayoi and Tomb ages. In the Yayoi period, primitive rice farming and bronze and iron metallurgy entered Japan; in the middle and late Tomb era, advanced agricultural, military, political, and cultural technologies came to Japan and spread. The Yamato state began to evolve in the Kinai. The first waves of Buddhism, the cornerstone of intellectual life in the ancient period, were introduced as well. By 645, Japanese population and the economy had been growing for almost a thousand years and many elements of the material culture of premodern Japan had come into being. The second phase began in 645 and lasted until approximately 800. During this century and a half, leaders created the basic political institutions that would hold sway for several hundred years and serve as a model of good government for a millennium. Increasingly unable to absorb culture through Korea, the Japanese court turned to the Middle Kingdom for guidance. This era saw some impressive achievements, such as the compilation of the Taihō and Yōrō codes and the construction of magnificent Chinese-style capitals.

In a word, the first half-millennium from the middle Yayoi to 645 witnessed substantial economic and demographic growth, the likes of which Japan may not have seen again until late medieval times; the second stage, the late seventh and eighth centuries, saw an institutionalization or codification of native practices with a view to enhancing the power of the former Yamato court.[3] In a provocative and insightful book, Tsude Hiroshi has endorsed this two-stage model. In his view the era from the middle Yayoi to 600 saw "a great turning point in farming productivity, such as expansion of the arable land or innovation in planting technology or improvement of farming tools." The Nara period, he says, "should be thought of as a great watershed in peasant control and landownership."[4]

It is no accident that Tsude is an archaeologist with knowledge of the written record: his command of the sources has enabled him to see that the surviving evidence also implicitly lends support to a two-stage model. Before 700, the preponderance of sources is archaeological, and sites and artifacts reveal the great technological and material changes in Japanese society. After 700, written sources play a much greater role, showing the impact of Chinese-style laws and institutions.[5] To gain a proper understanding of Japan's development in the first millennium A.D., one must use both sacred texts and buried treasures.

NOTES

Introduction

1. Peter Nosco, *Remembering Paradise*, pp. 71–248.

2. Carol Gluck, *Japan's Modern Myths*, pp. 73–156.

3. Kate Nakai, *Shogunal Politics*, pp. 235–264.

4. Fumiko Ikawa-Smith, "Co-traditions in Japanese Archaeology," *World Archaeology* 13 (February 1982): 296–309, discusses the premodern roots of postwar archaeology. The following brief history of Japanese archaeology comes from Teshigahara Akira, *Nihon kōkogaku shi*, pp. 2–24. See also J. Edward Kidder, *Ancient Japan*, pp. 15–22, and Vadime Elisseeff, *The Ancient Civilization of Japan*, pp. 15–66. Peter Bleed, "Almost Archaeology: Early Archaeological Interest in Japan," in Richard Pearson, ed., *Windows on the Japanese Past*, pp. 57–70, credits Edo scholars and naturalists for initiating Japanese interest in their ancient material culture, while Yamamoto Tadanao, "Reflections on the Development of Historical Archaeology in Japan," in Pearson, *Windows on the Japanese Past*, pp. 397–400, and Nishimura Masae, "A Study of Late Early Jomon Culture in the Tone River Area," in Pearson, *Windows on the Japanese Past*, pp. 421–448, treat the history of research into the historical and Jōmon eras, respectively.

5. Teshigahara, *Nihon kōkogaku shi*, p. 9.

6. On Toro and its impact see Walter Edwards, "Buried Discourse: The Toro Archaeological Site and Japanese National Identity in the Early Postwar Period," *Journal of Japanese Studies* 17 (Winter 1991): 1–23.

7. On the number of archaeologists see "Maizō bunka zai tantō sha sū no zōka," *Maizō bunka nyūsu* 67 (March 1990); on the number of site reports and excavations see "Maizō bunka zai kankei chōsa hōkoku sho to no kankō sū," *Maizō bunka nyūsu* 52 (December 1985). See also Richard Pearson, "Introduction," in Pearson, *Windows on the Japanese Past*, pp. 479–480; Tsuboi Kiyotari, "Problems Concerning the Preservation of Archaeological Sites in Japan," in Pearson, *Windows on the Japanese Past*, pp. 481–490; and Kobayashi Tatsuo, "Trends in Administrative Salvage Archaeology," in Pearson, *Windows on the Japanese Past*, pp. 491–496.

8. Tsuboi Kiyotari, "Issues in Japanese Archeology," *Acta Asiatica* 63 (1992): 3–5.

9. The following section is meant only as a brief summary of current thinking on complex societies. See Joseph Tainter, *The Collapse of Complex Societies*, pp. 22–38. William

McNeill, *A History of the Human Community*, vol. 1, pp. 58–71, prefers the terms "barbarism" and "civilization." Besides these two works, I have found the following studies helpful: V. Gordon Childe, *Man Makes Himself;* Jeremy Sabloff and C. C. Lamberg-Karlovsky, *The Rise and Fall of Civilizations;* Colin Renfrew, *Before Civilization;* and J. T. Robinson, Melvin Fowler, and Brian Fagan, *Human and Cultural Development.* Several world history texts also address this problem. See the Conclusion.

10. McNeill, *History of the Human Community*, vol. 1, pp. 22–25, 30–39, and 55.

11. The classic expression of the "hallmarks of civilization" is V. Gordon Childe's ten defining characteristics; see "The Urban Revolution," in Sabloff and Lamberg-Karlovsky, *Rise and Fall of Civilizations*, pp. 6–14. Since Childe, social scientists have differed on which aspects of complex society are critical. Albert Craig et al., *The Heritage of World Civilizations*, p. 6, cites writing, metallurgy, and cities; Renfrew, *Before Civilization*, p. 193, prefers towns, writing, and monumental architecture.

12. The following brief summary is drawn from J. Edward Kidder, "The Earliest Societies in Japan," in Delmer Brown, ed., *The Cambridge History of Japan*, vol. 1, pp. 48–107; Sahara Makoto, *Taikei Nihon no rekishi* 1: *Nihonjin no tanjō;* Tanaka Migaku, *Nihon no rekishi* 2: *Wajin sōran;* Inoue Mitsusada, *Nihon no rekishi* 3: *Asuka no chōtei;* and Yoshida Takashi, *Taikei Nihon no rekishi* 3: *Kodai kokka no ayumi.*

Prehistory designates the epoch before the advent of written records. Full-blown history begins with the era for which copious texts allow the construction of a detailed chronology verifiable through cross-referencing. Authors may often be known and the events described are usually written down not long after their occurrence. Protohistory belongs to an in-between realm. Records are primitive, authors are unknown, and a detailed chronology is impossible. Texts such as genealogies and myths, which may contain a kernel of truth, are staples of this research. Japanese scholars do not regularly employ the concept of protohistory.

13. For a recent treatment of the prehistoric eras see Keiji Imamura, *Prehistoric Japan,* pp. 19–125.

14. Mark Hudson, "From Toro to Yoshinogari—Changing Perspectives on Yayoi Period Archeology," in Gina Barnes, ed., *Hoabinhian: Jōmon, Yayoi, Early Korean States,* pp. 66–71.

15. This description of third-century political units follows Gina Barnes and Mark Hudson, "Yoshinogari: A Yayoi Settlement in Northern Kyushu," *Monumenta Nipponica* 46 (Summer 1991): 234.

16. Technically the term "Kinai" was not invented until the late seventh century, but historians and archaeologists alike commonly use it to refer to the Kyoto–Osaka–Nara area. Historically it includes the five home provinces of Yamato, Yamashiro, Kawachi, Izumi, and Settsu.

17. The nature of the *be* is a hotly debated issue. See Kamata Motokazu, "Ōken to bumin sei," in *Kōza Nihon rekishi* 1: *Genshi kodai*, pp. 255–256, and Yoshida, *Kodai kokka no ayumi*, pp. 43–47.

Chapter 1: The Lost Realm of Yamatai

1. See John Young, *The Location of Yamatai*, pp. 51–55.

2. Tanaka Migaku, *Nihon no rekishi* 2: *Wajin sōran*, pp. 237–239.

3. The following discussion comes from Mori Hiromichi and Sugimoto Kenji, "*Gishi* Wajin den o tsūdoku suru," in Mori Kōichi, ed., *Nihon no kodai* 1: *Wajin no tōjō*, pp. 93–156. Four good recent essays on Yamatai are J. Edward Kidder Jr., "The Earliest Societies in Japan," in Delmer Brown, ed., *The Cambridge History of Japan*, vol. 1, pp. 97–105; Kidder, "Yoshinogari and the Yamatai Problem," *Transactions of the Asiatic Society of Japan*, 4th series 6 (1991): 115–140; Okazaki Takashi, "Japan and the Continent," in Brown, *Cambridge History of Japan*, vol. 1, pp. 272–297; and Walter Edwards, "In Pursuit of Himiko: Postwar Archaeology and the Location of Yamatai," *Monumenta Nipponica* 51 (Spring 1996): 53–79.

4. Young, *Yamatai*, pp. 27–34.

5. The term "Wa" is troublesome, even though every scholar of repute acknowledges that Wa usually referred to the inhabitants of Kyushu and western Honshu. Inoue Hideo, *Wa Wajin Wakoku*, pp. 56–101, has argued that the Wa also lived along the coast of southern Korea. The vagueness of the Chinese description of the route to the land of the Wa precludes precise definition of the word, but for the purposes of this chapter Wa is synonymous with the people inhabiting western Japan, that is, west of central Honshu. One should not assume from the use of this single term that Japan was politically unified at this time.

6. For a translation of the "Account of the Wa" see *Japan in the Chinese Dynastic Histories*, trans. Ryusaku Tsunoda, pp. 8–21. All quotations from this record follow Tsunoda. On Korea see Sarah Nelson, *The Archaeology of Korea*, pp. 165–172.

7. Tanaka, *Wajin sōran*, pp. 237–239.

8. Mori and Sugimoto, "Wajin den," pp. 96–97.

9. Ōbayashi Taryō, *Yamatai koku*, pp. 146–154.

10. It should be noted that two other Chinese histories, *The History of the Liang Dynasty* (*Liang shu*) and *The History of the Northern Dynasties* (*Bei shi*), also list missions from Himiko to Wei China in A.D. 239 and 241, respectively. See *Chūgoku seishi Nihon den* 1 *Wei zhi Woren zhuan. Hou Han shu Wozhuan. Sung shu Woguo zhuan. Sui shu Woguo zhuan*, ed. Ishihara Michihiro, p. 151.

11. Young, *Yamatai*, pp. 51–55; Edwards, "In Pursuit of Himiko," pp. 58–61, also presents a brief history of the debate.

12. For convenience, all emperors and empresses are referred to by their more familiar posthumous names (*shigō*). One should keep in mind throughout this chapter that the position of emperor, here used as a translation for *tennō*, did not come into existence until the late sixth or early seventh century at the earliest.

13. There are several good books on the history of the Yamatai controversy. I have used Saeki Arikiyo, who developed the five-part periodization noted in the text. See *Kenkyū shi: Yamatai koku* and *Kenkyū shi: Sengo no Yamatai koku*. Note the collections of articles on Yamatai: Saeki Arikiyo, *Yamatai koku kihon ronbun shū*, and Mishina Akihide, *Yamatai koku kenkyū sōran*. Readers should refer to Young, *Yamatai*, pp. 43–171, for a detailed summary of prewar scholarship. In English see also Isamu Yonekura, "Himiko, Queen of Wa," *The East* 10 (June 1974): 44–51; and Saeki Arikiyo, "Studies on Ancient Japanese History," *Acta Asiatica* 31 (1977): 113–119.

14. Young, *Yamatai*, pp. 69–75, states that Arai favored the Kinai for the location of Yamatai. Later evidence in Saeki, *Yamatai koku*, pp. 8–9, contradicts Young's view.

15. Tanaka, *Wajin sōran*, p. 93.

16. Saeki, *Yamatai koku*, pp. 35–40. See also Okazaki, "Japan and the Continent," pp. 280–281.

17. See Ranke's Introduction to the *History of the Latin and Teutonic Nations*, in Roger Wines, ed., *The Secret of World History*, p. 58.

18. Young, *Yamatai*, pp. 89–93.

19. For an explanation of Naka's thinking see Young, *Yamatai*, pp. 93–96, or Gari Ledyard, "Galloping Along with the Horseriders: Looking for the Founders of Japan," *Journal of Japanese Studies* 1 (Summer 1975): 217–218.

20. Saeki, *Yamatai koku*, pp. 90–92. Miyake Yonekichi successfully read the Shiga seal, while Kume Kunitake declared an end to the controversy.

21. Young, *Yamatai*, pp. 118–121.

22. Kondō Kyōichi, *Sankakuen shinjū kyō*, pp. 5–7.

23. Ibid., pp. 4–10.

24. Saeki, *Yamatai koku*, pp. 171–190. The most vocal opponent of the Kyoto archaeologists was Hashimoto Masukichi. See also Young, *Yamatai*, pp. 130–143.

25. Since more reliable techniques had not yet been invented, Japanese archaeologists depended on relative sequences of pottery styles for dating. There were few absolute dates for sites or artifacts.

26. Okuno Masao, *Yamatai koku no kagami,* p. 30.

27. Saeki, *Yamatai koku,* pp. 164–171 and 190–208. In addition to the first research by archaeologists, the decade of the 1920s saw the appearance of a few other approaches. Nakayama Tarō compared Himiko to a legendary Okinawa queen who ruled with her brother; Sakima Takahide suggested that clothing described in the "Account of the Wa" matched articles worn by clay figurines (*haniwa*) of the later Tomb era. Scholars began discussing the definitions of terms such as *seikō* (slaves) and *jisai* (fortune-keeper), using new frameworks such as ethnography and economic history.

28. Ibid., pp. 224–228. Watanabe Yoshimichi was the historian arguing for a tribal confederacy.

29. Ibid., pp. 229–231. Higo Kazuo described Himiko as the occupant of Hashihaka Tomb, while Shida Fudomaro argued for women's political clout.

30. See ibid., p. 232, for a picture of a censored history monograph.

31. The following description relies on Saeki, *Sengo no Yamatai koku.*

32. Ibid., pp. 8–36. Mishina Akihide argued that the Wa were not a primitive society; the advocate of the Kyushu location was Enoki Kazuo; the historian who believed that Yamatai was a loose confederation overseen by the heroic Himiko was Tōma Seita.

33. Ibid., pp. 40–63.

34. Ibid., pp. 85–127.

35. Ibid., pp. 154–213.

36. Ibid., pp. 214–227. One prominent scholar on international relations was Ishimoda Shō.

37. See the Furuta Takehiko essay in Saeki, *Yamatai koku kihon ronbun shū,* vol. 3, pp. 305–339. Takemoto Tōru, "The Kyushu Dynasty," *Japan Quarterly* 30 (October–December 1983): 383–387, introduces Furuta's theory to the Western world. See also Matsumoto Seichō, "Japan in the Third Century," pp. 377–382 in the same volume.

38. See the article by Ozaki Yūjirō in Saeki, *Yamatai koku kihon ronbun shū,* vol. 3, pp. 341–354. See also Saeki, *Sengo no Yamatai koku,* pp. 244–253.

39. Saeki, *Sengo no Yamatai koku,* p. 265.

40. For Jōmon dates see Kidder, "The Earliest Societies in Japan," pp. 55–80. For the conventional dates for the Yayoi period see Gina Barnes, *China, Korea and Japan,* pp. 168–191; and Mark Hudson, "From Toro to Yoshinogari: Changing Perspectives on Yayoi Period Archeology," in Gina Barnes, ed., *Hoabinhian: Jōmon, Yayoi, Early Korean States,* p. 63. Barnes also argues for an earlier dating for the beginning of the Tomb age; see *Protohistoric Yamato,* pp. 195–200 and 237–238.

41. On the definition of Yayoi and the transition from Jōmon to Yayoi see Sahara, "The Yayoi Culture," in Tsuboi Kiyotari, ed., *Recent Archaeological Discoveries in Japan,* pp. 37–46; Sahara and Kanaseki, "The Yayoi Period," *Asian Perspectives* 19 (1978): 15–19; Peter Bleed, "Yayoi Cultures of Japan: An Interpretive Summary," *Arctic Anthropology* 9 (1972): 1–10; Peter Rowley-Conwy, "Postglacial Foraging and Early Farming Economies in Japan and Korea: A West European Perspective," *World Archaeology* 16 (1984): 28–42; Gary Crawford and Hiroto Takamiya, "The Origins and Implications of Late Prehistoric Plant Husbandry in Northern Japan," *Antiquity* 64 (1990): 889–911; Gary Crawford, "The Transitions to Agriculture in Japan," in *Transitions to Agriculture in Prehistory,* pp. 117–132; Akazawa Takeru, "Maritime Adaptation of Prehistoric Hunter-Gatherers and Their Transition to Agriculture in Japan," in *Affluent Foragers,* pp. 213–258; Akazawa, "Cultural Change in Prehistoric Japan: Receptivity to Rice Agriculture in the Japanese Archipelago," in F. Wendorf and A. Close, eds., *Advances in World Archaeology,* pp. 151–211; Akazawa, "Hunter-Gatherer Adaptations and the Transition to Food Production in Japan," in M. Zvebil, ed., *Hunters in Transition,* pp. 151–165; Akazawa Takeru and Maeyama Kiyoaki, "Discriminant Function Analysis of Later Jomon Settlements," in Richard Pearson, ed., *Windows on the Japanese Past,* pp. 279–292; W. W. Howells, "Physical Anthropology of the Prehistoric Japanese," in Pearson, *Windows on the Japanese Past,* pp. 85–99; Tsukada Matsuo, "Vegetation in Prehistoric Japan: The Last 20,000 Years," in Pearson, *Windows on the Japanese Past,* pp. 11–56; Melvin Aikens and Takayasu Higuchi, *Prehistory of Japan,* pp. 187–205; Keiji Imamura, *Prehistoric Japan,* pp. 9–17; and Patricia Hitchins, "A Cultural Synthesis of the Yayoi Period of Japan," Ph.D. dissertation, University of Toronto, 1977, pp. 16–128.

42. Shimakura Misaburō, "San seiki no shokubutsu," in Mori Kōichi, ed., *San seiki no kōkogaku* 1: *San seiki no shizen to ningen,* p. 159.

43. Ibid., p. 160.

44. Teramura Mitsuharu, "Tama," in Mori Kōichi, ed., *San seiki no kōkogaku* 2: *San seiki no iseki to ibutsu,* pp. 241–246.

45. Ibid., pp. 256–258 and 262. J. Edward Kidder has noted that the Japanese also used jade in the mid-Jōmon era.

46. Shimakura, "San seiki no shokubutsu," pp. 159–161; Barnes, *Protohistoric Yamato,* p. 214.

47. Yamamoto Takeo, "Ni san seiki to kikō," in Mori Kōichi, ed., *San seiki no kōkogaku* 1: *San seiki no shizen to ningen,* pp. 35–58. See also Ishino Hironobu, "Rites and Rituals of the Kofun Period," *Japanese Journal of Religious Studies* 19 (June–September 1992): 191–216.

48. Shimakura, "San seiki no shokubutsu," p. 161.

49. Sahara Makoto and Kanaseki Hiroshi, "Sōsetsu: kome to kinzoku no seiki," in

Sahara and Kanaseki, eds., *Kodai shi hakkutsu 4: Inasaku no hajimari*, p. 30; Imamura, *Prehistoric Japan*, pp. 156–157. On population see Hudson, "From Toro to Yoshinogari," p. 67. For Jōmon population see Sahara Makoto, *Taikei Nihon no rekishi* 1: *Nihonjin no tanjō*, pp. 170–172. Sahara's figures are based on Shūzō Koyama, "Jōmon Subsistence and Population," *Senri Ethnological Studies* 2 (1978): 1–65. By the late Jōmon, Japan's population had decreased to around 70,000 by one analysis, thus making the Yayoi demographic growth even more impressive.

50. Sahara, *Nihonjin no tanjō*, p. 171. See also Kanaseki Hiroshi, "The Evidence for Social Change Between the Early and Middle Yayoi," in Pearson, *Windows on the Japanese Past*, pp. 324–331, for a demographic analysis of the Doigahama site, including an estimate of the local death rate.

51. On Jōmon population see Sahara, *Nihonjin no tanjō*, pp. 168–169; for eighth-century populations see W. Wayne Farris, *Population, Disease, and Land in Early Japan, 645–900*, pp. 18–49.

52. The preceding discussion on the origins of the epithet "Wa" follows Sahara, *Nihonjin no tanjō*, pp. 302–304; see also Tanaka, *Wajin sōran*, pp. 12–14.

53. Ōbayashi, *Yamatai koku*, pp. 69–73.

54. Kōmoto Masayuki, "Yayoi jidai no shakai," in Sahara and Kanaseki, *Kodai shi hakkutsu 4: Inasaku no hajimari*, pp. 87–98. See also Kidder, "The Earliest Societies in Japan," pp. 86–87. Several English-language descriptions of Doigahama are available: Kanaseki, "Yayoi Social Change," pp. 324–331; Bleed, "Yayoi Cultures of Japan," p. 6; and Aikens and Higuchi, *Prehistory of Japan*, pp. 205–206.

55. Kōmoto, "Yayoi jidai no shakai," p. 91. Since ritual tooth pulling was a rite of passage undergone with one's birth cohort, it could only be performed at one's native village.

56. Yoshida Takashi, "Ritsuryō sei to sonraku," in *Iwanami kōza Nihon rekishi 3: Kodai 3*, pp. 156–161.

57. *Shintei zōho kokushi taikei, Sōsō-ryō no shūge, Fukuki no jō*, fourth, fifth, and eleventh *koki*, p. 972.

58. Tsude Hiroshi, *Nihon nōkō shakai no seiritsu katei*, pp. 442–465, is one of the few remaining opponents of bilateral kinship in the eighth century. Kōmoto, "Yayoi jidai no shakai," pp. 89–93, argues for bilateral kinship in the Yayoi period in Kyushu and the western tip of Honshu. William McCullough, "Japanese Marriage Institutions of the Heian Period," *Harvard Journal of Asiatic Studies* 27 (1967): 103–167, was a pioneer in analyzing the historic epoch, although he did not use the term "bilateral."

59. Tanaka, *Wajin sōran*, pp. 112–115.

60. Ibid., p. 116.

61. Tsunoyama Yukihiro, "Orimono," in Mori Kōichi, ed., *San seiki no kōkogaku* 2: *San seiki no iseki to ibutsu*, pp. 264–266.

62. Takakura Hiroaki, "Ifuku to sōshin gu," in Sahara and Kanaseki, *Kodai shi hakkutsu* 4: *Inasaku no hajimari*, pp. 70–71.

63. See also Junco Sato Pollack, "Looms," in *Kodansha Encyclopedia of Japan*, vol. 5, p. 73; and Hitchins, "Cultural Synthesis," pp. 114–117.

64. Sahara, *Nihonjin no tanjō*, pp. 313–314.

65. *Kangō shūraku Yoshinogari iseki: Gaihō*, p. 67.

66. Yasuda Hiroyoshi, "Shu tan to sono riyō," in Mori Kōichi, ed., *San seiki no kōkogaku* 2: *San seiki no iseki to ibutsu*, pp. 333–334.

67. For reconstructions of these two weapons see Tanaka, *Wajin sōran*, pp. 44–47.

68. This definition follows Tsude, *Nōkō shakai*, pp. 159–161. On wooden pedestals in Yayoi sites see Richard Pearson, *Ancient Japan*, p. 136. The best article on Yayoi pottery in English is Gina Barnes, "Ceramics of the Yayoi Agriculturalists (300 B.C.–A.D. 300)," in *The Rise of a Great Tradition*, pp. 28–39. See also Barnes, "The Structure of Yayoi and Haji Ceramic Typologies," in Pearson, *Windows on the Japanese Past*, pp. 449–476.

69. Tsude is the scholar arguing for Chen's tendency to emphasize the barbarity of the Wa. Sahara, *Nihonjin no tanjō*, p. 315, notes the absence of chopsticks in Yayoi sites.

70. Sahara, *Nihonjin no tanjō*, pp. 314–317. See also Mark Hudson, "Archaeological Approaches to Ritual and Religion in Japan," *Japanese Journal of Religious Studies* 19 (June–September 1992): 150–152.

71. Sahara, *Nihonjin no tanjō*, p. 261; Mori Kōichi, "Kōkogaku to uma," in Mori Kōichi, ed., *Nihon kodai bunka no tankyū* 9: *Uma*, p. 46.

72. Sahara, *Nihonjin no tanjō*, pp. 261–262. See also Imamura, *Prehistoric Japan*, pp. 144–146.

73. Mori, "Kōkogaku to uma," pp. 52–54.

74. Hayashida Shigeyoshi, "Nihon zairai uma no genryū," in Mori Kōichi, ed., *Nihon kodai bunka no tankyū* 9: *Uma*, pp. 234–235.

75. Sahara, *Nihonjin no tanjō*, pp. 262–265.

76. In my *Heavenly Warriors*, pp. 15–16, I followed Mori who believes that horses inhabited Japan in the Jōmon and Yayoi ages. At the time I did not have access to Sahara's work. Recent evidence shows that there were domesticated pigs and cattle; see Pearson, *Ancient Japan*, p. 134.

77. Instead of saying A.D. 1, for example, a Japanese archaeologist would describe the

period as "middle Yayoi." One may fault Japanese archaeologists for their use of such a relative dating scheme, but Japanese archaeologists argue that the duration for each pottery style (thirty to fifty years) is shorter than the "plus or minus sixty" usually tacked onto radiocarbon dates. Change, however, is coming from dendrochronology. Mitsutani Takumi of the Nara National Cultural Properties Research Institute has compiled master sequences for Japanese cedar (*sugi*) and cypress (*hinoki*) dating back to 1313 B.C. and 912 B.C., respectively; see *Mainichi shinbun*, May 16, 1996.

78. Farris, *Population, Disease, and Land*, pp. 5–6. On Toro see also Aikens and Higuchi, *Prehistory of Japan*, pp. 226–237; Gina Barnes, "Toro," in *Atlas of Archaeology*, pp. 198–201; Imamura, *Prehistoric Japan*, pp. 140–142; and Bleed, "Yayoi Cultures of Japan," pp. 12–15.

79. Kuraku Yoshiyuki, *Suiden no kōkogaku*, pp. 79–98.

80. "Suiden ikō shūsei," *Maizō bunka nyūsu* 62 (March 1988): 234–250. According to Imamura, *Prehistoric Japan*, p. 133, this number had swelled to 233 by 1996.

81. Farris, *Population, Disease, and Land*, pp. 5–6 and 101–105. Richard Pearson, *Ancient Japan*, p. 134, argues that the first rice paddies were not located in marshy areas, but as Tsude, *Nōkō shakai*, p. 55, notes, many rice paddies (such as Toro) rested in low-lying areas. Imamura, *Prehistoric Japan*, pp. 134–136, gives an example of both low-lying (Nabatake) and artificially irrigated (Itazuke) paddies. See also Kidder, "The Earliest Societies in Japan," p. 85.

82. The statement about the predominance of nonmetal tools comes from Sahara, *Nihonjin no tanjō*, pp. 250–251. See also "Nōgu," in Sahara Makoto and Kanaseki Hiroshi, eds., *Yayoi bunka no kenkyū* 5: *Dōgu to gijutsu* 1, pp. 77–135; and Imamura, *Prehistoric Japan*, pp. 168–169.

83. Sahara, *Nihonjin no tanjō*, pp. 245–247.

84. Personal communication, spring 1995.

85. Tsude, *Nōkō shakai*, pp. 53–56.

86. Ibid., pp. 9–43.

87. Date Muneyasu and Matsushita Masaru, "Nōkō," in Mori Kōichi, ed., *San seiki no kōkogaku* 2: *San seiki no iseki to ibutsu*, pp. 119–139.

88. Gina Barnes, "Paddy Soils Then and Now," *World Archaeology* 22 (1990): 1–17.

89. Sahara, *Nihonjin no tanjō*, pp. 247–251. According to one scholar, average daily intake of rice was merely 18 milliliters at the outset of the Yayoi era, between 108 and 180 milliliters in the middle, and 360 milliliters at the end. Rice supplied only 50 percent of a person's daily requirement of grain starch in A.D. 50 and 70 percent by A.D. 250.

90. While there are no dry fields from the Yayoi era, archaeologists find rice steamers in western and central Japan. As noted by Gina Barnes, "Ceramics of the Yayoi Agriculturalists," p. 31, the lack of such equipment in northeast Japan surely argues that rice growing was less common there in the Yayoi era. See also Hudson, "From Toro to Yoshinogari," p. 75, who notes the number of different domesticated plants, pp. 76–77. Imamura, *Prehistoric Japan*, p. 144, also discusses dry farming.

91. Wada Seigo, "Gyorō," in Sahara and Kanaseki, *Yayoi bunka no kenkyū* 2: *Seigyō*, p. 160.

92. Tanaka, *Wajin sōran*, pp. 122–133. See also Pearson, *Ancient Japan*, pp. 136 and 140, for evidence of specialization in glass and pottery. See also Kidder, "The Earliest Societies in Japan," pp. 99–100. For more on Tateiwa see Okazaki, "Japan and the Continent," pp. 277–279. On trade between Okinawa and northern Kyushu see Pearson, "Chiefly Exchange Between Kyushu and Okinawa, Japan, in the Yayoi Period," *Antiquity* 64 (1990): 912–922.

93. Exactly when western Japanese began to cast bronze weapons and bells remains unclear. Masahiro Saotome, "Bronze Weapons," *Kodansha Encyclopedia of Japan*, vol. 1, pp. 174–175, supports the first century A.D., as does Gina Barnes, "Early Japanese Bronze-Making," *Archaeology* 34 (May–June 1981): 38–46. Mark Hudson, "Rice, Bronze, and Chieftains," *Japanese Journal of Religious Studies* 19 (June–Sept. 1992): 153, follows Sahara with the date 100 B.C. for bells. I follow Tanaka, *Wajin sōran*, p. 172, on the dating of bronze manufacture. Hudson, p. 155, points out that molds for bells have been recovered in northern Kyushu and that bronze weapons have been discovered in the Kinai, thus undermining the prewar theory that northern Kyushu and the Kinai were two different ritual or political zones.

94. Tanaka, *Wajin sōran*, pp. 135–147; Pearson, *Ancient Japan*, pp. 141–142. Kidder, "The Earliest Societies in Japan," pp. 92–97, reveals strong evidence for trade. See also H. Mabuchi, Y. Hirao, and M. Nishida, "Lead Isotope Approach to the Understanding of Early Japanese Bronze Culture," *Archaeometry* 27 (February 1985): 131–159; and Patricia Hitchins, "Technical Studies on Materials from Yayoi Period Japan: Their Role in Archaeological Interpretation," *Asian Perspectives* 19 (1978): 162–167.

95. Tanaka, *Wajin sōran*, p. 150; Sahara, *Nihonjin no tanjō*, pp. 279–280.

96. This line of thinking follows Tanaka, *Wajin sōran*, pp. 150–151. See also Tsude, *Nōkō shakai*, pp. 366–369.

97. Tsude, *Nōkō shakai*, pp. 369–374.

98. Okazaki, "Japan and the Continent," pp. 291–297, makes a similar point.

99. See, for example, *Toro iseki shutsudo shiryō mokuroku 4: Shashin hen*, which lists only one bow among myriad finds.

100. See also, for example, the cache of bronze weapons uncovered in the secluded Kōjin Valley of Izumo described by Joan Piggott, "Sacral Kingship and Confederacy in Early Izumo," *Monumenta Nipponica* 44 (Spring 1989): 46–49 and 51.

101. Jacob Bronowski, *The Ascent of Man*, pp. 68–89; Kidder, "The Earliest Societies in Japan," pp. 91–92.

102. Ono Tadahiro, "Kōchi sei shūraku ron," in Mori Kōichi, ed., *San seiki no kōkogaku* 2: *San seiki no iseki to ibutsu*, p. 49. Note that Gina Barnes, *Protohistoric Yamato*, pp. 213–215, is somewhat more doubtful than most Japanese archaeologists. See Ono's *Kōchi sei shūraku ato no kenkyū: Shiryō hen*, pp. 792–793, for a good distribution map.

103. See, for example, Morioka Hideto, "Yama oka no Yayoi mura to okugai hitakiba," in *Kōkogaku ronshū*, vol. 1, pp. 33–68.

104. Ono still thinks that many highland settlements had agricultural functions; see Ono, "Kōchi sei shūraku ron," pp. 50–52. Three other archaeologists follow the military theme: see Tanaka, *Wajin sōran*, pp. 29–37; Sahara, *Nihonjin no tanjō*, pp. 288–291; and Tsude, *Nōkō shakai*, pp. 195–202.

105. Ono Tadahiro, "Kōchi sei shūraku kenkyū no kadai," in Ono, ed., *Kōchi sei shūraku to Wakoku tairan*, pp. 3–25. Tsude, Sahara, and Tanaka all follow Ono. See also Ono, "Tetsuzoku o shutsudo shita Yayoi shiki kōchi sei shūraku," *Kōkogaku jaanaru* 49 (October 1970): 21.

106. Tsude, *Nōkō shakai*, pp. 200–202.

107. Sahara, *Nihonjin no tanjō*, p. 289.

108. Tanaka, *Wajin sōran*, pp. 77–79.

109. On these villages see Ishiguro Tatsuhito, "Zenkoku kangō shūraku chimei hyō," *Kikan kōkogaku: Tokushū Kangō shūraku to kuni no okori* 31 (May 1990): 77–80. See also Pearson, *Ancient Japan*, pp. 143–144; Imamura, *Prehistoric Japan*, pp. 179–181; Hudson, "From Toro to Yoshinogari," p. 73; Aikens and Higuchi, *Prehistory of Japan*, pp. 210–215; and Barnes, *China, Korea and Japan*, pp. 188–189. Korea also had walled villages; see Nelson, *Archaeology of Korea*, p. 190.

110. Sahara, *Nihonjin no tanjō*, p. 285.

111. Tanaka, *Wajin sōran*, pp. 20–23; see also Pearson, *Ancient Japan*, pp. 143–144.

112. Tanaka, *Wajin sōran*, pp. 54–61; Tsude, *Nōkō shakai*, pp. 182–186.

113. For a detailed description of Yoshinogari see Gina Barnes and Mark Hudson, "Yoshinogari: A Yayoi Settlement in Northern Kyushu," *Monumenta Nipponica* 46 (Summer 1991): 211–235; *Kangō Shūraku Yoshinogari: Gaihō. Yoshinogari: Honbun hen* is a meticulous account of the excavation. See also Okazaki, "Japan and the Continent," pp. 284–286, and Kidder, "Yoshinogari and the Yamatai Problem," pp. 115–122.

114. Barnes and Hudson, "Yoshinogari," p. 234.

115. See *Kangō Shūraku Yoshinogari: Gaihō*, p. 42.

116. Barnes and Hudson, "Yoshinogari," p. 234.

117. Pearson, *Ancient Japan*, p. 150.

118. Tanaka, *Wajin sōran*, pp. 104–108. Imamura, *Prehistoric Japan*, pp. 186–196, also discusses the meaning of "country."

119. Barnes and Hudson, "Yoshinogari," p. 218.

120. Tanaka, *Wajin sōran*, pp. 111–112; see also Imamura, *Prehistoric Japan*, pp. 182–185.

121. Sahara, *Nihonjin no tanjō*, pp. 320–321; Pearson, *Ancient Japan*, p. 151.

122. Pearson, *Ancient Japan*, p. 151; Edwards, "In Pursuit of Himiko," pp. 68–72, emphasizes the degree of social stratification.

123. Pearson, *Ancient Japan*, p. 150. Piggott, "Sacral Kingship," pp. 54 and 73, argues that Izumo developed earlier and remained independent much later than is usually thought. See also Barnes, *Protohistoric Yamato*, pp. 1–5, for a description of eastern versus western Seto.

124. Barnes and Hudson, "Yoshinogari," p. 218.

125. Ibid., pp. 218 and 226; Pearson, *Ancient Japan*, p. 143.

126. Tsude, *Nōkō shakai*, pp. 204–205.

127. Kanaseki Hiroshi, "Yayoi jin no seishin seikatsu," in Sahara and Kanaseki, *Kodai shi hakkutsu 4: Inasaku no hajimari*, p. 80. On mirrors see also Kidder, "Yoshinogari and the Yamatai Problem," pp. 122–131.

128. Kondō, *Shinjū kyō*, pp. 12–13; Imamura, *Prehistoric Japan*, p. 188.

129. Kobayashi Yukio, *Kofun jidai no kenkyū*, p. 127; see also Edwards, "In Pursuit of Himiko," pp. 61–68. Walter Edwards has also provided scholars with a handy translation of Kobayashi's most important essay on this topic; see "Kobayashi Yukio's 'Treatise on Duplicate Mirrors': An Annotated Translation," *Tenri daigaku gakuhō* 178 (March 1995): 179–205.

130. Kobayashi, *Kofun jidai no kenkyū*, pp. 127–128.

131. Himiko's successor's name is usually given as Iyo, but the same Sung text that spells Himiko's land Yama*tai* (not Yamaichi) also gives Himiko's successor's name as *Daiyo*. See Mori and Sugimoto, "*Gishi* Wajin den o tsūdoku suru," p. 153. It should also be noted that as the supply of Chinese-made mirrors was used up, domestically cast imitations were substituted as gifts.

132. Kobayashi, *Kofun jidai no kenkyū*, p. 156. On Tsubai Ōtsukayama see also Aikens and Higuchi, *Prehistory of Japan*, pp. 255–263.

133. Kondō, *Shinjū kyō*, p. 86.

134. Ibid., pp. 1 and 15–19.

135. Mori Kōichi cited in Tanaka, *Wajin sōran*, p. 228.

136. Okuno Masao, *Yamatai koku no kagami*, pp. 7–54.

137. Wang Zhong-shu, *Nihon no sankakuen shinjū kyō mondai ni tsuite*, pp. 1–24, and "Nihon sankakuen shinjū kyō sōron," *Kōkogaku kenkyū* 122 (September 1984): 108–114. The original Chinese article is "Riben sanjue yuan shenshou jing zongji," *Kaogu* 200 (May 1984): 468–479. See also Pearson, *Ancient Japan*, p. 148. Okazaki, "Japan and the Continent," pp. 292–295, discusses the controversy over mirrors and places considerable weight behind Wang's arguments.

138. On this mirror see Tanaka, *Wajin sōran*, pp. 232–236; see also "Tokushū: keisho yo'nen no kagami o megutte," *Higashi Ajia no kodai bunka* 51 (1987): 2–75.

139. Tanaka, *Wajin sōran*, pp. 231–232.

140. Ibid., pp. 235–236.

141. Kobayashi, *Kofun jidai no kenkyū*, pp. 140–156.

142. On this point I disagree with the excellent analysis presented by Edwards, "In Pursuit of Himiko," p. 67. Moreover Gina Barnes, "The Archaeology of Protohistoric Yamato," *Beiträge zur Allgemeinen und Vergleichenden Archäologie* 16 (1996): 84–86, has expressed misgivings about the political implications of mirror distribution.

143. On the forms of Yayoi burial see "Bochi" in Sahara and Kanaseki, *Yayoi bunka no kenkyū* 8: *Matsuri to haka to yosoi*, pp. 91–164. See also Pearson, *Ancient Japan*, p. 144; Hudson, "Rice, Bronze, and Chieftains," pp. 156–168; Barnes, *China, Korea and Japan*, pp. 189–190. Walter Edwards, "In Pursuit of Himiko," pp. 68–77, provides a useful overview of Yayoi and Tomb burials and builds a chronology tied to pottery styles.

144. On elite and commoner subcultures see also Barnes, *Protohistoric Yamato*, pp. 225–238 and 242–246.

145. On Tatetsuki see Kondō Yoshirō, *Tatetsuki iseki*. Although archaeologists agree that Tatetsuki dates to the end of the Yayoi, the exact years of construction are subject to debate. Imamura, *Prehistoric Japan*, p. 191, briefly describes these Yayoi graves.

146. Kondō Yoshirō, *Zenpō kōen fun no jidai*, pp. 157–162. See also the Kondō essay in English, "The Keyhole Tumulus and Its Relationship to Earlier Forms of Burial," in Pearson, *Windows on the Japanese Past*, pp. 335–348; and Piggott, "Sacral Kingship and Confederacy," pp. 50–51. I have used Piggott's translation of this term.

147. Pearson, *Ancient Japan,* pp. 145–146.

148. Sahara, *Nihonjin no tanjō,* pp. 319–320.

149. Shiraishi Taichirō, "Kinki ni okeru kofun no nendai," *Kōkogaku jaanaru* 164 (August 1979): 21–26.

150. Shiraishi Taichirō, "Haka to bochi," in Mori Kōichi, ed., *San seiki no kōkogaku* 2: *San seiki no iseki to ibutsu,* pp. 94–95.

151. Ibid., p. 76.

152. See, for example, Shiomi Akira, "Tetsu tekki no seisan," in *Iwanami kōza Nihon kōkogaku* 3: *Seisan to ryūtsū,* p. 241; Tsude Hiroshi, "Nihon kodai no kokka keisei ron josetsu: Zenpō kōen fun taisei no teishō," *Nihon shi kenkyū* 343 (March 1991): 5–39. See also Nelson, *Archaeology of Korea,* p. 164, on a similar problem in Korea.

153. See Takakura Hiroaki for an excellent survey of work on iron technology: "Shoki tekki no fukyū to kakki," in *Kenkyū ronshū,* vol. 10, pp. 19–50. He argues that of the iron tools and weapons produced in the Yayoi period, woodworking tools appeared first about A.D. 1, followed by farming tools (A.D. 100) and lastly iron arrowheads in the late Yayoi. See also Hitchins, "A Cultural Synthesis of the Yayoi Period," pp. 92–101; and Imamura, *Prehistoric Japan,* pp. 168–169.

154. Sahara, *Nihonjin no tanjō,* pp. 271–272, admits the lack of evidence but argues for a major role for iron tools based on the shape of boards. Sarah Taylor, "Ploughshares into Swords: The Iron Industry and Social Development in Protohistoric Korea and Japan," Ph.D. dissertation, Cambridge University, 1990, p. 258, argues for some recycling in Yayoi Japan based on the plentitude of iron finds in burials compared with the metal's dearth in habitation sites.

155. Tsude, *Nōkō shakai,* pp. 30–32.

156. William McNeill, *A History of the Human Community,* vol. 1, pp. 94–95.

157. Kawagoe Tetsushi, "Yayoi jidai no chūzō teppu o megutte," *Kōkogaku zasshi* 65 (March 1980): 1–23. Note the evidence of iron production in southern Korea in Nelson, *Archaeology of Korea,* p. 174. Li Jing-hua, "On the Provenance of the Early Time Ironware Excavated in Kyushu, Japan," *Bulletin of the Metals Museum* 17 (1991): 32–39, argues that the earliest iron in Kyushu came from Han China as trade items.

158. Tsude, *Nōkō shakai,* p. 89; Shiomi, "Tetsu tekki no seisan," pp. 241–244. Archaeologists have, however, found smithies where iron tools were forged from prepared slabs; see Takakura, "Shoki tekki," pp. 26–27. Okazaki, "Japan and the Continent," pp. 279–280. Kidder, "The Earliest Societies in Japan," pp. 88–89, argues for the production of iron from native sources despite the lack of evidence. See also Taylor, "Ploughshares into Swords," pp. 59–61.

159. Okuno Masao, "Yamatai koku Kyushu ron," *Kikan Yamatai koku* 5 (April 1980): 137. Tsude, "Nihon kodai no kokka keisei ron josetsu," pp. 5–39, also notes that northern Kyushu has the lion's share of iron and posits a role for Han merchants distributing iron to natives of the area.

160. Sahara, *Nihonjin no tanjō*, pp. 326–328. See also Sahara Makoto, "Rice Cultivation and the Japanese," *Acta Asiatica* 63 (1992): 40–63. Since secondary burials existed in the Jōmon period, one could argue that they were a traditional element not unique to the Yayoi epoch.

Chapter 2: Ancient Japan's Korean Connection

1. In defining the term "Wa" I have consulted Chong-Hang Yi, "On the True Nature of 'Wae' in *Samguk sagi*," *Korea Journal* 17 (November 1977): 51–59; Gina Barnes, "Early Korean States," in Barnes, ed., *Hoabinhian: Jōmon, Yayoi Early Korean States*, pp. 113–162; Barnes, *China, Korea and Japan*, p. 244; Mark Hudson, "Ethnicity in East Asian Archaeology: Approaches to the Wa," *Archaeological Review from Cambridge* 8 (Spring 1989): 51–63; and Ch'on Kwan-U, "A New Interpretation of the Problems of Mimana," *Korea Journal* 14 (February 1974): 9–23 and 14 (April 1974): 31–44. For a translation of a relevant passage see Peter Lee, *Sourcebook of Korean Civilization*, vol. 1, p. 24.

2. *Nihongi*, trans. William Aston, vol. 1, p. 251; *Nihon koten bungaku taikei* (hereafter *NKBT*), *Nihon shoki*, vol. 1, Jingū kōgō 51/3, pp. 358–359. I have modified this translation slightly.

3. Aston, *Nihongi*, vol. 1, p. 338; *NKBT*, *Nihon shoki*, vol. 1, Yūryaku 2/7, pp. 463–464.

4. Aston, *Nihongi*, vol. 1, p. 354; *NKBT*, *Nihon shoki*, vol. 1, Yūryaku 9/3, pp. 480–481. I have modified this translation.

5. This early historiography is drawn from Saeki Arikiyo, *Kenkyū shi: Kokaido Ō hi*, pp. 1–179. Japanese scholars who believed the account of Jingū's subjugation of southern Korea include Aoe Hide (1884), Miyake Yonekichi (1889), Kan Masatomo (1891), and Nishikawa Ken (1910).

6. Ibid., pp. 111–114.

7. Ibid., pp. 123–125. The scholar was Kawasaki Hajime.

8. Ibid., pp. 143–157. On the history of the stele see also Yukio Takeda, "Studies on the King Kwanggaito Inscription and Their Basis," *Memoirs of the Research Department of the Toyo Bunko* 47 (1989): 63–68.

9. This part of the historiography follows Yamao Yukihisa, *Kodai no Nitchō kankei*, pp. 33–49.

10. Ibid., pp. 38–41.

11. Hamada Kōsaku, "Bunka shi jō no wa ga kuni no chii," in *Kōmin kyōiku taikei: Shōwa shichi nendo kaki kōshū kai kōen shū*, pp. 14–22; Gotō Shūichi, *Nihon kōkogaku*, pp. 283–285.

12. Egami Namio has rewritten his views several times; for the most recent view see *Kiba minzoku kokka*, especially pp. 144–304.

13. For criticisms see Inoue Mitsusada, *Nihon no rekishi* 1: *Shinwa kara rekishi e*, pp. 287–289. See also Walter Edwards, "Event and Process in the Founding of Japan: The Horserider Theory in Archeological Perspective," *Journal of Japanese Studies* 9 (Summer 1983): 265–295.

14. The best rewriting of Egami's theory is Gari Ledyard, "Galloping Along with the Horseriders: Looking for the Founders of Japan," *Journal of Japanese Studies* 1 (Summer 1975): 217–254. See also Cornelius Kiley's endorsement of the theory in "State and Dynasty in Archaic Yamato," *Journal of Asian Studies* 33 (November 1973): 25–49. Other writers using the theory include Jacques Kamstra, *Encounter or Syncretism*, pp. 186–223; Jonetta Covell and Alan Covell, *Korean Impact on Japanese Culture*, pp. 8–42; and James Grayson, "Mimana, A Problem in Korean Historiography," *Korea Journal* 17 (August 1977): 65–69. J. Russell Kirkland, "The Horseriders in Korea: A Critical Evaluation of a Historical Theory," *Korean Studies* 5 (1981): 109–128, raises many doubts about the theory. See also Wontack Hong, *Paekche of Korea and the Origin of Yamato Wa*, and Gina Barnes, *Protohistoric Yamato*, pp. 16–24.

15. Yamao, *Nitchō kankei*, pp. 41–47. Shades of this view are still visible in Delmer Brown, "The Yamato Kingdom," in Delmer Brown, ed., *The Cambridge History of Japan*, vol. 1, p. 108, although on p. 123 he retreats from this perspective somewhat. See also Inoue Mitsusada, "The Century of Reform," in Brown, *Cambridge History of Japan*, vol. 1, pp. 204 and 207.

16. See, for example, George Sansom, *A History of Japan to 1334*, pp. 41–48; Edwin Reischauer et al., *East Asia*, pp. 330–334; and Yasukazu Suematsu, "Japan's Relations with the Asian Continent and the Korean Peninsula (Before 950 A.D.)," *Cahiers d'histoire Mondiale* 4 (1958): 671–687. See also the criticisms of Wontack Hong in *Relationship Between Korea and Japan in Early Period: Paekche and Yamato Wa*, pp. 19–28.

17. All citations from Chinese dynastic histories follow Ishihara Michihiro, ed., *Chūgoku seishi Nihon den* 1: *Wei zhi Woren zhuan. Hou Han shu Wozhuan. Sung shu Woguo zhuan. Sui shu Woguo zhuan*, pp. 123–126. For an English version see *Japan in the Chinese Dynastic Histories*, trans. Ryusaku Tsunoda, pp. 22–24.

18. Kim's views are summarized in Saeki, *Kokaido Ō hi*, pp. 254–259; Yamao, *Nitchō kankei*, pp. 57–59; and Kim Sŏk-hyŏng, *Kodai Chōnichi kankei shi: Yamato seiken to Mimana*. In English see Ki-dong Lee, "Ancient Korean Historical Research in North Korea," *Korea Journal* 32 (Summer 1992): 35–36.

19. Lee, "Ancient Historical Research," p. 36.

20. On the quarrel among Japanese and North and South Koreans over the reading of the inscription on the monument see Takeda, "King Kwanggaito Inscription," pp. 57–63 and 68–72.

21. Yamao, *Nitchō kankei*, p. 58.

22. Saeki, *Kokaido Ō hi*, pp. 272–275.

23. See Seki Akira, *Kikajin*.

24. Saeki, *Kokaido Ō hi*, pp. 276–284. In English see Saeki, "Studies on Ancient Japanese History," *Acta Asiatica* 31 (1977): 126–129.

25. Some of these Korean interpretations began appearing in English in the 1970s. See Kim Jung-bae, "The Question of Horse-Riding People in Korea," *Korea Journal* 18 (September 1978): 39–50 and 18 (November 1978): 41–52; Ch'on, "Problems of Mimana."

26. Wang Jian-qun, *Kōtai ō hi no kenkyū*.

27. There is a growing literature on Korean archaeology in English. In addition to previously cited sources, I consulted general works like Kim Won-yong, "Korean Archaeology Today," *Korea Journal* 21 (September 1981): 22–43; Kim, "Impact of Ancient Korean Culture upon Japan," *Korea Journal* 12 (June 1972): 34–35; Kim, *Recent Archaeological Discoveries in the Republic of Korea;* Kim, *Art and Archaeology of Ancient Korea;* Gina Barnes, *China, Korea and Japan*, pp. 208–260; Sarah Nelson, "Korean Interpretations of Korean Archaeology," *Asian Perspectives* 27 (1990): 185–192; Kim Jung-bae, "Question of Horse-Riding People"; Sarah Nelson, "Recent Progress in Korean Archaeology," in F. Wendorf and A. Close, eds., *Advances in World Archaeology*, vol. 1, pp. 99–149; Ki-baik Lee, *A New History of Korea*, pp. 1–44; and Nelson, "Archaeological Discoveries in Korea," *Korean Culture* 14 (1993): 23–31.

28. This generalization may eventually need two qualifications. First, dates for primitive ironworking in China have been pushed back to 900 B.C. and earlier; see Tanaka Migaku, *Nihon no rekishi* 2: *Wajin sōran*, p. 134. Second, some are beginning to recognize Scythian influence on the Chinese *before* they developed iron casting; see Don Wagner, "The Beginning of Iron in China," *EAANnouncements* 17 (Autumn 1995): 6. See also Sarah Taylor, "Ploughshares into Swords: The Iron Industry and Social Development in Protohistoric Korea and Japan," Ph.D. dissertation, Cambridge University, 1990, pp. 5–23. Taylor's pioneering work informs my discussion throughout.

29. For routes of the diffusion of iron technology I consulted Chŏn Yŏng-nae, "Shoki tekki jidai," in Kim Wŏnyong, ed., *Kankoku no kōkogaku*, p. 82; Shiomi Akira, *Higashi Ajia no shoki tekki bunka*, pp. 225–226; Sarah Nelson, *The Archaeology of Korea*, pp. 164, 173–174, 191, and 199, for evidence of early iron production in Korea. Nelson argues for iron mines in Kaya by 200 B.C. Gina Barnes, "State Formation in the Southern Korea

Peninsula," *Archaeology in Korea* 10 (1983): 40–51, argues for primitive furnaces in southern Korea by the first to third century B.C. See also Sarah Taylor, "The Introduction and Development of Iron Production in Korea: A Survey," *World Archaeology* 20 (1989): 425; Dong Suk Yoon, "Early Iron Metallurgy in Korea," *Archaeological Review from Cambridge* 8 (1989): 92–99; and Taylor, "Ploughshares into Swords," pp. 31–40.

30. Gina Barnes, Don Wagner, Albert Dien, Sin Kyŏng-ch'ŏl, and Yoshimura Kazuaki, "Roundtable on Early Korean Armour," presented to the Association for Asian Studies in Los Angeles in March 1993; Taylor, "Ploughshares into Swords," pp. 242–281.

31. Taylor, "Iron Production in Korea," pp. 426–427, Kim, "Korean Archaeology Today," pp. 34–35, and Yoon, "Early Metallurgy," pp. 92–99, corroborate the timing of iron diffusion in southern Korea. Richard Pearson, "Lolang and the Rise of Korean States and Chiefdoms," *Journal of the Hong Kong Archaeological Society* 7 (1976–1978): 77–90, raises doubts about the impact of the commanderies on local inhabitants. On Lelang see also Pai Hyung Il, "Lelang and the 'Interaction Sphere'," *Archaeological Review from Cambridge* 8 (1989): 64–75; and Pai, "The Nangnang Triangle in China, Japan, Korea," *Korean Culture* 14 (Winter 1993): 32–41. See Chŏn, "Shoki tekki," pp. 84–86, on iron weapons and tools uncovered in Kyŏngju; Shiomi, *Higashi Ajia*, pp. 252–253, notes bellows and iron slag in a site near Seoul. See Han Pyŏng-sam, "Gen sankoku jidai," in Kim Wŏnyong, ed., *Kankoku no kōkogaku*, pp. 103–104.

32. Kim Chong-ch'ŏl, "Sankoku jidai: Kaya, Kyŏngsang North," in Kim, *Kankoku no kōkogaku*, pp. 178–183; Sim Pong-gŭn, "Sankoku jidai: Kaya Kyŏngsang South," in Kim, *Kankoku no kōkogaku*, pp. 198–199; Ch'oe Pyŏng-hyŏn, "Sankoku jidai: Silla," in Kim, *Kankoku no kōkogaku*, pp. 217–219, give examples of armor, knives, swords, arrowheads, and spear and pike points from Kaya and Silla territory. See Nelson, *Archaeology of Korea*, p. 216 (Koguryŏ) and p. 248 (Silla), for more examples. *Paekche üi chech'ŏl kongchŏng kwa kisul palchŏn*, pp. 12–16, lists nails, ax blades, sickles, spades, plowshares, and some weapons in Paekche territory. My chronology for iron production fits Taylor, "Ploughshares into Swords," pp. 24–72.

33. Cited in Yamao, *Nitchō kankei*, p. 265.

34. Tanaka, *Wajin sōran*, p. 321.

35. Tsude Hiroshi, "Nihon kodai no kokka keisei ron josetsu: Zenpō kōen fun taisei no teishō," *Nihon shi kenkyū* 343 (March 1991): 5–39, argues that chiefly leagues based in northern Kyushu and the Kinai fought a war over southern Korean iron during the late third and fourth centuries.

36. Furuse Kiyohide, "Tekki no seisan," in *Kofun jidai no kenkyū* 5: *Seisan to ryūtsū*, vol. 2, p. 42. In English see Aikens and Higuchi, *Prehistory of Japan*, pp. 263–277, and Lars Vargo, *Social and Economic Conditions for the Formation of the Early Japanese State*, pp. 15–31.

37. Tanaka, *Wajin sōran*, pp. 320–321. Other fifth-century caches of iron are described in Anazawa Wakō and Manome Jun'ichi, "Buki bugu to bagu," in Shiraishi Taichirō, ed., *Kodai o kangaeru kofun*, pp. 173–180. Vadime Elisseeff, *Ancient Civilization of Japan*, pp. 154–156, calls the Tomb period Japan's Iron Age.

38. Tanaka, *Wajin sōran*, pp. 322–323.

39. Written sources support this view as well. See Donald Philippi, trans., *Kojiki*, p. 285, for ironworkers sent to Japan from Paekche; see also Brown, "The Yamato Kingdom," pp. 121 and 144. Gotō Yoshiharu, "Kaji gijutsu dō'nyū ni okeru Silla Kaya kei toraijin," in *Kodai shi ronshū*, vol. 1, pp. 67–91, cites a source noting the high proportion of Kaya and Silla natives in ironworking.

40. On these tools see Matsui Kazuyoshi, "Kodai no kajigu," *Ko bunka ronsō*, pp. 560–585. See also Matsui Kazuyoshi, "Tetsu seisan," in *Kofun jidai no kenkyū 5: Seisan to ryūtsū* II, pp. 17–20. Taylor, "Ploughshares into Swords," pp. 208–280, argues for bloomeries in Japan based on the composition of iron artifacts.

41. On iron ingots see Azuma Ushio, "Tetsu sozai ron," in *Kofun jidai no kenkyū 5: Seisan to ryūtsū* II, pp. 22–35; Azuma Ushio, "Tettei no kisoteki kenkyū," in *Kashiwara kōkogaku kenkyū jo kiyō* 12: *Kōkogaku ronkō*, pp. 70–179. Tsude, "Nihon kodai no kokka keisei ron josetsu," pp. 5–39, also discusses these artifacts.

42. Okazaki Takashi, "Tettei," in *Munakata Okinoshima honbun*, pp. 335–363.

43. Okazaki, "Japan and the Continent," p. 309; Delmer Brown, "Introduction," in Delmer Brown, ed., *The Cambridge History of Japan*, vol. 1, p. 25.

44. Japan's ferrous industries began to grow after A.D. 550, when Kaya fell to Silla and iron-sand was discovered in Japan. Matsui, "Tetsu seisan," pp. 12–14, discusses ten iron-smelting sites uncovered in Kibi dating to the sixth and seventh centuries. Hanada Katsuhiro, "Wa seiken to kaji kōbō–Kinai no kaji seigyō shūraku o chūshin ni," *Kōkogaku kenkyū* 143 (December 1989): 68, has noted thirty-one blacksmith's shops located in the Kinai between A.D. 300 and 700. William Wayne Farris, *Heavenly Warriors*, pp. 155–156, indicates that the price of iron fluctuated widely by region in the 700s but had reached parity from Kyushu to the Kanto by 900.

45. Anazawa and Manome, "Buki," p. 177. For mention of Korean finds see Sŏ Sŏng-hun, "Sankoku jidai: Paekche, Chŏlla," in Kim, *Kankoku no kōkogaku*, p. 159; Sim, "Kaya, Kyŏngsang South," p. 199; Ch'oe, "Silla," p. 218. See also Niiro Izumi, "Buki," in *Kofun jidai no kenkyū 8: Kofun II: fukusōhin*, pp. 36–37.

46. See Yun Mu-byŏng, "Sankoku jidai: Paekche, Ch'ungch'ŏng," in Kim, *Kankoku no kōkogaku*, p. 146; Sŏ, "Paekche, Chŏlla," pp. 159–160; Kim, "Kaya, Kyŏngsang North," p. 178; Sim, "Kaya, Kyŏngsang South," p. 198; Ch'oe, "Silla," p. 218. Nelson, *Archaeology of Korea*, lists swords for Kaya on p. 242.

47. Machida Akira, "Kantō no keifu," in *Nara kokuritsu bunka zai kenkyū jo gakuhō* 28: *Kenkyū ronshū* 3, p. 90.

48. On loss of fighting capability see Machida, "Kantō," p. 92; on style variation see Anazawa and Manome, "Buki," p. 198.

49. Anazawa Wakō and Manome Jun'ichi, "Nihon ni okeru ryūhō kantō tachi no seisaku to haifu," *Kōkogaku jaanaru* 266 (August 1986): 20.

50. Niiro Izumi, "Sōshoku tsuki tachi to kofun jidai kōki no heisei," *Kōkogaku kenkyū* 119 (December 1983): 67; Anazawa and Manome, "Ryūhō kantō tachi," p. 20. For inscribed swords and their interpretation see Shinokawa Ken, "Eta Funayama kofun shutsudo no tachi mei," in Saeki Arikiyo, ed., *Kodai o kangaeru Yūryaku tennō to sono jidai,* pp. 104–107; Kishi Toshio, "Kodai no kakki Yūryaku chō kara no tenbō," in *Nihon no kodai 6: Ōken o meguru tatakai,* p. 13.

51. On prewar scholars see Anazawa and Manome, "Buki," p. 182. Nelson, *Archaeology of Korea,* pp. 239–241, indicates that as many as sixteen suits of armor have been found in one Kaya site. Gina Barnes, in "Discoveries of Iron Armour on the Korean Peninsula," in Gina Barnes and Beth McKillop, eds., *British Association for Korean Studies Papers* 5: *Korean Material Culture,* p. 106, suggests that the cuirass may have been inspired by Northern Wei armor. Although the two do not seem similar, the idea is reasonable given Japanese copying of Northern Wei models in other areas.

52. Kim, "Kaya, Kyŏngsang North," pp. 180–182, and Sim, "Kaya, Kyŏngsang South," pp. 198–199. See also Barnes, "Discoveries of Iron Armour," pp. 110–121, for a discussion of recent Korean finds.

53. Here I have summarized Chŏng Ching-wŏn and Sin Kyŏng-ch'ŏl, "Kodai KanNichi katchū dansō," *Kodai bunka* 38 (January 1986): 17–33; Sin Kyŏng-ch'ŏl, "Go seiki ni okeru Nihon to Kara hantō," in *Nihon kōkogaku kyōkai 1990 nendo taikai: kenkyū happyō yōshi,* pp. 30–36.

54. Sin Kyŏng-ch'ŏl, "Go seiki ni okeru Nihon to Kara hantō," p. 34. Barnes, "Discoveries of Iron Armour," pp. 123–127, endorses this point.

55. Tanaka Shinsaku, "Bugu," in *Kofun jidai no kenkyū 8: Kofun II: Fukusōhin,* pp. 41–50. The dating comes from Kobayashi Ken'ichi, "Hohei to kihei," in Shiraishi Taichirō, ed., *Kodai shi fukugen 7: Kofun jidai no kōgei,* pp. 142–146. The basic argument was first proposed by Kobayashi Ken'ichi, "Katchū seisaku gijutsu no hensen to kōjin no keitō," *Kōkogaku kenkyū* 80 (March 1974): 48–68 and 82 (September 1974): 37–49.

56. Kobayashi, "Katchū seisaku," 82:48.

57. Kobayashi Yukio, "Kofun jidai tankō no genryū," in *Nikkan kodai bunka no nagare,* pp. 32–33. I am deeply indebted to Gina Barnes, Don Wagner, Albert Dien, Sin Kyŏngch'ŏl, and Yoshimura Kazuaki for clarifying the complicated issues of East Asian armor

for me. Their "Roundtable on Early Korean Armour" presented to the Association for Asian Studies in Los Angeles in March 1993 informs my discussion throughout. See also Nishitani Tadashi, "The Kaya Tumuli: Windows on the Past," *Japan Foundation Newsletter* 21 (November 1993): 1–6, for further information on Kaya armor.

58. The following summary is drawn from Anazawa and Manome, "Buki," pp. 188–196. See also Farris, *Heavenly Warriors*, pp. 14–18.

59. Horita Keiichi, "Kodai Nitchō no bachū ni tsuite," in *Kashiwara kōkogaku kenkyū jo ronshū*, vol. 7, pp. 71–78; Anazawa and Manome, "Buki," p. 180.

60. For an example of a Korean scholar holding this view, see Sin Kyŏng-ch'ŏl, "Koshiki abumi kō," *Kodai bunka* 38 (June 1986): 37 and 39; for a Japanese example see Chiga Hisashi, "Nihon shutsudo shoki bagu no keifu," in *Kashiwara kōkogaku kenkyū jo ronshū*, vol. 9, p. 63. See also Kim Jung-bae, "The Question of Horse-Riding People in Korea," p. 47, for evidence that horses were virtually unknown in southern Korea before A.D. 300.

61. See Yun, "Paekche, Ch'ung'ch'ŏng," p. 146; Sŏ, "Paekche, Chŏlla," pp. 160–161, for evidence of Paekche stirrups and bridles. See also Kim Won-yong, *Recent Archaeological Discoveries in the Republic of Korea*, pp. 35–40. Most recent finds come from old Kaya territory: Kim, "Kaya, Kyŏngsang North," pp. 183–184, and Sim, "Kaya, Kyŏngsang South," pp. 199–200, write of stirrups, horse armor, gilded saddles, bridles, and decorations. Ch'oe, "Silla," pp. 218–219, describes gilt saddles, decorations, stirrups, and bridles.

62. Sin, "Koshiki abumi," pp. 22–43; Nelson, *Archaeology of Korea*, pp. 254–258.

63. Chiga Hisashi, "Bagu," in *Kofun jidai no kenkyū* 8: *kofun* II: *fukusōhin*, p. 55; Kobayashi, "Hohei," p. 150. As we shall see, there is also disagreement on timing. I consulted Sakamoto Yoshio, "Yon go seiki no bagu," *Kōkogaku jaanaru* 257 (December 1985): 12–15; see also Aikens and Higuchi, *Prehistory of Japan*, pp. 277–282.

64. Chiga, "Nihon shoki bagu," pp. 17–67; Chiga Hisashi, "Kofun jidai no shoki basō," in *Kashiwara kōkogaku kenkyū jo ronshū*, vol. 4, pp. 329–330.

65. Anazawa and Manome, "Buki," p. 195.

66. See *Ōtani kofun*, pp. 100–104. The tomb is located in Wakayama prefecture, but the Ki settled along the Inland Sea from northern Kyushu to central Honshu.

67. Sakamoto, "Bagu," p. 15.

68. Maekawa Akihisa, "Bagu shutsudo no kofun sū bunpu yori mita Yamato seiken no kiba senryoku," *Kodai bunka* 51 (January 1962): 1–2. See also Anazawa and Manome, "Buki," pp. 195–196.

69. Edwards, "Event and Process," pp. 287–292.

70. Kobayashi, "Hohei," p. 150.

71. See Kobayashi Yukio, *Kofun jidai no kenkyū*, pp. 265–274.

72. Tanaka, *Wajin sōran*, pp. 314–320.

73. Furuse Kiyohide, "Nō kōgu," in *Kofun jidai no kenkyū* 8: *Kofun* II: *Fukusōhin*, pp. 89–90.

74. Ibid., p. 81.

75. Tsude Hiroshi, *Nihon nōkō shakai no seiritsu katei*, pp. 87–88. I also used Joseph Needham's *Science and Civilization in China*, vols. 4 and 6, and Cho-yun Hsu, *Ancient China in Transition*, pp. 130–133.

76. I follow Needham, *Science and Civilization in China*, vol. 6, pt. 2, sec. 41, pp. 206–217.

77. Ibid., vol. 4, pt. 3, pp. 284–296. On plows see Yamada Masahiro, "Nihon ni okeru kofun jidai gyūba kō kaishi setsu sairon," *Rekishi jinrui* 17 (March 1989): 13–19; and Robert Temple, *The Genius of China*, pp. 15–28.

78. Some may argue that Yayoi sites like Toro had sophisticated ditch-digging technology, but according to Gina Barnes, "Toro," in *The Atlas of Archaeology*, p. 201, the canals at Toro were for draining the low-lying fields and not for gaining access to rivers.

79. Azuma Ushio, "Chōsen sankoku jidai no nōkō," in *Kashiwara kōkogaku kenkyū jo ronshū*, vol. 4, pp. 527–564; Nelson, *Archaeology in Korea*, pp. 223 and 236 (Paekche) and p. 242 (Kaya).

80. Azuma, "Chōsen nōkō," pp. 533–535; Yun, "Paekche, Ch'ungch'ŏng," p. 146; Sŏ, "Paekche, Chŏlla," p. 161; and Ch'oe, "Silla," p. 217.

81. Horio Hisashi and Iinuma Jirō, *Nōgu*, pp. 41–49.

82. Azuma, "Chōsen nōkō," p. 551. Kim Jung-bae, "Characteristics of Mahan in Ancient Korean Society," *Korea Journal* 14 (June 1974): 8, argues for dense population in early southern Korea, a fact that could be related to sophisticated wet-rice farming. See also Song Nai Rhee, "Emerging Complex Society in Prehistoric Southwest Korea," Ph.D. dissertation, University of Oregon, Eugene, 1984, pp. 229–232, for more evidence of Paekche irrigation works.

83. Farris, *Population, Disease, and Land*, pp. 94–101.

84. Azuma, "Chōsen nōkō," pp. 536–538.

85. Tsude, *Nōkō shakai*, pp. 9–16, 24–33, 68–75, and 89; Furuse, "Nō kōgu," pp. 74–76; Hirose Kazuo, "Doboku gijutsu," in *Kofun jidai no kenkyū* 5: *Seisan to ryūtsū* II, pp. 113–125; Nelson, *Archaeology in Korea*, p. 198; Vargo, *Social and Economic Conditions*, pp. 8–12 and 19–23.

86. On Furuichi see Tsude Hiroshi, "The Kofun Period," in Tsuboi Kiyotari, ed., *Recent Archaeological Discoveries in Japan*, pp. 66–68; Tsude, "The Kofun Period and State Formation," *Acta Asiatica* 63 (1992): 79–80. See also Brown, "The Yamato Kingdom," pp. 129–130, and Brown, "Introduction," pp. 27–28.

87. Farris, *Population, Disease, and Land*, pp. 6–7 and 95. See also Mun Sa-wi, "Chōsen sankoku no ijūmin shūdan ni yoru Kinai chihō no kaihatsu ni tsuite," *Rekishi gaku kenkyū* 374 (July 1971): 15–32.

88. Farris, *Population, Disease, and Land*, pp. 103–104.

89. Tsude, *Nōkō shakai*, pp. 18 and 284. Dana Morris, "Peasant Economy in Early Japan, 650–950," Ph.D. dissertation, University of California, Berkeley, 1980, pp. 135–146, argues for the diffusion of the plow after 900 based on two written references.

90. Farris, *Population, Disease, and Land*, pp. 8 and 50–73.

91. The following summary of ceramic technology comes from Nakamura Akira, *Kōkogaku raiburarii* 5: *Sue ki*, pp. 3–4, and J. E. Kidder, "Ceramics of the Burial Mounds (Kofun) (A.D. 258–646)," in *The Rise of a Great Tradition*, p. 40.

92. Nakamura, *Sue ki*, p. 4; Haraguchi Shōzō, *Nihon no genshi bijutsu* 4: *Sue ki*, p. 46. On Chinese stoneware see also Gina Barnes, "The Development of Stoneware Technology in Southern Korea," in Song Nai Rhee and C. M. Aikens, eds., *Pacific Northeast Asia in Prehistory*, pp. 201–204. In *China, Korea and Japan*, Barnes argues cogently that while the Chinese made some stoneware accidentally in the late Shang era, they could not produce it in quantity until the Late Zhou period.

93. On possible routes from China to southern Korea see Haraguchi, *Sue ki*, p. 46, which presents evidence of Chinese stoneware in Koguryŏ sites; and Tanaka Kiyomi, "Go seiki ni okeru Settsu Kawachi no kaihatsu to toraijin," *Hisutoria* 125 (December 1989): 2, which argues for a South China–Paekche–Wa route. See also Nelson, *Archaeology in Korea*, pp. 236–237 and 257. For a Korean debate on the timing of stoneware production see Barnes, "Stoneware Technology in Southern Korea," pp. 197–208. On Sue ware see Aikens and Higuchi, *Prehistory of Japan*, pp. 287–289, and Barnes, *China, Korea and Japan*, pp. 232–241.

Japanese archaeologists are divided on the issue of whether the first Japanese stoneware was shaped on the potter's wheel and whether it was an import from Korea. Nakamura, *Sue ki*, pp. 6–12, implies an affirmative answer in his discussion of transmission from southern Korea to Japan. Haraguchi, *Sue ki*, pp. 56–57, seems more doubtful. Narasaki Shōichi, "Nihon kodai no kama," in *Tōshitsu doki no kokusai kōryū*, pp. 9–11, states outright that Koreans from Kaya brought the potter's wheel with them to Japan.

94. For a recent summary of finds throughout Japan see *Tōshitsu doki no kokusai kōryū*, pp. 125–230.

95. Oda Fujio, "Kyushu chiiki no Sue ki to tōshitsu doki," in *Tōshitsu doki no kokusai kōryū*, p. 77; Kinoshita Wataru, "Tōshitsu doki to sono bunpu," in *Kofun jidai no kenkyū* 6: *Higashi Ajia to Sue ki*. See also Nishitani Tadashi, "Kara chiiki to hokubu Kyushu," in *Dazaifu ko bunka ronsō*, vol. 1, p. 50.

96. For Paekche see Sŏ, "Paekche, Chŏlla," p. 159; Chŏn Yŏng-nae,"Kudara chiiki no tōshitsu doki yōseki," in *Tōshitsu doki no kokusai kōryū*, p. 33. For Silla see Kondō Hiroshi, "Sōshoku tsuki Sue ki no denpan ni tsuite," *Hanazono shigaku* 8 (November 1987): 138–147.

97. Sin Kyŏng-ch'ŏl, "Kaya chiiki no tōshitsu doki," in *Tōshitsu doki no kokusai kōryū*, pp. 62–74.

98. See Kitano Kōhei, "Kofun jidai no Sue ki seisan to tekki seisan no setten," in *Tōshitsu doki no kokusai kōryū*, pp. 105–123; Tanaka, "Go seiki Settsu Kawachi," p. 8.

99. See Nishitani, "Kara chiiki," pp. 36–46; Hayashi Hiromichi, "Kamado shutsugen ni kansuru ni san mondai," in *Mizu to tsuchi no kōkogaku*, pp. 95–110; Ishino Hironobu, "Kōkogaku kara mita kodai Nihon no jūkyo," in Ōbayashi Taryō, ed., *Nihon kodai bunka no tankyū* 5: *Ie*, pp. 91–94; Nelson, *Archaeology in Korea*, pp. 183, 186, and 222. See also Aikens and Higuchi, *Prehistory of Japan*, pp. 293–304.

100. Tsude, *Nōkō shakai*, pp. 128–134.

101. All information in this paragraph comes from Nishitani, "Kara chiiki," pp. 41–45.

102. Ibid., pp. 43–45. The use of a special heating system in Korea may also be related to the development of the stove in Japan. See Lee, *New History of Korea*, p. 15.

103. The first estimate is from Kawakami Toshirō, "Kofun chikuzō no dōin sareta hito no kazu to jittai," *Kikan kōkogaku* 3 (Spring 1984): 71–72. The second is from Umehara Sueji, "Ōjin Nintoku Richū san tennō ryō no kibo to eizō," *Shoryōbu kiyō* 5 (March 1955): 14. Ōbayashi purojekuto chiimu, "Gendai gijutsu to kodai gijutsu no hikaku ni yoru Nintoku tennō ryō no kensetsu," *Kikan ōbayashi Mausoleum ōryō* 20 (April 1985): 20, has estimated that today it would cost $680 million and require sixteen years to build a keyhole tomb by ancient methods.

104. Kang In-gu, *Mugi san kwa Changgo san*.

105. For a critique of the Korean's work see Kim Ki-ung, "Kankoku shozai no zenpō kōen fun shingi ron," and Nishitani Tadashi, "Kankoku de hakken sareta 'zenpō kōen fun' ni tsuite," *Kōkogaku jaanaru* 23 (September 1984): 7–9.

106. See Ōuchi Mitsuzane, *Kankoku no zenpō kōen keifun*.

107. In my original analysis, "Ancient Japan's Korean Connection," *Korean Studies* 20 (1996): 11–12, I argued that stone chamber and corridor tumuli developed as Tomb-age engineers learned to use corbels. Subsequent study has suggested that some of the first

tombs with vertical-entrance chambers also employed corbels. It was not a technological improvement that led to the shift from one method of chamber construction to the next, but rather a change in funeral priorities. See note 120. Readers should also be aware that vertical-entrance tombs never hold more than one individual per trench, nor were sarcophagi normally lowered into the chamber, as previously stated.

108. Shiraishi Taichirō, "Kōki kofun no seiritsu to tenkai," in *Nihon no kodai 6: Ōken o meguru tatakai,* p. 211.

109. For opinions linking Japanese developments to Korea see Oda Fujio, "Yokoana shiki sekishitsu no dō'nyū to sono genryū," in *Chōsen sankoku to Wakoku,* pp. 280–291; Nagashima Kimichika, "Yokoana shiki sekishitsu no genryū o saguru," in *Nihon to Chōsen no kodai shi,* pp. 67–102; Yanagisawa Kazuo, "Kofun no henshitsu," in Shiraishi Taichirō, ed., *Kodai o kangaeru kofun,* pp. 125–134; Morishita Akiyuki, "Nihon ni okeru yokoana shiki sekishitsu no shutsugen to sono keifu," *Kodai gaku kenkyū* 111 (August 1986): 1–17; Mori Kōichi and Yokota Ken'ichi, "Taidan: bochi to kofun," in Mori Kōichi, ed., *Nihon kodai bunka no tankyū 10: Bochi,* pp. 298–301; and Nishitani Tadashi and Kim Ki-ung, "Yokoana shiki sekishitsu no shutsugen o megutte," in *Kyushu ni okeru kofun bunka to Chōsen hantō,* pp. 177–181. See also Nelson, *Archaeology in Korea,* pp. 222–233; note the corbels in Koguryŏ tombs, pp. 211–219. Doubters include Shiraishi, "Kōki kofun," pp. 215–218; Yun Hwan, "Kankō karyū iki ni okeru Paekche yokoana shiki sekishitsu," *Kobunka dansō,* vol. 20, pp. 178–179; and Habuta Sumiyuki, "Kyushu no shoki yokoana shiki sekishitsu," *Kobunka dansō* vol. 12, pp. 272–273. In English I consulted the following works: Nelson, "Recent Progress in Korean Archaeology," pp. 138–144; Kim Won-yong, *Recent Archaeological Discoveries in the Republic of Korea,* pp. 33–62; Vargo, *Social and Economic Conditions,* pp. 32–47; and Okauchi Mitsuzane, "Mounded Tombs in East Asia from the Third to Seventh Centuries A.D.," in Pearson, *Windows on the Japanese Past,* pp. 127–148.

110. See Yanagisawa, "Kofun no henshitsu," pp. 125–128; Shiraishi Taichirō, "Nihon ni okeru yokoana shiki sekishitsu no keifu," *Senshi gaku kenkyū* 5 (May 1965): 72–73. See also Byung-mo Kim, "Aspects of Brick and Stone Tomb Construction in China and South Korea, Ch'in to Silla Period," Ph.D. dissertation, Oxford University, 1978, pp. 41–47 and 72–141.

111. Gina Barnes argues for the transference from southern China to Paekche; see *China, Korea and Japan,* pp. 222–29. See also Okauchi, "Mounded Tombs in East Asia," pp. 132–141.

112. On the Koguryŏ tombs see Kim Wŏn-yong, "Sankoku jidai: Koguryŏ," in Kim, *Kankoku no kōkogaku,* pp. 117–127, and Byung-mo Kim, "Brick and Stone Tomb Construction," pp. 153–195.

113. Yanagisawa, "Kofun no henshitsu," pp. 131–132; Im Yŏng-jin, "Sankoku jidai: Paekche, Seoul," in Kim, *Kankoku no kōkogaku,* pp. 138–139. See also Byung-mo Kim, "Brick and Stone Tomb Construction," pp. 214–233.

114. Shiraishi, "Kōki kofun," p. 215; Yun, "Paekche yokoana sekishitsu," pp. 158–160. See also the comments of Kim Ki-ung in discussion with Nishitani, "Yokoana shiki sekishitsu no shutsugen o megutte," p. 180.

115. Okazaki, "Japan and the Continent," pp. 306–308, agrees that stone corridor and chamber tombs were not found in Silla until the sixth century but still argues for the possibility of influence from Silla to Yamato.

116. Shiraishi, "Nihon ni okeru yokoana shiki sekishitsu," pp. 75–76.

117. Oda, "Yokoana shiki sekishitsu no dō'nyū," pp. 264–280.

118. On stonecutting technology see Wada Seigo, "Sekkō gijutsu," in *Kofun jidai no kenkyū* 5: *Seisan to ryūtsū* II, pp. 127–143; and Wada, "Political Interpretations of Stone Coffin Production in Protohistoric Japan," in Pearson, *Windows on the Japanese Past*, pp. 349–374.

119. See Kobayashi Yukio, "Sōshoku kofun," in *Kofun bunka ronkō*, pp. 541–590. See also Elisseeff, *Ancient Civilization of Japan*, pp. 179–180, and Kim Won-yong, *Art and Archaeology of Ancient Korea*, pp. 389–399.

120. On Takamatsuzuka Tomb see Arimitsu Kyōichi, "Koguryŏ hekiga kofun no shishin zu," in *Hekiga kofun Takamatsu zuka*, pp. 140–150; J. E. Kidder, "The Newly Discovered Takamatsu Tomb," *Monumenta Nipponica* 27 (Summer 1972): 245–251. On other Korean aspects of Japanese tombs see Kirihara Takeshi, *Tsumiishi zuka to toraijin*, pp. 11–27 and 93–118.

Kobayashi Yukio, "Yomo tsu hegui," in *Kofun bunka ronkō*, pp. 263–281, and Shiraishi Taichirō, "Koto do watashi kō," in *Kashiwara kōkogaku kenkyū jo ronshū*, pp. 347–371, have argued that the adoption of the stone corridor and chamber tomb was associated with new attitudes toward death. Citing *NKBT, Nihon shoki*, vol. 1, pp. 92–93, and Aston, *Nihongi*, vol. 1, p. 25, they suggest that the new style of tomb gave rise to an incantation for taking leave of the deceased. In turn these archaeologists indicate that the idea of pollution from death, basic to Shinto, had finally taken firm root in Japan. See also Matsumae Takeshi, "Early Kami Worship," in Delmer Brown, ed., *The Cambridge History of Japan*, vol. 1, pp. 345 and 348–349. J. E. Kidder, however, has suggested that the idea of pollution from death could be as old as the Late Jōmon era.

121. Machida Akira, "Kodai obi kanagu kō," *Kōkogaku zasshi* 56 (September 1970): 35–36. The inference on earrings is drawn from Nogami Jōsuke, "Nihon shutsudo no tarekazari tsuki mimi kazari ni tsuite," in *Kobunka ronsō*, pp. 237–238. Belt buckles were not made totally of gold or silver because the metals are too soft. See also Lisa Kay Bailey, "Crowning Glory: Headdresses of the Three Kingdoms Period," in Barnes and McKillop, *Korean Material Culture*, pp. 83–103, who stresses ties to Central Asian nomads.

122. This generalization applies especially to belts. See Machida, "Obi kanagu," pp. 36–37. Few Jin models have survived. One burial found in Shanxi province and dated

A.D. 297 contains a military man and suggests the use of belt pieces as status markers. Two other examples are from Jiangsu and Hebei. On gold and silver refining in ancient China see Needham, *Science and Civilization in China,* vol. 5, pt. 2, sec. 33, pp. 47–71.

123. Ch'oe, "Sankoku jidai: Silla," pp. 212–217. In English I consulted Barnes, *China, Korea and Japan,* pp. 229–241; Kim, *Recent Archaeological Discoveries,* pp. 33–62; and Nishitani, "Kaya Tumuli," pp. 1–6.

124. On earrings see Nogami, "Mimikazari," p. 239; on shoes see Manome Jun'ichi, "Kindō shokuri," in *Kofun jidai no kenkyū* 8: *kofun* II: *fukusōhin,* p. 124. Shoes were made from fitted copper plates to which gilding was applied. Two styles are known in Japan, one made from two plates and the other from three; both styles have Korean prototypes.

125. Saotome Masahiro, "Imaki no gijutsu to kōgei," in *Kodai shi fukugen 7: Kofun jidai no kōgei,* pp. 137–140. See also Uno Masatoshi, "Nihon shutsudo kanbō to sono haikei," in *Kyūshū jōdai bunka ronshū,* pp. 289–291.

126. See the finds from King Muryŏng's tomb in Paekche: Yun, "Paekche, Ch'ungch'ŏng," pp. 151–152; Sŏ, "Paekche, Chŏlla," pp. 159–161; Kim, "Kaya, Kyŏngsang North," pp. 176–178; Sim, "Kaya, Kyŏngsang South," pp. 197–198. Okazaki, "Japan and the Continent," pp. 304–306, gives further details on the tomb. See also Nelson, *Archaeology of Korea,* pp. 231, 233, 239, 241–242, and 249–254.

127. On belts see Chiga Hisashi, "Nihon shutsudo obi kanagu no keifu," in *Kashiwara kōkogaku kenkyū ronshū,* vol. 6, p. 332.

128. Anazawa and Manome, "Buki," p. 186.

129. Kondō Kyōichi, "Chūdō seihin," in *Kofun jidai no kenkyū 5: Seisan to ryūtsū* II, pp. 62–65.

130. Morimitsu Toshihiko, "Seidō sei yōki, garasu yōki," in *Kofun jidai no kenkyū* 8: *Kofun* II: *Fukusōhin,* pp. 201–202. Insook Lee, "Ancient Glass Trade in Korea," in Barnes and McKillop, *Korean Material Culture,* pp. 65–82, stresses Korea's role as cultural intermediary.

131. See *Shinsen shōjiroku no kenkyū: honbun hen,* ed. Saeki Arikiyo, p. 279.

132. Seki Akira, *Kikajin,* pp. 95–97; Ueda Masaaki, *Kikajin,* pp. 69–72.

133. Tsunoyama Yukihiro, "Orimono," in *Kofun jidai no kenkyū 5: Seisan to ryūtsū* II, pp. 165–169. See also Mark Hudson, "From Toro to Yoshinogari—Changing Perspectives on Yayoi Period Archeology," in Gina Barnes, ed., *Hoabinhian: Jomon, Yayoi, Early Korean States,* p. 86, who mentions the introduction of the backstrap loom from Korea in the Tomb age. On sericulture in ancient China see Needham, *Science and Civilization in China,* vol. 5, pt. 9, sec. 31, pp. 285–417.

134. Philippi, *Kojiki*, p. 285.

135. *NKBT, Nihon shoki*, vol. 2, Bidatsu 1/5/15, pp. 132–135; Aston, *Nihongi*, vol. 2, p. 91.

136. Seki, *Kikajin*, p. 45; Okazaki, "Japan and the Continent," pp. 311–312. In English see Barnes, *China, Korea and Japan*, p. 243, and Ki-baik Lee, *A New History of Korea*, pp. 57–61.

137. On Tomb-period inscriptions see Yamao Yukihisa, "Kofun jidai no kinseki bun," *Nihon shi kenkyū* 130 (December 1972): 120–123. See also Inoue, "Century of Reform," pp. 170–171.

138. On these two inscriptions I follow the versions given in *Hakkutsu sareta kodai no zaimei ihō*, pp. 36–39 and 42–43. On Kawachi no Atai see Kasai Wajin, "Kawachi no Atai no keifu ni tsuite," in Mishina Akihide, ed., *Nihon shoki kenkyū*, vol. 5, pp. 156–158.

139. *Kodai no zaimei ihō*, pp. 45–47.

140. See Chŏng Cho-myo, "Chōsen sankoku to kodai Nihon moji," in *Kodai shi ron-shū*, vol. 1, pp. 46–65. On the Inariyama sword inscription see Anazawa and Manome, "Two Inscribed Swords from Japanese Tumuli: Discoveries and Research on Finds from the Sakitama-Inariyama and Eta-Funayama Tumuli," in Pearson, *Windows on the Japanese Past*, pp. 375–396; and Shichirō Murayama and Roy Miller, "The Inariyama Tumulus Sword Inscription," *Journal of Japanese Studies* 5 (1979): 405–438.

141. There is a proliferation of work on scholarly families of Korean origin. See Seki, *Kikajin*, pp. 26–50; Ueda, *Kikajin*, pp. 72–79; Katō Kenkichi, "Torai no hitobito," in Saeki Arikiyo, ed., *Kodai o kangaeru Yūryaku tennō to sono jidai*, pp. 220–227; and Ukeda Masayoshi, "Fuhito shūdan no ichi kōsatsu," in *Kodai shi ronshū*, vol. 1, pp. 179–202.

142. *NKBT, Nihon shoki*, vol. 2, Yūryaku 2/10/ *Kono toshi no jō*, p. 465; Aston, *Nihongi*, vol. 1, p. 340.

143. Maesono Ryōichi, "Uji to kabane," in Ōbayashi Taryō, ed., *Nihon no kodai* 11: *Uji to ie*, pp. 214–217. For a critique of Hirano and Abe (the conventional interpretation) see Shida Jun'ichi, "Uji ni tsuite," *Rekishi kōron* 58 (September 1980): 66–77. See also Maeda Akihisa, "Shisei sei e no michi," in Saeki Arikiyo, ed., *Kodai o kangaeru Yūryaku tennō to sono jidai*, pp. 190–197. On the Silla bone ranks see C. S. Kim, "The Kolp'um System: Basis for Sillan Social Stratification," *Journal of Korean Studies* 1 (1971): 43–69.

144. See Kiley, "State and Dynasty," pp. 29 and 34. See also Richard Miller's *Ancient Japanese Nobility* and Kiley's "Uji and Kabane in Ancient Japan," *Monumenta Nipponica* 32 (Autumn 1977): 365–376.

145. Yoshida Takashi, "Kodai shakai ni okeru uji," in *Nihon shakai shi* 6: *Shakaiteki sho shūdan*, pp. 40–42. See also Inoue Hideo, "Kodai Chōsen no seishi," *Rekishi kōron* 58 (September 1980): 104–116. Inoue downplays the similarities in Japanese and Korean systems of titles (*kabane*).

146. Inoue Mitsusada, *Nihon no rekishi* 3: *Asuka no chōtei*, pp. 231–233.

147. Takeda Sachiko, cited in Suzuki Yasutami, "Higashi Ajia no shominzoku no kokka keisei to Yamato ōken," in *Kōza Nihon rekishi* 1: *Genshi kodai* 1, p. 226.

148. Hirano Kunio, *Taika zendai shakai soshiki no kenkyū*, pp. 71–76; Inoue, "Century of Reform," p. 179; Vargo, *Social and Economic Conditions*, pp. 52–72. There is a debate over the date when Paekche established its service units. Several scholars now argue for the sixth century: Kamata Motokazu, "Ōken to bumin sei," in *Kōza Nihon rekishi* 1: *Genshi kodai* 1, p. 258; Yamao Yukihisa, "Be ni tsuite," *Kodai gaku kenkyū* 77 (September 1975): 40–41; and Kitō Kiyoaki, "Nihon no ritsuryō kansei no seiritsu to Kudara no kansei," in *Nihon no kodai shakai to keizai*, vol. 1, p. 207.

149. Tsuda, *Nihon jōdai shi no kenkyū*, p. 33; Kiley, "State and Dynasty," p. 28. Brown, "The Yamato Kingdom," pp. 138–139, makes the same point.

150. Kitō, "Ritsuryō kansei to Kudara no kansei," pp. 198–199.

151. Nishimoto Masahiro, "Tomo, tomo no o ni kansuru ichikōsatsu," *Shoku Nihongi kenkyū* 217 (March 1982): 1–28.

152. Kamata, "Bumin sei," pp. 255–259, was the first to voice this view. See also Hayakawa Man'nen, "Nihon to Chōsen no kodai seiji soshiki," *Kikan kōkogaku* 33 (November 1990): 85–88. Recently American scholars have come to reflect Kamata's perspective. See Gina Barnes, "The Role of the *be* in the Formation of the Yamato State," in Elizabeth Brumfiel and Timothy Earle, eds., *Specialization, Exchange and Complex Societies*, p. 100; Kidder, "Ceramics of the Burial Mounds," p. 40.

153. Some even argue for a tie between Korea and the *tomo*. See Maekawa Akihisa, "Kukadachi to tomo," *Higashi Ajia no kodai bunka* 32 (1982): 55–67.

154. On this technique see Hachiga Susumu, "Tojō zōei no gijutsu," in Kishi Toshio, ed., *Nihon no kodai* 9: *Tojō no seitai*, p. 174. Needham, *Science and Civilization in China*, vol. 4, pt. 3, pp. 38–57, describes the Chinese technique as using elongated boxes to form bricks and bamboo strips to aid in drying out the earth.

155. Yun Mu-byŏng, "Mokch'ŏn dojō no hanchiku kōhō," in *Higashi Ajia to Nihon: Kōko bijutsu hen*, pp. 569–581; Nelson, *Archaeology of Korea*, p. 223.

156. On the stamped earth method in the Yayoi period see Gina Barnes and Mark Hudson, "Yoshinogari: A Yayoi Settlement in Northern Kyushu," *Monumenta Nipponica* 46 (Summer 1991): 220.

157. *NKBT, Nihon shoki*, vol. 2, Suiko 32/9/3, pp. 210–211; Aston, *Nihongi*, vol. 2, pp. 153–154.

158. J. E. Kidder, *Early Buddhist Japan*, pp. 79–93. See also Inoue, "Century of Reform," pp. 174–175.

159. See *Toraijin no tera*. In English see Jacques Kamstra, *Encounter or Syncretism*, pp. 224–470; Covell and Covell, *Korean Impact*, pp. 44–112; and Donald McCallum, "Korean Influence on Early Japanese Buddhist Sculpture," *Korean Culture* 3 (March 1982): 22–29.

160. See *Asuka no genryū;* Inoue, "Century of Reform," p. 176. This point is missed by Brown, "Introduction," pp. 30–31.

161. On Koguryŏ see Lee, *New History of Korea*, p. 38. Inoue, *Asuka no chōtei*, p. 89, notes that Silla King Pŏphŭng distributed law codes (*ritsuryō*) in 520.

162. Suzuki Yasutami, "Nihon ritsuryō seiritsu to Chōsen sankoku," in *Nihon bunka to Chōsen*, vol. 3, pp. 28–29; Seki, *Kikajin*, p. 152; Inoue, "Century of Reform," pp. 208–209.

163. Seki, *Kikajin*, p. 153. For the Silla influence on eighth-century Japanese Buddhism see Sonoda Kōyū, "Early Buddha Worship," in Brown, *Cambridge History of Japan*, vol. 1, p. 391.

164. Farris, *Population, Disease, and Land*, pp. 116 and 139.

165. Seki, *Kikajin*, pp. 151–176.

166. Farris, *Heavenly Warriors*, pp. 36–37 and 46–47. On the tribute tax see Ishigami Eiichi, "Kodai ni okeru Nihon no zeisei to Shiragi no zeisei," in Hatada Takeshi, ed., *Kodai Chōsen to Nihon*, pp. 227–264.

167. Farris, *Heavenly Warriors*, pp. 41 and 113–116.

168. See Akiyama Hideo, "Koma jaku to jōri sei," in *Nihon bunka to Chōsen*, vol. 1, pp. 242–251.

169. Many historians write of the court's self-image, but none better than Hayakawa Shōhachi, "Higashi Ajia gaikō to Nihon ritsuryō sei no suii," in Kishi Toshio, ed., *Nihon no kodai 15: Kodai kokka to Nihon*, pp. 67–76.

170. *Shintei zōho kokushi taikei, Kushiki-ryō no shūge, Shōsho shiki no jō*, second *koki*, p. 774.

171. *The Chronicles* and other sources give many examples of technology transfer from the Korean kingdoms to Yamato as tribute items; for instance, see notes 178 and 180. One has only to read about the contents of the Kaya and Silla tombs to see why southern Korea was a precious jewel. See Nishitani, "The Kaya Tumuli," pp. 1–6; Kim, "Korean Archaeology Today," pp. 34–39; J. H. Grayson, "Excavation of Late Kaya Period Tumuli in So-ryong," *Indo-Pacific Prehistory Association Bulletin* 5 (1985): 64–73; and Kim, *Recent Archaeological Discoveries*, pp. 33–62. The Wa could also have learned of the wealth of the southern Korean states through Korean immigrants, traders, or returning soldiers.

172. Nishitani, "Kara chiiki," pp. 54–62; Yanagida Yasuo, "Chōsen hantō ni okeru Nihon kei ibutsu," in *Kyushu ni okeru kofun bunka to Chōsen hantō*, pp. 10–54.

173. Farris, *Heavenly Warriors*, p. 18, notes that according to *The Chronicles of Japan*, the Yamato court sent horses to Paekche's royal house.

174. Tsude, "Nihon kodai no kokka keisei ron josetsu," pp. 31–32, notes the increasingly common finds of Korean-style pottery and ovens in Japan.

175. Tanaka, *Wajin sōran*, pp. 64–65; Hudson, "From Toro to Yoshinogari," pp. 66–67. Hanihara Kazurō has expressed some of his views in "Estimation of the Number of Early Migrants to Japan: A Simulative Study," *Journal of the Anthropological Society of Nippon* 95 (July 1987): 391–403, and "Dual Structure Model for Population History of Japan," *Nichibunken Japan Review* 2 (1990): 1–33. For a thoughtful critique of Hanihara's theory see Keiji Imamura, *Prehistoric Japan*, pp. 149 and 155–157.

176. Tsude, *Nōkō shakai*, p. 453; Okazaki, "Japan and the Continent," p. 311.

177. Yamao, *Nitchō kankei*, pp. 286–305, and Mun Sa-wi, "Chōsen sankoku no ijūmin shūdan," pp. 15–32, are examples of works that stress immigration to the exclusion of other factors.

178. Aston, *Nihongi*, vol. 1, p. 350; NKBT, *Nihon shoki*, vol. 1, Yūryaku 7/kono toshi no jō, pp. 476–477.

179. Brown, "The Yamato Kingdom," p. 159; Inoue, "Century of Reform," pp. 171–172; and Okazaki, "Japan and the Continent," p. 306, all give implicit support to this notion.

180. Aston, *Nihongi*, vol. 2, p. 14; NKBT, *Nihon shoki*, Keitai 10/5 and 10/9, pp. 32–35.

181. Okazaki, "Japan and the Continent," pp. 309–310.

182. Conversation with Niiro Izumi, March 1992.

183. *Ōtani kofun*, pp. 67–125. See also Okazaki, "Japan and the Continent," p. 302.

184. *Oda Chausuzuka kofun*, vol. 4, pp. 17–56; *Ikenoue funbo gun*, pp. 121–142.

185. Hirano Kunio, "Yamato ōken to Chōsen," in *Iwanami kōza Nihon rekishi* 1: *Genshi oyobi kodai* 1, pp. 245–246, uses the ambiguous word "semi-independent." Hirano has expressed his views in English in "The Yamato State and Korea in the Fourth and Fifth Centuries," *Acta Asiatica* 31 (1977): 51–82. On Okinoshima and the Munakata no Kimi see Okazaki, "Japan and the Continent," pp. 312–316. Gina Barnes, "*Jiehao, tonghao*: Peer Relations in East Asia," in Colin Renfrew and John Cherry, eds., *Peer Polity Interaction and Socio-Political Change*, pp. 79–91, has raised the issue of Japan's centralization in this era. Joan Piggott, "Sacral Kingship and Confederacy in Early Izumo," *Monumenta Nipponica* 44 (Spring 1989): 53–54, has noted that scholars now believe Izumo was independent of Yamato at least until the sixth century, much later than previously believed.

186. Farris, *Heavenly Warriors*, pp. 26–27.

187. Kadowaki Teiji argues for Soga ties to Korean émigrés. See "Soga shi to toraijin," in Mori Kōichi et al., eds., *Kodai gōzoku to Chōsen*, pp. 169–212. Inoue, *Asuka no chōtei*, pp. 118–120, even suspects that Iname had a Paekche mother.

188. See also Okazaki, "Japan and the Continent," pp. 298–316. In addition to the sources cited later in the section, I consulted Barnes, "Early Korean States," pp. 113–162; Lee, *Sourcebook*, pp. 1–134; Lee, *New History of Korea*, pp. 1–65; Ch'on, "Problems of Mimana," pp. 9–23 and 31–44; Pearson, "Lolang," pp. 77–91; Grayson, "Mimana Problem," pp. 65–69; and Chong-wuk Lee, "The Formation and Growth of Paekche," *Korea Journal* 18 (October 1978): 35–40. I am especially indebted to Professor Ned Shultz for sharing the papers from the *Samguk sagi* Conference held in Honolulu, February 15–19, 1996. In particular, "Troubled Histories: A Study of Silla's Relations with Paekche and Kaya," by Jonathan Best of Wesleyan University presents a detailed analysis of a valuable source.

I chose 676 rather than 663 for the terminus of this survey primarily to provide background for later chapters. The year 663 may have been more important in Japanese domestic politics, but 676 marked the end of the centuries of conflict on the peninsula and the dawning of a new era of diplomacy in East Asia.

189. Okazaki, "Japan and the Continent," pp. 298–303.

190. Kenneth Gardiner, *Early History of Korea*, p. 40.

191. On the Chinese sources see Yamao, *Nitchō kankei*, pp. 275–276.

192. The issue of state formation in Japan is subject to varying interpretations based often on differences between written and material sources. See Tsude, "Nihon kodai no kokka keisei ron josetsu," pp. 5–39. In critiquing Tsude's view of a "keyhole tomb system" (*zenpō kōen fun taisei*), I would note three further points. First, his reading of political meaning into archaeological materials is reminiscent of Kobayashi's mirror theory presented in Chapter 1. Second, Tsude's interpretation results in an idealized status hierarchy similar to that ingrained in Japanese society since the Tokugawa era. Third, the idea of a hierarchy with Yamato at the pinnacle bears an uncanny resemblance to the ideology of *The Chronicles*.

193. Hirano, "Yamato ōken to Chōsen," pp. 231–236; Suzuki, "Higashi Ajia to Yamato ōken," p. 202. Okazaki too uses the vague term "foothold" in "Japan and the Continent," pp. 308–309.

194. Inoue Hideo, *Wa Wajin Wakoku*, especially pp. 70–78; Hirano, "Yamato ōken to Chōsen," p. 242.

195. Several scholars have noted the inclusion of the *Paekche pongi* in *The Chronicles of Japan*. I agree with Hirano, "Yamato ōken to Chōsen," pp. 231–236, who argues that the

source is to be treated with caution, since nothing prevented editors from altering it to suit their purposes.

196. Brown, "The Yamato Kingdom," pp. 121–122. On Paekche's victory and Koguryŏ's reforms see Okazaki, "Japan and the Continent," pp. 298–299. On the rise of Paekche see Okazaki, "Japan and the Continent," pp. 303–304.

197. Hirano, "Yamato ōken to Chōsen," p. 238.

198. Ibid., pp. 238–239. Brown, "The Yamato Kingdom," p. 123, misses Silla's stance.

199. Hirano, "Yamato ōken to Chōsen," pp. 252–253. The *Samguk sagi* notes a Koguryŏ attack against Paekche in 392, a Wa battle against Silla in 393, the alliance of Wa, Paekche, and Silla in 397, more battles between Silla and Wa, and Paekche's gratitude to Wa in 405. On the monument I follow Saeki Arikiyo, *Rekishi shinsho 1: Kodai no higashi Ajia to Nihon*, pp. 146–148. Okazaki, "Japan and the Continent," pp. 302–303 also accepts the authenticity of the monument. See also Ueda Masaaki, "A Fresh Look at Ancient History," *Japan Quarterly* 33 (October–December 1986): 406–409, and Takeda, "Studies on the King Kwanggaito Inscription," pp. 72–87, for recent international attempts to agree on a reading of the monument. On the Korean sources I follow most recent scholars who believe they are generally reliable, especially when corroborated by other texts. See Hirano, "Yamato ōken to Chōsen," pp. 239–241; Best, "Troubled Histories," pp. 1–10; and Saeki Arikiyo, "Kaisetsu," in Saeki, ed., *Samguk sagi wajin den ta roppen*, pp. 15–28.

200. Saeki, *Kodai no higashi Ajia to Nihon*, pp. 147–148, suggests that several unclear phrases on the stele may refer to a 407 battle between the Wa and Koguryŏ. Hirano, "Yamato ōken to Chōsen," p. 253, argues that after their defeats the Wa turned to diplomatic means to dominate Korea, despite occasional evidence of hostilities in the *Samguk sagi* and elsewhere.

201. Hirano, "Yamato ōken to Chōsen," pp. 252–253; Saeki, *Kodai no higashi Ajia to Nihon*, pp. 149–150.

202. Okazaki, "Japan and the Continent," pp. 310–311, agrees that the Chinese recognized the dominant Japanese position. See also Brown, "The Yamato Kingdom," pp. 140–144.

203. Hirano, "Yamato ōken to Chōsen," pp. 256–257; Suzuki, "Higashi Ajia to Yamato ōken," pp. 217–219.

204. Hirano, "Yamato ōken to Chōsen," pp. 258–259. The Korean sources are *Samguk sagi* (Paekche Annals) and inscriptions from the tomb of King Muryŏng. *Nihon shoki* lists these points under Yūryaku 5, 20, and 23; Buretsu 4; and Keitai 17.

205. See Kishi Toshio, "Kakki toshite no Yūryaku chō," in *Nihon seiji shakai shi kenkyū*, vol. 1, pp. 9–49.

206. Okazaki, "Japan and the Continent," pp. 306–307.

207. Suzuki, "Higashi Ajia to Yamato ōken," pp. 216–219. Suzuki emphasizes Paekche's dependence on Yamato, a position that seems doubtful.

208. Yamao, *Nitchō kankei*, pp. 25–31.

209. Suzuki, "Higashi Ajia to Yamato ōken," pp. 219–221; Brown, "The Yamato Kingdom," pp. 146 and 154–156.

210. Inoue, "Century of Reform," pp. 164–169, 182–188, 193–194, and 201–209. Inoue discusses two abortive Yamato attempts to invade Silla and "reestablish Mimana" in 591 and 600. Note also the attempt in 623.

211. Suzuki, "Higashi Ajia to Yamato ōken," pp. 228–230.

212. Anazawa and Manome, "Buki," p. 172.

213. Henri Pirenne, *Mohammed and Charlemagne*.

Chapter 3: Capitals

1. This section summarizes excavation and research until the early 1980s. For more recent information see the following sections. There is little in English on the current archaeology of ancient Japanese capitals. I have consulted J. Edward Kidder, *Early Buddhist Japan*, pp. 61–78; Tanaka Migaku, "The Early Historical Period," in Tsuboi Kiyotari, ed., *Recent Archaeological Discoveries in Japan*, pp. 72–76; Kōichi Yokoyama, "Early Historic Archaeology in Japan," *Asian Perspectives* 19 (1976): 27–34; Gina Barnes, *China, Korea and Japan*, pp. 246–251; Yamamoto Tadanao, "Reflections on the Development of Historical Archaeology in Japan," in Richard Pearson, ed., *Windows on the Japanese Past*, pp. 397–403; and Tsuboi Kiyotari and Tanaka Migaku, *The Historic City of Nara*, pp. 101–142. See also Edwina Palmer, "Land of the Rising Sun: The Predominant East-West Axis among the Early Japanese," *Monumenta Nipponica* 46 (Spring 1991): 69–90, and Minoru Senda, "Territorial Possession in Ancient Japan: The Real and the Perceived," in *Geography of Japan*, pp. 101–120.

2. Machida Akira, *Kōkogaku raiburarii* 44: *Heijō-kyō*, pp. 3–7. On the history of Japanese archaeology see also Gina Barnes, *Protohistoric Yamato*, pp. 44–55. On excavations see Tsuboi Kiyotari, "The Excavation of Ancient Palaces and Capitals," *Acta Asiatica* 63 (1992): 87–98.

3. On Naniwa see Nakao Yoshiharu, *Kōkogaku raiburarii* 46: *Naniwa-kyō*, p. 25; on Ōtsu see Hayashi Hiromichi, *Kōkogaku raiburarii* 27: *Ōtsu-kyō*, pp. 50–52; on Fujiwara see Kanō Hisashi and Kinoshita Masashi, *Kodai Nihon o hakkutsu suru* 1: *Asuka Fujiwara no miyako*, pp. 92–93.

4. For ancient and medieval sources on Heian see Inoue Mitsuo, *Kenkyū shi: Heian-kyō*, pp. 1–10. Kume Kunitake was the first to raise questions about the move to Heian. See also Tsuji Hiroshi, "Heian-kyō," in Tsuboi Kiyotari, ed., *Kodai o kangaeru kyūto hakkutsu*, pp. 218–219.

5. Inoue, *Heian-kyō*, pp. 42–51. I refer to the various Japanese rulers listed in *The Chronicles* by the title "emperor" (*tennō*) along with their posthumous names. This is a matter of convenience. Technically, neither appellation was invented until at least the late seventh century.

6. On Ōtsu see Hayashi, *Ōtsu-kyō*, p. 53; on Fujiwara see Kanō and Kinoshita, *Fujiwara*, pp. 93–95.

7. Inoue, *Heian-kyō*, pp. 46–49.

8. Machida, *Heijō-kyō*, pp. 7–10.

9. Nakao, *Naniwa-kyō*, pp. 25–28.

10. Tsuboi Kiyotari, "Kodai kyūto hakkutsu," in Tsuboi Kiyotari, ed., *Kodai o kangaeru kyūto hakkutsu*, pp. 9–11.

11. Ibid., pp. 11–12.

12. Hayashi, *Ōtsu-kyō*, pp. 61–81.

13. Inoue, *Heian-kyō*, pp. 69–141.

14. Kanō and Kinoshita, *Fujiwara*, pp. 96–105.

15. Tsuboi, "Kodai kyūto hakkutsu," pp. 14–15. On the postwar research on capitals see also Kidder, *Early Buddhist Japan*, pp. 61–78.

16. The following history of Heijō's preservation draws from Tsuboi, "Kodai kyūto hakkutsu," pp. 15–16, and from *Heijō-kyō ten*, pp. 8–9.

17. On the Eastern Grounds see Tanaka Migaku, *Kodai Nihon o hakkutsu suru 3: Heijō-kyō*, pp. 1–44. See also Tsuboi and Tanaka, *Historic City of Nara*, pp. 1–66.

18. Nakao, *Naniwa-kyō*, pp. 28–42.

19. Tsuboi, "Kodai kyūto hakkutsu," pp. 18–19; Kanō and Kinoshita, *Fujiwara*, pp. 11–76. See also Richard Pearson, *Ancient Japan*, pp. 278–281. Japanese-style buildings could be built with their floors elevated above the ground on posts.

20. Tsuboi, "Kodai kyūto hakkutsu," p. 20.

21. Ibid., pp. 20–21.

22. Ibid., pp. 21–22. Studies of written records of Heian boomed for a few years after the war, but in the 1960s scholarship entered a confused phase; see Inoue, *Heian-kyō*, pp.

197–264. Another history of Kyoto excavations may be found in Namigai Tsuyoshi, "Kōkogaku kara no Heian-kyō kenkyū," in Tsunoda, *Heian-kyō teiyō*, pp. 863–868.

23. Tsuboi, "Kodai kyūto hakkutsu," pp. 22–24.

24. Ping-ti Ho, "Lo-yang, A.D. 495–534: A Study of Physical and Socio-Economic Planning of a Metropolitan Area," *Harvard Journal of Asiatic Studies* 26 (1966): 52. On Chinese capitals I have also consulted Arthur Wright, "The Sui Dynasty (581–617)," in Denis Twitchett, ed., *The Cambridge History of China*, vol. 3, pt. 1, pp. 48–149; Tonami Mamoru, "Chūgoku tojō no shisō," in Kishi Toshio, ed., *Nihon no kodai* 9: *Tojō no seitai*, pp. 81–114; Michael Loewe, "The Former Han Dynasty," in Denis Twitchett and Michael Loewe, eds., *The Cambridge History of China*, vol. 1, pp. 103–222; Hans Bielenstein, "Wang Mang, the Restoration of the Han Dynasty, and Later Han," in Twitchett and Loewe, *Cambridge History of China*, vol. 1, pp. 223–290; and Victor Cunrui Xiong, "Sui Yangdi and the Building of Sui-Tang Luoyang," *Journal of Asian Studies* 52 (February 1993): 66–89.

25. John Hall, "Kyoto as Historical Background," in John Hall and Jeffrey Mass, eds., *Medieval Japan: Essays in Institutional History*, p. 3.

26. Ibid., p. 12.

27. Kishi, *Kodai kyūto no tankyū*, pp. 40–41. The Rites of Zhou (*Zhou li*) of the Late Zhou period was a valuable guide to Japan's first planners. It presented a utopian vision of a capital: a walled square laid out along the points of the compass with three gates to a side, nine avenues east-west and north-south, and the emperor's residence in the center.

28. Kishi Toshio, "Nihon tojō sei sōron," in Kishi Toshio, ed., *Nihon no kodai* 9: *Tojō no seitai*, pp. 49–52; Sarah Nelson, *The Archaeology of Korea*, p. 211 (Koguryŏ), p. 222 (Paekche), and p. 259 (Silla).

29. Kishi Toshio, *Nihon kodai kyūto no kenkyū*, pp. 495–522. Bruce Batten, "State and Frontier in Early Japan," Ph.D. dissertation, Stanford University, 1989, pp. 111–117, argues that Dazaifu had a grid when it was created.

30. On this topic see also Richard Posonby-Fane, *Imperial Cities;* Paul Wheatley and Thomas See, *From Court to Capital*, pp. 103–109; and Takeo Yazaki, *Social Change and the City in Japan*, pp. 1–18. In *Protohistoric Yamato*, pp. 265–267, Gina Barnes recognizes "urbanizing trends" in fifth-century Japan. One can only speculate how settlement patterns from the Yayoi and Tomb eras influenced the adaptation of Chinese-style capitals to the Japanese environment. Certainly building materials and architectural styles show many continuities. See also note 33.

31. Ōwaki Kiyoshi, "Shin'yaku-kyō no kensetsu," in Machida Akira and Kitō Kiyoaki, eds., *Shinpan Kodai no Nihon* 6: *Kinki* II, pp. 67–68.

32. Kishi, *Nihon kodai kyūto no kenkyū*, pp. 239–242. Kishi cites other entries beside those listed in the text.

33. Japanese archaeologists attach great significance to the appearance of north-south orientations for large-scale buildings recently discovered at middle Yayoi sites such as Ikegami-Sone in Osaka. Many read this as a sign of the influence from the same ideology that informed later capitals. If this is true, the description of Oharida in *The Chronicles* may not have been fanciful.

34. *Japan in the Chinese Dynastic Histories,* trans. Ryusaku Tsunoda, p. 29.

35. Ueki Hisashi, "Yamato e no genkan," in Machida Akira and Kitō Kiyoaki, eds., *Shinpan kodai no Nihon 6: Kinki II,* pp. 22–28. Much of what follows is from this source.

36. In the following discussion of Japan's palaces, I prefer "imperial residence" as the translation for *"dairi,"* the word applied by Japanese experts to all royal domiciles from Naniwa on. Technically the use of the adjective "imperial" for the early palaces is not appropriate, since the title of emperor was probably not adopted until later. My translation is mostly a matter of convenience and clarity.

37. Yagi Hisae, "Naniwa no miya," in Tsuboi Kiyotari, ed., *Kodai o kangaeru kyūto hakkutsu,* p. 91.

38. Kishi, *Nihon kodai kyūto no kenkyū*, pp. 411–433. See also *Naniwa kyūseki Ōsaka-jōseki hakkutsu chōsa chūkan hōkoku,* vol. 1, pp. 16–21; see vol. 2, pp. 10–12, for more recent information.

39. Ueki, "Yamato e no genkan," p. 24; Yoshida Akira, *Nihon shi 37: Kodai no Naniwa,* pp. 168–169; Kishi, *Nihon kodai kyūto no kenkyū*, pp. 360–361. Both Inoue Mitsusada, "The Century of Reform," in Delmer Brown, ed., *The Cambridge History of Japan,* vol. 1, p. 192, and Naoki Kōjirō, "The Nara State," in Brown, *Cambridge History of Japan,* vol. 1, p. 229, believe there was an audience hall in the palace at the lower level of Naniwa, but they give no basis for their beliefs.

40. The uncertainty in dating the levels of Naniwa Palace may be changing. In 1995 a catalog for an exhibit at Osaka City Museum proclaimed the lower stratum belonged to the mid-seventh century (Kōtoku's time), based upon "recent advances in research on the dating of pottery recovered from postholes and from the soil used for making the foundation for the site." Personal communication from Walter Edwards, January 1997.

41. William Aston, trans., *Nihongi: Chronicles of Japan from the Earliest Times to A.D. 697,* vol. 2, p. 242; *Nihon koten bungaku taikei* (hereafter *NKBT*), *Nihon shoki,* vol. 2, Hakuchi 3/9, pp. 318–319.

42. Nakao, *Naniwa-kyō,* pp. 97–98, discusses the possible Buddhist influences.

43. Nakao, *Naniwa-kyō*, pp. 59–62 and 97–103; Ueki, "Yamato e no genkan," pp. 26–27; Yoshida, *Kodai no Naniwa*, pp. 169–172. Kishi, *Nihon kodai kyūto no kenkyū*, pp. 361–371, argues for pre-Sui elements in Nagara Toyosaki's design, all drawn up by Korean engineers.

44. Nakao, *Naniwa-kyō*, pp. 50–52; Kidder, *Early Buddhist Japan*, pp. 74–76.

45. Naoki Kōjirō, "Naniwa Ogori-no-miya to Nagara Toyosaki," in *Naniwa no miya to Nihon kodai kokka*, pp. 41–78.

46. Hayakawa Shōhachi, *Nihon kodai kanryō sei no kenkyū*, pp. 317–324.

47. Kishi, *Nihon kodai kyūto no kenkyū*, pp. 353–354; see also Kajiyama Hikotarō, *Naniwa kokyō kō*; Nakao, *Naniwa-kyō*, pp. 106–119, who summarize the various attempts at reconstruction.

48. Yagi, "Naniwa no miya," p. 93.

49. Prince Naka's precise status during the period 645–668 is a hotly debated matter. Although *The Chronicles* states that he assumed the title of heir apparent after the Taika coup, it is doubtful that such a position existed. See *NKBT*, *Nihon shoki*, vol. 2, *Kōtoku tennō sokui zenki*, pp. 270–271, and the notes on pp. 539 and 556–557. See also Araki Toshio, *Nihon kodai no kōtai shi*. Whatever his exact standing, there is little doubt that Naka played an influential role.

50. *NKBT*, *Nihon shoki*, vol. 2, Tenji 6/3, pp. 366–367; Aston, *Nihongi*, vol. 2, pp. 285–286. I have modified Aston's translation. See also Inoue, "Century of Reform," p. 203.

51. Hayashi Hiromichi, "Ōtsu no miya," in Tsuboi Kiyotari, ed., *Kodai o kangaeru kyūto hakkutsu*, p. 98.

52. Hayashi, *Ōtsu-kyō*, pp. 114–118. A 1993 investigation uncovered the remains of a few buildings north of what may be the imperial residence. Personal communication from Yamanaka Akira, January 1997.

53. Ibid., pp. 86–87.

54. Fujioka Kenjirō, "Kodai no Ōtsu kyōiki to sono shūhen no jiwari ni kansuru jakkan no rekishi chirigakuteki kōsatsu," *Jinbun chiri* 23 (December 1971): 9–14. Recently Abe Yoshihira, "Nihon rettō ni okeru tojō keisei-2," *Kokuritsu rekishi minzoku hakubutsu-kan kenkyū hōkoku* 45 (December 1992): 2–47, has attempted a reconstruction of the capital grid using 500 "Korean feet" (*Koma jaku*) per unit, but his estimate has been met with skepticism. Personal communication from Yamanaka Akira, January 1997.

55. Hayashi, *Ōtsu-kyō*, citing archaeologists' views on tile designs on pp. 140–141, dates these four temples to Tenji's reign.

56. Ibid., pp. 140–145.

57. As in Chinese and Korean sources, "Wa" refers to Japan. Unlike those sources, the term may also be read "Yamato" and is synonymous with the court in the southern Kinai. See *NKBT, Nihon shoki*, Hakuchi 4/*kono toshi no jō*, pp. 320–321.

58. For these debates and the scholars involved in them see notes 59, 60, and 61. On the roads see Kishi, *Nihon kodai kyūto no kenkyū*, pp. 29–46. See also Barnes, *Protohistoric Yamato*, pp. 166–170.

59. Kishi, *Nihon kodai kyūto no kenkyū*, p. 158; Ōwaki Kiyoshi, "Shin'yaku-kyō no kensetsu," p. 78; Akiyama Hideo, "Fujiwara-kyō to Asuka-kyō no kyōiki kō," *Chiri* 25 (September 1980): 36–37.

60. Imaizumi Takao, "Ritsuryō sei tojō no seiritsu to tenkai," in *Kōza Nihon rekishi* 2: *kodai* 2, pp. 54–55.

61. See Ōwaki, "Shin'yaku-kyō no kensetsu," p. 78, on grid layout; see Kishi, *Nihon kodai kyūto no kenkyū*, pp. 150–156, on administration.

62. Ōwaki, "Shin'yaku-kyō no kensetsu," pp. 65–77. Most of what follows comes from Ōwaki. Another interesting palace for which archaeological information is available is Ikaruga, home of Shōtoku Taishi. See Nitō Atsushi, "Jōgū ōke to Ikaruga," in Machida and Kitō, *Shinpan kodai no Nihon* 6: *Kinki* II, pp. 47–50.

63. Note that *mokkan* have confirmed that the uppermost layer is from Temmu's age. Like Ōwaki, Kishi thinks that the uppermost level is Kiyomihara; see "Nihon tojō sei sōron," p. 64.

64. Ibid., pp. 64–65. My view of the historical context for Fujiwara follows Kishi, *Nihon kodai kyūto no kenkyū*, pp. 454–456.

65. Aston, *Nihongi*, vol. 2, p. 335. He also translates two other passages, p. 354, in like manner.

66. Ōwaki, "Shin'yaku-kyō no kensetsu," p. 80; the *mokkan* may be found in *Fujiwara-kyū mokkan* 2: *Kaisetsu*, p. 55.

67. *NKBT, Nihon shoki*, vol. 2, Temmu 12/12/17, pp. 460–461; see also Aston, *Nihongi*, vol. 2, p. 362.

68. Nakao, *Naniwa-kyō*, pp. 82–87.

69. Kishi, *Nihon kodai kyūto no kenkyū*, pp. 380–381. See also Ueki, "Yamato e no genkan," pp. 35–38.

70. Yoshida, *Kodai no Naniwa*, pp. 174–178. The evidence on the road from Shitennōji to the palace and east-west avenues comes from personal communication with Osaka archaeologist Ueki Hisashi.

71. Kishi, *Nihon kodai kyūto no kenkyū*, pp. 58–66.

72. Yagi, "Naniwa no miya," p. 77.

73. *NKBT, Man'yōshū,* vol. 1, no. 50, pp. 34–37; *The Man'yoshu,* trans. Nippon gaku-jutsu shinkōkai, p. 68.

74. The detailed description of Fujiwara Palace that follows is taken from Satō Kōji, "Fujiwara no miya," in Tsuboi Kiyotari, ed., *Kodai o kangaeru kyūto hakkutsu,* pp. 122–130.

75. Ōwaki, "Shin'yaku-kyō no kensetsu," pp. 84–86.

76. The middle gate on the southern side measured 26 by 10 meters. Wooden tablets show gates named after families charged with guarding the monarch.

77. Satō, "Fujiwara no miya," p. 26.

78. Ōwaki, "Shin'yaku-kyō no kensetsu," pp. 85–86. Archaeologists make judgments about the age of tiles, as with pots, based on relative patterns.

79. Kishi, *Nihon kodai kyūto no kenkyū,* pp. 14–22. See also Naoki, "The Nara State," pp. 229–230. A "league" measures 530 meters.

80. Satō, "Fujiwara no miya," pp. 130–131.

81. Kishi, *Nihon kodai kyūto no kenkyū,* pp. 307–352. See also Wang Zhong–shu, "Nihon no kodai tojō seido no genryū ni tsuite," *Kōkogaku zasshi* 69 (October 1983): 1–30.

82. Kishi Toshio, "Tojō no genryū o tazuneru," in Kishi Toshio, ed., *Nihon no kodai* 9: *Tojō no seitai,* pp. 31–32. See also Naoki, "The Nara State," pp. 243–245.

83. Ōwaki, "Shin'yaku-kyō no kensetsu," pp. 80–84. For new theories on the grid plan of Fujiwara see Akiyama, "Fujiwara-kyō to Asuka-kyō," pp. 31–33, and Abe Yoshihira, "Shin'yaku-kyō ni tsuite," *Chiba shigaku* 9 (1986): 13–43.

84. The *Asahi shinbun* for July 28, 1996, reports that even more ditches have turned up on the eastern and western edges of the city, making it wider by two more files. If these were part of the original metropolis, then Fujiwara would be the largest of all Japan's Chinese-style capitals.

85. Kanō and Kinoshita, *Asuka Fujiwara no miyako,* pp. 127–133.

86. Satō, "Fujiwara no miya," p. 131.

87. *NKBT, Man'yōshū,* vol. 4, no. 4260, pp. 374–375; *The Man'yoshu,* p. 60.

88. Yagi Atsuru, *Kodai Nihon no miyako,* pp. 128–130.

89. *Shoku Nihongi,* Wadō 1/2/11, p. 34, in *Shintei zōho kokushi taikei* (hereafter *SZKT*). A handy reference to the historical context for Nara is the chronology found in *Heijō-kyū hakkutsu chōsa hōkoku,* vol. 3, pp. 71–86.

90. Machida Akira, "Heijō-kyō," in Machida Akira and Kitō Kiyoaki, eds., *Shinpan kodai no Nihon 6: Kinki* II, p. 114. On the move to Heijō see also Joan Piggott, "Tōdaiji and the Nara Imperium," Ph.D. dissertation, Stanford University, 1987, pp. 22–24.

91. For a translation of this order see William Wayne Farris, *Population, Disease, and Land in Early Japan, 645–900*, p. 121.

92. Aoki Kazuo, "Koeki sei no seiritsu," *Shigaku zasshi* 67 (April 1958): 45.

93. Machida, "Heijō-kyō," p. 114.

94. *SZKT, Shoku Nihongi,* Wadō 4/9/4, p. 46.

95. Ibid., Wadō 5/1/16, p. 47.

96. Machida, "Heijō-kyō," pp. 114–115.

97. Ibid., p. 116.

98. Tanaka Tetsuo, "Heijō-kyō," in Tsuboi Kiyotari, ed., *Kodai o kangaeru kyūto hakkutsu,* pp. 162–163.

99. Kishi, *Nihon kodai kyūto no kenkyū,* pp. 477–493.

100. Machida, "Heijō-kyō," pp. 119–124. See also Tsuboi and Tanaka, *Historic City of Nara,* pp. 101–131.

101. See *Nagaya ō teitaku to mokkan,* pp. 39–82. See also Joan Piggott, "*Mokkan* Wooden Documents from the Nara Period," *Monumenta Nipponica* 45 (Winter 1990): 452–458, and Cornelius Kiley, "Wooden Tags and Noble Houses: The Household(s) of Prince Nagaya as Revealed by *Mokkan.*" For more examples of aristocratic houses see Tanaka, "Heijō-kyō," pp. 164–166. While archaeologists at the Nara National Cultural Properties Research Institute state in *Nagaya ō teitaku to mokkan,* p. 109, that Nagaya and Kibi owned and lived in this residence, not everyone agrees. See Chapter 4.

102. Machida, *Heijō-kyō,* pp. 82–83.

103. *Fujiwara-kyōseki no toire ikō.*

104. On this toilet see Kanehara Masaaki, Kanehara Masako, and Matsui Akira, "Toire no kōkogaku," in Tanaka Migaku and Sahara Makoto, eds., *Hakkutsu o kagaku suru,* pp. 47–62.

105. For Sawada's estimate see his *Nara chō jidai minsei keizai no sūteki kenkyū,* pp. 164–165 and 276–283. The first scholar to redo Sawada's pioneering work was Kishi, *Kodai kyūto no tankyū,* pp. 152–168. See also Tanaka Migaku, *Heijō-kyō,* pp. 150–161, and Tsuboi and Tanaka, *Historic City of Nara,* pp. 128–129.

106. Machida, "Heijō-kyō," pp. 117–18.

107. Kaneko Hiroyuki, "Heijō-kyū," in Tsuboi Kiyotari, ed., *Kodai o kangaeru kyūto hakkutsu*, p. 143.

108. Machida, "Heijō-kyō," pp. 133–136. In the early 1990s, archaeologists excavated the probable locations for the ministries of war and rites in greater detail. Personal communication from Yamanaka Akira, January 1997.

109. Tanaka, *Heijō-kyō*, pp. 33–36.

110. Kaneko, "Heijō-kyū," pp. 151–155.

111. Machida, "Heijō-kyō," pp. 126–128.

112. Thus almost all English-language descriptions of Nara Palace are somewhat inaccurate, even Tsuboi and Tanaka, *Historic City of Nara*, pp. 60–66. The lone exception to this rule is William Coaldrake, "City Planning and Palace Architecture in the Creation of the Nara Political Order: The Accommodation of Place and Purpose at Heijō-kyō," *East Asian History* 1 (1991): 37–54.

113. Machida, "Heijō-kyō," pp. 126–133. The roofed wall was 177 by 318 meters, while the main building measured 35 by 29.5 meters.

114. Information in this paragraph comes from Machida, "Heijō-kyō," pp. 128–129. This section is customarily called the "official compound," but such an appellation is now outdated.

115. The open space measured 214 by 284 meters and the longest of the four buildings was 4 by 10 *ken*. A *ken* is the distance between postholes and varies with each structure.

116. Machida, "Heijō-kyō," pp. 129–131. Imaizumi Takao wrote on ceremonies; Asano Atsuru wrote on the likeness to the Chinese structure.

117. Ibid., p. 129.

118. Ibid.

119. These theories are found in Machida, ibid., pp. 130–131. The first scholars mentioned are Machida and Asano; the second, Kanō Hisashi; and the third, Machida and Terasaki Yasuhiro.

120. This northern section measured 184 square meters.

121. Machida, "Heijō-kyō," p. 133.

122. The new compound for the audience hall measured 122 by 88 meters and the area of the imperial residence was 279 by 373 meters.

123. Machida, "Heijō-kyō," p. 68.

124. Kaneko, "Heijō-kyū," pp. 150–151.

125. On the tiles see *Heijō-kyūseki hakkutsu chōsa bu: hakkutsu chōsa gaihō*, 1992, pp. 4–19, and 1990, pp. 32–33. On the wooden tablet see Tateno Kazumi, "Nara: Heijō-kyūseki," *Mokkan kenkyū* 14 (1992): 7–16.

126. *Muchimaro den*, in *Nihon shisō taikei* (hereafter *NST*) 8: *Kodai seiji shakai shisō*, pp. 35 and 276.

127. See also *Dai Nihon komonjo* (hereafter *DNK*), vol. 1, p. 376.

128. *Heijō-kyū hakkutsu chōsa hōkoku*, vol. 3, pp. 77–81.

129. Aoki, "Koeki sei," pp. 47–50.

130. Ueki, "Yamato e no genkan," pp. 32–34. The description of Naniwa's layout follows this author.

131. Information on the historical context comes from Nakatani Masaharu, "Kuni-kyō (Shigaraki no miya, Hora no miya, Yuge no miya)," in Tsuboi Kiyotari, ed., *Kodai o kangaeru kyūto hakkutsu*, pp. 175–176; *Heijō-kyū hakkutsu chōsa hōkoku*, vol. 3, pp. 76–77; *SZKT, Shoku Nihongi*, Tenpyō 12/12/6, p. 162–Tenpyō 17/5/5, p. 183; and Yoshida Takashi, *Taikei Nihon no rekishi 3: Kodai kokka no ayumi*, pp. 217–218.

132. Yoshida, *Kodai kokka no ayumi*, p. 218.

133. *SZKT, Shoku Nihongi*, Tenpyō 12/12/6, p. 162.

134. Ibid., Tenpyō 15/12/24, p. 176.

135. Ibid., Tenpyō 17/5/6, p. 183.

136. Nakatani, "Kuni-kyō," pp. 176–178. On the layout of Kuni see Ashikaga Takaakira, *Nihon kodai chiri kenkyū*, pp. 59–111. See also Nakatani Masaharu, "Kuni-kyū no zōsaku kōji ni tsuite," in *Kodai gaku sōron*, pp. 171–187; and Kubo Tetsumasa, "Kuni-kyū no zōei ni tsuite," in *Nagaoka-kyō kobunka ronsō*, vol. 2, pp. 97–107. See Sonoda Kōyū, "Early Buddha Worship," in Brown, *Cambridge History of Japan*, vol. 1, p. 405, for a point that substantially supports the argument of this chapter. See Piggott, "Tōdaiji and the Nara Imperium," pp. 57–59, for the politics of this era.

137. Nakatani, "Kuni-kyō," pp. 179–191; conversation with archaeologists of the Yamashiro Regional Museum (Yamashiro kyōdo shiryō kan), fall 1991. In 1995 archaeologists uncovered a ditch along the western boundary of the palace, but the ditch did not extend beyond the palace into the city; communication from Tateno Kazumi, January 1997.

138. Nara was 5.5 by 4.5 kilometers, while Nagaoka was 4.3 by 5.3 kilometers and Heian measured 4.5 by 5.2 kilometers. Heijō Palace measured 1.1 by 1.4 kilometers; Nagaoka was 1.05 by 1.6 kilometers, while Heian was 1.15 by 1.4 kilometers.

139. See Satō Makoto, "Nagaoka-kyō kara Heian-kyō e," in Sasayama Haruo, ed., *Kodai*

o kangaeru Heian no miyako, pp. 52–54. See also Ronald Toby, "Why Leave Nara?" *Monumenta Nipponica* 40 (Autumn 1985): 331–347, and Piggott, "Tōdaiji and the Nara Imperium," pp. 248–250. Conrad Totman, *The Green Archipelago,* pp. 12–16, argues that the location of timber sources helped shape the choice of sites.

140. The following description of the historical context derives from Satō, "Nagaoka-kyō kara Heian-kyō e," pp. 46–54, and Yamanaka Akira, "Nagaoka-kyō kara Heian-kyō e," in Machida Akira and Kitō Kiyoaki, eds., *Shinpan kodai no Nihon 6: Kinki* II, pp. 218–219. These essays are good starting places for those desiring more information.

141. Aoki, "Koeki sei," pp. 55–56. Recently the authors of *Yomigaeru Heian-kyō,* p. 70, have concurred in this interpretation.

142. See *Nagaoka-kyō mokkan* 1: *Kaisetsu,* pp. 55–64, for construction tablets and pp. 186–187 for the impressment of Buddhist acolytes.

143. In addition to the death of Sawara, Satō, "Nagaoka-kyō kara Heian-kyō e," pp. 68–69, suggests that several factors—the slow pace of construction following Tane-tsugu's death; Kammu's anxiety and feelings of pollution deriving from the deaths of two imperial consorts and the illness of the heir apparent Prince Ate; repeated unnatural occurrences including epidemics; two major floods in 792; and the lack of urban conveniences—all played a role in the decision to leave Nagaoka.

144. Yamanaka, "Nagaoka-kyō kara Heian-kyō e," p. 208. The quote is from an obituary of a key official overseeing Nagaoka.

145. Ibid., pp. 223–225. Residential lots at Nagaoka were usually 40 *jō* square. One *jō* is 2.96 meters. The smaller lots were 35 or 37.5 *jō* on two sides. At Heian, all lots were 40 *jō* square. While wealthier residents might own a full 3.5-acre lot, it was not uncommon for individuals to live in one-sixteenth or even one-thirty-second of a lot.

146. Momose Chidori, "Nagaoka-kyō jōbō sei shōron," in *Nagaoka-kyō kobunka ronsō,* pp. 77–94.

147. Yamanaka Akira and Shimizu Miki, "Nagaoka-kyō," in Tsuboi Kiyotari, ed., *Kodai o kangaeru kyūto hakkutsu,* p. 208.

148. Ibid., p. 211, for more information on dwellings in Nagaoka. See also Yamanaka, "Nagaoka-kyō kara Heian-kyō e," pp. 226–228, and Yamanaka Akira, "Nagaoka–kyō no kenchiku ikō to takuchi no haichi," in *Nagaoka-kyō kobunka ronsō,* pp. 249–288, for evidence of maintenance buildings near the imperial palace and other dwellings. On the markets at Nagaoka see Yamanaka and Shimizu, "Nagaoka-kyō," pp. 211–212. Archaeologists have found a canal, storage bins, and a wooden tablet referring to market officials.

149. See Yamanaka and Shimizu, "Nagaoka-kyō," pp. 200–206; Yamanaka, "Nagaoka-kyō kara Heian-kyō e," pp. 211–216.

150. A 1996 excavation uncovered evidence of the grid plan in an area 500 meters north of the imperial residence. Wooden tablets suggest that it was the domicile for a later heir apparent, Kammu's son Prince Ate. Personal communication from Yamanaka Akira, January 1997.

151. Yamanaka and Shimizu, "Nagaoka-kyō," pp. 201–202; Yamanaka, "Nagaoka-kyō kara Heian-kyō e," p. 208.

152. See *Fujiwara no miya to miyako*, pp. 68–69.

153. Yamanaka, "Nagaoka-kyō kara Heian-kyō e," pp. 211–215.

154. Kishi, *Nihon kodai kyūto no kenkyū*, pp. 523–531.

155. The following description of the historical context for Heian derives from Satō, "Nagaoka-kyō kara Heian-kyō e," pp. 65–69; *Yomigaeru Heian-kyō*, pp. 66–73; Murai Yasuhiko, "Heian zenki," in Tsunoda Bun'ei, ed., *Heian-kyō teiyō*, pp. 59–70; and Yamanaka, "Nagaoka-kyō kara Heian-kyō e," pp. 216–223. Readers desiring more information should start with these sources.

156. *SZKT, Nihon kōki*, Enryaku 24/12/7, pp. 48–49.

157. On the complicated politics of this affair see Sasayama Haruo, "Heian shoki no seiji kaikaku," in *Iwanami kōza Nihon rekishi* 3: *Kodai* 3, p. 248, and references on p. 266.

158. Taira Yasuhisa, "Chichū no Heian-kyo," in Sasayama Haruo, ed., *Kodai o kangaeru Heian no miyako*, p. 101. For a general overview of sites and artifacts see Sugiyama Shinzō and Nagata Nobukazu, "Heian-kyō no iseki to ibutsu," in Tsunoda, *Heian-kyō teiyō*, pp. 93–100.

159. The information in this paragraph derives from Taira, "Chichū no Heian-kyō," pp. 105–106 and 120–122. On the *rashō mon* see *Heian-kyōseki hakkutsu chōsa gaihō*, 1977, p. 20. More data for reconstructing the checkerboard layout may be found in Horiuchi Akihiro, *Miyako o horu*, pp. 67–69; Tsuji Jun'ichi, "Jōbōsei to sono fukugen," in Tsunoda, *Heian-kyō teiyō*, pp. 103–116; Yamada Kunikazu, "Sakyō zenchō no gaiyō" and "Ukyō zenchō no gaiyō," in Tsunoda, *Heian-kyō teiyō*, pp. 187–358; and *Yomigaeru Heian-kyō*, p. 32. The last work also notes that Suzaku and Second Rank Great Roads measured 85 and 51 meters in width, respectively. On the markets see Sugeta Kaoru, "Tōzai ichi," in Tsunoda, *Heian-kyō teiyō*, pp. 359–372.

160. Yamanaka, "Nagaoka-kyō kara Heian-kyō e," p. 230; Taira, "Chichū no Heian-kyō," pp. 124–128.

161. Yamanaka, "Nagaoka-kyō kara Heian-kyō e," pp. 231–232.

162. Takinami Sadako, "Heian-kyō no kōzō," in Sasayama Haruo, ed., *Kodai o kangaeru Heian no miyako*, p. 90. *Yomigaeru Heian-kyō*, pp. 18, 43, and 79–80, also stresses the low population density of early Heian city.

163. Tōno Haruyuki, "Nanto shoden kyūjō zu zanketsu ni tsuite," *Komonjo kenkyū* 20 (February 1983): 1–12. *Yomigaeru Heian-kyō*, p. 16, and Teramasu Hatsuyo, "Heian-kyū no fukugen," in Tsunoda, *Heian-kyō teiyō*, pp. 143–170, also raise the problem of reconstructing ninth-century Heian Palace.

164. Taira, "Chichū no Heian-kyō," pp. 108–115; *Yomigaeru Heian-kyō*, pp. 34–35; Horiuchi, *Miyako o horu*, pp. 57–60. On pp. 65–67 Horiuchi summarizes information on the recent discovery of one corner of the imperial villa called the Shinsen'en. On the festivities hall see also Teramasu, "Heian-kyū no fukugen," pp. 155–157; on the population ministry and central ministry see the same article, pp. 161–165.

165. Taira, "Chichū no Heian-kyō," pp. 115–118; Kondō Kyōichi, *Kawara kara mita Heian-kyō*, pp. 38–41. See also *Heian-kyōseki hakkutsu chōsa gaihō*, 1987, pp. 19–25. Uehara Mahito, "Zenki no kawara," in Tsunoda, *Heian-kyō teiyō*, pp. 625–628, provides the best discussion of this topic so far.

166. Yamanaka, "Nagaoka-kyō kara Heian-kyō e," pp. 218–223.

167. Farris, *Population, Disease, and Land*, pp. 18–73.

168. On this point see Totman, *Green Archipelago*, pp. 9–33; and Okita Masaaki, "Yamato seiken ka no shizen to ningen," in Shiraishi Taichirō et al., eds., *Kōkogaku ni yoru Nihon rekishi* 16: *Shizen kankyō to bunka*, pp. 55–56.

169. On Miyoshi see his *Iken jūnikajō* in Takeuchi Rizō et al., eds., *NST* 8: *Kodai seiji shakai shisō*, pp. 78–79; the information on abandoned fields comes from Tsude, *Nihon nōkō shakai no seiritsu katei*, pp. 67–68. It should be noted that Tsude uses the term "medieval" (*chūsei*) when he means Heian.

170. Kozo Yamamura, "The Decline of the *Ritsuryō* System: Hypothesis on Economic and Institutional Change," *Journal of Japanese Studies* 1 (Autumn 1974): 30–37, also describes ancient Japan as a labor-short economy, although he believes that the population was growing.

171. On this system see Iyanaga Teizō, *Nihon kodai shakai keizai shi kenkyū*, pp. 427–493.

172. *Heijō-kyū mokkan* 2: *Kaisetsu*, pp. 75–76. A cook may have gathered firewood as part of his duties, but only for his own partner and not for the emperor.

173. Iyanaga, *Kodai keizai shi*, p. 451.

174. On this institution see Kishi Toshio, *Nihon kodai sekichō no kenkyū*, pp. 453–464; Yoshida Takashi, *Ritsuryō kokka to kodai no shakai*, pp. 349–410.

175. Yoshida, *Ritsuryō kokka*, p. 385.

176. *SZKT, Ruijū sandai kyaku*, Daidō 3/2/5, p. 270.

177. Ibid., Kōnin 14/2/21, p. 436; Jōgan 6/1/9, p. 518.

178. On this system I follow Aoki, "Koeki sei," *Shigaku zasshi* 67 (March 1958): 1–30 and 67 (April 1958): 35–66. Readers should not confuse this corvée institution with the like-sounding *kōeki* (written with different characters and meaning trade).

179. Archaeological evidence suggests that a corvée labor system similar to *edachi* may have been in place as early as the late third century, perhaps for construction of the first colossal keyhole tombs. For example, the area around Hashihaka Tomb yields large amounts of pottery dating to the late third century. Between 15 and 25 percent of the ceramics have been identified stylistically as coming from regions outside of Nara, such as western and central Honshu. One explanation is that the pots were brought by workers recruited from these regions. Communication from Walter Edwards, January 1997.

180. Note that Yamamura, "Decline of the *Ritsuryō* System," p. 8, interprets the ten-day corvée as a real levy.

181. Aoki, "Koeki sei," p. 64.

182. Harry Miskimin, *The Economy of Early Renaissance Europe, 1300–1460*, p. 33; Michael Postan, *The Medieval Economy and Society*, p. 152. Paid corvée was applied to provinces outside the Kinai in the 800s and 900s for raising small labor gangs. See Takinami, "Heian-kyō no kōzō," p. 84.

183. *Heijō-kyū hakkutsu chōsa shutsudo mokkan gaihō*, vol. 8, p. 8.

184. SZKT, *Shoku Nihongi*, Tenpyō Hōji 7/1/15, p. 292. The eventual abolition of the draft in 792 is also consistent with the termination of the corvée systems, which policies attempted to reduce enforcement costs amidst a depleted and resistant population.

185. As evidence of the severity of epidemics during the ninth century see SZKT, *Nihon sandai jitsuroku*, Jōgan 12/8/5, p. 276, which states that in 865 and 866 Oki province lost 3,189 people due to an epidemic outbreak. If one uses Sawada's estimate of 9,400 persons as Oki's total population around 810, then in two years almost 34 percent of Oki's population died. See Sawada, *Sūteki kenkyū*, p. 188. On the harsh agrarian conditions see Farris, *Population, Disease, and Land*, pp. 91–93 and 158–160.

186. Fukuyama Toshio, *Nara chō no Tōdaiji*, pp. 21–67.

187. SZKT, *Shoku Nihongi*, Tenpyō 19/11/7, pp. 193–194.

188. Ibid., Tenpyō Shōhō 8/12/20, p. 227.

189. See, for example, "Kokubunji nado hakkutsu chōsa kankei bunken mokuroku," *Maizō bunka zai nyūsu* 22 (December 1979): 3–44; *Kokubunji*.

190. Farris, *Population, Disease, and Land*, pp. 129–130.

191. Aoki, "Koeki sei," pp. 54–55.

192. On the difficulties involved in land clearance in early Japan see Farris, *Population, Disease, and Land,* pp. 74–93, and *Heavenly Warriors,* pp. 206–222.

193. Takinami, "Heian-kyō no kōzō," p. 84. The end to large-scale construction and reliance on elite sources of wealth at a time of depopulation are trends that find parallels in late fourteenth- and fifteenth-century Western Europe, where the construction of Gothic cathedrals stopped and newly enriched nobles and churches paid for the official building that did occur.

Chapter 4: Wooden Tablets

1. Kishi Toshio, *Iseki ibutsu to kodai shigaku,* p. 162. The rough estimate of 170,000 was derived as follows. As of early 1988, Kanō Hisashi, "Kodai mokkan gaisetsu," in *Nihon kodai mokkan sen,* p. 236, reports 51,782 tablets. The Prince Nagaya and Second Rank Great Avenue *mokkan* added over 100,000 to that number by early 1990, according to Machida Akira, cited in *Nagaya Ō teitaku to mokkan,* p. 36. Finds have increased greatly over the last few years.

2. The following description is based on Kitō Kiyoaki, *Kōkogaku raiburarii* 57: *Mokkan,* pp. 18–45; Kanō, "Kodai mokkan gaisetsu," pp. 236–240; Hirano Kunio, "Mokkan to kodai shigaku," in *Nihon kodai mokkan sen,* pp. 240–245; Tanaka Migaku, "Mokkan to kōkogaku," in *Nihon kodai mokkan sen,* pp. 245–249; Satō Makoto, "Mokkan kenkyū no ayumi to kadai," in *Nihon kodai mokkan sen,* pp. 249–252; and Satō Makoto, "Moji shiryō toshite no mokkan," in Okimori Takuya and Satō Makoto, eds., *Jōdai mokkan shiryō shūsei,* pp. 175–183.

There is little in English on wooden tablets. See Michael Loewe, "Note: Wooden Documents from China and Japan: Recent Finds and Their Value," *Modern Asian Studies* 14 (1980): 159–162; Joan Piggott, "Keeping Up with the Past: New Discoveries Enrich Our Views of History," *Monumenta Nipponica* 33 (Autumn 1983): 313–319; Tanaka Migaku, "The Early Historical Period," in Tsuboi Kiyotari, ed., *Recent Archaeological Discoveries in Japan,* pp. 76–82; and Tsuboi Kiyotari and Tanaka Migaku, *The Historic City of Nara,* pp. 67–83. There also reports of tablets in Korea; see Kim Won-yong, *Recent Archaeological Discoveries in the Republic of Korea,* pp. 68–69.

3. Yamanaka Akira, "Kōko shiryō toshite no kodai mokkan," *Mokkan kenkyū* 14 (1992): 148–154.

4. Scholars in Japan have worked out a complex taxonomy of surviving tablets according to shape:

Of the fifteen designated types, two of the most familiar are long strips with square corners (*tansaku gata*), a form later applied to paper for Japanese poetry. Short rectangles with and without rounded tops constitute two more categories. Six types have differing sorts of pointed ends or indentations for attachment to goods as tags, while essentially illegible shaved pieces (*kezuri kuzu*) and other damaged remnants compose five unfortunately large categories. About 80 percent of all tablets unearthed by archaeologists have been broken or damaged and convey only incomplete information. Only seven types are pictured in this figure.

5. Kitō, *Mokkan,* pp. 39–45.

6. On this subject the best work is Tōno Haruyuki, *Nihon kodai mokkan no kenkyū,* pp. 255–299, and *Shōsōin monjo to mokkan no kenkyū,* pp. 115–122. See also Kitō Kiyoaki, *Kodai mokkan no kisoteki kenkyū,* pp. 88–94.

7. Tōno, *Nihon kodai mokkan no kenkyū,* pp. 268 and 291–295.

8. Takigawa Masajirō, "Tansaku kō," *Kodai gaku* 7 (October 1958): 147–154. See also Satō, "Ayumi to kadai," pp. 250–251, for a periodization of research.

9. Kate Nakai, *Shogunal Politics,* p. 260.

10. Tsuda Sōkichi, *Nihon jōdai shi no kenkyū,* pp. 185–218.

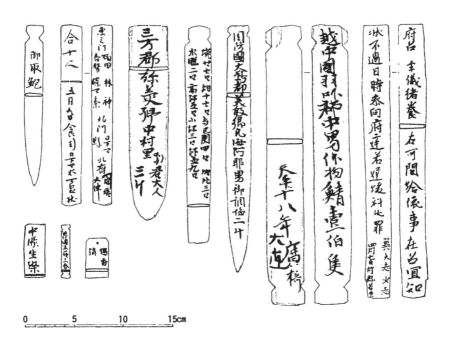

Types of Wooden Tablets. *Source: Mokkan kenkyū* 4 (1982): 6. © Nara Kokuritsu Bunkazai Kenkyūjo.

11. Nomura Tadao, *Kenkyū shi: Taika no kaishin*, pp. 7–8; Wayne Farris, "Taika no kaishin," in *The Encyclopedia of Japan*, vol. 7, pp. 295–297. For background on Taika see Bruce Batten, "Foreign Threat and Domestic Reform," *Monumenta Nipponica* 41 (1986): 199–219. Batten shows how the Taika Reform may have affected regional government in "State and Frontier in Early Japan: The Imperial Court and Northern Kyushu, 645–1185," Ph.D. dissertation, Stanford University, 1989, pp. 55–65 and 139–167.

12. For the classic expression of this view see Sakamoto Tarō, *Taika kaishin no kenkyū*.

13. See Inoue Mitsusada, "Taika no kaishin to higashi Ajia," in *Iwanami kōza Nihon no rekishi 2: Kodai 2*, pp. 139–155. See also Inoue Mitsusada, *Nihon no rekishi 3: Asuka no chōtei*, pp. 305–329, and Inoue Mitsusada, "The Century of reform," in Delmer Brown, ed., *The Cambridge History of Japan*, vol. 1, pp. 197–199.

14. See Hara Hidesaburō, "Taika no kaishin ron hihan josetsu," *Nihon shi kenkyū* 86 (September 1966): 25–45 and 88 (January 1967): 23–48, and Kadowaki Teiji, *Taika no kaishin ron*.

15. Tsuda, *Nihon jōdai shi*, p. 201; Inoue, "Century of reform," p. 198.

16. Inoue Mitsusada, "Gunji seido no seiritsu nendai ni tsuite," *Kodai gaku* 2 (April 1952): 104–119. Because nothing concrete is known about the organization or powers of the *hyō*, either in Japan or Korea, the *gunpyō ronsō* is to some extent an argument about vocabulary.

17. *Fujiwara kyūseki shutsudo mokkan gaihō*, pp. 12–38.

18. *Fujiwara-kyū mokkan 1: Kaisetsu*.

19. Nomura Tadao, *Kodai kanryō no sekai*, pp. 57–58.

20. *Asuka-kyōseki dai gojū ichiji hakkutsu chōsa shutsudo mokkan gaihō*.

21. Kishi Toshio, *Kyūto to mokkan*, pp. 1–15.

22. *Fujiwara-kyū mokkan 2: Kaisetsu*.

23. *Asuka Fujiwara-kyū hakkutsu chōsa shutsudo mokkan gaihō*, vols. 5–10; Hashimoto Yoshinori, "Nara: Fujiwara-kyōseki," *Mokkan kenkyū* 14 (1992): 24–28, 15 (1993): 22–25, and 16 (1994): 37–39; Takeda Masataka and Wada Atsumu, "Nara: Fujiwara-kyō Ukyō gojō yonbō," *Mokkan kenkyū* 15 (1993): 26–33; and Hashimoto Yoshinori and Tsuyuguchi Naohiro, "Nara: Fujiwara-kyōseki Ukyō kujō yonbō," *Mokkan kenkyū* 16 (1994): 40–45.

24. Single tablets bearing the Korean-style word have also appeared from excavations at Dazaifu in northern Kyushu, the Izumo provincial headquarters, and Iba in Shizuoka. See *Dazaifu shiseki shutsudo mokkan gaihō*, vol. 1, p. 14. See also Hirano, "Mokkan to kodai shigaku," p. 242.

25. The following paragraphs are drawn from Inoue, "Taika no kaishin to higashi Ajia," pp. 129–174, and Hayakawa Shōhachi, "Ritsuryō sei no keisei," in *Iwanami kōza Nihon no rekishi 2: Kodai 2*, pp. 222–252.

26. Inoue, "Taika no kaishin to higashi Ajia," pp. 150–152.

27. Nomura, *Kodai kanryō*. Richard Miller was the foremost Western expert on the bureaucracy; see *Ancient Japanese Nobility*, pp. 1–10, and *Japan's First Bureaucracy: A Study of Eighth-Century Government*. See also Batten, "State and Frontier in Early Japan," pp. 15–24. I find Batten's discussion to be the best so far available in English.

28. This list could go on forever, but there are three particularly noteworthy sources: Yoshida Takashi, *Ritsuryō kokka to kodai no shakai*, pp. 289–347; Sakaehara Towao, "Heijō-kyō jūmin no seikatsu shi," in Kishi Toshio, ed., *Nihon no kodai 9: Tojō no seitai*, pp. 187–266; and Joan Piggott, "Tōdaiji and the Nara Imperium," Ph.D. dissertation, Stanford University, 1987, pp. 142–156.

29. These *mokkan* appear in *Heijō-kyū mokkan 4: Kaisetsu*.

30. Nomura, *Kodai kanryō*, pp. 17–18.

31. Terasaki Yasuhiro, "Kōka mokkan no saikentō," in *Ritsuryō kokka no kōzō*, pp. 223–234.

32. Nomura, *Kodai kanryō*, pp. 16–21. See also Inoue Mitsusada, "Saikin shutsudo shita Heijō-kyō no mokkan," *Gekkan bunka zai* 42 (March 1967): 4–9, and Kitō Kiyoaki, "Shōwa yon jū ichi nendo Heijō-kyū shutsudo no mokkan," in *Nara kokuritsu bunka zai kenkyū jo nenpō*, pp. 31–34.

33. *Shintei zōho kokushi taikei* (hereafter *SZKT*), *Kōka-ryō no gige, Bunpan no jō*, pp. 156–157.

34. Nomura, *Kodai kanryō*, p. 21.

35. Ibid.

36. *SZKT, Senjo-ryō no gige, Sentai no jō*, pp. 136–137. See also Inoue, "Heijō-kyō no mokkan," pp. 6 and 8, for examples of tablets dealing with rank advancement or dismissal.

37. The agonizingly slow trek up the rank ladder was difficult for many officials to bear. By the late eighth century, unranked persons paid cash to receive promotion. On this system see Inoue, "Heijō-kyū no mokkan," p. 7.

38. For Tablets 1 and 2 see Nomura, *Kodai kanryō*, p. 22; for Tablet 3, see *Heijō-kyū mokkan 4: Kaisetsu*, p. 41. A string of dots indicates illegible parts of *mokkan*. Like others in the cache, these three showed evidence of recycling—writing something in ink on the surface, then shaving them down and reusing them. All three were rectangular

(*tansaku gata*), with a hole drilled in the top, because they were meant to hang from a string in an office where bureaucrats could refer to them as needed.

39. See Nomura, *Kodai kanryō*, pp. 152–153, for a description how evaluations were converted into rank advancements.

40. Nomura, ibid., p. 37, argues that Hirone had risen in rank while doing shift work for the ministry of rites and waiting for a full-time post to open.

41. Robert Borgen, *Sugawara no Michizane and the Early Heian Court*, pp. 69–80.

42. Nomura, *Kodai kanryō*, pp. 24–27. It should be noted that Borgen, *Sugawara no Michizane*, p. 78, asserts that the Japanese model was more egalitarian and less dependent on heredity than the Tang, a conclusion that Nomura does not share.

43. On the university I follow Nomura, *Kodai kanryō*, p. 29. See also Naoki Kōjirō, "The Nara State," in Brown, *Cambridge History of Japan*, vol. 1, p. 236.

44. Terasaki, "Kōka mokkan," pp. 238–239, stresses Japanese experience with cap ranks, possibly of Korean derivation.

45. John Hall, *Government and Local Power in Japan, 500 to 1700*, pp. 99–128. One might make the distinction between the principle of authority and actual power and argue that Hall was referring to the former and Farris to the latter. But as Sakamoto Shōzō and others have shown since the time Hall wrote his classic study, law was the source of authority and actual power was based on the family in both the Nara and Heian periods.

46. Nomura, *Kodai kanryō*, pp. 31–36.

47. Hayakawa Shōhachi, "Ritsuryō zaisei no kōzō to sono tokushitsu," in Iyanaga Teizō, ed., *Nihon keizai shi taikei 1: kodai*, pp. 221–280, has written the most comprehensive overview of the Chinese-style tax system. In English see Dana Morris, "Peasant Economy in Early Japan, 650–950," Ph.D. dissertation, University of California, Berkeley, 1980, pp. 42–64.

48. Denis Twitchett, *Financial Administration Under the Tang Dynasty*, pp. 24–40. The theory and practice of head taxes paid in kind originated in northern China during the Northern and Southern dynasties.

49. Naoki Kōjirō, "Nie ni kansuru ni san no kōsatsu," in *Ritsuryō kokka to kizoku shakai*, pp. 173–200.

50. Kitō, *Kisoteki kenkyū*, p. 142.

51. *Heijō-kyū mokkan 1: Kaisetsu*, p. 138–139.

52. Naoki, "Nie," pp. 197–198; Tōno, *Nihon kodai mokkan no kenkyū*, pp. 99–125. See also Higuchi Tomoji, "'Nijō ōji mokkan' to kodai shokuryō hin kōshin seido," *Mokkan*

kenkyū 13 (1991): 190–193, who argues that pre-Taika control mechanisms remained prominent until the 730s.

53. *Nihon kodai mokkan sen,* p. 129; Kitō, *Kisoteki kenkyū,* pp. 227–250.

54. Kitō, *Kisoteki kenkyū,* pp. 252–259. On Izu see also Naotake Hashiguchi, "The Izu Islands: Their Role in the Historical Development of Ancient Japan," *Asian Perspectives* 33 (1994): 121–149.

55. Kitō, *Kisoteki kenkyū,* pp. 259–268; Kanō Hisashi, "Miketsu kami to Kashiwade shi," in Tsuboi Kiyotari and Kishi Toshio, eds. *Kodai no Nihon* 5: *Kinki,* pp. 263–281.

56. According to William Aston, trans., *Nihongi: Chronicles of Japan from Earliest Times to A.D. 697,* vol. 2, p. 119; *NKBT, Nihon shoki,* vol. 2, Sushun 5/11/3, pp. 170–171, the Yamato king played a ceremonial role when *mitsuki* was delivered to the court. Imazu Katsunori, "Chō yō bokusho mei to nifuda mokkan," *Nihon shi kenkyū* 323 (July 1989): 15–20, suggests that in the eighth century court bureaucrats reduced this ritual to the pressing of an imperial seal upon documents listing goods coming into the court.

57. All information in this paragraph follows Ishigami Eiichi, "Nihon kodai ni okeru chō yō sei no tokushitsu," *Rekishi ni okeru minzoku to minshushugi Rekishi gaku kenkyū bessatsu tokushū* (November 1973): 28.

58. On the Japanese grain tax see Hayakawa Shōhachi, "Ritsuryō sozei sei ni kansuru ni san no mondai," in Okazaki Takashi and Hirano Kunio, eds., *Kodai no Nihon* 9: *Kenkyū shiryō,* pp. 128–144.

59. On Japanese and Tang labor statutes see Aoki Kazuo, "Koeki sei no seiritsu," *Shigaku zasshi* 67 (March 1958): 1–30 and 67 (April 1958): 35–66.

60. *Heijō-kyū hakkutsu chōsa shutsudo mokkan gaihō,* vol. 14, p. 8. One *to* equals 0.2 U.S. bushel.

61. Kanō Hisashi, "Yōmai tsukefuda ni tsuite," *Mokkan kenkyū* 3 (1981): 99–113.

62. Satō Makoto, "Kome no yūkō sei ni miru ritsuryō zaisei no tokushitsu," in *Bunka zai ronsō,* pp. 530–535.

63. *Nagaoka-kyō mokkan* 1: *Kaisetsu,* p. 155.

64. For more information on these two discoveries and the careers of Nagaya and Maro see *Nagaya ō teitaku to mokkan,* pp. 33–36 and 107–112; Joan Piggott, "*Mokkan* Wooden Documents from the Nara Period," *Monumenta Nipponica* 45 (Winter 1990): 452–463. For the most authoritative version of the Nagaya *mokkan* see *Heijō-kyō mokkan* 1.

65. Satō, "Ayumi to kadai," p. 250.

66. *Nagaya ō teitaku to mokkan,* p. 99. Nagaya's sustenance households would not have been located on his forty *chō* of land.

67. Ibid., p. 106.

68. See Yagi Atsuru, "Nagaya ōke mokkan to kōshin keryō sho," *Nihon shi kenkyū* 353 (January 1992): 16, on the relatives; see Piggott, "Wooden Documents," p. 453, on the excavation.

69. *Nagaya ō teitaku to mokkan*, p. 100. The evidence for horses from eastern Honshu comes in *Heijō-kyū hakkutsu chōsa shutsudo mokkan gaihō*, vol. 21, *Nagaya ōke mokkan* I, p. 21.

70. *Nagaya ō teitaku to mokkan*, pp. 103–106.

71. Ibid., pp. 131–133.

72. Ibid., pp. 99–100.

73. Not all historians agree with this conclusion. See, for example, Ōyama Seiichi, "Iwayuru 'Nagaya ōke mokkan' no saikentō," *Mokkan kenkyū* 11 (1989): 137–155. See also *Heijō-kyō mokkan* 1: *Kaisetsu*, pp. viii–ix.

74. On this point see Ōyama, "'Nagaya ōke mokkan,'" p. 144, and *Nagaya ō teitaku to mokkan*, pp. 99–100. Yagi Atsuru, "Nagaya ōke mokkan," pp. 36–37, speculates that the head of the more elaborate administration was Princess Minabe, Prince Takechi's widow and Nagaya's mother. While Yagi raises many doubts about the attribution to Kibi, he marshals no direct evidence to support Minabe. No matter which woman was in charge, the point about the alteration of Tang law to allow for women's greater economic power in Japan remains valid. See also Watanabe Akihiro, "Nagaya ōke mokkan to futatsu no kasei kikan," in *Nara kodai shi ronshū*, vol. 2, pp. 61–68.

75. *Nagaya ō teitaku to mokkan*, p. 97; on the Yamashiro lands, see p. 100.

76. As Yagi notes, pp. 24–33, this is one point against the Kibi thesis, but there is no evidence that Minabe ever held the Second Degree, the rank apparently held by one resident of the mansion uncovered in the excavation.

77. Sekiguchi Hiroko, "Nihon kodai no gō kizoku sō ni okeru kazoku no tokushitsu ni tsuite," in *Genshi kodai shakai kenkyū*, vol. 5, pp. 197–202.

78. Ibid., p. 197. To flesh out her argument, Sekiguchi believes eighth-century elite kinship was bilateral. In a prestige society, both men and women possessed status and possessions according to their ascriptive stature (bloodlines). Degrees of royalty were only faintly defined in the early 700s.

79. *Nagaya ō teitaku to mokkan*, pp. 103–104.

80. Ibid.

81. Kitō Kiyoaki, "Nagaya ōke mokkan nidai," *Hakusan shigaku* 26 (April 1990): 87–89.

82. See, for example, the case of Miwa no Fumiya no Kimi and Prince Yamashiro in Farris, *Heavenly Warriors*, p. 11.

83. *Nagaya*, vol. 1, p. 5 of *Heijō gaihō*, vol. 21.

84. All information in this paragraph comes from Hirano, "Mokkan to kodai shigaku," p. 244. See also the interesting essay by Okimori Takuya, "Mokkan ni arawareta kodai Nihongo," in Okimori Takuya and Satō Makoto, eds., *Jōdai mokkan shiryō shūsei*, pp. 184–193.

85. Misapplication of the term *"shinnō"* (referring to the brother or son of an emperor) to Nagaya in several tablets could have the same meaning, as could calling the followers of the prince *"chōdai"* (a word reserved for attendants of the sibling or child of the emperor). Indeed as Piggott, "Wooden Documents," p. 461, has written, the use of all these words could even indicate that at some point Prince Nagaya may have held the position of heir apparent.

86. *Nagaya ō teitaku to mokkan*, p. 111.

87. Tateno Kazumi, "Monjo mokkan no kenkyū kadai," *Kōkogaku jaanaru* 339 (November 1991): 7–15. See also Terasaki Yasuhiro, "Nagaya ōke no monjo mokkan," *Nihon rekishi* 500 (January 1990): 110–115.

88. Yoshida Takashi, "Ritsuryō to kyaku," in Okazaki Takashi and Hirano Kunio, eds., *Kodai no Nihon* 9: *Kenkyū shiryō*, pp. 245–248.

89. Edwin Reischauer et al., *East Asia*, p. 337; Hall, *Government and Local Power*, p. 60.

Conclusion

1. On remnants of simple society in Japan see Amino Yoshihiko, *Nihon no rekishi* 10: *Mōko shūrai*, pp. 441–445.

2. Sahara Makoto, *Taikei Nihon no rekishi* 1: *Nihonjin no tanjō*, pp. 328–330.

3. Scholars are just starting to analyze population and the economy during the Heian and Kamakura periods; for support for this hypothesis see Kitō Hiroshi, *Nihon nisen nen no jinkō shi*, pp. 39–60.

4. Tsude Hiroshi, *Nihon nōkō shakai no seiritsu katei*, p. 93.

5. This point is not meant to minimize the importance of the introduction of writing to Japan. Jack Goody has shown that the use of writing can have a significant impact on the way a society organizes its religion, economy, and polity. Certainly the spread of literacy is an important variable in social change. See Jack Goody, *The Logic of Writing and the Organization of Society*.

CHARACTER LIST

anagama 穴窯
ashiba 足場
bankoku 蕃国
bansei ikkei 万世一系
banzai 万歳
be 部
Bei shi 北史
biao 表
bō 坊
bunka zai hogo hō 文化財保護法
bunpan 分番
buraku den (in) 豊楽殿・院
chō (diao) 調
chō 町
chōdai 帳内
chōdōin 朝堂院
chōjō 長上
Chōsen kei bunkoku ron 朝鮮系分国論
chōshū den 朝集殿
chūgū 中宮
chūka 中華
chūsei 中世
chūtō 中等
daian den 大安殿
daigoku den (tai ji dian) 太極殿
daijin 大人
daika-ge 大花下
dairi 内裏
Daiyo 台与
daizen shiki 大膳職
dajō kan 大政官
dōtaku 銅鐸
edachi エダチ
ekifu 役夫
ekimin 役民
fu 符

fuko 封戸
fukurō 複廊
fu(mi)hito 史
funkyū bo 墳丘墓
gaikaku 外廓
gaku-ryō 学令
geko 下戸
gekyō 外京
genze riyaku 現世利益
getō 下等
gisen setsu 偽僭説
gō 郷
gun 郡
gunpyō ronsō 郡評論爭
guo 国
gyōyō 杏葉
hachijō 八条
hakucho 白丁
hanchiku hō 版築法
haniwa 埴輪
hanniku bori shinjū kyō 半肉刻神獸鏡
Hanyuan dian 含元殿
hei 塀
Heijō-kyū 平城宮
heishi 兵士
hekiga kofun 壁画古墳
hinoki 檜
hisashi 庇
hon 品
hoppen 北辺
hyō (kohori) 評
i (document) 移
i (rank) 位
iden 位田
ifuku-ryō 衣服令
ishi 位子

jikamaki 直播

Jingchu (*Keisho*) 景初

jisai 持衰

jō (measure) 丈

jō (rank) 条

jōbō sei 条坊制

jōri sei 条里制

jōtō 上等

juan 巻

jūjō 十条

kabane 姓

kabuto 冑

kafu 家扶

kagami ita 鏡板

kairō 回廊

kakibe o sadamu 部曲を定む

kamado 竈

kanbō 冠帽

kanden 官田

kangō shūraku 環濠集落

kan'i-ryō 官位令

kanmuri 冠

kantō tachi 環頭大刀

(*Kara*) *kamado* 韓竈

karamushi 苧

kashiwade 膳

keikō 挂甲

keiseki 景迹

ken 間

keryō 家令

keryō sho 家令所

kezuri kuzu 削屑

kika(jin) 帰化人

kishi 吉士

kita no miya 北の宮

kō 考

kōbetsu 皇別

kōchisei shūraku 高地性集落

Kodai kanryō no sekai 古代官僚の世界

kōden 公田

koeki (corvée) 雇役

kōeki (trade) 交易

kofun jidai 古墳時代

kōgō 皇后

kōhai 光背

Kojiki 古事記

kōka-ryō 考課令

koki 古記

koku 石

kokubunji 国分寺

kokugaku 国学

Koma jaku 高麗尺

konrō 軒廊

kōō 侯王

koto 琴

kumaso 熊襲

kuni no miyatsuko 国造

kurage 水母

kurahito 蔵人

kurai 位

kusagusa no miyuki クサグサノ御行

kushiki-ryō 公式令

kyŏngjil togi 硬質土器

kyōshiki 京職

li (*ri*) 里

Liang shu 梁書

machi 町

magatama 勾玉

Mantetsu chōsa bu 満鉄調査部

Man'yōshū 万葉集

meryō 馬寮

Mimana Nihon fu 任那日本府

mimikazari 耳飾り

minbu shō 民部省

minie 御贄

miso 㽵

mitsuki 調

miyake 官家；屯倉；御宅；三宅

miyako 都

mochiokuri gihō 持ち送り技法

mokkan 木簡

mokkan gakkai 木簡学会

monjo mokkan 文書木簡

mōretsu ni 猛烈に

Nagaya ōke mokkan 長屋王家木簡

nai shinnō 内親王

naizen shi 內膳司

nakatsukasa shō 中務省

nakatsu michi 中ツ道

nie 贄

nifuda 荷札

Nihon 日本

nihon 二品

Nihon ko bunka kenkyū jo 日本古文化
研究所

Nihon no naka no Chōsen bunka 日本の
中の朝鮮文化

Nihon shoki 日本書紀

nijō (ōji) 二条大路

nijō ōji mokkan 二条大路木簡

Nissen dōso ron 日鮮同祖論

oba 伯母・叔母

obi kanagu 帶金具

ōgaki 大垣

Okamoto taku no tsukasa 岡本宅の司

ōmikoto 大命

ōnie 大贄

onshi 陰子

onson 陰孫

on'yō-ryō 陰陽寮

Paekche pongi 白済本記

rakugaki 落書き

rashō (mon) 羅城門

ri (village) 里

rinkoku 隣国

ritsuryō 律令

ro 炉

rokujō 六条

roku-ryō 祿令

sakan 主典

Samguk sagi 三国史記

Samguk yusa 三国遺事

sanjō 三条

sankakuen shinjū kyō 三角緣神獸鏡

seikō 生口

senchi 壖地

senjo-ryō 選叙令

senmyō 宣命

sesshō 摂政

shaku 尺

shichishi no katana 七支の刀

shichō 仕丁

shigō 諡号

shijin 資人

shijō 四条

shikibu shō 式部省

shimotsu michi 下ツ道

shinbetsu 神別

shinden zukuri 寢殿造り

shinjō 新城

shinnō 親王

Shinsen shōjiroku 新選姓氏録

shin'yaku-kyō 新益京

shō 升

shoban 諸蕃

Shoku Nihongi 続日本紀

shokuri 飾履

shori 書吏

shōrin'en 松林苑

shō shori 少書吏

shubun 主文

shūsho 習書

Si ji 史記

so (zu) 租

sōshoku kofun 裝飾古墳

sōtaiteki dorei sei 総体的奴隷制

sugi 柱

suguri 村主

sukashi-bori 透かし彫り

Suzaku mon 朱雀門

suzu 鈴

taima 大麻

Tai ping yu lan 大平御覧

takatsuki 高杯

tankō 短甲

tansaku gata 短冊形

tatara 踏鞴

tateana kei yokoguchi shiki sekishitsu
竪穴系横口式石室

tateana shiki sekishitsu 竪穴式石室

taue 田植之

Teito 帝都

tennō 天皇
tettei 鉄鋌
to 斗
tōen 東園
tōgoku 東国
tōgū 東宮
tōin 東院
tojō 都城
tomo 伴
tomo no miyatsuko 伴造
toneri 舎人
tōshitsu doki 陶質土器
tsubo 坪
tsuiji 築地
tsukefuda 付け札
ubasoku 優婆塞
uji 氏
Wa (Wo) 倭
Wajin den 倭人伝
wakame 稚海藻

Wa-kyō 倭京
wang 王
Yamashiro kyōdo shiryō kan 山城郷土
　史料館
Yamatai 邪馬台
yō (*yung*) 庸
yokoana shiki sekishitsu 横穴式石室
yoko ōji 横大路
yōmai 庸米
yosumi tosshutsu bo 四隅突出墓
zei shi 税司
zenpō kōen fun (*taisei*) 前方後円墳体制
zhi 志
Zhou li (*Rites of Zhou*) 周礼
zōgū kyō 造宮卿
zōgū shiki 造宮職
zōgū shō 造宮省
zōshū shi 造酒司
zōyō 雑徭

BIBLIOGRAPHY

All Japanese publishers are in Tokyo unless indicated otherwise.

Primary Sources

Asuka Fujiwara-kyū hakkutsu chōsa shutsudo mokkan gaihō. Vols. 5–10. Nara: Nara kokuritsu bunka zai kenkyū jo, 1980–1991.

Asuka-kyōseki dai gojū ichiji hakkutsu chōsa shutsudo mokkan gaihō. Kashiwara: Nara kenritsu Kashiwara kōkogaku kenkyū jo, 1977.

Chūgoku seishi Nihon den 1: *Wei zhi Woren zhuan. Hou Han shu Wozhuan. Sung shu Woguo zhuan. Sui shu Woguo zhuan.* Edited by Ishihara Michihiro. Rev. ed. Iwanami shoten, 1985.

Dai Nihon komonjo. Vols. 1–25. Tokyo daigaku shuppan kai, 1901.

Dazaifu shiseki shutsudo mokkan gaihō. Vol. 1. Fukuoka: Kyushu shiryō kan, 1976.

Fujiwara-kyōseki no toire ikō. Nara: Nara kokuritsu bunka zai kenkyū jo, 1992.

Fujiwara-kyū mokkan: kaisetsu. 2 vols. Nara: Nara kokuritsu bunka zai kenkyū jo, 1978 and 1981.

Fujiwara-kyūseki shutsudo mokkan gaihō. Nara: Nara-ken kyōiku iinkai, 1968.

Hakkutsu sareta kodai no zaimei ihō. Nara: Nara kokuritsu hakubutsu kan, 1989.

Heian-kyōseki hakkutsu chōsa gaihō. 2 vols. Kyoto: Kyoto-shi maizō bunka zai kenkyū jo, 1977 and 1987.

Heijō-kyō mokkan. Vol. 1. Nara: Nara kokuritsu bunka zai kenkyū jo, 1995.

Heijo-kyū hakkutsu chōsa hōkoku. Vol. 3. Nara: Nara kokuritsu bunka zai kenkyū jo, 1963.

Heijō-kyū hakkutsu chōsa shutsudo mokkan gaihō. Vols. 4–25. Nara: Nara kokuritsu bunka zai kenkyū jo, 1965–1992.

Heijō-kyū mokkan: Kaisetsu. 4 vols. Nara: Nara kokuritsu bunka zai kenkyū jo, 1969–1986.

Heijō-kyūseki hakkutsu chōsa bu: Hakkutsu chōsa gaihō. 2 vols. Nara: Nara kokuritsu bunka zai kenkyū jo, 1990 and 1992.

Ikenoue funbo gun. Amaki: Amaki-shi kyōiku iinkai, 1979.

Kangō shūraku Yoshinogari iseki: gaihō. Yoshikawa kōbunkan, 1990.

Man'yōshū. In *Nihon koten bungaku taikei,* edited by Gomi Tomohide et al. Vols. 7–10. Iwanami shoten, 1959.

Miyoshi Kiyoyuki. *Iken jūnikajō.* In *Nihon shisō taikei: Kodai seiji shakai shisō,* edited by Takeuchi Rizō. Vol. 7. Iwanami shoten, 1979.

Muchimaro den. In *Nihon shisō taikei: Kodai seiji shakai shisō,* edited by Ōzone Shōsuke. Vol. 8. Iwanami shoten, 1979.

Nagaoka-kyō mokkan 1: *Kaisetsu.* Kyoto: Shin'yō sha, 1984.

Naniwa-kyūseki Osaka-jōseki hakkutsu chōsa chūkan hōkoku. 2 vols. Osaka: Osaka-shi bunka zai kyōkai, 1989 and 1990.

Nihon kōki. In *Shintei zōho kokushi taikei.* Vol. 3. Yoshikawa kōbunkan, 1934.

Nihon sandai jitsuroku. In *Shintei zōho kokushi taikei.* Vol. 4. Yoshikawa kōbunkan, 1934.

Nihon shoki. In *Nihon koten bungaku taikei,* edited by Sakamoto Tarō et al. Vols. 67–68. Iwanami shoten, 1965.

Oda Chausuzuka kofun. Vol. 4. Amaki: Amaki-shi kyōiku iinkai, 1979.

Ōtani kofun. Wakayama: Wakayama-ken kyōiku iinkai, 1959.

Ruijū sandai kyaku. In *Shintei zōho kokushi taikei.* Vol. 25. Yoshikawa kōbunkan, 1936.

Ryō no gige. In *Shintei zōho kokushi taikei.* Vol. 22. Yoshikawa kōbunkan, 1939.

Ryō no shūge. In *Shintei zōho kokushi taikei.* Vols. 22–24. Yoshikawa kōbunkan, 1966.

Samguk sagi wajin den ta roppen. Edited by Saeki Arikiyo. Iwanami shoten, 1988.

Shinsen shōjiroku no kenkyū: honbun hen. Edited by Saeki Arikiyo. Yoshikawa kōbunkan, 1962.

Shoku Nihongi. In *Shintei zōho kokushi taikei.* Vol. 2. Yoshikawa kōbunkan, 1935.

Toro iseki shutsudo shiryō mokuroku 4: *shashin hen.* Shizuoka: Shizuoka shiritsu Toro hakubutsukan, 1989.

Yoshinogari: honbun hen. Saga: Saga kyōiku iinkai, 1994.

Secondary Sources

Abe Yoshihira. "Nihon rettō ni okeru tojō keisei." *Kokuritsu rekishi minzoku hakubutsukan kenkyū hōkoku* 45 (December 1992): 1–47.

————. "Shin'yaku-kyō ni tsuite." *Chiba shigaku* 9 (1986): 13–43.

Aikens, Melvin, and Takayasu Higuchi. *Prehistory of Japan.* New York: Academic Press, 1982.

Akazawa Takeru. "Cultural Change in Prehistoric Japan: Receptivity to Rice Agriculture in the Japanese Archipelago." In F. Wendorf and A. Close, eds., *Advances in World Archaeology.* New York: Academic Press, 1982.

————. "Hunter-Gatherer Adaptations and the Transition to Food Production in Japan." In M. Zvebil, ed., *Hunters in Transition: Mesolithic Societies of Temperate Eurasia and Their Transition to Farming.* Cambridge: Cambridge University Press, 1986.

————. "Maritime Adaptation of Prehistoric Hunter-Gatherers and Their Transition to Agriculture in Japan." In Shuzo Koyama and David Thomas, eds., *Affluent Foragers.* Osaka: National Museum of Ethnology, 1981.

Akiyama Hideo. "Fujiwara-kyō to Asuka-kyō no kyōiki kō." *Chiri* 25 (September 1980): 29–37.

————. "Koma jaku to jōri sei." In *Nihon bunka to Chōsen.* Vol. 1. Shin jinbutsu ōrai sha, 1973.

Amino Yoshihiko. *Nihon no rekishi* 10: *Mōko shurai*. Shōgakkan, 1974.

Anazawa Wakō and Manome Jun'ichi. "Buki bugu to bagu." In Shiraishi Taichirō, ed., *Kodai o kangaeru kofun*. Yoshikawa kōbunkan, 1989.

———. "Nihon ni okeru ryūhō kantō tachi no seisaku to haifu." *Kōkogaku jaanaru* 266 (August 1986): 16–22.

Aoki Kazuo. "Koeki sei no seiritsu." *Shigaku zasshi* 67 (March 1958): 1–30; 67 (April 1958): 35–66.

Araki Toshio. *Nihon kodai no kōtai shi*. Yoshikawa kōbunkan, 1985.

Arimitsu Kyōichi. "Koguryŏ hekiga kofun no shishin zu." In *Hekiga kofun Takamatsu zuka*, vol. 2. Nara: Nara kyōiku iinkai, 1972.

Ashikaga Takakira. *Nihon kodai chiri kenkyū*. Daimyō dō, 1985.

Asuka no genryū. Nara: Nara kokuritsu bunka zai kenkyū jo, 1992.

Asuka shiryō kan: annai. Nara: Nara kokuritsu bunka zai kenkyū jo, 1977.

Azuma Ushio. "Chōsen sankoku jidai no nōkō." In *Kashiwara kōkogaku kenkyū jo ronshū*, vol. 4. Yoshikawa kōbunkan, 1978.

———. "Tetsu sozai ron." In *Kofun jidai no kenkyū* 5: *Seisan to ryūtsū* II. Yūzan kaku, 1991.

———. "Tettei no kisoteki kenkyū." In *Kashiwara kōkogaku kenkyū jo kiyō* 12: *Kōkogaku ronkō*. Nara: Nara kenritsu Kashiwara kōkogaku kenkyū jo, 1987.

Bailey, Lisa Kay. "Crowning Glory: Headdresses of the Three Kingdoms Period." In Gina Barnes and Beth McKillop, eds., *British Association for Korean Studies Papers* 5: *Korean Material Culture*. London: University of London Press, 1994.

Barnes, Gina. "The Archaeology of Protohistoric Yamato." *Beiträge zur Allgemeinen und Vergleichenden Archäologie* 16 (1996): 79–90.

———. "Ceramics of the Yayoi Agriculturalists (300 B.C.–A.D. 300)." In *The Rise of a Great Tradition: Japanese Archaeological Ceramics from the Jōmon Through the Heian Periods (10,500 B.C.–A.D. 1185)*. New York: Japan Society, 1991.

———. *China, Korea and Japan: The Rise of Civilization in East Asia*. London: Thames & Hudson, 1993.

———. "The Development of Stoneware Technology in Southern Korea." In Song Nai Rhee and C. M. Aikens, eds., *Pacific Northeast Asia in Prehistory*. Pullman: Washington State University Press, 1993.

———. "Discoveries of Iron Armour on the Korean Peninsula." In Gina Barnes and Beth McKillop, eds., *British Association for Korean Studies Papers* 5: *Korean Material Culture*. London: University of London Press, 1994.

———. "Early Japanese Bronze-Making." *Archaeology* 34 (May–June 1981): 34–38.

———. "Early Korean States." In Gina Barnes, ed., *Hoabinhian: Jōmon, Yayoi Early Korean States*. Oxford: Oxbow Books, 1990.

———. "*Jiehao, tonghao*: Peer Relations in East Asia." In Colin Renfrew and John Cherry, eds., *Peer Polity Interaction and Socio-Political Change*. Cambridge: University of Cambridge Press, 1986.

———. "Paddy Soils Then and Now." *World Archaeology* 22 (1990): 1–17.

———. *Protohistoric Yamato*. Ann Arbor: University of Michigan Press, 1988.

―――. "The Role of the *be* in the Formation of the Yamato State." In Elizabeth Brumfiel and Timothy Earle, eds., *Specialization, Exchange and Complex Societies.* Cambridge: Cambridge University Press, 1987.

―――. "State Formation in the Southern Korea Peninsula." *Archaeology in Korea* 10 (1983): 40–51.

―――. "Toro." In *The Atlas of Archaeology.* New York: St. Martin's Press, 1982.

Barnes, Gina, and Mark Hudson. "Yoshinogari: A Yayoi Settlement in Northern Kyushu." *Monumenta Nipponica* 46 (Summer 1991): 211–235.

Barnes, Gina, Don Wagner, Albert Dien, Sin Kyŏng-ch'ŏl, and Yoshimura Kazuaki. "Roundtable on Early Korean Armour." Papers presented at the Association of Asian Studies conference, Los Angeles, April 1993.

Batten, Bruce. "Foreign Threat and Domestic Reform." *Monumenta Nipponica* 41 (1986): 199–219.

―――. "State and Frontier in Early Japan: The Imperial Court and Northern Kyushu, 645–1185." Ph.D. dissertation, Stanford University, 1989.

Best, Jonathan. "Troubled Histories: A Study of Silla's Relations with Paekche and Kaya." Paper presented at the *Samguk sagi* Conference, Honolulu, February 1996.

Bielenstein, Hans. "Wang Mang, the Restoration of the Han Dynasty, and Later Han." In Denis Twitchett and Michael Loewe, eds., *The Cambridge History of China,* vol. 1: *The Ch'in and Han Empires, 221 B.C.–A.D. 220.* Cambridge: Cambridge University Press, 1978.

Bleed, Peter. "Yayoi Cultures of Japan: An Interpretive Summary." *Arctic Anthropology* 9 (1972): 1–23.

"Bochi." In Sahara Makoto and Kanaseki Hiroshi, eds., *Yayoi bunka no kenkyū* 8: *Matsuri to haka to yosoi.* Yūzan kaku, 1988.

Borgen, Robert. *Sugawara no Michizane and the Early Heian Court.* Cambridge, Mass.: Harvard University Press, 1986.

Bronowski, Jacob. *The Ascent of Man.* Boston: Little, Brown, 1973.

Brown, Delmer. "Introduction." In Delmer Brown, ed., *The Cambridge History of Japan,* vol. 1: *Ancient Japan.* Cambridge: Cambridge University Press, 1992.

―――. "The Yamato Kingdom." In Delmer Brown, ed., *The Cambridge History of Japan,* vol. 1: *Ancient Japan.* Cambridge: Cambridge University Press, 1992.

Chiga Hisashi. "Bagu." In *Kofun jidai no kenkyū* 8: *Kofun* II: *Fukusōhin.* Yūzan kaku, 1991.

―――. "Kofun jidai no shoki basō." In *Kashiwara kōkogaku kenkyū jo ronshū,* vol. 4. Yoshikawa kōbunkan, 1978.

―――. "Nihon shutsudo obi kanagu no keifu." In *Kashiwara kōkogaku kenkyū ronshū,* vol. 6. Yoshikawa kōbunkan, 1984.

―――. "Nihon shutsudo shoki bagu no keifu." In *Kashiwara kōkogaku kenkyū jo ronshū,* vol. 9. Yoshikawa kōbunkan, 1988.

Childe, V. Gordon. *Man Makes Himself.* London: Watts, 1936.

Ch'oe Pyŏng-hyŏn. "Sankoku jidai: Silla." In Kim Wŏnyong, ed., *Kankoku no kōkogaku.* Kōdan sha, 1989.

Ch'on Kwan-U. "A New Interpretation of the Problems of Mimana." *Korea Journal* 14 (February 1974): 9–23; 14 (April 1974):31–44.

Chŏn Yŏng-nae. "Shoki tekki jidai." In Kim Wŏnyong, ed., *Kankoku no kōkogaku.* Kōdan sha, 1989.

Chŏng Ching-wŏn and Sin Kyŏng-ch'ŏl. "Kodai KanNichi katchū dansō." *Kodai bunka* 38 (January 1986): 17–33.

Chŏng Cho-myo. "Chōsen sankoku to kodai Nihon moji." In *Kodai shi ronshū,* vol. 1. Hanawa shobō, 1988.

Coaldrake, William. "City Planning and Palace Architecture in the Creation of the Nara Political Order: The Accommodation of Place and Purpose at Heijō-kyō." *East Asian History* 1 (1991): 37–54.

Covell, Jonetta, and Alan Covell. *Korean Impact on Japanese Culture.* Elizabeth, N.J., and Seoul: Hollym International, 1984.

Craig, Albert, et al. *The Heritage of World Civilizations.* Vol. 1. New York: Macmillan, 1986.

Crawford, Gary. "The Transitions to Agriculture in Japan." In *Transitions to Agriculture in Prehistory.* Madison: Prehistory Press, 1992.

Crawford, Gary, and Hiroto Takamiya. "The Origins and Implications of Late Prehistoric Plant Husbandry in Northern Japan." *Antiquity* 64 (1990): 889–911.

Date Muneyasu and Matsushita Masaru. "Nōkō." In Mori Kōichi, ed., *San seiki no kōkogaku* 2: *San seiki no iseki to ibutsu.* Gakusei sha, 1981.

Duiker, William, and Jackson Spielvogel. *World History.* Minneapolis: West, 1994.

Edwards, Walter. "Buried Discourse: The Toro Archeological Site and Japanese National Identity in the Early Postwar Period." *Journal of Japanese Studies* 17 (Winter 1991): 1–23.

———. "Event and Process in the Founding of Japan: The Horserider Theory in Archeological Perspective." *Journal of Japanese Studies* 9 (Summer 1983): 265–295.

———. "In Pursuit of Himiko: Postwar Archaeology and the Location of Yamatai." *Monumenta Nipponica* 51 (Spring 1996): 53–79.

———. "Kobayashi Yukio's 'Treatise on Duplicate Mirrors': An Annotated Translation." *Tenri daigaku gakuhō* 178 (March 1995): 179–205.

Egami Namio. *Kiba minzoku kokka.* Rev. ed. Chūō kōron, 1991.

Elisseeff, Vadime. *The Ancient Civilization of Japan.* London: Barrie & Jenkins, 1974.

Farris, W. Wayne. "Ancient Japan's Korean Connection." *Korean Studies* 20 (1996): 1–22.

———. *Heavenly Warriors: The Evolution of Japan's Military, 500–1300.* Cambridge, Mass.: Harvard University Press, 1992.

———. *Population, Disease, and Land in Early Japan, 645–900.* Cambridge, Mass.: Harvard University Press, 1985.

———. "Taika no kaishin." In *The Encyclopedia of Japan,* vol. 7. Kōdan sha, 1983.

Fujioka Kenjirō. "Kodai no Ōtsu kyōiki to sono shūhen no jiwari ni kansuru jakkan no rekishi chirigakuteki kōsatsu." *Jinbun chiri* 23 (December 1971): 1–15.

Fujiwara no miya to miyako. Asuka: Nara kokuritsu bunka zai kenkyū jo, 1991.

Fukuyama Toshio. *Nara chō no Tōdaiji.* Kyoto: Kōdō shoin, 1947.

Furuse Kiyohide. "Nō kōgu." In *Kofun jidai no kenkyū* 8: *kofun* II: *fukusōhin.* Yūzan kaku, 1991.

————. "Tekki no seisan." In *Kofun jidai no kenkyū* 5: *Seisan to ryūtsū* II. Yūzan kaku, 1991.

Gardiner, Kenneth. *Early History of Korea.* Honolulu: University of Hawaiʻi Press, 1969.

Gluck, Carol. *Japan's Modern Myths.* Princeton: Princeton University Press, 1985.

Goody, Jack. *The Logic of Writing and the Organization of Society.* Cambridge: Cambridge University Press, 1986.

Gotō Shuichi. *Nihon kōkogaku.* Shikai shobō, 1927.

Gotō Yoshiharu. "Kaji gijutsu dō'nyū ni okeru Silla Kaya kei toraijin." In *Kodai shi ronshū,* vol. 1. Hanawa shobō, 1988.

Grayson, James. "Excavation of Late Kaya Period Tumuli in So-ryong." *Indo-Pacific Prehistory Association Bulletin* 5 (1985): 64–73.

————. "Mimana, A Problem in Korean Historiography." *Korea Journal* 17 (August 1977): 65–69.

Habuta Sumiyuki. "Kyushu no shoki yokoana shiki sekishitsu." In *Ko bunka dansō,* vol. 12. Kita Kyushu: Kyushu kobunka kenkyū kai, 1983.

Hachiga Susumu. "Tojō zōei no gijutsu." In Kishi Toshio, ed., *Nihon no kodai* 9: *Tojō no seitai.* Chūō kōron, 1987.

Hall, John. *Government and Local Power in Japan, 500 to 1700.* Princeton: Princeton University Press, 1966.

————. "Kyoto as Historical Background." In John Hall and Jeffrey Mass, eds., *Medieval Japan: Essays in Institutional History.* New Haven: Yale University Press, 1974.

Hamada Kōsaku. "Bunka shi jō no waga kuni no chii." In *Kōmin kyōiku taikei: Shōwa shichi nendo kaki kōshū kai kōen shū.* Teikoku kōmin kyōiku kyōkai, 1932.

Han Pyŏng-sam. "Gen sankoku jidai." In Kim Wŏnyong, ed., *Kankoku no kōkogaku.* Kōdan sha, 1989.

Hanada Katsuhiro. "Wa seiken to kaji kōbō—Kinai no kaji seigyō shūraku o chūshin ni." *Kōkogaku kenkyū* 143 (December 1989): 67–97.

Hanihara Kazurō. "Dual Structure Model for Population History of Japan." *Nichibunken Japan Review* 2 (1990): 1–33.

————. "Estimation of the Number of Early Migrants to Japan: A Simultative Study." *Journal of the Anthropological Society of Nippon* 95 (July 1987): 391–403.

Hara Hidesaburō. "Taika no kaishin ron hihan josetsu." *Nihon shi kenkyū* 86 (September 1966): 25–45; 88 (January 1967): 23–48.

Haraguchi Shōzō. *Nihon no genshi bijutsu* 4: *Sue ki.* Kōdan sha, 1979.

Hashiguchi, Naotake. "The Izu Islands: Their Role in the Historical Development of Ancient Japan." *Asian Perspectives* 33 (1994): 121–149.

Hashimoto Yoshinori. "Nara: Fujiwara kyōseki." *Mokkan kenkyū* 14 (1992): 24–28.

————. "Nara: Fujiwara kyōseki." *Mokkan kenkyū* 15 (1993): 22–25.

————. "Nara: Fujiwara kyōseki." *Mokkan kenkyū* 16 (1994): 37–39.

Hashimoto Yoshinori and Tsuyuguchi Naohiro. "Nara: Fujiwara-kyōseki Ukyō kujō yonbō." *Mokkan kenkyū* 16 (1994): 40–45.

Hayakawa Man'nen. "Nihon to Chōsen no kodai seiji soshiki." *Kikan kōkogaku* 33 (November 1990): 85–88.

Hayakawa Shōhachi. "Higashi Ajia gaikō to Nihon ritsuryō sei no suii." In Kishi Toshio, ed., *Nihon no kodai* 15: *Kodai kokka to Nihon*. Chūō kōron, 1988.

————. *Nihon kodai kanryō sei no kenkyū*. Iwanami shoten, 1986.

————. "Ritsuryō sei no keisei." In *Iwanami kōza Nihon rekishi* 2: *Kodai* 2. Iwanami shoten, 1975.

————. "Ritsuryō sozei sei ni kansuru ni san no mondai." In Okazaki Takashi and Hirano Kunio, eds., *Kodai no Nihon* 9: *Kenkyū shiryō*. Kadokawa shoten, 1971.

————. "Ritsuryō zaisei no kōzō to sono tokushitsu." In Iyanaga Teizō, ed., *Nihon keizai shi taikei* 1: *Kodai*. Tokyo daigaku shuppan kai, 1965.

Hayashi Hiromichi. "Kamado shutsugen ni kansuru ni san mondai." In *Mizu to tsuchi no kōkogaku*. Jōyō City: Kōyū kai, 1973.

————. *Kōkogaku raiburarii* 27: *Ōtsu-kyō*. Nyū saiensu sha, 1984.

————. "Ōtsu no miya." In Tsuboi Kiyotari, ed., *Kodai o kangaeru kyūto hakkutsu*. Yoshikawa kōbunkan, 1987.

Hayashida Shigeyoshi. "Nihon zairai uma no genryū." In Mori Kōichi, ed., *Nihon kodai bunka no tankyū* 9: *Uma*. Shakai shisō sha, 1974.

Heijo-kyō ten. Asahi shinbun, 1989.

Higuchi Tomoji. "'Nijō ōji mokkan' to kodai shokuryō hin kōshin seido." *Mokkan kenkyū* 13 (1991): 186–220.

Hirano Kunio. *Taika zendai shakai soshiki no kenkyū*. Yoshikawa kōbunkan, 1969.

————. "Yamato ōken to Chōsen." In *Iwanami kōza Nihon rekishi* 1: *Genshi oyobi kodai* 1. Iwanami shoten, 1974.

————. "The Yamato State and Korea in the Fourth and Fifth Centuries." *Acta Asiatica* 31 (1977): 51–82.

Hirose Kazuo. "Doboku gijutsu." In *Kofun jidai no kenkyū* 5: *Seisan to ryūtsū* II. Yūzan kaku, 1991.

Hitchins, Patricia. "A Cultural Synthesis of the Yayoi Period of Japan." Ph.D. dissertation, University of Toronto, 1977.

————. "Technical Studies on Materials from Yayoi Period Japan: Their Role in Archaeological Interpretation." *Asian Perspectives* 19 (1978): 156–171.

Ho, Ping-ti. "Lo-yang, A.D. 495–534: A Study of Physical and Socio-Economic Planning of a Metropolitan Area." *Harvard Journal of Asiatic Studies* 26 (1966): 52–101.

Hong, Wontack. *Paekche of Korea and the Origin of Yamato Wa*. Seoul: Kudara International, 1994.

————. *Relationship Between Korea and Japan in Early Period: Paekche and Yamato Wa*. Seoul: Seoul University Press, 1988.

Horio Hisashi and Iinuma Jirō. *Nōgu*. Hōsei daigaku shuppan kyoku, 1976.

Horita Keiichi. "Kodai Nitchō no bachū ni tsuite." In *Kashiwara kōkogaku kenkyū jo ronshū*, vol. 7. Yoshikawa kōbunkan, 1984.

Horiuchi Akihiro. *Miyako o horu*. Tankō sha, 1996.

Hsu, Cho-yun. *Ancient China in Transition*. Palo Alto: Stanford University Press, 1965.

Hudson, Mark. "Archaeological Approaches to Ritual and Religion in Japan." *Japanese Journal of Religious Studies* 19 (June–September 1992): 139–189.

———. "Ethnicity in East Asian Archaeology: Approaches to the Wa." *Archaeological Review from Cambridge* 8 (Spring 1989): 51–63.

———. "From Toro to Yoshinogari—Changing Perspectives on Yayoi Period Archeology." In Gina Barnes, ed., *Hoabinhian: Jōmon, Yayoi Early Korean States*. Oxford: Oxbow Books, 1990.

———. "Rice, Bronze, and Chieftains—An Archaelogy of Yayoi Ritual." *Japanese Journal of Religious Studies* 19 (June–Sept. 1992): 189.

Ikawa-Smith, Fumiko. "Co-traditions in Japanese Archaeology." *World Archaeology* 13 (February 1982): 296–309.

Im Yŏng-jin. "Sankoku jidai: Paekche, Seoul." In Kim Wŏnyong, ed., *Kankoku no kōkogaku*. Kōdan sha, 1989.

Imaizumi Takao. "Ritsuryō sei tojō no seiritsu to tenkai." In *Kōza Nihon rekishi* 2: *Kodai* 2. Tokyo daigaku shuppan kai, 1984.

Imamura, Keiji. *Prehistoric Japan: New Perspectives on Insular East Asia*. Honolulu: University of Hawai'i Press, 1996.

Imazu Katsunori. "Chō yō bokusho mei to nifuda mokkan." *Nihon shi kenkyū* 323 (July 1989): 1–31.

Inoue Hideo. "Kodai Chōsen no seishi." *Rekishi kōron* 58 (September 1980): 104–116.

———. *Wa Wajin Wakoku*. Kyoto: Jinbun shoin, 1991.

Inoue Mitsuo. *Kenkyū shi: Heian-kyō*. Yoshikawa kōbunkan, 1978.

Inoue Mitsusada. "The Century of Reform." In Delmer Brown, ed., *The Cambridge History of Japan*, vol. 1: *Ancient Japan*. Cambridge: Cambridge University Press, 1992.

———. "Gunji seido no seiritsu nendai ni tsuite." *Kodai gaku* 2 (April 1952): 104–119.

———. *Nihon no rekishi* 3: *Asuka no chōtei*. Shōgakkan, 1974.

———. *Nihon no rekishi* 1: *Shinwa kara rekishi e*. Chūō koron, 1965.

———. "Saikin shutsudo shita Heijō-kyō no mokkan." *Gekkan bunka zai* 42 (March 1967): 4–9.

———. "Taika no kaishin to higashi Ajia." In *Iwanami kōza Nihon no rekishi* 2: *kodai* 2. Iwanami shoten, 1975.

Ishigami Eiichi. "Kodai ni okeru Nihon no zeisei to Shiragi no zeisei." In Hatada Takashi, ed., *Kodai Chōsen to Nihon*. Ryūkei shosha, 1974.

———. "Nihon kodai ni okeru chō yō sei no tokushitsu." *Rekishi ni okeru minzoku to minshushugi Rekishi gaku kenkyū bessatsu tokushū* (November 1973): 23–34.

Ishiguro Tatsuhito. "Zenkoku kangō shūraku chimei hyō." *Kikan kōkogaku: tokushū Kangō shūraku to kuni no okori* 31 (May 1990): 77–80.

Ishino Hironobu. "Kōkogaku kara mita kodai Nihon no jūkyo." In Ōbayashi Taryō, ed., *Nihon kodai bunka no tankyū* 5: *Ie*. Shakai shisō sha, 1975.

———. "Rites and Rituals of the Kofun Period." *Japanese Journal of Religious Studies* 19 (June–September 1992): 191–216.

Iyanaga Teizō. *Nihon kodai shakai keizai shi kenkyū*. Iwanami shoten, 1980.

Japan in the Chinese Dynastic Histories: Later Han through Ming Dynasties. Translated by Ryusaku Tsunoda and edited by L. Carrington Goodrich. New York: P. D. and Ione Perkins, 1951.

Kadowaki Teiji. "Soga shi to toraijin." In Mori Kōichi et al., eds., *Kodai gōzoku to Chōsen*. Shinjinbutsu ōrai sha, 1991.

———. *Taika no kaishin ron*. Tokuma shoten, 1967.

Kajiyama Hikotarō. *Naniwa kokyō kō*. Osaka: Ko monmotsu gaku kenkyū kai, 1981.

Kamata Motokazu. "Ōken to bumin sei." In *Kōza Nihon rekishi* 1: *Genshi kodai*. Tokyo daigaku shuppan kai, 1984.

Kamstra, Jacques. *Encounter or Syncretism*. Leiden: Brill, 1967.

Kanaseki Hiroshi. "Yayoi jin no seishin seikatsu." In Sahara Makoto and Kanaseki Hiroshi, eds., *Kodai shi hakkutsu* 4: *Inasaku no hajimari*. Kōdan sha, 1975.

Kanehara Masaaki, Kanehara Masako, and Matsui Akira. "Toire no kōkogaku." In Tanaka Migaku and Sahara Makoto, eds., *Hakkutsu o kagaku suru*. Iwanami shoten, 1994.

Kaneko Hiroyuki. "Heijō-kyū." In Tsuboi Kiyotari, ed., *Kodai o kangaeru kyūto hakkutsu*. Yoshikawa kōbunkan, 1987.

Kang In-gu. *Mugi san kwa Changgo san*. Sŏngnam: Han'guk chŏngshin munhwa yŏn'gu wŏn, 1986.

Kanō Hisashi. "Miketsu kami to Kashiwade shi." In Tsuboi Kiyotari and Kishi Toshio, eds., *Kodai no Nihon* 5: *Kinki*. Kadokawa shoten, 1970.

———. "Yōmai tsukefuda ni tsuite." *Mokkan kenkyū* 3 (1981): 99–113.

Kanō Hisashi and Kinoshita Masashi. *Kodai Nihon o hakkutsu suru* 1: *Asuka Fujiwara no miyako*. Iwanami shoten, 1985.

Kasai Wajin. "Kawachi no Atai no keifu ni tsuite." In Mishina Akihide, ed., *Nihon shoki kenkyū*, vol. 5. Hanawa shobō, 1971.

Katō Kenkichi. "Torai no hitobito." In Saeki Arikiyo, ed., *Kodai o kangaeru Yūryaku tennō to sono jidai*. Yoshikawa kōbunkan, 1988.

Kawagoe Tetsushi. "Yayoi jidai no chūzō teppu o megutte." *Kōkogaku zasshi* 65 (March 1980): 1–23.

Kawakami Toshirō. "Kofun chikuzō no dōin sareta hito no kazu to jittai." *Kikan kōkogaku* 3 (Spring 1984): 71–72.

Kibi no kyofun. Okayama: San'yō shinbun sha, 1980.

Kidder, J. Edward, Jr. *Ancient Japan*. Oxford: Elsevier-Phaidon, 1977.

———. "Ceramics of the Burial Mounds (Kofun) (A.D. 258–646)." In *The Rise of a Great Tradition: Japanese Archeological Ceramics from the Jōmon through Heian Periods (10,500 B.C.–A.D. 1185)*. New York: Japan Society, 1991.

————. "The Earliest Societies in Japan." In Delmer Brown, ed., *The Cambridge History of Japan*, vol. 1: *Ancient Japan*. Cambridge: Cambridge University Press, 1992.

————. *Early Buddhist Japan*. New York: Praeger, 1972.

————. "The Newly Discovered Takamatsu Tomb." *Monumenta Nipponica* 27 (Summer 1972): 245–251.

————. "Yoshinogari and the Yamatai Problem." *Transactions of the Asiatic Society of Japan*, 4th series, 6 (1991): 115–140.

Kiley, Cornelius. "State and Dynasty in Archaic Yamato." *Journal of Asian Studies* 33 (November 1973): 25–49.

————. "Uji and Kabane in Ancient Japan." *Monumenta Nipponica* 32 (Autumn 1977): 365–376.

————. "Wooden Tags and Noble Houses: The Household(s) of Prince Nagaya as Revealed by *Mokkan*." Paper presented at the Association of Asian Studies at Washington, D.C., April 1995.

Kim, Byung-mo. "Aspects of Brick and Stone Tomb Construction in China and South Korea, Ch'in to Silla Period." Ph.D. dissertation, Oxford University, 1978.

Kim Chong-ch'ŏl. "Sankoku jidai: Kaya, Kyŏngsang North." In Kim Wŏnyong, ed., *Kankoku no kōkogaku*. Kōdan sha, 1989.

Kim, C. S. "The Kolp'um System: Basis for Sillan Social Stratification." *Journal of Korean Studies* 1 (1971): 43–69.

Kim Jung-bae. "Characteristics of Mahan in Ancient Korean Society." *Korea Journal* 14 (June 1974): 4–10.

————. "The Question of Horse-Riding People in Korea." *Korea Journal* 18 (September 1978): 39–50; 18 (November 1978):41–52.

Kim Ki-ung. "Kankoku shozai no zenpō kōen fun shingi ron." *Kōkogaku jaanaru* 23 (September 1984): 7.

Kim Sŏk-hyŏng. *Kodai Chōnichi kankei shi: Yamato seiken to Mimana*. Keisō shobō, 1969.

Kim Wŏn-yong. *Art and Archaeology of Ancient Korea*. Seoul: Taekwang, 1986.

————. "Impact of Ancient Korean Culture upon Japan." *Korea Journal* 12 (June 1972): 34–35.

————. "Korean Archaeology Today." *Korea Journal* 21 (September 1981): 22–43.

————. *Recent Archaeological Discoveries in the Republic of Korea*. Tokyo and Paris: UNESCO, 1983.

————. "Sankoku jidai: Koguryŏ." In Kim Wŏnyong, ed., *Kankoku no kōkogaku*. Kōdan sha, 1989.

Kinoshita Wataru. "Tōshitsu doki to sono bunpu." In *Kofun jidai no kenkyū* 6: *Higashi Ajia to Sue ki*. Yūzan kaku, 1991.

Kirihara Takeshi. *Tsumiishi zuka to toraijin*. Tokyo daigaku shuppan kai, 1989.

Kirkland, J. Russell. "The Horseriders in Korea: A Critical Evaluation of a Historical Theory." *Korean Studies* 5 (1981): 109–128.

Kishi Toshio. *Iseki ibutsu to kodai shigaku*. Yoshikawa kōbunkan, 1980.

———. "Kakki toshite no Yūryaku chō." In *Nihon seiji shakai shi kenkyū*, vol. 1. Hanawa shobō, 1983.

———. *Kodai kyūto no tankyū*. Hanawa shobō, 1984.

———. "Kodai no kakki Yūryaku chō kara no tenbō." In Kishi Toshio, ed., *Nihon no kodai 6: Ōken o meguru tatakai*. Chūō kōron, 1986.

———. *Kyūto to mokkan*. Yoshikawa kōbunkan, 1977.

———. *Nihon kodai kyūto no kenkyū*. Iwanami shoten, 1988.

———. *Nihon kodai sekichō no kenkyū*. Hanawa shobō, 1973.

———. "Nihon tojō sei sōron." In Kishi Toshio, ed., *Nihon no kodai 9: Tojō no seitai*. Chūō kōron, 1987.

———. "Tojō no genryū o tazuneru." In Kishi Toshio, ed., *Nihon no kodai 9: Tojō no seitai*. Chūō kōron, 1986.

Kitō Hiroshi. *Nihon nisen nen no jinkō shi*. Kyoto: PHP Paperbacks, 1983.

Kitō Kiyoaki. *Kodai mokkan no kisoteki kenkyū*. Hanawa shobō, 1993.

———. *Kōkogaku raiburarii 57: Mokkan*. Nyū saiensu sha, 1990.

———. "Nagaya ōke mokkan nidai." *Hakusan shigaku* 26 (April 1990): 87–103.

———. "Nihon no ritsuryō kansei no seiritsu to Kudara no kansei." In *Nihon no kodai shakai to keizai*, vol. 1. Yoshikawa kōbunkan, 1978.

———. "Shōwa yon jū ichi nendo Heijō-kyū shutsudo no mokkan." In *Nara kokuritsu bunka zai kenkyū jo nenpō*. Nara: Nara kokuritsu bunka zai kenkyū jo, 1967.

Kobayashi Ken'ichi. "Hohei to kihei." In Shiraishi Taichirō, ed., *Kodai shi fukugen 7: Kofun jidai no kōgei*. Kōdan sha, 1990.

———. "Katchū seisaku gijutsu no hensen to kōjin no keitō." *Kōkogaku kenkyū* 80 (March 1974): 48–68; 82 (September 1974): 37–49.

Kobayashi Yukio. *Kofun jidai no kenkyū*. Aoki shoten, 1961.

———. "Kofun jidai tankō no genryū." In *Nikkan kodai bunka no nagare*. Osaka: Tezukayama kōkogaku kenkyū jo, 1982.

———. "Sōshoku kofun." In *Kofun bunka ronkō*. Heibon sha, 1976.

———. "Yomo tsu hegui." In *Kofun bunka ronkō*. Heibon sha, 1976.

Kojiki. Translated by Donald Philippi. University of Tokyo Press, 1968.

Kokubunji. Nara: Nara kokuritsu hakubutsu kan, 1980.

"Kokubunji nado hakkutsu chōsa kankei bunken mokuroku." *Maizō bunka zai nyūsu* 22 (December 1979): 3–44.

Kōmoto Masayuki. "Yayoi jidai no shakai." In Sahara Makoto and Kanaseki Hiroshi, eds., *Kodai shi hakkutsu 4: Inasaku no hajimari*. Kōdan sha, 1975.

Kondō Hiroshi. "Sōshoku tsuki Sue ki no denpan ni tsuite." *Hanazono shigaku* 8 (November 1987): 138–147.

Kondō Kyōichi. "Chūdō seihin." In *Kofun jidai no kenkyū 5: Seisan to ryūtsū* II. Yūzan kaku, 1991.

———. *Kawara kara mita Heian-kyō*. Kyōiku sha, 1985.

———. *Sankakuen shinjū kyō*. Tokyo daigaku shuppan kai, 1988.

Kondō Yoshirō. *Tatetsuki iseki*. Okayama: San'yō shinbun sha, 1980.

———. *Zenpō kōen fun no jidai*. Iwanami shoten, 1983.

Koryŏ taehakkyo saengsan kisul yŏn'gu so. *Paekche ŭi chech'ŏl kongchŏng kwa kisul balchŏn*. Seoul: Koryŏ taehakkyo, 1985.

Koyama, Shūzō. "Jōmon Subsistence and Population." *Senri Ethnological Studies* 2 (1978): 1–65.

Kubo Tetsumasa. "Kuni-kyū no zōei ni tsuite." In *Nagaoka-kyō kobunka ronsō*, vol. 2. Kyoto: Sansei shuppan, 1992.

Kuraku Yoshiyuki. *Suiden no kōkogaku*. Tokyo daigaku shuppan kai, 1991.

Kyoto-shi, ed. *Yomigaeru Heian-kyō*. Kyoto: Kyoto-shi, 1994.

Ledyard, Gari. "Galloping Along with the Horseriders: Looking for the Founders of Japan." *Journal of Japanese Studies* 1 (Summer 1975): 217–254.

Lee, Chong-wuk. "The Formation and Growth of Paekche." *Korea Journal* 18 (October 1978): 35–40.

Lee, Insook. "Ancient Glass Trade in Korea." In Gina Barnes and Beth McKillop, eds., *British Association for Korean Studies Papers* 5: *Korean Material Culture*. London: University of London Press, 1994.

Lee, Ki-baik. *A New History of Korea*. Cambridge, Mass.: Harvard University Press, 1984.

Lee, Ki-dong. "Ancient Korean Historical Research in North Korea." *Korea Journal* 32 (Summer 1992): 22–41.

Lee, Peter. *Sourcebook of Korean Civilization*. Vol. 1. New York: Columbia University Press, 1993.

Li Jing-hua. "On the Provenance of the Early Time Ironware Excavated in Kyushu, Japan." *Bulletin of the Metals Museum* 17 (1991): 32–39.

Loewe, Michael. "The Former Han Dynasty." In Denis Twitchett and Michael Loewe, eds., *The Cambridge History of China*, vol. 1: *The Ch'in and Han Empires, 221 B.C.–A.D. 220*. Cambridge: Cambridge University Press, 1978.

———. "Note: Wooden Documents from China and Japan: Recent Finds and Their Value." *Modern Asian Studies* 14 (1980): 159–162.

Mabuchi, H., Y. Hirao, and M. Nishida. "Lead Isotope Approach to the Understanding of Early Japanese Bronze Culture." *Archaeometry* 27 (February 1985): 131–159.

Machida Akira. "Heijō-kyō." In Machida Akira and Kitō Kiyoaki, eds., *Shinpan kodai no Nihon* 6: *Kinki* II. Kadokawa shoten, 1991.

———. "Kantō no keifu." In *Nara kokuritsu bunka zai kenkyū jo gakuhō* 28: *Kenkyū ronshū* 3. Nara: Nara kokuritsu bunka zai kenkyū jo, 1976.

———. "Kodai obi kanagu kō." *Kōkogaku zasshi* 56 (September 1970): 33–60.

———. *Kōkogaku raiburarii* 44: *Heijō-kyō*. Nyū saiensu sha, 1986.

McCallum, Donald. "Korean Influence on Early Japanese Buddhist Sculpture." *Korean Culture* 3 (March 1982): 22–29.

McCullough, William. "Japanese Marriage Institutions of the Heian Period." *Harvard Journal of Asiatic Studies* 27 (1967): 103–167.

McNeill, William. *A History of the Human Community*. Vol. 1. 2nd ed. Englewood Cliffs, N.J.: Prentice-Hall, 1987.

Maeda Akihisa. "Shisei sei e no michi." In Saeki Arikiyo, ed., *Kodai o kangaeru Yūryaku tennō to sono jidai.* Yoshikawa kōbunkan, 1988.

Maekawa Akihisa. "Bagu shutsudo no kofun sū bunpu yori mita Yamato seiken no kiba senryoku." *Kodai bunka* 51 (January 1962): 1–31.

———. "Kukadachi to tomo." *Higashi Ajia no kodai bunka* 32 (1982): 55–67.

Maesono Ryōichi. "Uji to kabane." In Ōbayashi Taryō, ed., *Nihon no kodai* 11: *Uji to ie.* Chūō kōron, 1987.

"Maizō bunka zai kankei chōsa hōkoku sho to no kankō sū to hakkutsu todoke to kensū no suii." *Maizō bunka nyūsu* 52 (December 1985).

"Maizō bunka zai tantō sha su no zōka." *Maizō bunka nyūsu* 67 (March 1990).

Manome Jun'ichi. "Kindō shokuri." In *Kofun jidai no kenkyū* 8: *Kofun* II: *Fukusōhin.* Yūzan kaku, 1991.

The Manyoshu. Translated by Nippon gakujutsu shinkō kai. New York: Columbia University Press, 1965.

Matsui Kazuyoshi. "Kodai no kajigu." *Ko bunka ronsō.* Fukuoka: Kojima Takato sensei kijū kinen jigyō kai, 1991.

———. "Tetsu seisan." In *Kofun jidai no kenkyū* 5: *Seisan to ryūtsū* II. Yūzan kaku, 1991.

Matsumae Takeshi. "Early Kami Worship." In Delmer Brown, ed., *The Cambridge History of Japan,* vol. 1: *Ancient Japan.* Cambridge: Cambridge University Press, 1992.

Matsumoto Seichō. "Japan in the Third Century." *Japan Quarterly* 30 (October–December 1983): 377–382.

Miller, Richard. *Ancient Japanese Nobility.* Berkeley: University of California Press, 1974.

———. *Japan's First Bureaucracy: A Study of Eighth-Century Government.* Ithaca: Cornell University Press, 1979.

Mishina Akihide. *Yamatai koku kenkyū sōran.* Sōgen sha, 1970.

Miskimin, Harry. *The Economy of Early Renaissance Europe, 1300–1460.* Cambridge: Cambridge University Press, 1975.

Miyamoto Nagajirō. *Nihonjin wa dono yō ni kenzō butsu o tsukutte kita ka* 7: *Heijō kyō. Kodai no toshi keikaku to kenchiku.* Sōshi sha, 1986.

Mokkan gakkai, ed. *Mokkan kenkyū.* 1–16 (1979–1994).

Momose Chidori. "Nagaoka-kyō jōbō sei shōron." In *Nagaoka-kyō kobunka ronsō,* vol. 1. Kyoto: Dōhō sha, 1986.

Mori Hiromichi and Sugimoto Kenji. "*Gishi* Wajin den o tsūdoku suru." In Mori Kōichi, ed., *Nihon no kodai* 1: *Wajin no tojō.* Chūō kōron, 1985.

Mori Kōichi. "Kōkogaku to uma." In Mori Kōichi, ed., *Nihon kodai bunka no tankyū* 9: *Uma.* Shakai shisō sha, 1974.

Mori Kōichi and Yokota Ken'ichi. "Taidan: bochi to kofun." In Mori Kōichi, ed., *Nihon kodai bunka no tankyū* 10: *Bochi.* Shakai shisō sha, 1975.

Morimitsu Toshihiko. "Seidō sei yōki, garasu yōki." In *Kofun jidai no kenkyū* 8: *Kofun* II: *Fukusōhin.* Yūzan kaku, 1991.

Morioka Hideto. "Yama oka no Yayoi mura to okugai hitakiba." In *Kōkogaku ronshū,* vol. 1. Osaka: Rekibun dō, 1985.

Morishita Akiyuki. "Nihon ni okeru yokoana shiki sekishitsu no shutsugen to sono keifu." *Kodai gaku kenkyū* 111 (August 1986): 1–17.

Morris, Dana. "Peasant Economy in Early Japan, 650–950." Ph.D. dissertation, University of California, Berkeley, 1980.

Mun Sa-wi. "Chōsen sankoku no ijūmin shūdan ni yoru Kinai chihō no kaihatsu ni tsuite." *Rekishi gaku kenkyū* 374 (July 1971): 15–32.

Murayama, Shichirō, and Roy Miller. "The Inariyama Tumulus Sword Inscription." *Journal of Japanese Studies* 5 (1979): 405–438.

Nagashima Kimichika. "Yokoana shiki sekishitsu no genryū o saguru." In *Nihon to Chōsen no kodai shi.* Sansei dō, 1979.

Nagaya ō teitaku to mokkan. Yoshikawa kōbunkan, 1991.

Nakai, Kate. *Shogunal Politics: Arai Hakuseki and the Premises of Tokugawa Rule.* Cambridge, Mass.: Harvard University Press, 1988.

Nakamura Akira. *Kōkogaku raiburarii* 5: *Sue ki.* Nyū saiensu sha, 1988.

Nakao Yoshiharu. *Kōkogaku raiburari-* 46: *Naniwa-kyō.* Nyū saiensu sha, 1986.

Nakatani Masaharu. "Kuni-kyō (Shigaraki no miya, Hora no miya, Yuge no miya)." In Tsuboi Kiyotari, ed., *Kodai o kangaeru kyūto hakkutsu.* Yoshikawa kōbunkan, 1987.

———. "Kuni-kyū no zōsaku kōji ni tsuite." In *Kodai gaku sōron.* Kyoto: Tsunoda Bun'ei sensei koki kinen jigyō kai, 1983.

Naoki Kōjirō. "Naniwa Ogori-no-miya to Nagara Toyosaki." In *Naniwa no miya to Nihon kodai kokka.* Hanawa shobō, 1977.

———. "The Nara State." In Delmer Brown, ed., *The Cambridge History of Japan,* vol. 1: *Ancient Japan.* Cambridge: Cambridge University Press, 1992.

———. "Nie ni kansuru ni san no kōsatsu." In *Ritsuryō kokka to kizoku shakai.* Yoshikawa kōbunkan, 1969.

Needham, Joseph. *Science and Civilization in China.* Vols. 4–6. Cambridge: Cambridge University Press, 1965–1988.

Nelson, Sarah. "Archaeological Discoveries in Korea." *Korean Culture* 14 (Winter 1993): 23–31.

———. *The Archaeology of Korea.* Cambridge: Cambridge University Press, 1993.

———. "Korean Interpretations of Korean Archaeology." *Asian Perspectives* 27 (1990): 185–192.

———. "Recent Progress in Korean Archaeology." In F. Wendorf and A. Close, eds., *Advances in World Archaeology.* New York: Academic Press, 1982.

Nihongi: Chronicles of Japan from the Earliest Times to A.D. 697. Translated by William Aston. 2 vols. London: Kegan, Paul, Trench and Trubner, 1896.

Nihon kodai mokkan sen. Iwanami shoten, 1990.

Niiro Izumi. "Buki." In *Kofun jidai no kenkyū* 8: *kofun* II: *fukusōhin.* Yūzan kaku, 1991.

———. "Sōshoku tsuki tachi to kofun jidai kōki no heisei." *Kōkogaku kenkyū* 119 (December 1983): 50–70.

Nishimoto Masahiro. "Tomo, tomo no o ni kansuru ichikōsatsu." *Shoku Nihongi kenkyū* 217 (March 1982): 1–28.

Nishitani Tadashi. "Kankoku de hakken sareta 'zenpō kōen fun' ni tsuite." *Kōkogaku jaanaru* 23 (September 1984): 8–9.

———. "The Kaya Tumuli: Windows on the Past." *Japan Foundation Newsletter* 21 (November 1993): 1–6.

———. "Kara chiiki to hokubu Kyushu." In *Dazaifu ko bunka ronsō*, vol. 1. Yoshikawa kōbunkan, 1983.

Nishitani Tadashi and Kim Ki-ung. "Yokoana shiki sekishitsu no shutsugen o megutte." In *Kyushu ni okeru kofun bunka to Chōsen hantō*. Gakusei sha, 1989.

Nitō Atsushi. "Jōgū ōke to Ikaruga." In Machida Akira and Kitō Kiyoaki, eds., *Shinpan Kodai no Nihon* 6: *Kinki* II. Kadokawa shoten, 1991.

Nogami Jōsuke. "Nihon shutsudo no tarekazari tsuki mimikazari ni tsuite." In *Kobunka ronsō*. Osaka: Fujisawa Kazuo sensei koki kinen ronshū kankō kai, 1983.

"Nōgu." In Sahara Makoto and Kanaseki Hiroshi, eds., *Yayoi bunka no kenkyū* 5: *Dōgu to gijutsu* I. Yūzan kaku, 1988.

Nomura Tadao. *Kenkyū shi: Taika no kaishin*. Yoshikawa kōbunkan, 1973.

———. *Kodai kanryō no sekai*. Hanawa shobō, 1969.

Nosco, Peter. *Remembering Paradise: Nativism and Nostalgia in Eighteenth-Century Japan*. Cambridge, Mass.: Harvard University Press, 1990.

Ōbayashi purojekuto chiimu. "Gendai gijutsu to kodai gijutsu no hikaku ni yoru Nintoku tennō ryō no kensetsu." *Kikan ōbayashi Mausoleum ōryō* 20 (April 1985): 2–21.

Ōbayashi Taryō. *Yamatai koku*. Chūō kōron, 1977.

Oda Fujio. "Yokoana shiki sekishitsu no dō'nyū to sono genryū." In *Chōsen sankoku to Wakoku*. Gakusei sha, 1980.

Okazaki Takashi. "Japan and the Continent." In Delmer Brown, ed., *The Cambridge History of Japan*, vol. 1: *Ancient Japan*. Cambridge: Cambridge University Press, 1992.

———. "Tettei." In *Munakata Okinoshima honbun*. Fukuoka: Munakata taisha fukko ki seikai, 1979.

Okimori Takuya and Satō Makoto, eds. *Jōdai mokkan shiryō shūsei*. Ōfū sha, 1994.

Okita Masaaki. "Yamato seiken ka no shizen to ningen." In Shiraishi Taichirō, ed., *Kōkogaku ni yoru Nihon rekishi* 16: *Shizen kankyō to bunka*. Yūzan kaku, 1996.

Okuno Masao. "Yamatai koku Kyushu ron." *Kikan Yamatai koku* 5 (April 1980): 77–187.

———. *Yamatai koku no kagami*. Shin jinbutsu ōrai sha, 1982.

Ono Tadahiro. *Kōchi sei shūraku ato no kenkyū: shiryō hen*. Gakusei sha, 1979.

———. "Kōchi sei shūraku kenkyū no kadai." In Ono Tadahiro, ed., *Kōchi sei shūraku to Wakoku tairan*. Yūzan kaku, 1984.

———. "Kōchi sei shūraku ron." In Mori Kōichi, ed., *San seiki no kōkogaku* 2: *San seiki no iseki to ibutsu*. Gakusei sha, 1981.

———. "Tetsuzoku o shutsudo shita Yayoi shiki kōchi sei shūraku." *Kōkogaku jaanaru* 49 (October 1970): 21.

Ōuchi Mitsuzane. *Kankoku no zenpō kōen keifun*. Yūzan kaku, 1996.

Ōwaki Kiyoshi. "Shin'yaku-kyō no kensetsu." In Machida Akira and Kitō Kiyoaki, eds., *Shinpan kodai no Nihon* 6: *Kinki* II. Kadokawa shoten, 1991.

Ōyama Seiichi. "Iwayuru 'Nagaya ōke mokkan' no saikentō." *Mokkan kenkyū* 11 (1989): 137–155.

Pai Hyung Il. "Lelang and the 'Interaction Sphere.'" *Archaeological Review from Cambridge* 8 (1989): 64–75.

———. "The Nangnang Triangle in China, Japan, and Korea." *Korean Culture* 14 (Winter 1993): 32–41.

Palmer, Edwina. "Land of the Rising Sun: The Predominant East-West Axis Among the Early Japanese." *Monumenta Nipponica* 46 (Spring 1991): 69–90.

Pearson, Richard. *Ancient Japan.* Washington, D.C.: Smithsonian Institution, 1992.

———. "Chiefly Exchange between Kyushu and Okinawa, Japan, in the Yayoi Period." *Antiquity* 64 (1990): 912–922.

———. "Lolang and the Rise of Korean States and Chiefdoms." *Journal of the Hong Kong Archaeological Society* 7 (1976–1978): 77–90.

———, ed. *Windows on the Japanese Past.* Ann Arbor: University of Michigan Press, 1986.

Piggott, Joan, "Keeping Up with the Past: New Discoveries Enrich Our Views of History." *Monumenta Nipponica* 33 (Autumn 1983): 313–319.

———. "*Mokkan* Wooden Documents from the Nara Period." *Monumenta Nipponica* 45 (Winter 1990): 449–470.

———. "Sacral Kingship and Confederacy in Early Izumo." *Monumenta Nipponica* 44 (Spring 1989): 45–74.

———. "Tōdaiji and the Nara Imperium." Ph.D. dissertation, Stanford University, 1987.

Pirenne, Henri. *Mohammed and Charlemagne.* New York: Barnes and Noble, 1955.

Pollack, Junco Sato. "Looms." *Kodansha Encyclopedia of Japan,* vol. 5. Kōdan sha, 1983.

Posonby-Fane, Richard. *Imperial Cities: The Capitals of Japan from Oldest Times Until 1229.* Washington, D.C.: University Publications of America, 1979.

Postan, Michael. *The Medieval Economy and Society.* Berkeley: University of California Press, 1972.

Ranke, Leopold von. *The Secret of World History.* Edited by Roger Wines. New York: Fordham University Press, 1981.

Reischauer, Edwin, John Fairbank, and Albert Craig. *East Asia: Tradition and Transformation.* Boston: Houghton Mifflin, 1989.

Renfrew, Colin. *Before Civilization.* Cambridge: Cambridge University Press, 1973.

Robinson, J. T., Melvin Fowler, and Brian Fagan. *Human and Cultural Development.* Indianapolis: Indiana Historical Society, 1974.

Rowley-Conwy, Peter. "Postglacial Foraging and Early Farming Economies in Japan and Korea: A West European Perspective." *World Archaeology* 16 (1984): 28–42.

Sabloff, Jeremy, and C. C. Lamberg-Karlovsky. *The Rise and Fall of Civilizations.* Menlo Park: Cummings, 1974.

Saeki Arikiyo. *Kenkyū shi: Kokaido Ō hi.* Yoshikawa kōbunkan, 1974.

———. *Kenkyū shi: Sengo no Yamatai koku.* Yoshikawa kōbunkan, 1972.

———. *Kenkyū shi: Yamatai koku.* Yoshikawa kōbunkan, 1971.

————. *Rekishi shinsho* 1: *Kodai no higashi Ajia to Nihon.* Kyōiku sha, 1977.

————. "Studies on Ancient Japanese History." *Acta Asiatica* 31 (1977): 113–129.

————. *Yamatai koku kihon ronbun shū.* 3 vols. Sōgen sha, 1982.

Sahara Makoto. "Rice Cultivation and the Japanese." *Acta Asiatica* 63 (1992): 40–63.

————. *Taikei Nihon no rekishi* 1: *Nihonjin no tanjō.* Shōgakkan, 1987.

————. "The Yayoi Culture." In Tsuboi Kiyotari, ed., *Recent Archaeological Discoveries in Japan.* Tokyo and Paris: UNESCO, 1987.

Sahara Makoto and Kanaseki Hiroshi. "Sōsetsu: kome to kinzoku no seiki." In Sahara Makoto and Kanaseki Hiroshi, eds., *Kodai shi hakkutsu* 4: *Inasaku no hajimari.* Kōdan sha, 1975.

————. "The Yayoi Period." *Asian Perspectives* 19 (1978): 15–26.

Sakaehara Towao. "Heijō-kyō jūmin no seikatsu shi." In Kishi Toshio, ed., *Nihon no kodai* 9: *Tojō no seitai.* Chūō kōron, 1987.

Sakamoto Tarō. *Taika kaishin no kenkyū.* Jibun dō, 1938.

Sakamoto Yoshio. "Yon go seiki no bagu." *Kōkogaku jaanaru* 257 (December 1985): 12–15.

Sansom, George. *A History of Japan to 1334.* Palo Alto: Stanford University Press, 1958.

Saotome, Masahiro. "Bronze Weapons." *Kodansha Encyclopedia of Japan,* vol. 1. Kōdan sha, 1983.

————. "Imaki no gijutsu to kōgei." In *Kodai shi fukugen* 7: *Kofun jidai no kōgei.* Kōdan sha, 1990.

Sasayama Haruo. "Heian shoki no seiji kaikaku." In *Iwanami kōza Nihon rekishi* 3: *Kodai.* Iwanami shoten, 1975.

Satō Kōji. "Fujiwara no miya." In Tsuboi Kiyotari, ed., *Kodai o kangaeru kyūto hakkutsu.* Yoshikawa kōbunkan, 1987.

Satō Makoto. "Kome no yūkō sei ni miru ritsuryō zaisei no tokushitsu." In *Bunka zai ronsō.* Kyoto: Dōhō sha, 1983.

————. "Nagaoka-kyō kara Heian-kyō e." In Sasayama Haruo, ed., *Kodai o kangaeru Heian no miyako.* Yoshikawa kōbunkan, 1991.

Sawada Goichi. *Nara chō jidai minsei keizai no sūteki kenkyū.* Kashiwa shobō, 1972.

Scarre, Chris. *Smithsonian Timelines of the Ancient World.* New York: Dorling Kindersley, 1993.

Seki Akira. *Kikajin.* Jibun dō, 1966.

Sekiguchi Hiroko. "Nihon kodai no gō kizoku sō ni okeru kazoku no tokushitsu ni tsuite." In *Genshi kodai shakai kenkyū,* vol. 5. Azekura shobō, 1979.

Senda, Minoru. "Territorial Possession in Ancient Japan: The Real and the Perceived." In *Geography of Japan.* Teikoku shoin, 1980.

Shida Jun'ichi. "Uji ni tsuite." *Rekishi kōron* 58 (September 1980): 66–77.

Shimakura Misaburō. "San seiki no shokubutsu." In Mori Kōichi, ed., *San seiki no kōkogaku* 1: *San seiki no shizen to ningen.* Gakusei sha, 1980.

Shinokawa Ken. "Eta Funayama kofun shutsudo no tachi mei." In Saeki Arikiyo, ed., *Kodai o kangaeru Yūryaku tennō to sono jidai.* Yoshikawa kōbunkan, 1988.

Shiomi Akira. *Higashi Ajia no shoki tekki bunka.* Yoshikawa kōbunkan, 1983.

————. "Tetsu tekki no seisan." In *Iwanami kōza Nihon kōkogaku* 3: *Seisan to ryūtsū.* Iwanami shoten, 1986.

Shiraishi Taichirō. "Haka to bochi." In Mori Kōichi, ed., *San seiki no kōkogaku* 2: *San seiki no iseki to ibutsu.* Gakusei sha, 1981.

————. "Kinki ni okeru kofun no nendai." *Kōkogaku jaanaru* 164 (August 1979): 21–26.

————. "Kōki kofun no seiritsu to tenkai." In *Nihon no kodai* 6: *Ōken o meguru tatakai.* Chūō kōron, 1986.

————. "Koto do watashi kō." In *Kashiwara kōkogaku kenkyū jo ronshū.* Yoshikawa kōbunkan, 1975.

————. "Nihon ni okeru yokoana shiki sekishitsu no keifu." *Senshi gaku kenkyū* 5 (May 1965): 61–78.

Sim Pong-gŭn. "Sankoku jidai: Kaya, Kyŏngsang South." In Kim Wŏnyong, ed., *Kankoku no kōkogaku.* Kōdan sha, 1989.

Sin Kyŏng-ch'ŏl. "Go seiki ni okeru Nihon to Kara hantō." In *Nihon kōkogaku kyōkai 1990 nendo taikai: Kenkyū happyō yōshi.* Fukuoka: Nihon kōkogaku kyōkai, 1990.

————. "Koshiki abumi kō." *Kodai bunka* 38 (June 1986): 22–43.

Sŏ Sŏng-hun. "Sankoku jidai: Paekche, Chŏlla." In Kim Wŏnyong, ed., *Kankoku no kōkogaku.* Kōdan sha, 1989.

Song Nai Rhee. "Emerging Complex Society in Prehistoric Southwest Korea." Ph.D. dissertation, University of Oregon, Eugene, 1984.

Sonoda Kōyū. "Early Buddha Worship." In Delmer Brown, ed., *The Cambridge History of Japan,* vol. 1: *Ancient Japan.* Cambridge: Cambridge University Press, 1992.

Suematsu Yasukazu. "Japan's Relations with the Asian Continent and the Korean Peninsula (Before 950 A.D.)." *Cahiers d'histoire Mondiale* 4 (1958): 671–687.

"Suiden ikō shūsei." *Maizō bunka nyūsu* 62 (March 1988): 234–250.

Suzuki Yasutami. "Higashi Ajia no shominzoku no kokka keisei to Yamato ōken." In *Koza Nihon rekishi* 1: *Genshi kodai.* Tokyo daigaku shuppan kai, 1984.

————. "Nihon ritsuryō seiritsu to Chōsen sankoku." In *Nihon bunka to Chōsen,* vol. 3. Shin jinbutsu ōrai sha, 1978.

Tainter, Joseph. *The Collapse of Complex Societies.* Cambridge: Cambridge University Press, 1988.

Taira Yasuhisa. "Chichū no Heian-kyō." In Sasayama Haruo, ed., *Kodai o kangaeru Heian no miyako.* Yoshikawa kōbunkan, 1991.

Takakura Hiroaki. "Ifuku to sōshin gu." In Sahara Makoto and Kanaseki Hiroshi, eds., *Kodai shi hakkutsu* 4: *Inasaku no hajimari.* Kōdan sha, 1975.

————. "Shoki tekki no fukyū to kakki." In *Kenkyū ronshū,* vol. 10. Kyushu rekishi shiryō kan, 1985.

Takeda Masataka and Wada Atsumu. "Nara: Fujiwara-kyō Ukyō gojō yonbō." *Mokkan kenkyū* 15 (1993): 26–33.

Takeda, Yukio. "Studies on the King Kwanggaito Inscription and Their Basis." *Memoirs of the Research Department of the Toyo Bunko* 47 (1989): 57–87.

Takemoto Tōru. "The Kyushu Dynasty." *Japan Quarterly* 30 (October–December 1983): 383–387.

Takigawa Masajirō. "Tansaku kō." *Kodai gaku* 7 (October 1958): 147–154.

Takinami Sadako. "Heian-kyō no kōzō." In Sasayama Haruo, ed., *Kodai o kangaeru Heian no miyako*. Yoshikawa kōbunkan, 1991.

Tanaka Kiyomi. "Go seiki ni okeru Settsu Kawachi no kaihatsu to toraijin." *Hisutoria* 125 (December 1989): 1–25.

Tanaka Migaku. "The Early Historical Period." In Tsuboi Kiyotari, ed., *Recent Archaeological Discoveries in Japan*. Tokyo and Paris: UNESCO, 1987.

———. *Kodai Nihon o hakkutsu suru* 3: *Heijō-kyō*. Iwanami shoten, 1984.

———. *Nihon no rekishi* 2: *Wajin sōran*. Shūei sha, 1991.

Tanaka Shinsaku. "Bugu." In *Kofun jidai no kenkyū* 8: *Kofun* II: *Fukusōhin*. Yūzan kaku, 1991.

Tanaka Tetsuo. "Heijō-kyō." In Tsuboi Kiyotari, ed., *Kodai o kangaeru kyūto hakkutsu*. Yoshikawa kōbunkan, 1987.

Tateno Kazumi. "Monjo mokkan no kenkyū kadai." *Kōkogaku jaanaru* 339 (November 1991): 7–15.

———. "Nara: Heijō-kyūseki." *Mokkan kenkyū* 14 (1992): 7–16.

Taylor, Sarah. "The Introduction and Development of Iron Production in Korea: A Survey." *World Archaeology* 20 (1989): 422–433.

———. "Ploughshares into Swords: The Iron Industry and Social Development in Protohistoric Korea and Japan." Ph.D. dissertation, Cambridge University, 1990.

Temple, Robert. *The Genius of China*. New York: Simon & Schuster, 1989.

Teramura Mitsuharu. "Tama." In Mori Kōichi, ed., *San seiki no kōkogaku* 2: *San seiki no iseki to ibutsu*. Gakusei sha, 1981.

Terasaki Yasuhiro. "Kōka mokkan no saikentō." In *Ritsuryō kokka no kōzō*. Yoshikawa kōbunkan, 1989.

———. "Nagaya ōke no monjo mokkan." *Nihon rekishi* 500 (January 1990): 110–115.

Teshigahara Akira. *Nihon kōkogaku shi*. Tokyo daigaku shuppan kai, 1988.

Toby, Ronald. "Why Leave Nara?" *Monumenta Nipponica* 40 (Autumn 1985): 331–347.

"Tokushū: keisho yo'nen no kagami o megutte." *Higashi Ajia no kodai bunka* 51 (1987): 2–75.

Tonami Mamoru. "Chūgoku tojō no shisō." In Kishi Toshio, ed., *Nihon no kodai* 9: *Tojō no seitai*. Chūō kōron, 1987.

Tōno Haruyuki. "Nanto shoden kyūjō zu zanketsu ni tsuite." *Komonjo kenkyū* 20 (February 1983): 1–12.

———. *Nihon kodai mokkan no kenkyū*. Hanawa shobō, 1983.

———. *Shōsōin monjo to mokkan no kenkyū*. Hanawa shobō, 1977.

Toraijin no tera. Nara: Nara kokuritsu bunka zai kenkyū jo, 1983.

Tōshitsu doki no kokusai kōryū. Kashiwa shobō, 1989.

Totman, Conrad. *The Green Archipelago*. Berkeley: University of California Press, 1989.

Tsuboi Kiyotari. "The Excavation of Ancient Palaces and Capitals." *Acta Asiatica* 63 (1992): 87–98.

———. "Issues in Japanese Archeology." *Acta Asiatica* 63 (1992): 1–20.

———. "Kodai kyūto hakkutsu." In Tsuboi Kiyotari, ed., *Kodai o kangaeru kyūto - hakkutsu.* Yoshikawa kōbunkan, 1987.

Tsuboi Kiyotari and Tanaka Migaku. *The Historic City of Nara.* Translated by Gina Barnes. Tokyo and Paris: UNESCO, 1991.

Tsuda Sōkichi. *Nihon jōdai shi no kenkyū.* Iwanami shoten, 1947.

Tsude Hiroshi, ed. *Kodai shi fukugen 6: Kofun jidai no ō to minshū.* Kōdan sha, 1989.

———. "The Kofun Period." In Tsuboi Kiyotari, ed., *Recent Archaeological Discoveries in Japan.* Paris and Tokyo: UNESCO, 1987.

———. "The Kofun Period and State Formation." *Acta Asiatica* 63 (1992): 40–63.

———. "Nihon kodai no kokka keisei ron josetsu: Zenpō kōen fun taisei no teishō." *Nihon shi kenkyū* 343 (March 1991): 5–39.

———. *Nihon nōkō shakai no seiritsu katei.* Iwanami shoten, 1989.

Tsuji Hiroshi. "Heian-kyō." In Tsuboi Kiyotari, ed., *Kodai o kangaeru kyūto hakkutsu.* Yoshikawa kōbunkan, 1987.

Tsunoda Bun'ei, ed. *Heian-kyō teiyō.* Kadokawa shoten, 1994.

Tsunoyama Yukihiro. "Orimono." In *Kofun jidai no kenkyū 5: Seisan to ryūtsū.* Yūzan kaku, 1991.

———. "Orimono." In Mori Kōichi, ed., *San seiki no kōkogaku 2: San seiki no iseki to ibutsu.* Gakusei sha, 1981.

Twitchett, Denis. *Financial Administration under the T'ang Dynasty.* Cambridge: Cambridge University Press, 1970.

Ueda Masaaki. "A Fresh Look at Ancient History." *Japan Quarterly* 33 (October–December 1986): 403–410.

———. *Kikajin.* Chūō kōron, 1965.

Ueki Hisashi. "Yamato e no genkan." In Machida Akira and Kitō Kiyoaki, eds., *Shinpan kodai no Nihon 6: Kinki* II. Kadokawa shoten, 1991.

Ukeda Masayoshi. "Fuhito shūdan no ichi kōsatsu." In *Kodai shi ronshū,* vol. 1. Hanawa shobō, 1988.

Umehara Sueji. "Ōjin Nintoku Richū san tennō ryō no kibo to eizō." *Shoryōbu kiyō* 5 (March 1955): 1–15.

Uno Masatoshi. "Nihon shutsudo kanbō to sono haikei." In *Kyushu jōdai bunka ronshū.* Kumamoto: Otomasu Shigetaka sensei koki kinen ronbun shū kankō kai, 1990.

Upshur, Jiu-hwa, et al. *World History.* Minneapolis: West, 1991.

Vargo, Lars. *Social and Economic Conditions for the Formation of the Early Japanese State.* Stockholm: Japanological Studies, 1982.

Wada Seigo. "Gyorō." In Sahara Makoto and Kanaseki Hiroshi, eds., *Yayoi bunka no kenkyū 2: seigyō.* Yūzan kaku, 1988.

———. "Sekkō gijutsu." In *Kofun jidai no kenkyū 5: seisan to ryūtsū* II. Yūzan kaku, 1991.

Wagner, Don. "The Beginning of Iron in China." *EAANnouncements* 17 (Autumn 1995): 6.

Wang Jian-qun. *Kōtai ō hi no kenkyū.* Yūkon sha, 1984.

Wang Zhong-shu. "Nihon no kodai tojō seido no genryū ni tsuite." *Kōkogaku zasshi* 69 (October 1983): 1–30.

———. *Nihon no sankakuen shinjū kyō mondai ni tsuite.* Tō a shoten, 1981.

———. "Nihon sankakuen shinjū kyō sōron." *Kōkogaku kenkyū* 122 (September 1984): 108–114.

———. "Riben sanjue yuan shenshou jing zongji." *Kaogu* 200 (May 1984): 468–479.

Watanabe Akihiro. "Nagaya ōke mokkan to futatsu no kasei kikan." In *Nara kodai shi ronshū,* vol. 2. Kyoto: Shin'yō sha, 1991.

Wheatley, Paul, and Thomas See. *From Court to Capital.* Chicago: University of Chicago Press, 1978.

Wright, Arthur. "The Sui Dynasty (581–617)." In Denis Twitchett, ed., *The Cambridge History of China,* vol. 3: *Sui and T'ang China 589–906,* pt. 1. Cambridge: Cambridge University Press, 1979.

Xiong, Victor Cunrui. "Sui Yangdi and the Building of Sui-Tang Luoyang." *Journal of Asian Studies* 52 (February 1993): 66–89.

Yagi Atsuru. *Kodai Nihon no miyako.* Kōdan sha, 1974.

———. "Nagaya ōke mokkan to kōshin keryō sho." *Nihon shi kenkyū* 353 (January 1992): 1–37.

Yagi Hisae. "Naniwa no miya." In Tsuboi Kiyotari, ed., *Kodai o kangaeru kyūto hakkutsu.* Yoshikawa kōbunkan, 1987.

Yamada Masahiro. "Nihon ni okeru kofun jidai gyūba kō kaishi setsu sairon." *Rekishi jinrui* 17 (March 1989): 3–29.

Yamamoto Takeo. "Ni san seiki to kikō." In Mori Kōichi, ed., *San seiki no kōkogaku* 1: *San seiki no shizen to ningen.* Gakusei sha, 1980.

Yamamura, Kozo. "The Decline of the *Ritsuryo* System: Hypothesis on Economic and Institutional Change." *Journal of Japanese Studies* 1 (Autumn 1974): 1–37.

Yamanaka Akira. "Kōko shiryō toshite no kodai mokkan." *Mokkan kenkyū* 14 (1992): 147–188.

———. "Nagaoka-kyō kara Heian-kyō e." In Machida Akira and Kitō Kiyoaki, eds., *Shinpan kodai no Nihon* 6: *Kinki* II. Kadokawa shoten, 1991.

———. "Nagaoka-kyō no kenchiku ikō to takuchi no haichi." In *Nagaoka-kyō kobunka ronsō,* vol. 1. Kyoto: Dōhō sha, 1986.

Yamanaka Akira and Shimizu Miki. "Nagaoka-kyō." In Tsuboi Kiyotari, ed., *Kodai o kangaeru kyūto hakkutsu.* Yoshikawa kōbunkan, 1987.

Yamao Yukihisa. "Be ni tsuite." *Kodai gaku kenkyū* 77 (September 1975): 40–41.

———. *Kodai no Nitchō kankei.* Hanawa shobō, 1989.

———. "Kofun jidai no kinseki bun." *Nihon shi kenkyū* 130 (December 1972): 120–123.

Yanagida Yasuo. "Chōsen hantō ni okeru Nihon kei ibutsu." In *Kyushu ni okeru kofun bunka to Chōsen hantō.* Gakusei sha, 1989.

Yanagisawa Kazuo. "Kofun no henshitsu." In Shiraishi Taichirō, ed., *Kodai o kangaeru kofun.* Yoshikawa kōbunkan, 1989.

Yasuda Hiroyoshi. "Shu tan to sono riyō." In Mori Kōichi, ed., *San seiki no kōkogaku* 2: *San seiki no iseki to ibutsu.* Gakusei sha, 1981.

Yazaki, Takeo. *Social Change and the City in Japan.* Japan Publications, 1968.

Yi, Chong-Hang. "On the True Nature of 'Wae' in *Samguk sagi.*" *Korea Journal* 17 (November 1977): 51–59.

Yokoyama, Kōichi. "Early Historic Archaeology in Japan." *Asian Perspectives* 19 (1976): 27–41.

Yonekura, Isamu. "Himiko, Queen of Wa." *The East* 10 (June 1974): 44–51.

Yoon, Dong Suk. "Early Iron Metallurgy in Korea." *Archaeological Review from Cambridge* 8 (1989): 92–99.

Yoshida Akira. *Nihon shi* 37: *kodai no Naniwa.* Kyōiku sha, 1982.

Yoshida Takashi. "Kodai shakai ni okeru uji." In *Nihon shakai shi* 6: *Shakaiteki sho shūdan.* Iwanami shoten, 1988.

———. *Ritsuryō kokka to kodai no shakai.* Iwanami shoten, 1983.

———. "Ritsuryō sei to sonraku." In *Iwanami kōza Nihon rekishi* 3: *kodai* 3. Iwanami shoten, 1975.

———. "Ritsuryō to kyaku." In Okazaki Takashi and Hirano Kunio, eds., *Kodai no Nihon* 9: *kenkyū shiryō.* Kadokawa shoten, 1971.

———. *Taikei Nihon no rekishi* 3: *Kodai kokka no ayumi.* Shōgakkan, 1988.

Young, John. *The Location of Yamatai: A Case Study in Japanese Historiography, 720–1945.* Baltimore: Johns Hopkins University Press, 1957.

Yun Hwan. "Kankō karyū iki ni okeru Paekche yokoana shiki sekishitsu." *Kobunka dansō,* vol. 20. Kita Kyushu: Kyushu kobunka kenkyū kai, 1989.

Yun Mu-byŏng. "Mokch'ŏn dojō no hanchiku kōhō." In *Higashi Ajia to Nihon: Kōko bijutsu hen.* Yoshikawa kōbunkan, 1987.

———. "Sankoku jidai: Paekche, Ch'ungch'ŏng." In Kim Wŏnyong, ed., *Kankoku no kōkogaku.* Kōdan sha, 1989.

INDEX

Page numbers followed by 'f' refer to figures; 'm' to maps; 'n' to notes; and 't' to tables.

ABOUT THE AUTHOR

William Wayne Farris is currently professor of history and chair of the Asian Studies Program at the University of Tennessee at Knoxville. He received his M.A. and Ph.D. from Harvard. He is the author of two other books dealing with the social and economic history of premodern Japan: *Population, Disease, and Land in Early Japan, 645–900* examines peasant life during the age of Japanese apprenticeship to Chinese civilization; *Heavenly Warriors: The Evolution of Japan's Military, 500–1300* considers the origins of the samurai class and its rise to political prominence. Farris has spent four years in Kyoto conferring with scholars and traveling to archaeological sites.